PAX ECONOMICA

Pax Economica

LEFT-WING VISIONS OF A
FREE TRADE WORLD

MARC-WILLIAM PALEN

PRINCETON UNIVERSITY PRESS

PRINCETON & OXFORD

Published by Princeton University Press
41 William Street, Princeton, New Jersey 08540
99 Banbury Road, Oxford OX2 6JX

press.princeton.edu

All Rights Reserved

Library of Congress Cataloging-in-Publication Data

Names: Palen, Marc-William, author.
Title: Pax economica: left-wing visions of a free trade world / Marc-William Palen.
Description: Princeton: Princeton University Press, 2024 |
    Includes bibliographical references and index.
Identifiers: LCCN 2023017887 (print) | LCCN 2023017888 (ebook) |
    ISBN 9780691199320 (hardback) | ISBN 9780691205137 (ebook)
Subjects: LCSH: Free trade—Political aspects—History. | Imperialism—
    Economic aspects—History. | Radicalism—Economic aspects—History. |
    International relations—History. | BISAC: BUSINESS & ECONOMICS /
    Economic History | HISTORY / Modern / 19th Century
Classification: LCC HF1711.P35 2024 (print) | LCC HF1711 (ebook) |
    DDC 382/.71—dc23/eng/20230705
LC record available at https://lccn.loc.gov/2023017887
LC ebook record available at https://lccn.loc.gov/2023017888

British Library Cataloging-in-Publication Data is available

Editorial: Hannah Paul and Josh Drake
Production Editorial: Theresa Liu
Jacket/Cover Design: Heather Hansen
Production: Erin Suydam
Publicity: James Schneider and Kate Farquhar-Thomson

Jacket image: "—and peace shall rule," Udo J. Keppler, 1872–1956. Published by Keppler & Schwarzmann, 1899 May 3. Library of Congress Prints and Photographs Division, Washington, DC.

This book has been composed in Classic Arno

Printed on acid-free paper. ∞

Printed in the United States of America

10 9 8 7 6 5 4 3 2 1

To Rachel

CONTENTS

ILLUSTRATIONS

ACKNOWLEDGEMENTS

THIS BOOK owes a great debt to all those who graciously provided feedback along the way, be it by email exchanges, conversations over coffee, or close readings of draft chapters. After eight years, this has become quite a list: Duncan Bell, Bill Brands, Cathie Carmichael, Emily Conroy-Krutz, Thomas Conti, Mike Cullinane, Julio Decker, Chris Dietrich, Dexter Fergie, Katarina Friberg, Ben Gallaway, Bernard Gissibl, Sarah Hamilton, Ryan Hanley, Kristin Hoganson, Tony Hopkins, Tony Howe, Richard Huey, Jon Hunt, Julia Irwin, Josh Keidaish, Elisabeth Leake, James Mark, Steve Meardon, Jamie Miller, Jessica Moody, Simon Morgan, Jimmy Myers, Chris Nichols, Ned Richardson-Little, Natt Ringer, Aviel Roshwald, Tobias Rupprecht, Ilaria Scaglia, Cyrus Schayegh, Jay Sexton, David Thackeray, Martin Thomas, Andrew Thompson, Michael Thompson, Megan Threlkeld, Richard Toye, Heidi Tworek, James Vaughn, Daniel Whittall, Donald Winch, Krisna Wymore, the Press's anonymous reviewers, and the brilliant students at Exeter who undertook my final-year course 'Critics of Empire' and joined me in investigating some of the book's themes between Autumn 2016 and Spring 2022. And, of course, I will forever be indebted to my partner in life, Rachel Herrmann, for her keen edits, culinary sustenance, and intellectual inspiration along the way.

I am grateful to the editors and outlets that provided venues to test the book's argument. An earlier version of chapter 1 appeared in *The Cambridge History of Nationhood and Nationalism*. A preliminary draft of chapter 3 appeared in the *International History Review*. An early condensed version of chapter 4 appeared in *Imagining Britain's Economic Future, c. 1800–1975*. Ideas and themes explored in *Diplomatic History* and *Crossing Empires* have also been incorporated.[1] On the editorial front, I also owe many thanks to my wonderful editors at Princeton University Press, Hannah Paul and Josh Drake, for their patience, guidance, and support throughout, as well as to Princeton's marketing team, to my production editor Theresa Liu, and to Francis Eaves for his careful copyediting.

I also want to thank those who supported the book's archival research. Research support from the History Department and the College of Humanities at the University of Exeter was invaluable, as were short-term archival fellowships from the Sophia Smith Library at Smith College, the Historical Society of Pennsylvania, the Hoover Institution Library and Archives at Stanford, and UT Austin's Harry Ransom Center. Geneva-based research was made possible thanks to the Global Humanitarianism Research Academy, which I was fortunate to contribute to during its run from 2015 to 2019. A long-term fellowship at the Massachusetts Historical Society in 2022 allowed me to finish my archival research and manuscript writing; a big shout-out to Kid Wongsrichanalai and the MHS's amazing research team, archivists, and donors that made this possible.

ABBREVIATIONS

AAUW	American Association of University Women
ACLL	Anti–Corn Law League
AFTL	American Free Trade League
AIL	Anti-Imperialist League
APS	American Peace Society
CCRWT	Citizens' Committee for Reciprocal World Trade
CAIP	Catholic Association for International Peace
CECWT	Consumer Education Council on World Trade
CEIP	Carnegie Endowment for International Peace
CEIPR	Carnegie Endowment for International Peace Records, Columbia University, New York
CPU	Church Peace Union
CWU	Church Women United
DAR	Daughters of the American Revolution
EEC	European Economic Community
EU	European Union
FCC	Federal Council of Churches
FOR	Fellowship of Reconciliation
GATT	General Agreement on Tariffs and Trade
GHS	German Historical School
HSP	Historical Society of Philadelphia, PA
IAPA	International Arbitration and Peace Association
IAW	International Alliance of Women for Suffrage and Equal Citizenship

ICA	International Co-Operative Alliance
ICDP	International Confederation for Disarmament and Peace
ICPUFT	International Committee to Promote Universal Free Trade
IFTL	International Free Trade League
IFTU	International Federation of Trade Unions
ILP	Independent Labour Party
IMF	International Monetary Fund
INC	Indian National Congress
IPC	International Peace Campaign
ISI	Import Substitution Industrialization
ITO	International Trade Organization
LON	League of Nations Archives, Geneva, Switzerland
LSI	Labour and Socialist International
MECW	*Karl Marx/Frederick Engels Collected Works,* 50 vols (New York: International Publishers, 1975–2004)
MHS	Massachusetts Historical Society, Boston, MA
NAACP	National Association for the Advancement of Colored People
NAFTA	North American Free Trade Agreement
NCCCW	National Committee on the Cause and Cure for War
NCJW	National Council of Jewish Women
NCL	National Consumers' League
NCNW	National Council of Negro Women
NIEO	New International Economic Order
NLWV	National League of Women Voters
OECD	Organization for Economic Co-operation and Development
OEEC	Organization for European Economic Co-operation
PSA	Argentine Socialist Party (Partido Socialista Argentino)
RTAA	Reciprocal Trade Agreements Act
SPA	Socialist Party of America
SPD	[German] Social Democratic Party (Sozialdemokratische Partei Deutschlands)

SSC	Sophia Smith Collection, Smith College, Northampton, MA
TPP	Trans-Pacific Partnership
UCCW	United Council of Church Women
UN	United Nations
UNCTAD	United Nations Conference on Trade and Development
USAID	United States Agency for International Development
WAP	World Alliance for International Friendship through the Churches Papers, Swarthmore Peace Collection, Swarthmore, PA
WCC	World Council of Churches
WCG	Women's Co-operative Guild
WILPF	Women's International League for Peace and Freedom
WPC	World Peace Council
WPF	World Peace Foundation
WPP	Woman's Peace Party
WPS	Women's Peace Society
WTFA	World Trade Foundation of America
WTO	World Trade Organization
YMCA	Young Men's Christian Association
YWCA	Young Women's Christian Association

PAX ECONOMICA

Introduction

If you believe you are a citizen of the world, you are a citizen of nowhere.

—BRITISH CONSERVATIVE PRIME MINISTER
THERESA MAY, BIRMINGHAM, UK, 2016

The future does not belong to the globalists. The future belongs to patriots.

—REPUBLICAN US PRESIDENT DONALD TRUMP,
UN GENERAL ASSEMBLY, NEW YORK, 2019

IN 1927, George and Ira Gershwin put on a musical satire about trade and war entitled *Strike Up the Band*. The plot centres around a middle-aged US cheesemaker, Horace J. Fletcher of Connecticut, who wants to corner the domestic dairy market. When Fletcher hears that the US government has just slapped a fifty per cent tariff on foreign-made cheese, he sees dollar signs. High tariffs mean his fellow citizens will have little choice but to 'buy American'. What's more, the tariff's impact soon reaches beyond the national market to sour the country's trade relationships. Swiss cheesemakers are particularly sharp in their demands for retaliation. Fletcher surmises that a prolonged Swiss–American military conflict would provide the necessary fiscal and nationalistic incentives to maintain the costly tariff on foreign cheese in perpetuity.

To make his monopolistic dream of market control a reality, Fletcher sees to it that the tariff spat between the two countries leads to all-out war. He first creates the Very Patriotic League to drum up support for the Alpine military adventure, as well as to weed out any 'un-American' agitation at home. The Very Patriotic League's members, donning white hoods reminiscent of the Ku Klux Klan, go about excising all things Swiss from the nativist nation. Not even the classic adventure tale *The Swiss Family Robinson* escapes notice: it gets rebranded *The American Family Robinson*. With domestic anti-war dissent quelled, Fletcher next orchestrates a military invasion of Switzerland. The farcical imperial intervention ends with a US victory. But just as the war with Switzerland winds down and a peaceful League of Cheese established, an ultimatum arrives from Russia objecting to a US tariff on caviar. And, it's implied, the militant cycle repeats.

The Gershwins' late-1920s lampoon was praised by theatre critics but panned by the public. 'The masses in general still believe in patriotism,' one theatre critic explained. 'People are going to be hurt and resentful [. . .] to say nothing of the American Legion and patriotic societies.'[1] He was right. The musical's 1927 road tour was cancelled after just three weeks owing to the nationalistic blowback. A watered-down version of *Strike Up the Band* was churned out a couple years later. Apparently to make the story more palatable to the US sweet tooth, the tariff on cheese was switched for one on chocolate. Fletcher's war with Switzerland, real in the original score, was downgraded to a dream sequence. Even with these ameliorative changes, however, critics once again warned that 'the more aggressive American patriotic organizations' might 'threaten reprisals'.[2]

Strike Up the Band's satirical association of US protectionism with nationalism, militarism, and imperialism may have gone too far for the average 'patriotic' American, but it would have struck a sympathetic chord with many left-wing peace workers. After all, during and after the First World War, the country's peace activists—liberal radicals, socialists, feminists, Christians—had similarly witnessed with alarm the uptick of these very same 'isms' at home and abroad. And in seeking to curb these trends, left-wing peace workers often faced persecution, even imprisonment, at the hands of deputized 'patriotic' organizations and the US government. The peace movement's common association of trade wars with geopolitical conflict, as in the Gershwin musical, is central to the story that follows. Leading peace activists envisioned instead a free trade world as promising a new prosperous economic order devoid of imperialism and war: what they increasingly referred to as their 'Pax Economica'. *Strike Up the Band*'s libretto tongue-lashing of 'patriotic' protectionism can thus be recast as a musical accompaniment to what was, by the late 1920s, a long-standing international left-wing tradition that connected economic cosmopolitanism with anti-imperialism and peace—and economic nationalism with imperialism and war.

Writing this book amid a pandemic and mounting nationalist demands for economic self-sufficiency has been instructive. The COVID-19 pandemic itself has heightened the tensions wrought from greater interdependence. Covid's rapid spread illustrates a doomsday scenario that the Cassandras of globalization have long warned about. The ensuing stringent travel restrictions, broken supply chains, resurgent xenophobia, and further protectionist retrenchment that have followed demonstrate how the coronavirus has ratcheted up the political forces of anti-globalism that had been making headway in the years since the 2008 Great Recession.[3] This economic nationalist revival has most strikingly transpired within the two nations most responsible for creating the more liberal and open economic order after the Second World War, the United States and Britain.[4]

In the years following the 2016 presidential election, US political leaders from both major parties have renounced the pro–free market 'Washington Consensus'. Republican president Donald Trump kicked things off with the unveiling of his 'America First' foreign trade policy, replete with xenophobia, tariff wars against trading partners, and anti-immigration policies. Trump pulled the United States out of the massive Asia-Pacific trade agreement called the Trans-Pacific Partnership, scrapped the North American Free Trade Agreement, levied punitive tariffs against the country's closest allies, and even attempted to build a giant wall along the US–Mexico border to deter migrants. Democratic president Joe Biden's 'Buy American' programme and industrial policy echo Trump's, and Biden has also continued the trade war with China. In some areas, Biden's protectionist policies are even more extreme than his predecessor's.

Brexit Britain's bipartisan 'Buy British' campaign, in turn, has followed close on the heels of the UK's chaotic and nationalistic dislocation from the European Union (EU), accompanied by severe immigration restrictions to 'take back control' of British sovereignty. Some Conservative Party Brexit champions have promised that former British colonies such as India will replace the EU single market; others have proffered a more selective racialized vision called CANZUK, an economic union between the UK and its former 'white' settler colonies Canada, Australia, and New Zealand. Both proposals drip with imperial nostalgia.[5] The consequent creation of new trade barriers between the UK and the EU and between Northern Ireland and the rest of the UK, in turn, have upset the European peace project.

Nationalistic onlookers have been fast to follow the Anglo-American protectionist cue. Right-wing governments in Italy, Hungary, Poland, Turkey, Brazil, the Philippines, India, China, and Japan, among others, have taken inspiration from the burgeoning protectionist consensus. Then came Russia's brazen imperial incursion into Ukraine in 2022, accompanied by crippling Western economic sanctions in retaliation. The economic nationalist and imperial backdrop of the present volume no longer looks all that distant or alien.

Pax Economica's spectrum of left-wingers broadly encompasses those whose politics were left of centre. Some sought reform, others revolution, but all shared the belief that economic interdependence could foster democratization, economic and social justice, and world harmony. For some left-wingers like Karl Marx writing in the 1840s, the envisaged interconnectivity wrought from free trade signalled the next progressive step in capitalism's march towards proletarian revolution, and therefore deserved support. But for many other left-wing internationalists, universal free trade came to be seen as the economic bedrock of a more peaceful, prosperous, and democratic world order. Left-leaning liberal radical reformers such as Richard Cobden, Henry George, Mark Twain, Leo Tolstoy, Norman Angell, Abe Isoo, J. A. Hobson, Jane Addams, Rosika Schwimmer, and Fanny Garrison Villard connected free trade with democracy promotion, antislavery, universal suffrage, civil rights, prosperity, anti-imperialism, and peace. Socialist internationalist peace workers such as Florence Kelley, Eduard Bernstein, Karl Kautsky, Crystal Eastman, Toyohiko Kagawa, Norman Thomas, and Kirby Page leaned further left in their critiques of capitalism and economic inequality. But these same social democrats, democratic socialists, and communists nevertheless often found themselves working alongside their more moderate liberal radical contemporaries to realise their shared vision of a peaceful, free trade world.

Pax Economica's motley crew of left-wing free traders were the leading globalists of their age, in contrast to the right-wing free-market advocacy more commonly associated with globalism's champions today. The disjuncture between then and now offers an opportunity to correct a historical imbalance. The past couple of decades have witnessed a flurry of scholarship tracing the right-wing origins of today's free-market ideas back to the interwar years.[6] By recovering the shared world of left-wing radicalism and free trade, this book tells a very different story, with a much earlier starting point: the 1840s. Back then, the left-leaning free-trade ideology of anti-imperialism and peace was famously known as 'Manchester liberalism' or 'the Manchester School', owing to its roots in Manchester, England. It was also referred to as 'Cobdenism', after the school's most prominent British spokesman, Richard Cobden. Cobdenism took on various left-wing guises and varieties, suffusing the international peace and anti-imperial movements from the mid-nineteenth century onward.

The terminology used to describe the book's left-wingers accordingly reflect their intersectional fight for free trade, anti-imperialism, and peace. Their movement is referred to interchangeably throughout the book as 'the free-trade-and-peace movement', 'the commercial peace movement', and 'the economic peace movement'. So too 'internationalism' is used interchangeably with 'cosmopolitanism', because of their shared intellectual property for much of the period between the mid-nineteenth and mid-twentieth centuries. During this time, even the most extreme cosmopolitans recognized the existence and staying power of the nation state; and even the staunchest internationalists, while recognizing that nationalism was an entrenched reality, also saw it as the most powerful stumbling block to a more peaceful, interdependent world order. Internationalism and cosmopolitanism back then were both also closely associated with 'interdependence': what we now more often refer to as 'globalization'.[7]

'Free trade' and 'protectionism' also had meanings particular to the century preceding the Second World War. This was a time when governments relied largely on tariffs for generating revenue. *Pax Economica*'s cast of characters accordingly understood free trade to mean low tariffs for revenue purposes only, rather than their near absence as free trade is commonly thought of today. Left-wing free traders back then sought to lower government expenditures on imperial defence and militaries to keep revenue tariffs as low as possible for the consumer—with imperial devolution, peace, and prosperity a natural by-product. Most protectionists, believing war and imperialism to be immutable, instead sought discriminatory or prohibitive tariffs on foreign products both to insulate domestic producers from unfettered international competition and to pay for expanding their nation's militaries and empires. This form of economic nationalism, often accompanied by government subsidies for domestic businesses and internal improvements, became popularly known by the mid-nineteenth century as the 'American System' in the United States. The close late-nineteenth and twentieth-century association of protectionism and colonialism, in turn, is sometimes referred to as 'neomercantilism'. As Eric Helleiner has argued, neomercantilism was an updated version of the older mercantilist system of imperial trading blocs and monopolies common among early modern empires.[8]

The left-wing economic cosmopolitan fight for anti-imperialism and peace begins with the mid-nineteenth-century transatlantic free-trade movement. At first glance, it might seem ironic that the leading peace and anti-imperial theories emanated outward from Britain, the dominant empire of the day. The

British Empire of the Victorian age likely brings to mind ambitions of world-wide market access and a British world system controlled through naval supremacy, pith helmets, and diplomatic persuasion. This depiction is in keeping with what is now a prodigious body of literature examining the complex relationship between British imperialism and modern liberalism.[9] This volume adds further complexity by exploring how liberal ideas spurred transnational anti-imperial and peace activism; for many politically left-of-centre adherents, free-trade liberalism contained a hard-nosed critique of imperialism, militarism, and war.

And yet the radical left-wing free-trade fight to end imperialism and war, if recognized at all, is treated as a mere curiosity: what Stephen Howe describes as 'a minority current, and a limited and conditional stance'.[10] This marginalization stems in part from a long-standing tendency to misremember the half-century leading up to the First World War as 'a golden era of globalization', as Tara Zahra puts it.[11] *Pax Economica*'s study of the commercial peace movement paints a very different political economic picture. Recovering the pacifistic efforts of left-wing free traders thus provides a new transnational history of peace activism and its complex relationship to global capitalism between the mid-nineteenth century and today. Excepting British peace historiography, most national histories of pre-1945 peace movements (and most are national histories) grant little more than a passing reference, if any, to free trade. They also exclude the numerous organizations for which peace through free trade was their main purpose.

Free trade's marginalization and exclusion has a long lineage within peace studies. Helen Bosanquet, in her 1924 study of the relationship between free trade and peace in the nineteenth century, went so far as to state that peace societies had 'lost even their mild interest in Free Trade' after a brief flirtation in the 1840s and 1850s.[12] The doyen of peace studies Merle Curti has argued that the 'slow advance of peace' over the late nineteenth and early twentieth centuries owed much to the fact that 'peacemakers have not adequately fought the economic forces that make for war'. He goes on to argue that 'most friends of peace [...] have naturally accepted the existing economic order and have not seen the threats to peace inherent in it'. Others have held that peace activists didn't think about economic matters at all. Gorham Munson, for instance, asserts that 'as a movement pacifism has been notoriously innocent of economics'. These observations, John Nelson concludes, 'hold true for the peace movement prior to the First World War', and to a large extent after it.[13] The disjuncture works both ways. Those histories of world governance and liberal internationalism that have recognized the sizeable role played by free-trade ideas and their left-wing adherents have isolated them from their peace activism.[14] This book turns these long-held assumptions, exclusions, and dissociations on their heads by showing how free trade remained a central tenet among left-wing internationalists working within the era's anti-imperial and peace movements to overturn the neomercantilist order.

Free trade's historiographical exclusion is more surprising still considering that commercial peace workers were well recognized in their day, not least by Nobel Peace Prize committees. The first ever Nobel Peace Prize, in 1901, was awarded to two individuals. Of the two names, Henri Dunant is the more familiar today, as the founder of the International Committee of the Red Cross in Geneva. The other, the leader of the turn-of-the-century French peace movement Frédéric Passy, is less remembered. Passy was a French disciple of Britain's mid-nineteenth-century 'apostle of free trade' Richard Cobden. Like Cobden, Passy believed that universal free trade was an essential ingredient for a more peaceful world and accordingly helped create numerous European economic peace organizations. The Nobel committee's interest in the economic cosmopolitan connection to peace only grew stronger after the First World War. In the summer of 1919 the Nobel Institute even ran an international competition to provide 'An Account of the History of the Free Trade Movement in the Nineteenth Century and its Bearing on the International Peace Movement'.[15] Other left-leaning leaders of the commercial peace movement to receive the prize thereafter included Chicago's Jane Addams (1931), Britain's Norman Angell (1933), former Democratic US secretary of state Cordell Hull (1945), and Boston's Emily Green Balch (1946).

Along the way, *Pax Economica* traces how the global vision of left-wing economic cosmopolitans came to embrace supranational oversight as a prerequisite for their pacifistic free-trade order. As Glenda Sluga describes it, by the end of the First World War 'steam, electricity, and trade had socialized a new kind of international man' who put greater faith in supranational governance to maintain the peace.[16] The book's 'cosmopolitan internationalists' well understood that this meant weakening national borders and diminishing national sovereignty and allegiances. This globalist mindset and worldview paved the way for the likes of the League of Nations and, eventually, the United Nations, the EU, and the World Trade Organization, key institutions that would underpin subsequent post-1945 economic ordering.

The book's thematic approach highlights the multifaceted growth and evolution of this left-wing free-trade tradition within transnational anti-imperial and peace networks spanning a century and more. Its structure allows for the telling of six distinct but overlapping stories. The first chapter provides the protectionist and imperial backdrop to the rest of the book. The chapter focuses on how the American System of protectionism—popularized by Alexander Hamilton, Henry Clay, Henry Carey, and Friedrich List—most shaped the economic makeup of the world's empires from around 1870. This allows us to see the global economic order in the way that both its leading supporters and its leading critics saw it: as one dominated by extreme protectionism, nationalism, militarism, and colonialism. The subsequent four chapters trace the role of free trade within the international anti-imperial and peace movements from the left-wing perspective of liberal radicals, socialists, feminists, and Christians, groups that tend to be treated disparately or even as oppositional. The final chapter carries the story forward from the end of the Second World War to today. During this time, the United States is commonly understood to have taken the lead from Britain in liberalizing global trade even as the decolonizing world fought to obtain a seat at the decision-making table.

Treated individually, the chapters allow for a more focused engagement with debates and questions surrounding the international peace histories of liberal radicals, socialists, feminists, and Christians. Taken as a whole, the chapters provide a wide-ranging landscape depicting how visions of free trade helped tie these left-wing peace workers together, and how they overlapped with other left-leaning reform movements. As *Strike Up the Band* illustrates, by the 1920s free trade's association with peace had seeped into wider left-wing culture and discourses, and controversially so. *Pax Economica* accordingly includes how left-wing visions of a more peaceful interdependent world intersected with a variety of other nineteenth- and twentieth-century initiatives such as the abolition of slavery, women's suffrage, civil rights, the Esperanto movement, and the New International Economic Order.

Liberal ideas connecting free-trade universalism with peace not only preceded the Cold War; they predated the 1840s. We can find earlier such iterations of economic cosmopolitanism in the Enlightenment thought of Immanuel Kant, the French physiocrats, Adam Smith, and Thomas Paine, perhaps even as far back as the ancient Greeks.[17] But massive mid-nineteenth-century transformations of the global economy heralded something new for the modernizing world. Universalistic theories of free trade became potential political realities upon the creation of a global food system, global transport and communication networks, and mass industrialization. These globalizing trends evolved and grew between the 1840s and 1940s, underpinning post-1945 left-wing visions of world citizenship, the international division of labour, de-colonization, economic interdependence, prosperity, social justice, and peace.[18]

The left-wing fight for free trade, anti-imperialism, and peace was a transim-perial one, meaning a transnational struggle that more often than not criss-crossed imperial boundaries.[19] This was an uphill struggle during an era in which empires were key movers, shakers, and innovators of globalization: what A. G. Hopkins describes as 'imperial globalization'.[20] The transimperial story that follows therefore corrects the all too common misimpression that this first age of modern globalization was one of free trade and laissez-faire run amok, culminating in the First World War. Apart from the British case, this imperial phase of integration was protectionist, regional, and quite often co-ercive, as pre-modern or undeveloped economies were forced to become integrated within a Euro-American dominated global market system. The protagonists of this book understood the economic nationalist makeup of the imperial order only too well.

Their pacifistic visions of a liberal order of open trade and world fraternity evolved throughout the last half of the nineteenth century and the first half of the twentieth, but even so, the era in which its protagonists lived imposed certain limitations. For many Victorian-era economic peace workers, their universalistic worldview was constrained by their Euro-American-centrism and the limitations of nascent global transportation and communication net-works. The Victorian-era commercial peace movement also showed itself to be more susceptible to the era's white supremacist ideas of Anglo-Saxonism and 'civilization' than its twentieth-century successors. These biases further limited left-wing economic cosmopolitan and anti-imperial visions.[21] For some utopians at the extreme end of this Anglo-Saxonist spectrum, for ex-ample, the global dominance of a free-trading Anglosphere— 'Anglobalization'—even promised an 'Anglotopia': perpetual peace through Anglo-American democratic imperialism.[22] This liberal imperialist dimension later reinforced the League of Nations mandates system.[23] Granted, few of this book's protagonists fell into this peace-through-empire camp. But nor were the era's left-wing economic peace workers able to break free entirely from the constraints of this racialized Euro-American-centric worldview. This tendency would noticeably weaken during the interwar years amid the global turn towards authoritarianism and autarky, during which a more radical generation of commercial peace workers threw themselves into creating a new interde-pendent economic order more sympathetic to the demands of the decoloniz-ing world.

Euro-American-centrism also informed the free-trade and protectionist theories of economic development emanating from the imperial metropoles.[24] Many of the leading theorists of capitalism, from Adam Smith to Friedrich List to Karl Marx, followed this line of thought. These developmental stage theories drew the attention of not only imperial-minded nationalists but also anti-colonial nationalists, who embraced and adapted these same theories to undermine the Euro-American imperial order. As explored in chapter 1, almost paradoxically, anti-colonial nationalists such as Liang Qichao, Ma Yinchu, Arthur Griffith, Mahatma Gandhi, Benoy Kumar Sarkar, and W.E.B. Du Bois saw the Western developmental model as both the source of their humiliation and the means of their salvation.[25] That the colonized and decolonizing world often borrowed from, imitated, and adapted the ideas, texts, languages, and policies of the colonizers—a nineteenth-century process that Christopher Hill refers to as 'conceptual universalization'—should not be surprising.[26] Recognizing this unequal power relationship does not dismiss the unique and significant ways that anti-colonial nationalists incorporated local settings and traditions to retool the racialized developmental ideologies of the West into emancipatory weapons of independence.

Pax Economica therefore reflects the imbalanced dissemination of economic ideologies during this era of Western-dominated colonialism, globalization, and industrialization. Although not one-way streets during this period, the most popular ideological roads invariably led back to Rome or, more often than not, London, Paris, Berlin, New York, Geneva, and Boston. The intrinsic power dynamics of imperial globalization meant that the West's near monopoly control of global transportation and communication networks, and thus of knowledge transfer, allowed for few exceptions to this Euro-American-centred rule. As a result, while this is a globe-trotting book, its Euro-American connections remain prominent. Yet the story that unfolds seeks to avoid falling into the pitfall of narrating merely how the West shaped the rest. What follows is in no small part about how Western ideas framed the global battle between economic cosmopolitanism and economic nationalism. But it is also about how 'the rest'—including anti-colonial nationalists in India, Ireland, Egypt, Ghana, the USA, China, Cuba, the Philippines, and Argentina—refashioned these ideas and policies to make them their own. These same efforts would, in turn, gradually make left-wing economic cosmopolitans more accepting of the developmentalist trade policy visions of the Global South after 1945.

The ensuing transimperial struggle between economic cosmopolitanism and economic nationalism over the future course of global capitalism often made for strange bedfellows. Before the Cold War conflict between capitalism and communism, capitalist and socialist radicals found common cause in their efforts to overturn the economic nationalist imperial order. By the early twentieth century, a shared belief in trade liberalization as a mechanism for peace, prosperity, and social justice had socialist internationalists joining hands with left-leaning capitalist reformers. The latter—liberal radicals—were willing to work closely with more centrist elements within the peace establishment like the Carnegie Endowment for International Peace, as well as with Marxist revolutionaries, international feminists, and ecumenical Christians. The pageantry of the left-wing economic peace movement included a colourful cast of characters that readers might find surprising.

Pax Economica's interventions challenge a wide scholarship that has tended not to look earlier than the 1930s and 1940s to understand the origins of post-1945 economic globalization.[27] Limited understanding has bred understandable confusion. Cold War lenses have blurred the historical depiction of modern left-wing radicalism, displacing the economic peace movement from its previously prominent position. In the US context, for example, since the 1950s historians have recast late nineteenth- and early twentieth-century free-trade radicals as supporters of the very corporate monopolies and empires that they sought to dismantle, and have shoehorned them into histories of US conservatism rather than of US liberalism. Still others depict all US socialists as economic nationalists, overlooking the pacifistic free-trade alliances between socialist internationalists and capitalist liberal radicals.[28] This book's unorthodox narrative upends many such common Cold War–driven misconceptions surrounding modern liberalism, free trade, anti-imperialism, and peace.

In sum, *Pax Economica* illustrates most vividly how the global spread of imperial ideas was never limited to imperial rule; it also advanced anti-imperial dissent. Free-trade cosmopolitanism provided the economic fuel needed to fire up the international peace and anti-imperialist movements working between the mid-nineteenth century and today. This anti-imperialism of free trade was a transimperial phenomenon that came to encompass the political left-wing within the British, US, Spanish, German, Dutch, Belgian, Italian, Russian, French, and Japanese empires, where economic cosmopolitans struggled to replace the neomercantilist and nationalist realist logics that undergirded imperialism and war with the free-trade principles they believed would undermine empires and promote peace. Travelling across imperial boundaries, trade wars, and military conflicts, free-trade theories of anti-imperialism and peace sought to undo the world that had produced them.

The book's findings help explain how we got 'there and back again' (to borrow a phrase from J.R.R. Tolkien). Today's ongoing economic nationalist backlash against free-market globalism has once again shaken the economic order, contributing to the growth of authoritarian regimes, the search for self-sufficiency, trade wars, geopolitical turmoil, and imperial expansion. The book's examination of the economic peace movement and its close affinity with democratization therefore also provides a new history of what in the field of international relations is referred to as 'democratic peace theory' and 'capitalist peace theory', although the book's economic cosmopolitans would be perplexed to see these theories treated separately rather than as mutually reinforcing. They would also be surprised to discover that their contributions to these theories are nearly forgotten.[29]

The book concludes by emphasising how the ideological origins of post-1945 battles over neocolonialism, neomercantilism, and neoliberalism lay in the 1840s and the century that followed. The Cold War has obfuscated a much older ideological struggle that pitted the industrializing imperial powers against each other, while also giving birth to anti-colonial nationalist demands for political autonomy and economic development that would later prevail in the Global South. Long before the Cold War divided much of the globe into socialist and capitalist camps, the capitalist system itself was riven in two between those cosmopolitan idealists who wanted the world's markets to become peaceably interdependent through free trade, and those nationalist realists who viewed geopolitics as a matter of perpetual war, wherein tariff walls were needed to buttress national boundaries and insulate infant domestic industries from unfettered international competition. As an intellectual and political history, this battle between economic cosmopolitanism and economic nationalism encapsulates what David Armitage describes as 'a collision of competing universalisms'. This same collision course once again appears cataclysmic three decades after Cold War's end.[30] Today's visions of a more peaceful economic order arose long before the cheese war that played out upon the Gershwins' interwar stage. They began to take shape within the century-long political and ideological fight over the future course of trade, imperialism, and war that gripped the industrializing and colonial world from the 1840s.

1

The Imperialism of Economic Nationalism

GLOBALIZING THE AMERICAN SYSTEM OF PROTECTIONISM

The highest means of development of the manufacturing power [...] are colonies. [...] England owes her immense colonial possessions solely to her surpassing manufacturing power. If the other European nations wish also to partake of the profitable business of cultivating waste territories and civilizing barbarous nations [...] they must commence with the development of their own internal manufacturing powers, of their mercantile marine, and of their naval power.

—FRIEDRICH LIST, 1841[1]

Modern protectionism is, both in theory and in practice, largely an American product. [...] Modern protectionism is the economic policy, not of nascent nationality [...] but of young imperialism.

—SYDNEY SHERWOOD, 1897[2]

BRITAIN'S EMBRACE of free trade in the 1840s got the 'cosmopolitical' imagination running wild. The era's leading internationalists began predicting that the rest of the industrializing world, seeing the widespread benefits the island nation gained from trade liberalization, would soon follow suit. The United States, Britain's resource-rich former colony, looked like it would provide the most fertile soil for free trade's mid-nineteenth-century transplantation; even as Britain was striking down its protective tariffs on foreign grain (the Corn

Laws) in 1846, Democrats in the United States were slashing tariff rates.[3] The timing appeared fortuitous, leading Richard Cobden, the Liberal radical figurehead of the British free-trade movement, to declare that the consummation of their efforts was at hand.[4] The Anglo–French Treaty of 1860, or Cobden-Chevalier Treaty, thereafter lowered tariff barriers across much of Europe, promising the arrival of a new era of economic liberalism, market integration, affordable food, and regional prosperity.[5] Left-leaning supporters of free trade augured that greater economic interdependence would eventually erode national rivalries, and perhaps, some day, even national boundaries, resulting in a more peaceful and prosperous world federation. And their liberal vision of global interdependence left little, if any, room for imperial projects. With the glimmer of mid-century trade liberalization across both the English Channel and the Atlantic Ocean, a brave new economic cosmopolitan world order appeared to be just over the horizon.

But this left-wing free-trade vision proved to be a mirage conjured from hubristic optimism. Such pacifistic cosmopolitan speculations underappreciated the value of economic nationalism in an era of unprecedented nation-state formation, industrialization, militarism, and empire building. German-American economic theorist Friedrich List penned his famous neomercantilist book *The National System of Political Economy* (1841), which would fast become a secular bible of free-market sceptics the world over. The United States then became the first major power to buck the free-trade trend in 1861 when, with input from political economist Henry Carey, the Republican Party began implementing its protectionist programme known as the American System. By the 1870s, Britain's presumed free-trade trump card had received an unanticipated counter from most of its competitors. Drawing inspiration from List and other US protectionist prophets, one rival after another instead turned to economic nationalism to foster infant industries at home and to expand closed colonial markets abroad. Even Britain's own settler colonies would abandon free trade by the turn of the century. Economic nationalism, not free trade, became the predominant political economic force underpinning imperial expansion and consolidation from the mid-nineteenth century to the Second World War.

And yet one of the more enduring myths surrounding the half-century leading up to the First World War remains the mistaken assumption that free trade and laissez-faire prevailed over the tail end of this 'first era of globalization'. The reality was quite different. Commodity flows and exchanges

increased across this period *despite* the growing demand for economic nationalism. Alongside the British-led gold standard, government-backed technological developments in transport and communications—railways, canals,
steamships, telegraph lines—and a corresponding decline in transport costs
deserve much of the credit.[6] So, too, does the era's coercive incorporation of
new colonial markets into the global capitalist system. By around 1870, the
'cosmopolitical school' of free trade had little to show for its propagandistic
efforts beyond Britain itself, whereas the American System's nationalistic
brand of infant industrial protectionism could claim global popularity, especially among Britain's imperial rivals.

This widespread preference for the American System of protectionism over
British-style free trade can be seen at once as a response to Britain's hegemonic
power and an uncomfortable reminder of its limitations. Fears of unfettered
competition with the more industrially developed British allowed infant industrial protectionism to become a formidable countermovement, especially
when coupled with imperial expansion. From North America to continental
Europe to the Near East, Australia, and Japan, economic nationalist ideas and
policies prevailed over the imperial economic order of the late nineteenth
and early twentieth centuries. As a result, this century of global market integration, nationalism, militarism, and empire building—imperial globalization—
derived in far larger part from the imperialism of economic nationalism than
from the imperialism of free trade.[7] In other words, instead of opening up the
world's markets under the British-heralded banner of free trade for all, Britain's
imperial rivals demonstrated a predilection for extending their market access
through informal means of high tariff walls, closed markets, and tariff retaliation where possible, and by formal annexation when necessary.

This Western-dominated age of imperial globalization meant that ideological exchanges, as well as capital flows, were often Euro-American-centric. The
modernizing ideas of economic nationalism, developmentalism, and imperial
expansion that most shaped this era drew upon a rich Euro-American ideological tradition. The Anglophobic US political system proved remarkably
resistant to British-inspired economic cosmopolitan ideas, to the consterna-
tion of Anglo-American free traders. Thanks to the homegrown efforts of economic nationalist theorists such as Alexander Hamilton, Friedrich List, Henry
Clay, and Henry Carey, most US politicians instead preferred a protectionist
doctrine that combined a strong fiscal-military state with subsidies for internal
improvements and infant industrial protectionism: what became known as the

'American System' in the decades preceding the country's civil war (1861–1865). By the 1840s, the American System had evolved into a global export, a consumption driven in no small part by an urge to counteract the contemporaneous free-trade ideas emanating from Britain.

By the late nineteenth century, the American System of protectionism was in high demand. Nationalists across the globe—in France, Germany, Canada, Australia, Russia, the Ottoman Near East, and Japan—found the American System's ideological connection of protectionism, nationalism, industrialism, militarism, and empire-building seductive. As so often happens during times of economic crisis, the onset of the Long Depression (c. 1873–1896) exacerbated this neomercantilist turn, as nation after nation sought to insulate itself from the full force of world market competition. For Britain's imperial rivals, the new norm combined high tariff walls with monopolization of colonial markets to secure access to raw materials and to export surplus capital and populations. The seeming successes of late nineteenth-century US economic nationalism and continental conquest made the American System, rather than British-style free trade, the preferred developmental model.[8] The years leading up to and during the First World War witnessed a speeding up of these trends towards nationalism, protectionism, and imperialism. Desire for economic self-sufficiency and imperial consolidation thereafter became paramount, once the Great Depression struck in 1929, even within 'Free Trade England' itself. And in exceptional cases where states fell under the direct coercive influence of British free-trade imperial policies, as in China, Ireland, India, and Egypt, leading nationalists instead looked upon the successful implementation of the American System as an anti-colonial exemplar for economic development within a British world system. Pan-Africanist leader W.E.B. Du Bois's calls for Black self-sufficiency also drew from this burgeoning anti-colonial economic nationalist tradition. The American System thus cast its long protectionist shadow over the imperial order from the mid-nineteenth century to the Second World War.

The American System and Imperial Globalization, 1783–1861

The American System's roots became entangled with Britain and its empire in the decades immediately following the American Revolution. The eighty-year period preceding the US Civil War was one of formal US independence from

Britain, as well as continued informal economic dependence.[9] As a partial remedy for the latter, Alexander Hamilton, the newly minted nation's first treasury secretary, sought to replicate British mercantilism and military fiscalism in order to create a stronger federal government and a continental American empire.[10] Such protectionist and fiscal-military reforms included a modernized central banking system styled after the Bank of England, alongside protective tariffs for American infant industries and farmers, coupled with subsidies for internal improvements of roads and canals to facilitate continental trade.[11] Along the way, Hamilton also coined the term 'the American System' and introduced it into domestic circulation.[12] With the adoption of the British-style fiscal-military state, the United States was thereafter better able to maintain and expand its military, facilitating US westward expansion and the establishment of a continental empire by mid-century.

Hamilton's American System received a big boost in the 1820s and 1830s from Kentucky senator Henry Clay, the Whig Party's most prominent congressional protectionist defender. To create 'a genuine American System', Clay argued, federal and state governments needed to enact protectionism, which had by then become synonymous with the American System. To strengthen and maintain it, he and other American System advocates supported westward expansion through a public land policy. Clay was also wont to point out Britain's continued application of the Corn Laws, which from 1815 until 1846 placed high protective tariffs on foreign grain, as evidence that even the era's most industrially advanced nation remained reliant upon economic nationalism to maintain its empire and to protect its domestic economic interests.[13] Clay believed that the expansion of the American System was manifest destiny: that the American System would one day encompass all of the western hemisphere. And Clay's pan-American vision contained a sharp imperial edge; Latin America, once devoid of the influence of the European imperial powers, would become part of a protectionist hemispheric *Zollverein*, with the United States sitting 'at the head of the American system.'[14]

Clay's protectionist efforts on behalf of the American System and US imperial expansion received propagandistic support from the antebellum era's most influential publisher, Philadelphia's Mathew Carey. Carey's mistreatment and persecution at the hands of the British government while coming of age in Ireland helped shape his Anglophobic desire to nurture US industries so that they might eventually overtake the British. Mathew's son Henry Charles Carey eventually took up his father's protectionist mantle and played a central role in making the American System a key tenet of the Republican Party upon its founding in 1856.[15]

From within this same circle of American System advocates arose the most authoritative of nineteenth-century protectionist theorists: Friedrich List. This German-born US citizen's economic ideas were 'made in America', Boston's *Protectionist* reflected.[16] During his residency in Pennsylvania (1825–1831), List left his indelible mark domestically on the likes of Henry Charles Carey and the subsequent Republican Party. List's American System-inspired ideas first appeared in *Outlines of American Political Economy* (1827), establishing him as an authority on US fiscal policy and a champion of protectionism. He fleshed out his protectionist vision further in *The National System of Political Economy* (*Das national System der politischen Oekonomie*, 1841). List's ideas went far in shaping imperial globalization by at once (1) attacking British free trade, (2) encouraging high tariffs and subsidies to foster national industrial development, and (3) contending that Western industrializing powers such as the United States, Belgium, France, and Germany required colonial expansion to obtain national security, raw materials, and new export markets for surplus capital. Undeveloped, 'uninstructed, indolent' nations such as those of Latin America, Asia, and eastern Europe, in turn, needed to be colonized by these same nations and needed to focus upon the production of raw materials for their industrializing colonial masters.[17]

After all, List emphasized, this combination of economic nationalism and colonialism was precisely what Britain had used to ascend to industrial preeminence in the decades preceding its post-1846 embrace of free trade, whereupon it now sought to 'kick away the ladder'. British free traders and their international disciples—the era's advocates of what List derided as 'cosmopolitical economy'—duplicitously downplayed the power of political and economic nationalism at their own peril.[18] Free-trade radicals, in their heady idealism, promised that international trade liberalization would bring cheap food to the starving masses, prosperity for all, and even world peace. But List the realist claimed to see through their universalistic and pacifistic language. He believed it to be little more than an ideological smokescreen to hide their true intentions: to forever keep Britain the 'manufacturer of the world'. If the rest of the industrializing world followed suit and precipitously threw open its markets, he warned, Britain would maintain its hegemony by strangling rival nations' infant industries in the cradle. List prescribed his Anglophobic protectionist product as a cure-all to counteract a British-dominated economic system— and it fast found a receptive global market.

Transimperial Exportation of the
American System, 1861–1890

From imperial metropoles to colonial peripheries, the American System, rather than British-style free trade, became the economic model of choice. The late nineteenth-century industrializing world of nation states looked on with a mixture of envy, imitation, and emulation at the Republican Party's successful establishment of the American System and its consequent centralization of federal power during and immediately after the US Civil War.[19] This was on clear display when the Republicans subsidized the transcontinental railroad and doled out massive tracts of land to encourage westward settlement, despite the fact that Native Americans, collectively, already owned much of the territory. As Carl Mosk puts it, the GOP's support for a centralized banking system, domestic manufactures, and mass production over the coming decades 'was revolutionary not only in shaping consumption but also in reducing the relative cost of exerting military force'. In other words, the American System's establishment made US militarism cheaper, and US imperial expansion easier.[20] Its establishment also created geopolitical conflict between the United States and its Gilded Age rivals. This included numerous trade wars with Canada, its British colonial neighbour to the north, that very nearly came to all-out military conflict.[21] The model of the American System appeared ripe for exportation throughout the late nineteenth-century industrializing world: a nationalistic consumer demand that only grew stronger following the onset of the Long Depression in 1873.[22]

By the early 1870s, theorists of the American System had become the protectionist prophets of the industrializing world. From mid-century their ideas fed into fiscal debates worldwide, as best reflected in the popularization of Friedrich List's work. List's 1841 *National System of Political Economy* was translated into numerous nationalist contexts, among them those of Hungary (1843), France (1851), the USA (1856), Australia (1860), Britain (1885), Romania (1887), Sweden (1888), Japan (1889), Russia (1891), Bengal (1912–16), Bulgaria (1926), China (1927), Finland (1846, 1935), and Spain (1942). List's growing popularity illustrates how the American System was in high demand across the globe—especially among the industrializing Western imperial powers.

The American System doctrine was exported most immediately to post-Napoleonic France through Friedrich List himself. Following his exile years in Pennsylvania, List returned to continental Europe an American citizen.

While residing in Paris in the late 1830s, he penned much of *National System*. List's ideas had a direct impact upon French protectionist politics once his close friend Adolphe Thiers became premier in 1840. Thiers even offered List the job of overseeing the building of a French national rail network, although List declined in order to return to Germany.[23]

The combined protectionist work of List and Thiers helped shape the political economic makeup of the French Empire in a reverse image of what was unfolding in 1840s Britain. Despite the efforts of French liberals such as Richard Cobden's friend Frédéric Bastiat and British liberals such as John Bowring to spread the free-trade gospel, the infant industrial lobbyists and Anglophobic protectionist politicians of 'Fortress France' reigned triumphant.[24] And they soon began looking to expand the French colonial system. They added colonizing Algeria to their obsession with industrial development, along lines laid out by List and French right-wing protectionist politicians.[25] Largely in imitation of the USA's American System and continental colonization, Fortress France built its tariff walls ever higher over the coming decades, and then extended them to encircle its colonies; tariff protection from foreign competition was granted to Algeria in 1884 and to French Indochina in 1887. Jules Ferry, the former colonial premier of Tonkin and Tunis and the empire's 'apostle of the colonial renaissance', summarized it thus in 1890: 'Colonial policy is the daughter of industrial policy. [...] The protectionist system is a steam-engine without safety valve if it does not have as correlative and auxiliary a healthy and serious colonial policy.' His expansionist sentiments were shared by Emile Chautemps, the minister of colonies; Foreign Minister Théophile Delcassé, 'the guiding genius of French imperialism'; and influential academics, such as Sorbonne historian Alfred Rambaud and Collège de France economist Pierre Paul Leroy-Beaulieu, through the 1880s and 1890s.[26] The empire-wide expansion of the nineteenth-century French economic nationalist system culminated in the passage of the Méline Tariff of 1892, partly in response to an ongoing trade war with Italy, and partly in retaliatory response to the US protectionist passage of the McKinley Tariff of 1890. The French bill's author, conservative politician Jules Méline, would continue to look to the United States and its American System as a model for emulation.[27]

German economic nationalists were not far behind France in embracing the American System and adapting it to the *Zollverein*. Upon List's return to his fatherland in 1841, as US consul for the Kingdom of Württemberg, he designed the intellectual blueprint for subsequent German unification, protectionism, and imperial expansion with the publication of his *National System*. List's nationalist vision for Germany was, according to one recent biographer, 'a "transatlantic" idea that List had brought back with him from his exile in the USA'.[28] Praise came pouring in from some of his German contemporaries, including Wilhelm Roscher, professor of political economy at the University of Göttingen, who would help found the late nineteenth-century German Historical School (GHS). List's reception among free traders in Britain and certain liberal segments of the German press was less enthusiastic, to put it mildly, contributing to his depression and subsequent suicide in 1846.[29]

Application of List's American System manifested itself in German imperial politics after his death.[30] According to Matthew Fitzpatrick, List's work established 'many of the tropes of imperialist discourse in Germany. [...] Constantly repeated and reinscribed, the central tenets of his belief in the necessity of imperialism as a national mission were transmitted to the next generation.'[31] As early as 1844, List's *National System* was rumoured to have become Otto von Bismarck's 'bedside reading'.[32] German imperialist Alexander von Bülow, quoting List, wrote one of the strongest defences of German colonialism in 1849, with an expansionist eye towards Latin America. He then founded the Berliner Kolonisationsverein, which in 1853 was granted a contract to send German settlers to colonize Costa Rica, resulting in the short-lived colony of Angostura. Mid-century imperial theorist Karl Gaillard and the former Prussian envoy to Brazil Johann Jacob Sturz devised further colonial schemes for Latin America on this Listian model.[33] In 1867, Lothar Bucher of the Prussian foreign office called for the acquisition of St. Thomas, Timor, and the Philippines to complete List's envisaged colonial project.[34] Wilhelm Hübbe-Schleiden—lawyer, publicist, African explorer, and member of the Westdeutscher Verein für Kolonisation und Export (West German association for colonization and export)—demanded in the late 1870s and early 1880s that Germany extricate itself from Anglo-Saxon cosmopolitanism and instead embrace a colonial *Weltpolitik* encompassing South America and Ethiopia. Investments in steamship lines connecting Germany with its African colonies picked up pace from the 1880s—and were backed up with a stronger navy.[35] These trends led the German economist Julius Lehr to proclaim List 'the father of the young theory that forms the basis of all protective tariff policies in Germany'.[36] Illustrating the growing transatlantic reach of the American School, Henry Carey's influence began rivalling that of List's within German protectionist circles, not least because of Carey's advocacy of agricultural protectionism.[37]

Bismarck's support proved crucial to the Listian development of Germany's imperialism of economic nationalism. Carey's German disciples increasingly had Bismarck's ear.[38] List's daughter Emilie took it upon herself to send a three-volume edition of *National System* to Bismarck and the crown prince in 1877, and she viewed the country's protectionist turn after 1879 as an affirmation of her father's enduring influence.[39] Both Bismarck's newfound favour for the Conservatives and German colonial expansion provided further affirmation. This confluence of German protectionism, conservative nationalism, and colonialism, first under Bismarck and then under Wilhelm II, is, according to Cornelius Torp, broadly considered to be 'a turning point of crucial importance [. . . and] a key element in the conservative "refoundation" of the German Empire'.[40] It also resulted in a series of trade wars with Germany's main protectionist rivals, Russia and the United States, in the decades to come, as well as promoting the common idea that Germany needed to become a leading imperial power in its own right. By around 1890 more and more financial investments were being funnelled into German colonial projects in Africa, with the goal of exploiting raw materials for home industries.[41] Such Listian colonial schemes for strengthening the German nation epitomized this period of imperial globalization by necessitating not only emigration and colonial expansion, but also the creation of a strong German navy and German–South American steamship lines.

The German unification that followed the Franco–Prussian War (1870–1871), and the economic depression that struck soon thereafter, cemented Friedrich List's envisioned national system and tariff union at home not only through its imperial governors, but also within German universities via the influential GHS. This self-described anti-*Manchestertum* intellectual movement considered List its ideological progenitor. The GHS accordingly emphasized centralization of the German state, a programme of economic nationalism, anti-internationalist state socialism, and imperial expansion. The GHS was also more amenable to agricultural protectionism alongside tariffs and subsidies for German industries. The Listian school dominated German universities and threw its support behind the German imperial government. Professor Wilhelm Roscher, for example, supported colonial expansion in order to alleviate German overpopulation, surplus of capital, and political conflict. German imperialism was 'a necessary consequence of the new development in business' and essential in order for Germany to take its rightful place among the modern industrial nations of the world.[42] Its leading lights created the Verein für Sozialpolitik (Association for social policy) in 1872 to counteract Manchester liberalism, Judaism, internationalism, anti-imperialism, and democratic socialism, all of which were seen as existential threats to the nascent German nation and its imperial future.[43] The 1873 onset of the Long Depression and the GHS's conspiratorial attacks on *Manchestertum* also helped spark a new wave of anti-Semitism. Berlin journalist Otto Glagau abandoned liberalism at this time because 'Jewry is applied *Manchestertum* carried to its logical extreme. Similar sentiments appeared in Conservative and Catholic publications, and the Anglophobic writings of right-wing GHS historian Henrich von Treitschke, a longtime proponent of German colonialism at the University of Berlin.[44] Thanks to Roscher, Treitschke, and their GHS circle, by the latter part of the century such economic nationalistic—and often anti-Semitic—defences of German imperial expansion had become mainstream.[45]

The American System and the GHS became more enmeshed by the turn of the century. Italian economist Luigi Cossa went so far as to suggest at the time that the two should be rebranded the 'German-American school of economics'.[46] This amalgamation came about owing to a second wave of Listian nationalism crashing upon US shores during the late nineteenth century. In droves, US university students began studying history and economics at German universities, the beating heart of the GHS, in the last decades of the century. And these same students returned home infused with a progressive desire to use an activist government to undermine the doctrine of the Manchester School that was then so commonly trumpeted within the hallowed halls of the US ivory tower.[47] US disciples of the GHS began their assault on *Manchestertum's* university strongholds from their base camp, the University of Pennsylvania's Wharton School (founded in 1881), so named after its wealthy protectionist benefactor, industrialist Joseph Wharton. A frequent attendee of Henry Carey's Sunday 'Vespers', Wharton sought to counteract the academy's free-trade 'infection which healthy political organisms can hardly afford to tolerate'.[48] From their newfound bully pulpit in Philadelphia, economists Richard T. Ely, Simon Patten, and Robert Ellis Thompson, 'much influenced by Friedrich List's nationalism in political economy', taught their students in the tradition of 'the German-American school of economists founded by List and represented by H. C. Carey'. In 1885, the three men also co-founded the American Economic Association—originally proposed as the Society for the Study of National Economy—to act as the US branch of the GHS's Verein für Sozialpolitik. Republican opposition to Cobdenism grew as a result. The Anti-Cobden Club of Philadelphia, for instance, laid claim to over 1,500 members by the end of the 1880s, landing the club's president a prominent federal post in the 1889–1893 GOP administration of Benjamin Harrison.[49]

The American System first became a British imperial import by way of Canada, an unsurprising transimperial border-crossing considering the British colony's geographical proximity to, and growing economic dependence upon, its southern neighbour. By the 1850s, Canadian merchants were agitating for economic nationalism by citing the writings of Horace Greeley, the pro-Republican protectionist editor of the *New York Tribune*, and, of course, Friedrich List. Dominion politicians also continued to advocate construction of high tariff walls, emulating the American System, and nowhere were they to be built higher than along the long border that Canada shared with its southern neighbour. Toronto's Isaac Buchanan, the self-styled 'father of the National Policy' of Canada, helped found the Association for the Promotion of Canadian Industry (forerunner of the Canadian Manufacturer's Association) in 1858. With Henry Carey's writings as guide, he believed the 'Patriotic or Social Economy' of protectionism to be superior to the 'English Political Economy' of free trade. Canadian protectionists secured higher tariff rates during the depression years of 1858–1859 via the Galt Tariff, around the same time that Republican congressmen were beginning to push through the protectionist Morrill Tariff in the United States.[50]

The American System's appeal, including designs for a Canadian transcontinental railway, picked up more steam following Confederation in 1867, amid a growing sense of national identity. As Mel Watkins touches upon, the American System's emphasis on industrialization, homesteading, and railway promotion 'imprinted itself on the Canadian consciousness' as well as through 'high tariffs and lavish railway subsidies'.[51] The mid-1870s economic depression garnered further protectionist support for nurturing Canadian industries from the Dominion Boards of Trade. The Manufacturers' Association of Ontario thereafter helped craft the 1879 tariff bill, the same year that John A. Macdonald introduced the Conservative Party's protectionist National Policy.[52] In 1885 the last spike of the Canadian Pacific Railway was driven in, strengthening lines of transport and communication between the British Atlantic and the empire's colonies across the Pacific. By 1890, the American System had thus been emulated through the transcontinental railway and protectionist Canadian legislation, culminating in the entrenchment of the Conservative Party's National Policy and a series of trade wars with Canada's southern neighbour. Many of these same Canadian economic nationalists also took the lead in the late nineteenth-century British imperial trade preference movement and helped spark similar calls in Australia.[53]

Thanks in no small part to the efforts of North American economic nationalists, the American System soon took hold of the Australian nationalist imagination. With List, Clay, and Henry Carey as inspiration, protectionists in the British colony of Victoria were fighting a political and ideological battle with the free traders of New South Wales throughout the latter half of the nineteenth century.[54] Victorian protectionist William Bryson argued for infant industrial protectionism using US economic growth under the American System as testament and the work of Clay and List as scripture. The mid-century protectionist editor of the Melbourne *Age*, David Syme, also drew upon List and Carey. Melbourne politician and merchant George Ward Cole similarly reproduced sections of List's *National System* and Clay's speeches to highlight the prosperity to be derived were the American System to be implemented in Australia.[55] Following passage of a protective tariff in 1865 in Victoria, Australian colonial demands for imitation and retaliation only grew louder with the deepening of the Long Depression and passage in the United States of the extremely protectionist 1890 McKinley Tariff. The new Republican tariff indirectly injured Australian wool exports, sparking demands for retaliation and for strengthening of the economic bonds of the British Empire. Free traders throughout the Australian colonies found themselves outnumbered. The protectionist Melbourne *Age* celebrated how even New South Wales had become intolerant of 'the policy of the Manchester School'.[56]

The growing popularity of the American System in the British settler colonies of Canada and Australia, coupled with the Long Depression, gave succour to imperial protectionists in Britain itself. Whereas British economic nationalists had feared speaking above a whisper in the 1860s and 1870s owing to the hegemonic hold of the Manchester School, protectionist rumblings became a tumult by the late 1880s.[57] Unsurprisingly, a British variant of the GHS arose at this time, in Oxford: the derivatively named English Historical School. Then in 1885 Sampson Samuel Lloyd, a prominent Conservative politician and Birmingham manufacturer, published the first British translation of List's *National System*. His global tour of the settler colonies had inspired the undertaking. During his travels, he had discovered how List's work had 'directly inspired the commercial policy of two of the greatest nations of the world, Germany and the United States of America', as well as 'our English-speaking colonies' and 'some commercial economists in this country'. List's economic nationalist theories of forty years earlier were thus 'applicable at one time as at another', including 'the present moment' in Britain.[58]

With List as muse, Lloyd helped revive the imperialism of economic nationalism in Britain. This included the National Fair Trade League in 1881, 'fair trade' at this time referring to tariff retaliation and imperial trade preference.[59]

The Imperial Federation League was created a few years later to argue on behalf of greater imperial consolidation, with local chapters spread throughout Britain and the settler colonies.[60] A mounting desire to retaliate against the 1890 McKinley Tariff, even more than these imperial advances, legitimated their position; fair traders found a new home within the United Empire Trade League in 1891 under the leadership of Sheffield's anti-immigration Conservative MP Howard Vincent.[61] Whether through inspiration, emulation, or retaliation, disciples of the American System were to be found arrayed across the imperial world system.

The Imperialism of Economic Nationalism, 1890–1945

The American System's combination of economic nationalism and imperial expansion was becoming ever more popular across the industrializing world by the turn of the century, with the United States leading the way with the 1890 McKinley Tariff. This revolutionary Republican tariff bill was authored by two of the most forward-looking of the GOP's American System advocates, Ohio congressman William McKinley and secretary of state James G. Blaine of Maine. The tariff allowed the United States to expand its informal empire through its protectionist reciprocity provision. For years to come, the GOP slogan became 'protection and reciprocity', a clear call for foreign market expansion under an economic nationalist umbrella. In contrast to the *unconditional* most favoured nation principle backed by free traders—which allowed for any other interested parties to sign on, thereby expanding trade liberalization—Republican reciprocity was *conditional*. This meant that the 1890 tariff allowed for the signing of a series of bilateral reciprocity treaties, mostly in undeveloped regions of Latin America, so as to expand US market access while also curtailing the ability of signatories to sign similar treaties with the American empire's European rivals. This coercive reciprocal element, along with the looming threat of massive tariff retaliation should a signatory step out of line, restricted its application, making sure that US trade expansion at this time occurred under protectionist principles.[62]

At the dawn of the twentieth century, the Republican Party next oversaw the acquisition of a colonial empire. This included shoring up the country's transcontinental conquest, followed by the acquisition of a formal and informal colonial empire encompassing various islands in the Caribbean and the Asia-Pacific region—Puerto Rico, Cuba, Guam, Samoa, the Philippines, Hawai'i—where a succession of Republican administrations maintained coercive control

FIGURE 1.1. 'The Rapid Growth of Prosperity'. President McKinley pushes the massive imperial 'Protection Snowball', on its way to absorbing 'Extension of Territory'. *American Economist*, 23 February 1900, 89.

over colonial trade, finance, and migration.[63] As Johns Hopkins economist Sidney Sherwood described it at the turn of the century, the USA's 'young imperialism' of national political union alongside 'a tariff wall of fortification around the imperial boundaries' owed much to that 'successor of Hamilton', Friedrich List, whose ideas were 'rightly regarded as American' in origin.[64]

With the mythical 'China market' drawing Republican expansionist attentions, the GOP's styling of the protectionist empire's trade policy as an 'open door' was prime Orwellian doublespeak. Hence the unfortunate historiographical tendency to misconstrue the Republican open-door policy as free-trade in character. Observers at the time, by contrast, understood it for what it was; the open door meant equal access to foreign-controlled Chinese markets, not free trade. The door into the US domestic market would remain tightly closed, even for its newly acquired colonies. The Republican Party's 'magnificent open-door policy' aimed at the China market 'is Protection for American Industry', the *American Economist* clarified in 1901 (see Figs. 1.1, 1.2, and 1.3). Benjamin Wallace of the US Tariff Commission reiterated as much in 1921: 'The open door does not mean and should not mean free trade.'[65]

FIGURE 1.2. 'The White Light of Protection'. The American protectionist colonial empire shines with prosperous 'white light' at the dawning of the twentieth century. *American Economist*, 28 December 1900, 305.

FIGURE 1.3. 'Oh Mother, May I Go Out to Swim?' Uncle Sam, in maternal garb and carrying a disciplinary birch rod, warns a childlike Philippines to stay away from the water labelled 'free trade in tobacco in sugar'. *Puck* 58 (24 Jan. 1906).

GOP fears of a deluge of immigration from the newly acquired US colonies played a non-trivial part in the turn-of-the-century Listian playbook. 'Your votes for Free-Trade, your votes for the phantom politics of the flag following the Constitution,' warned Ohio congressman Charles Grosvenor in 1900, 'is but a declaration that the Sulus, the Tagals, the Filipinos and all the enormous horde of foreigners in Asia that have come to us as a possession' could pour into the United States in 'overwhelming columns of cheap—oh, how cheap!—low, degraded labor'.[66] Similar fears were raised about migrants from the nation's Caribbean colonies. The protectionist news organ *American Economist* reiterated *Gunton's Magazine*'s racialist demand that Puerto Rico and Hawai'i 'be permanently annexed as colonies, with no rights of American citizenship or statehood', so as to restrict immigration and foreign representation in Congress, and to set an imperial 'precedent for Cuba, if it should eventually be annexed'.[67] The US Supreme Court gave the xenophobic closed-door empire its legal seal of approval beginning with its 1901 decision in *Downes v. Bidwell*, which effectively ruled that the US government could enforce ad hoc tariff policies upon its colonies, in contrast to the internal policy of free trade that existed among the US states.[68]

The GOP's haphazard maintenance of the closed-door imperial project continued until the onset of the Great Depression. Fallout from both the First World War and the 1918 'Spanish' Flu aided and abetted the Republican Party's 1920s retreat from globalism.[69] Along Listian lines, US protectionists proudly announced their opposition to the League of Nations. The American Protective Tariff League highlighted that it was 'the first national organization in the United States to oppose the covenant of the League of Nations'. Why? Because the League was a 'foreign-controlled super-government' hell-bent upon enshrining free trade within its charter. 'Freedom of trade between the different states of the United States' only worked because they were all on the same 'economic level'. The same principle did not hold true, the *American Economist* argued, for trade among nations.[70] Republican passage of the Fordney-McCumber Tariff in 1922 helped get the country back on a protectionist track following a slight lowering of tariff rates under the Democratic pro–free trade presidency of Woodrow Wilson. The tariff was, along with quotas on immigration, a key part of the GOP's 'America First' unilateralist programme.[71] The increasingly nativist interwar nation would also place more stringent quotas on 'undesirable' European immigration, and by the end of the decade similarly racist associations would be imputed to Filipinos to curtail their migration to the continental United States, a policy that Rick Baldoz calls 'racial protectionism'.[72]

The beginning of the end of the US closed-door empire arrived in 1930. Republican passage of the infamous 1930 Hawley-Smoot Tariff so soon after the onset of the Great Depression contributed to the shrinking of world trade just when it most needed to expand. The protectionist legislation incurred a series of European retaliatory tariffs and a rise in anti-American sentiment.[73] The Foreign Policy Association's Raymond Leslie Buell, writing from Boston in 1938, went so far as to connect this blowback to the 1931 Japanese invasion of Manchuria, the 1935 Italian annexation of Ethiopia, and Nazi designs upon Central Europe; the last ditch efforts to maintain the American System in the USA had created a domino effect, as one desperate country after another, seeking economic self-sufficiency, turned to tariff retaliation alongside formal colonialism.[74] For many Americans, even some Republican stalwarts like Buell, protectionism now became synonymous with economic instability, an association that eased the way for a liberalization of US trade under the direction of Roosevelt's secretary of state, Cordell Hull. This reversal of long-standing protectionist politics also signalled a serious challenge to the imperial expansion of the American System that had taken place between the Civil War era and the early 1930s. The closed door of the expansive empire—implemented through high tariff walls, immigration restrictions, government subsidies, jingoism, militarism, and trade wars—was finally beginning to swing open.

In turn-of-the-century Britain, the US closed-door empire had already begun sparking renewed right-wing calls for retaliation from economic nationalists. They drew further encouragement from the settler colonies' continued support for protectionism and imperial trade preference. Joseph Chamberlain's Tariff Reform movement (1903–1913) was the result.[75] The Birmingham manufacturer-turned-politician spearheaded the movement, which emphasized tariff retaliation and immigration restrictions alongside British imperial trade preference as a retaliatory response to the American System's global popularity.

The prolific British political economist Joseph Shield Nicholson, Scottish businessman-turned-pundit F. S. Oliver, and Conservative journalist Leopold Amery all lent Listian firepower to the Tariff Reform arsenal. Nicholson oversaw the British republication of List's *National System* in 1904, and followed this up in 1909 with *A Project of Empire*, which sought to recast Adam Smith as an advocate of British protectionism and imperial expansion. Nicholson also made sure to include a scheme for an imperial customs union based upon the American System.[76] Oliver, a supporter of imperial preference and federation since the 1880s, drew upon the federalist vision of Alexander Hamilton as an example for unifying the empire under Tariff Reform.[77] Fears of German navalism and protectionism in turn were used to bolster the Tariff Reform movement, even as it brought leading lights of the English Historical School such as Birmingham University economic historian William Ashley into closer alliance with GHS counterparts in Germany.[78] And Leo Amery, among Chamberlain's staunchest supporters, began lashing out at the Manchester School in the pages of the London *Times*. Then, in 1906, with List as explicit inspiration, he published *The Fundamental Fallacies of Free Trade* amid his assault upon Adam Smith and Richard Cobden's Edwardian disciples. Amery continued to pursue his protectionist reformation as dominions secretary (1924–1929), when he pushed Empire Shopping and 'Buy British' campaigns through the London-based Empire Marketing Board (1926–1933).[79] Amery's defence of imperial protectionism was such that he once admitted to preferring the 'new order' of Hitler to the free-trade order of Cordell Hull.[80] Although Joseph Chamberlain's Tariff Reform movement was unsuccessful in the near term, it claimed a Pyrrhic victory in the early 1930s, when Britain abandoned free trade and joined the empire's trade preference system. Protectionist promotion of 'Buying British' would remain a staple within the Dominions until 1945.[81]

Edwardian Tariff Reformers were keen to point out with wry self-satisfaction that even under those few regimes that had remained bastions of economic liberalism longer than most, such as the Austro-Hungarian Empire, the 'circumstances have changed'. As Austrian economist Leo Petritsch recognized in his 1904 response to Chamberlain's movement, 'now there exists neither in Austria nor in Hungary any political party that would fly the banner of free trade'.[82] What became known as the 'Pig War' (1906–1909) began two years later when Austria-Hungary put prohibitive tariffs on Serbia's main export, pork. A sharp decrease in trade and a desire to curb Serbian expansionist ambitions motivated Austria-Hungary to annex Bosnia and Herzegovina from the Ottomans in 1908, sparking an Ottoman boycott of Austrian goods. The geopolitical groundwork had been laid for Austrian archduke Franz Ferdinand's 1914 assassination in Sarajevo at the hands of a young Bosnian Serb.[83]

The 'young' US closed-door empire remained a *fin de siècle* model for modernizing states like Australia. Following federation in 1900, the newly united antipodal British colony immediately embraced infant industrial protectionism and imperial trade preference. Sydney played host to the Intercolonial Protectionist Conference that same year, where the attendees emphasized the growth of the protected markets of Canada and the United States, while warning of the looming threat of Asian competition. The president of the New South Wales Chamber of Manufacturers referenced Henry Clay amid his calls for making protectionism a permanent Australian fixture, and the Melbourne *Age* did likewise by reprinting passages from Henry Carey and List.[84] In 1904 Benjamin Hoare, Melbourne journalist and secretary of the Protectionists' Association, abashedly admitted to having once been 'half caught by the fascinations of some of the Cobdenic theories', particularly those of the radical US political economist Henry George. But luckily for Hoare, 'the profounder reasonings of the German school of economics came as a corrective', and the teachings of List and Henry Carey as 'a very saving prophylactic'. In *Preferential Trade* (1904), Hoare outlined how Australian economic nationalism should go hand in hand with Joseph Chamberlain's newly proposed system of impe-rial trade preference in Britain.[85] Australia's economic nationalist investment paid imperial dividends; in 1907, federated Australia established trade prefer-ence with Britain, much as had Canada, New Zealand, and South Africa over the previous decade.

Not to be outdone, leading French and Italian imperialists took their cues from their protectionist counterparts across the English Channel and the Atlantic. Imperial expansionist Jules Méline, in his efforts to acquire new ex-ploitable agricultural lands at the turn of the century, looked in part to Joseph Chamberlain's contemporary Listian imperial preference scheme. But Méline found even more inspiration in the US continental empire. As David Todd puts it, Méline 'preferred to compare France's colonial demesne to the prosperous agricultural West of America'.[86] The empire's closed-door system thereafter was bolstered in the mid-1930s by the French government's establishment of a Maghreb customs union. French intra-imperial trade grew even as colonial food security crumbled amidst wider depression-era protectionist retrenchment; French colonial subjects from North Africa to northern Vietnam faced famine by the Second World War.[87] From around the same time, Italian imperialists began enacting similar exploitative neomercantilist policies in Ethiopia, culmi-nating in a campaign for Italian imperial 'wheat autarky' from 1938 to 1941.[88]

The Russian Empire followed its own Listian trajectory at the turn of the century. Throughout the latter half of the nineteenth century, the Russian academy became suffused with the teachings of the GHS.[89] And not long be-fore the Japanese and Russian empires came into conflict over Manchuria and Korea, Count Sergei Witte began repurposing the American System for the Russian Empire. Witte viewed himself as the Friedrich List of imperial Russia. His ideas, laid out in his popular 1889 pamphlet *The National Economy and Friedrich List*, were soon followed up with policy action. As director of railway affairs from 1889 to 1891, minister of ways and communications in 1892, finance minister from 1892 to 1903, and prime minister between 1905 and 1906, Witte oversaw the Russian Empire's Listian turn-of-the-century industrialization programme, high tariff policies, and the construction of the Trans-Siberian Railway to place Russia on a par with its rival imperial powers.[90] The high tariff of 1891 served as the cornerstone of Russian trade policy until the empire's demise, and sparked a two-year trade war with Germany.[91] Following Chinese defeat in the 1895 Sino–Japanese War, Witte negotiated a treaty with the Chinese government by which the Russian Empire would service China's debt to Japan in exchange for a railway concession in Manchuria: to build the Chinese Eastern Railway.

With support from the Russian Empire's leading industrialists, Witte's autocratic Listian endgame was to create a colonial space to strengthen the Russian continental imperial project. As Chia Yin Hsu notes, Witte's vision for Manchuria within the Russian Empire 'was an outgrowth of his contemplation on nationhood, articulated in a pamphlet on "nationalism" and the "national economy" that was both a translation of and a tribute to' Friedrich List, emphasizing 'the "colonial" dimension of this concept'. Russia would become the industrialized imperial metropole and Manchuria its agricultural colonial 'handmaiden' to set Russia on an equal footing with Japan and the European imperial powers. European economic nationalism and militarism, in turn, threatened Russian grain exports, worsening relations with its European rivals in the years leading up to the Great War.[92]

During the First World War, the Russian Empire's economic nationalism spilled over into violent policies of expulsion and property seizures of ethnic minority groups (Jews and Germans) seen as sympathetic to the enemy and a hindrance to economic development.[93] Listian disciple Dmitrii Mendeleev (of periodic table fame) and Russian industrialists comprising the Association of Industry and Trade, an influential lobbying group, continued to look to the neomercantalist doctrines of the United States and Germany for inspiration in the years leading up to and immediately following the 1917 Russian Revolution, paving the way for the increasingly autarkic interwar economic policies of the Soviet Empire. V. I. Lenin—who according to Roman Szporluk 'translated List into a Marxist language and adapted him to the Russian political tradition'—laid the groundwork for Joseph Stalin, whose industrial-military system was more Listian than Marxist.[94]

Turn-of-the-century German protectionists warned of the 'American peril'— a triple threat that included the US export invasion of Europe, heightened tariff walls, and economic encroachment into Latin America—and called for a customs war between the two empires. As Georg Oertel, editor of *Deutsche Tageszeitung*, argued to a gathering of agricultural protectionists in 1907 to riotous applause, a 'brisk and breezy war' was far better 'than a foul and musty peace [...] bought at the expense of German honour, at the price of German prosperity. There should be no attempt to avoid a customs war at all costs!' Some among Gustav Schmoller's GHS circle became more boastful about

German investments in China and Turkey, and even concocted plans for carving out a German colonial sphere from the remains of the Spanish and Portuguese empires in Latin America.[95] The increased duties on German exports implemented through the Republican tariff of 1909 only worsened German–American relations on the eve of the First World War.[96] The German Empire's protectionist response to the global spread of the American System, however, was imitative as well as retaliatory.

Through the expansionist efforts of Friedrich Naumann and his circle, Listian imperial visions for a German-led united *Mitteleuropa* became more and more popular in the years leading up to the First World War. As the nineteenth century wound down, the German Colonial Department was already beginning to consider the economic exploitation of eastern Europe along Listian lines.[97] The scheme received further support once Naumann, a Lutheran theologian by training, became involved with the GHS's distinctly secular Verein für Sozialpolitik from 1890. He thereafter established a name for himself among the German working class as an influential patriot-advocate of German navalism and colonial expansion. In 1906 Naumann argued for reconciling German industrial capitalism with democratization at home and imperial expansion abroad. In so doing, as Henry Meyer observes, 'he was following in the footsteps of Friedrich List'. Naumann's Listian vision emphasized the growth of German railway networks, and his circle also made sure to keep at least one expansionist eye on the Ottoman-controlled Christian Near East. Naumann and other like-minded turn-of-the-century 'patriot imperialists' viewed the Baghdad Railway as the ideal colonial prize, much as the Trans-Siberian Railway was to the Russian Empire. According to Meyer, 'many a Reich-German finger followed the thin black lines from Berlin southeastward and many a patriotic heart beat faster at the mention of *"unsere Bagdadbahn"*'.[98]

From the beginning of the Great War to the end of the Third Reich, this Listian pan-German vision infused German imperial policies and discourses. In 1914, Naumann's group began lobbying the imperial government to add *Mittelafrika* to its war aims. A year later, Naumann's widely popular book *Mitteleuropa* became his pan-Germanist magnum opus.[99] Continued anti-colonial unrest in the African colonies persuaded wartime an-German theorists and organizations such as the Pan-German League and German Eastern Marches Society to look elsewhere to achieve German hegemony, particularly Russian-controlled Poland. Some German colonialists during and after the Great War even began portraying Poland as more African or Asiatic than European, in order to justify its acquisition on grounds of racial superiority.[100] Soon after the onset of the Great Depression, Adolf Hitler's Third Reich put Naumann's Listian theories into imperial practice, coupled with Adolf Wagner's earlier anti-Semitic socialist (economic) nationalism via the GHS.[101] Hitler's economic nationalist Nazi empire accordingly adopted German colonial methods and ideas from south-west Africa as it looked to Latin America and eastern Europe for colonial exploitation. These 'indolent' regions were to have become peripheral agricultural producers to feed the German industrial centre, much as List had first recommended in 1841. In the case of Nazi-occupied Poland, this is effectively what transpired.[102]

The Ottoman Empire took its comparatively late Listian turn amid the First World War. As urged within the List-inspired publications of Ottoman economist Akyiğitzade Musa and Young Turk intellectuals such as Ömer Seyfeddin, Yusuf Akçura, and Mehmed Ziya Gökalp, economic nationalists within the empire pushed back against classical liberal theories as both an anti-colonial mechanism for extricating Ottoman finances from western European control, and as a last-ditch effort to resuscitate the empire's agriculture and industry through pan-Turkish consolidation. The coercive free-trade treaties that the western European powers had forced upon the Ottomans in the 1830s and 1840s allowed little room for protectionism throughout the late nineteenth century, outside of intellectual circles.[103] Investment in internal improvements such as telegraph lines and the Damascus–Hijaz Railway (1900–1908) laid an integrative path for Ottoman development. These were coupled with, as Cyrus Schayegh puts it, 'a "systematic colonization" policy of purchasing land [. . .] to stem Western economic inroads and expand agricultural output'. The empire's inability to raise tariff rates gave rise to an urban grassroots 'Buy Ottoman' campaign by the 1890s, and an Ottoman boycott of Austro-Hungarian goods followed Austria's 1908 annexation of Bosnia-Herzegovina.[104] The Great War itself allowed for substantive tariff increases in 1914. The subsequent wartime dislocation, persecution, exclusion, boycott, and property confiscation of Ottoman Armenians occurred under this widening economic nationalist standard that was carried forward into the post-Ottoman period; the national government's embrace of the 'New Turkish Economic School' included big increases in tariffs and quotas after 1929, once Turkey regained complete control over its tariff rates.[105] Through the 1930s leading Turkish intellectuals continued to draw on the GHS, alongside Marx, in advocating for a self-sufficient Turkish national economy.[106] Middle Eastern states not under the Mandatory thumb of the League of Nations joined Turkey in this 1930s protectionist trend.[107] By the 1920s, high tariff walls thus separated the nations and empires of Europe, as famously depicted by British Conservative politician Clive Morrison-Bell in 1926.[108]

Finally, economic nationalist intellectuals and politicians in the Japanese Empire found much to emulate in the American System. United States gunboats had coercively prised open Japanese markets in 1854, and until the 1890s the country stuck to a policy of free trade. But dissension from this laissez-faire establishment grew following the 1868 Meiji Restoration. It ushered in a new era of national consolidation and industrialization, with infant industrial protectionism soon to follow. Henry Carey's colleague the US economist Erasmus P. Smith began popularizing the American System in the early 1870s during his brief tenure as adviser to Japan's Ministry of Foreign Affairs.[109] Takahashi Korekiyo, who had undertaken studies in California as a teenager in the late 1860s, thereafter began arguing in the mid-1870s that protective tariffs were in Japan's national interest, with 'Fortress France' and the United States as models. Henry Carey's work was referenced as early as 1871, and then translated into Japanese between 1884 and 1888 (*Keishi no keizigaku*, or *Mr Carey's Economics*). Shiba Shirō wrote the preface. Shiba had received a finance degree from the University of Pennsylvania's Wharton School, part of the GHS-inspired school's first graduating class. During his studies, he was prone to consulting Carey's personal library. List was taught alongside Carey at the University of Tokyo by way of an American professor, Ernest Fenollosa. Financial reformer and politician Matsukata Masayoshi drew on List in advocating for Japanese infant industrial protectionism and central banking; according to Eric Helleiner, he was 'following in the footsteps of Alexander Hamilton'. The *National System* thereafter appeared in Japanese in 1889 at the request of Tomita Tesunosuke, the pro-centralization governor of the Bank of Japan, and an acquaintance of Henry Carey. List's translator, Oshima Sadamusu, the 'Friedrich List of Japan', was a staunch protectionist in his own right and was also an acquaintance of Carey. At around this time, disciples of the GHS such as Kanai Noburu and Kuwata Kumazō, following their studies at German universities, began preaching the gospel of economic nationalism from their bully pulpits at Tokyo's Imperial University. Takahashi himself went on to serve as prime minister from 1921 to 1922 and as minister of agriculture and commerce from 1924 to 1925. The protectionist Ministry of Commerce and Industry was created in 1925 under Takahashi's direction, inspired by his understanding of List's ideas and of how he saw Japan's late-developing position in the 1920s as analogous to that of interwar Germany.[110]

The growth of Japanese late nineteenth- and early twentieth-century economic nationalism led to colonial consolidation following the empire's successful wars against China (1894–1895) and Russia (1904–1905). Japanese tariff
walls were extended to its colonies of Taiwan in 1898 and Korea in 1920, at
which point, according to Kazuo Hori, Tokyo had effectively 'constructed a
tariff wall surrounding the whole empire to reinforce the economic unity of
the empire'.[111] The Japanese Empire's economic nationalism and its colonial
expansion in Asia in the years leading up to the Second World War contributed
in no small part to the growing tensions between Japan and the Western empires, particularly those of Britain and Russia.[112]

Japan's imperialism of economic nationalism became more systematized
during the Second World War. Mōri Hideoto, the right-wing division chief of
the economic section of the Foreign Ministry's newly established Asian Development Board, drew explicitly upon Friedrich List in outlining his imperial
vision for the Japanese national economy: 'the New Order of East Asia'.[113] The
wartime Japanese minister of foreign affairs, Matsuoka Yōsuke, unveiled
the subsequent Greater East Asia Co-Prosperity Sphere in August 1940. Along
Listian lines, the Sphere involved both a defensive and an offensive hierarchical programme of regional self-sufficiency and colonial exploitation, whereby
Japan's colonies in the 'South' such as Burma and the Philippines were to provide raw materials—petroleum, tin, nickel, cotton, wool hemp, lumber, rice,
sugar—for Japanese military industries and food needs.[114] The move was seen
as essential following punitive US economic sanctions in 1940–1941. The sanctions also helped provoke the surprise Japanese offensive against US colonial
holdings in the Asia-Pacific region, thereby drawing the United States into the
Second World War on the side of the Allies. Japan's militant response was a
predictable outcome of what Michael Barnhart describes as 'the vicious cycle
of Japan's pursuit of self-sufficiency'.[115]

Anti-Colonial Exceptions:
The Anti-imperialism of Economic Nationalism

List had not intended his infant industrial policies to be implemented in colonial spaces such as China, Ireland, India, and Egypt. For him, 'uninstructed,
indolent' regions like these were meant to remain exploitable colonial sources
of raw materials and export markets for surplus manufactured goods and
populations, not anti-colonial sites of infant industrial protectionist

agitation.[116] And yet this was precisely what unfolded during the late nine-teenth and early twentieth centuries. These colonial spaces exhibited unusual circumstances wherein economic nationalism along the American System model was embraced primarily as a defensive tool to counter free-trade impe-rial policies emanating from Britain. The US pan-Africanist intellectual W.E.B. Du Bois's adaptation of the American System to advocate for Black economic self-sufficiency provided a further anti-colonial bulwark from the turn of the century. His radical reinterpretation of white exploitation of Black labour as internalized US colonialism helped inspire his subsequent pan-African vision. Du Bois's Listian endorsement of a 'negro nation within a nation' stemmed from this, aided by his own ideological grounding in the GHS as a university student in 1890s Berlin and from growing pan-Africanist affinities with British Caribbean intellectuals. These anti-colonial exceptions to the imperial rule highlight a burgeoning early twentieth-century network of anti-colonial eco-nomic nationalists working within the empires of Britain, Germany, and the United States to undermine them. These anti-colonial advance guards laid the economic nationalist footpath for the decolonizing world to follow.

The era's systemic racial hierarchical structures contributed not only to the political and economic exploitation of Du Bois's Black America, but also to coercive British fiscal policies applied to China, Ireland, India, and Egypt. One key aspect of late nineteenth- and early twentieth-century British imperial rule was the commonly held belief that the empire's settler colonies were an ex-tension of the metropole, whereas 'uncivilized' colonies, by contrast, were considered racially inferior and therefore unable to be entrusted with fiscal autonomy.[117] Racism thus helped justify British free-trade imperialism in China, Ireland, India, and Egypt.

Whereas Britain's 'white' settler colonies of Canada, Australia, New Zea-land, and South Africa took greater control over their own fiscal policies from the mid-nineteenth century, the tariff policies of China, India, Ireland, and Egypt remained under the coercive free-trade dictates of the British imperial government.[118] Or as the Indian nationalist economist Romesh Dutt put it in 1902, 'in India the Manufacturing Power of the people was stamped out by protection against her industries, and then free trade was forced on her so as to prevent a revival'.[119] Lacking fiscal autonomy, Irish, Indian, and Egyptian anti-colonial nationalists would turn to an alternative method of protectionist protest: the boycott. The term 'boycott' itself became part of the English lexi-con by way of Ireland, stemming from the colony's late Victorian anti-colonial protests against British monopolization of Irish lands; a British land agent in

Ireland named Charles Cunningham Boycott became the main target, and the term's inspiration.[120] The United States's own successful nineteenth-century protectionist counter to British free-trade imperialism also provided an enticing model for anti-colonial nationalists to imitate if and when they gained control over their own tariff policies. By focusing narrowly on the defensive anti-imperial aspects of the American System, in turn, anti-colonial nationalists within the British Empire's remit were able to sidestep the imperial expansionist impulse that so often accompanied the American System's implementation elsewhere at this time.

China's Listians made their political presence felt from the turn of the century. Nationalist leader Liang Qichao helped pave the way. Liang's endorsement of economic nationalism as both an anti-colonial tool and an imperial weapon, however, departed from the purely defensive posture taken by Irish, Indian, and Egyptian anti-colonial nationalists. Following an unsuccessful attempt to reform the government in 1898, Liang landed in Japan, where he first encountered the writings of the GHS. They complemented an older tradition of Chinese neomercantilist thought, and Liang thereafter self-identified as an anti-Smithian disciple of 'national economics'. He saw the world as one of perpetual warfare, and believed that China's very survival rested on its ability to win a global trade war. The European-controlled treaty ports were clear examples of free-trade imperialism in China. 'If the whole country becomes a free-trade zone,' he mused, 'then is that not equivalent to making the whole country a colony?' Liang sought to create for China the economic nationalist system that had worked so well in Europe and the United States—including massive corporate monopolies and imperial expansion. Upon returning to China in 1911, he threw himself into Chinese nationalist politics, rivalling Sun Yat-Sen, the provisional president of the Republic of China in 1912. Liang also wore his 'national economics' on his sleeve at the 1919 Paris Peace Conference, where he demanded that China be given control over its tariff policies.[121]

Three years later, Chinese Listian reinforcements arrived. Ma Yinchu—future president of Peking University—returned to China following his studies at Yale, Columbia, and New York universities. In Peking (Beijing), he gave a speech arguing that China needed List's protectionist prescription because of the country's long-standing exploitation at the hands of European imperial powers, which continued to force open the nation's markets. Without tariff autonomy and industrialization, 'China would forever remain a supplier of raw materials and a consumer of manufactured goods'. His answer apparently did not go unnoticed. In 1925, after his studies at the University of Berlin and the

University of London (1920–1925), Liu Binglin authored a Chinese biography of List to undermine the common British-influenced belief that 'economic undertakings have no national boundaries'. That same year, Wang Kaihua undertook the first Chinese translation of List's National System as a PhD student at the University of Tübingen, which appeared in print in 1927. The Chinese minister to the German Legation, Wei Chenzu, in the preface to the 1929 edition, noted that List's work remained applicable to China because the country had been 'deprived of the right to set its tariffs' and flooded with foreign goods: 'It is highly proper that List's theory should be adopted in China.' The successful rise of the United States and Germany at the very high-water mark of British naval and commercial power underlined these points for Chinese 'patriots and political economists'.[122]

Even as British imperialists were busy forcing open the China market for opium, early stirrings of Irish anti-imperialist economic nationalism were detectable in the years leading up to the Great Famine (1845–1849). Economic crises afflicting Ireland between 1838 and 1842 had hit Dublin's own infant industries hard, sparking protectionist rumblings.[123] At this time, however, Ireland's nationalist movement yet remained under the free-trade leadership of 'the Liberator', Daniel O'Connell. A liberal radical on many issues—including Irish Home Rule, antislavery, religious freedom, suffragism, and protection of Aborigines—O'Connell tied the mid-century Irish nationalist movement's political coat-tails to the middle-class radicalism of Richard Cobden and John Bright's Anti–Corn Law League and its promise of cheap food for the British Isles. As Pickering and Tyrell put it, 'no public figure outside the ranks of the League leadership was received more warmly at Anti-Corn Law gatherings than the "Liberator" of Ireland'.[124] O'Connell's death in 1847, however, created a vacuum waiting to be filled by a younger generation of Irish nationalists more amenable to protectionist politics.[125]

American System policies began making more anti-colonial nationalist headway in Ireland once Arthur Griffith launched the Sinn Féin Party in 1905. In his now famous 1905 Dublin speech, Griffith acknowledged List's influence upon his own anti-colonial critique of the Manchester School: 'I am in economics largely a follower of the man who thwarted England's dream of the commercial conquest of the world [. . .] Frederich [sic] List.' Griffith 'would wish to see [The National System] in the hands of every Irishman' and thereby brush aside 'the fallacies of Adam Smith and his tribe'. Drawing upon List alongside Henry Carey, Griffith put forward a bold protectionist plan for obtaining Irish independence.[126]

A mounting trade conflict between Britain and the Irish Free State came to a head in 1932. That year, right-wing nationalist Seán Lemass was appointed minister of industry and commerce with the principal goal of attaining Irish economic self-sufficiency. So began what became known as the Economic War (1932–1938) of tariff retaliation between the two states.[127] The British government—fresh from repudiating the nation's long-standing adherence to the gold standard in 1931 and then free trade at the 1932 Ottawa Conference— kicked the conflict off with severe tariffs on Ireland's main exports to Britain. It added salt to the wounds by excluding Ireland from the Commonwealth preferential tariff agreements devised at the conference. The Economic War continued for six years, finally winding down with the signing of the Anglo– Irish Trade Agreement in 1938, but the Irish nationalist desire for economic self-sufficiency would remain.[128]

Ireland's economic nationalist movement had much in common with India, where late Victorian and Edwardian British free-trade imperial policies simi- larly helped fuel anti-colonial nationalist fires. And much as in Ireland, for many Indian nationalist leaders the American System's successful implementa- tion in the United States, Germany, and Japan also came to represent how underdeveloped economies like India's might thwart British free-trade impe- rial machinations.[129] So too would key cities in the United States and Germany become, as Kris Manjapra describes it, 'the most important centers for Indian anti-colonial internationalism', leading to the development of 'a highly articu- lated international imagination [. . .] after 1905, by which Bengali thinkers saw their own experiences mirrored back in political events that had occurred, or were occurring, in China, Japan, the United States, and Germany'.[130]

Indian anti-imperialism of economic nationalism started in the early 1860s when the British Raj reduced tariffs on imported cotton to five per cent. The low- tariff policy was then applied to general import duties between 1864 and 1875. Even such minimal revenue tariffs soon came under attack from Lancashire cotton manufacturers and the Manchester Chamber of Commerce. This led to the effective elimination of Indian import duties by the early 1880s, despite Indian nationalist protestations that doing so would undermine industrial de- velopment. The exemption of an excise tax on manufactured cotton goods in 1894 was viewed in a similar light by granting British cotton manufacturers an effective monopoly over the Indian market. That year's Indian National Con- gress (INC) put 'on record its firm conviction that [. . .] the interests of India have been sacrificed to those of Lancashire'. One nationalist leader, Pheroze- shah Mehta, charged that the motivation behind the tax exemption was to

strangle 'the infant industries of India [. . .] in their birth'. This coercive enforcement of free trade upon India, he continued, represented the culmination
of decades of British economic exploitation, which had long since gutted India's centuries-old 'indigenous industries'.[131]

British free-trade imperialism in India sparked late nineteenth- and early
twentieth-century anti-colonial protectionist grassroots action. Calcutta-born
nationalist Bholanath Chandra sought to 'dethrone King Cotton of Manchester' in the 1870s, popularizing the boycotting of British goods as anti-colonial
protest. Demands for anti-British boycotts became commonplace in Bombay
newspapers throughout the 1880s and 1890s. Mahadev Govind Ranade helped
organize the Industrial Association of Western India and convened the first
annual Industrial Conference in 1890. In 1900 the INC formed an Industrial
Committee to explore how best to nurse India's long-malnourished industries
back to health. Amid yet another famine, nationalists also emphasized canal
projects over the British Raj's preference for railway lines, arguing that the latter
may have increased foreign trade, but had done little to develop indigenous
agriculture and industry.[132] Indian economic nationalist dissent culminated in
the Swadeshi (home rule) movement, which arose in direct response to Lord
Curzon's partition of Bengal in 1905, the same year Arthur Griffith launched
Sinn Féin in Ireland. By mid-century, Swadeshi's anti-colonialism had evolved
into a national expression of economic patriotism.[133]

Turn-of-the-century Indian nationalist leaders viewed the global protectionist turn as evidence of Swadeshi's universalism. M.G.K. Gokahle, speaking
before the 1906 INC, even held up Joseph Chamberlain's Tariff Reform movement alongside the protectionist policies of Germany, France, and the United
States as evidence that 'the *Swadeshi* movement is one which all nations on
earth are seeking to adopt in the present day'.[134] The anti-colonial end-goal of
the Swadeshi movement, meanwhile, confounded subsequent attempts to
align it with the empire's advocates of imperial trade preference such as Joseph
Chamberlain and his protectionist successors.[135]

At this time, Sinn Féin's Listian programme came to be seen as a reflection
of Swadeshi's anti-colonial appeal. Griffith's List-inspired 1905 speech-turned-
pamphlet *The Sinn Féin Policy* was republished a year later in Hindustani and
mass-distributed in Indian nationalist news outlets, demonstrating both the
ideological affinity between and similar fiscal colonial circumstances of India
and Ireland at this time. One such newspaper went on to explain that 'Mr
Griffith's scheme is thus of great service to us just now. [. . .] The new policy is
called 'Sinn Féin' policy, which is only another name for our 'Swadeshi' policy.'

At around this time, Mahatma Gandhi too, although critical of the violence of the Irish nationalist movement, expressed his appreciation for Griffith's anti-colonial protest through economic non-cooperation. Griffith's own subsequent endorsement of non-violence, in turn, illustrated the reciprocal nature of their relationship.[136] Gandhi would soon rise to even greater prominence as a leading interwar advocate of non-violent anti-colonial activism that emphasized Indian economic development through boycotts and non-cooperation.[137] The 1919 Fiscal Autonomy Act in turn allowed for Indians to begin levying tariffs on British-made textiles, reaching twenty-five per cent by 1931.[138]

Britain's stifling of India's industrial development through coercive free-trade imperial policies also drew Indian nationalists to the GHS. The GHS's transimperial crossings became common from the turn of the century. German scholars were often invited to Calcutta University, and young Indian academics attended German universities to bolster Indian nationalist research programmes upon their return home.[139] Manu Goswami explores how at this time Friedrich List's *National System* became a 'foundational text' for South Asian anti-colonial nationalists like Kashinath Trimbak Telang, Ganesh Vyankatesh Joshi, Gopal Krishna Gokhale, Subramania Aiyer, Ranade, Romesh Chunder Dutt, Benoy Kumar Sarkar, Vaman Govind Kale, and Radhakamal Mukherjee. To a lesser extent, Henry Carey and the heads of the GHS such as Wilhelm Roscher and Adolf Wagner also gained an Indian nationalist following.[140] As Kale of the 'Bombay School' described it in 1910, 'almost all our industries are in the infancy stage. How are they to grow in the face of the formidable rivalry of foreign manufacturers? [. . .] The national and historical school of economists, has successfully demonstrated the abstract and impractical nature of the doctrines of the old school [of Adam Smith and Manchester liberalism].' Meanwhile, Japan had 'demonstrated to the world what Protection can do for a backward country—and Asiatic country too, not to speak of Germany, the most formidable rival England has in Europe today'.[141] The transimperial intellectual confluence of the American System within India thus helped cement the ideological foundations of the early twentieth-century Swadeshi anti-colonialist movement.

Socialist Jawaharlal Nehru's rise to prominence within the Indian nationalist movement propelled demands for independence and anti-imperialism throughout the 1930s and 1940s, as well as closer coordination with the international peace movement. Nehru was one of the authors of the INC's 1923 Boycott Resolution, which tied economic non-cooperation to the nationalist *swaraj* (self-rule) movement.[142] In 1936, Nehru succeeded in persuading the

INC to join the Geneva-based International Peace Campaign (IPC, 1936–1940). The IPC's wide membership also included numerous feminist, socialist, and Christian economic peace organizations, such as the International Co-Operative Alliance (see chapter 3), the International Co-Operative Women's Guild, the Women's International League for Peace and Freedom (see chapter 4), and the World Alliance for Promoting International Friendship through the Churches (see chapter 5). Perhaps owing to these growing affinities with the economic peace movement, Nehru did not see any contradiction in connecting 1930s Euro-American economic nationalism with monopolies and war, even as he supported boycotts and other forms of economic nationalism for the colonial world.[143] Nehru's anti-colonial affinities with China reached such a point in 1937 that he organized a boycott of Japanese goods following the launching of a major Japanese military offensive there.[144] Ever the consummate diplomat, Nehru proved adept at reconciling his wider support for the economic peace movement with the anti-imperialism of his economic nationalism.

Thanks to Benoy Kumar Sarkar, the interwar Swadeshi movement continued to draw upon List and the American System for ideological inspiration. Sarkar undertook the first Bengali translation of List's *National System* following his travels around the world. His transimperial journey began in Japan in 1915, and ended in Berlin. From his temporary base in Germany, Sarkar lectured on the similarities between India and 'Euro-America'. Upon his return to Calcutta, he was numbered among Bengal's most prominent interwar intellectuals. In 1932 he described how List's *National System* was 'the Bible of a people seeking a rapid transformation of the country from the agricultural to the industrial tage'.[145] This was a remarkably prescient observation, and not just for India; Listian infant industrial policies would become a popular model for economic nationalists throughout the decolonizing world after 1945 (see chapter 6). Sarkar's strong sympathies with Germany also helped draw him further to the political right, leading to his supporting the Nazi Party.[146]

During and after the First World War, the Swadeshi movement began looking not only to the anti-colonial leadership of Gandhi, Nehru, and Sarkar, but also to local Indian women spinners. Gandhi himself emphasized the importance of women in the struggle for *swaraj* and economic self-sufficiency. The boycotting of Lancashire-made cotton goods to bolster local production of homespun textiles (*khadi*) became key. 'In this struggle for freedom,' Gandhi argued, 'the contribution of women will exceed that of men. Swaraj is tied to a strand of yarn [. . . and] it is the women who are the spinners.' Women also tended to be the ones on the picket lines of the cloth markets. Their roles expanded still further in 1930, when protests arose against the long-standing British monopoly on the manufacture and sale of salt. Members of the Indian female intelligentsia such as Uma Nehru and Swarup Rani joined Gandhi at the forefront of the non-violent march against the salt tax, in the course of which Gandhi and over sixty thousand others were arrested. To break the British monopoly, they called for the domestic manufacture of salt. 'If you are true to your motherland,' Swarup Rani argued before ten thousand fellow activists gathered near Allahabad in April 1930, 'then you should start manufacturing salt in every household.' The salt *satyagraha* (truth force) movement thus provided a further feminist additive to the quarter-century-old Swadeshi fight for *swaraj*.[147]

Early twentieth-century Egyptian anti-colonial nationalist women and men drew inspiration from the Indian nationalist movement in British-occupied Egypt. The Swadeshi connection was hinted at as early as 1905 in an Indian cartoon that was reported as a 'seditious image' to the India Office (Fig. 1.4). The actual title of the cartoon was 'Rashtriya Jagruti', or 'National Awakening'. It recast the mythical Hindu battle between the multi-weaponed Devi Mahalakshmi and her lion against a horde of Mahishasura's evil demons. Devi is armed with 'a sword labelled "Swadeshi", a mace labelled "Aikya" (Unity), a knife labelled "Atma Viswas" (Self-reliance) [, and] a trident labelled "Svatantrya" (Self-Government), which the goddess has thrust into the mouth of a demon labelled "Partantrya" (Government by Others)'. Devi's lion, 'labelled "Bahishkar" (Boycott)', is lashing out at a 'bovine monster labelled "'Pardeshi Vyapar" (Foreign Trade)'. Visages of Indian nationalist leaders such as Gandhi and Dutt create a border around the cartoon. Included among them, notably, was the Egyptian nationalist Mustapha Kamil Pasha (top row, furthest right).[148]

The Swadeshi movement continued to provide inspiration as Egyptian nationalist agitation grew during the First World War, leading to revolution in 1919. Its rallying cry was 'Egypt for the Egyptians'. Mass protests and boycotts became commonplace, as did corresponding acts of British colonial violence. The independence movement's Women's Boycott Committee played a central role.[149] Egyptian demands for boycotts and non-cooperation against the British picked up pace in the early 1920s, in conjunction with Gandhi's movement, but waned after the ending of the Egyptian protectorate in 1922. A visit from Gandhi himself in 1931 helped spark the nationalist Wafd Party's 'Buy Egyptian' campaign, political non-cooperation, and an economic boycott of British goods to protest the authoritarian policies of

FIGURE 1.4. C. R. Cleveland, 'A Seditious Image'. London, British Library, Mss.Eur.D.709/12, India Office Records and Private Papers. © British Library Board. All Rights Reserved / Bridgeman Images.

the British-backed Egyptian government. Fabrics made from Egyptian cotton were prioritized, and British-made clothing was burned in public bonfires. New Egyptian industries rose from the ashes. As Nancy Reynolds puts it, 'the boycotts acted as steppingstones toward the establishment of a completely independent nation-state.'[150]

Gandhi's non-violent, anti-imperial, economic nationalist ideology, or 'Gandhism', in turn gave succour to Black activists in Jamaica, southern Africa, and the United States, resulting in a closer association between pan-Africanism and pan-Asianism. Gandhi's non-cooperation movement—the mass boycott of British products and political institutions between 1920 and 1922—accentuated to Black activists in the United States, including pan-Africanist leaders W.E.B. Du Bois and Jamaican-born Marcus Garvey, that economic self-sufficiency could create political empowerment.[151] In 1921, for example, the West Indian editors of the *Crusader* asked Black Americans, 'How long will we Negroes of America remain indifferent to the sufferings of our kindred under "British" rule and blind to the vast power of the economic boycott to chastise our enemy and effect reprisals for the wrongs and insults heaped upon us by the supercilious Anglo-Saxons?' The magazine noted that they would also have Irish nationalist allies, 'whose boycott the British are already beginning to feel.'[152] A year later James Weldon Johnson, the executive secretary of the NAACP, argued in a *New York Age* editorial that 'if non-cooperation brings the British to their knees in India, there is no reason why it should not bring the white man to his knees in the South.'[153]

W.E.B. Du Bois drew up his own evolving political economic blueprint for undermining Euro-American colonial exploitation of people of color from within this growing sense of solidarity between anti-colonial nationalists across the British, US, and German empires.[154] During his studies with the intellectual leaders of the GHS in 1890s Berlin, Du Bois 'began to see the race problem in America, the problem of the peoples of Africa and Asia, and the political development of Europe as one.'[155] For Du Bois, the US system of internal Black colonial exploitation had first existed under the slave system before the US Civil War and was thereafter perpetuated under Jim Crow. 'Like Nemesis of Greek tragedy,' he wrote in *Black Reconstruction* (1935), 'the central problem of America after the Civil War, as before, was the black man: those four million souls whom the nation had used and degraded, and on whom the South had built an oligarchy similar to the colonial imperialism of today, rested on cheap colored labor and raising raw material for manufacture'. He later described the post–Civil War programme of Reconstruction as 'a vast and powerful Mandates Commission [...] to apply to our colonial population', followed by ongoing attempts 'to suppress the Negro [... and] to push him back toward slavery'.[156] Drawing more on pan-Africanist and GHS influences than upon Marxism, he called his anti-colonial vision for Black economic self-sufficiency within the United States 'a negro nation within the nation'.[157]

Du Bois, the most influential early twentieth-century Black American writer, first began theorizing about Black nationalism and self-sufficiency during his graduate studies in Berlin between 1892 and 1894, at the high tide of the GHS's influence.[158] Those years in imperial Germany were among the happiest and most liberating of Du Bois's life; the warm welcome he received there provided a stark contrast to the lynching, disfranchisement, and discrimination of Jim Crow America. In Berlin, he 'sat under the voice of the fire-eating Pan-German, von Treitschke', and professors Adolf Wagner and Gustav Schmoller granted him access to their elite doctoral research seminars. They thereafter wrote in support of Du Bois to extend his studies with them rather than at Harvard, where 'the tendency was toward English free trade and against the American tariff policy'.[159] With encouragement from the two dons of the GHS, Du Bois began to apply their 'scientific' approach to re-examine Black history, sociology, and political economy in the United States. He also became a member of the Verein für Sozial Politik. As Lawrence Oliver notes, from here on Du Bois viewed the US 'race problem' as being 'inextricably connected to racism suffered by peoples of color around the world and impelled him to begin to 'unite [his] economics and [his] politics. [. . . H]e would have to challenge not only proponents of laissez-faire economics but also the Color Line.'[160]

Du Bois's GHS-inspired critique of 'English free trade' remained visible within his subsequent pan-Africanist economic nationalism. His envisioned self-sufficient and separate Black economic community was made explicit in his 1911 novel *The Quest of the Silver Fleece*; the tragic tale ended with a white mob setting fire to the community and the lynching of two Black men. In *Black Reconstruction* (1935), within a pan-African Marxist/Listian framework, Du Bois made sure to acknowledge the successful scientific industrialization promotion of Henry Carey during the Civil War era, as well as Carey's attacks on free trade, joining 'the German Liszt [*sic*] in a demand for a self-contained national economy'.[161] Du Bois's Marxist/Listian emphasis upon a separate, self-sufficient Black economic system remained part of his evolving pan-Africanist ideology and his growing interwar opposition to European imperialism in Africa and Asia. His radicalism and ideas would also continue to influence the anti-colonial world after 1945. As Walter Rucker observes, 'Du Bois' conceptualization of "self-segregation" became the basis for a revolutionary Pan-Africanist tradition that would be espoused later by the likes of Malcolm X, Kwame Nkrumah, and Kwame Turé.'[162] Thanks to anti-colonial nationalists in China, Ireland, India, Egypt, and the USA, the American System, for so long the economic nationalist model of modern empires, was starting to be refashioned to dismantle them.

Conclusion

The American System arose as the preferred late nineteenth-century economic programme of Britain's rival industrializing imperial powers as well as for some leading anti-colonial nationalists by the turn of the century. One empire after another—the United States, France, Germany, Russia, Austria-Hungary, the Ottomans, and Japan—embraced protectionism and colonial expansion along lines laid out by the American System. Even Britain, the last free-trade holdout, ultimately succumbed to the siren song of self-sufficiency and colonial consolidation amid the depression-ridden early 1930s. Imperial globalization was thus largely a protectionist, piecemeal, regionalized process, within which anti-colonial nationalist networks across the British, US, and German empires provided unusual exceptions to the American System's imperial application, as illustrated in the cases of China, Ireland, India, Egypt, and Du Bois's Pan-Africanism.

From the mid-nineteenth to the mid-twentieth century, the American System of protectionism was far more synonymous with militarism, jingoism, war, and imperial expansion. And this was precisely how the vast majority of both the American System's economic nationalist supporters and its economic cosmopolitan critics understood it. Left-wing peace activists and anti-imperialists accordingly sought to undermine the protectionist imperial order. Their mid-nineteenth-century mobilization saw the creation of a radical cosmopolitan pacifistic alliance of capitalists, socialists, feminists, and Christians, marking the beginning of their century-long left-wing free-trade fight for a more peaceful, anti-imperial world order.

2

The Anti-imperialism of Free Trade

THE LIBERAL RADICAL CRITIQUE OF IMPERIALISM AND WAR

The Colonial system, with all its dazzling appeals to the passions of the people, can never be got rid of except by the indirect process of Free Trade which will gradually and imperceptibly loose the bonds which unite our colonies to us by a mistaken notion of self-interest.

—RICHARD COBDEN (BRITAIN), 1842[1]

Richard Cobden has said: 'Free-Trade is the best peace-maker.' We make bold to say: 'Free-Trade has become the only possible peace-maker.' ... To those who have a justified horror of an autocratic Pax Germanica, who do not want a Pax Britannica—nor wish for a Pax Americana—there remains one hope, that of the advent of the democratic Pax Economica.

—HENRI LAMBERT (BELGIUM), 1918[2]

Peace waves her olive-branch, and summons round her,
Array of heads unhelmed, unweaponed hands;
Commerce, late lightened of the chains that bout her,
Speeds hitherwards the gifts of many lands.

So began *Punch*'s pacifistic paean to London's Great Exhibition of 1851.[3] The 'Exhibition of Industry' set up shop at the Crystal Palace. The enormous glass architectural wonder along the north bank of Hyde Park's Serpentine Lake had been constructed just for the occasion. The six million visitors who arrived to ogle the wares of the fifteen thousand exhibitors between May and October were greeted with 'songs of "peace on earth and good-will towards men"' meant to cement 'the great idea of fraternity' more than 'at any time within the period of recorded history'.[4] The exhibition promised the world. It claimed to display goods from nearly every nation. Such a global feat was made possible, the *Illustrated London News* reported, thanks to the 'civilizing agencies' of the age: railroads, steamships, telegraphs. These modern marvels had annihilated 'space and time' by breaking down 'the ancient barriers of jealousy and exclusiveness', by obliterating 'the rancourous remembrances of bygone wars', and by making 'Europe one large country'. Playing host recast London as 'the metropolis of the world. The Exhibition [...] deprived it of its local character, and rendered it no longer English merely, but cosmopolitan'.[5] *Punch* nicknamed the Crystal Palace the 'Temple of Peace'.[6] London's *Morning Chronicle* instead dubbed it 'the inaugural festival of free trade'.[7] Both were fitting descriptors.

The exhibition's more liberal organizers well understood its intimate association between free trade and peace. For such left-leaning liberals (liberal radicals), the festival of free trade tapped into a deep wellspring of Enlightenment-era economic ideas that had come to be known by this time as the Manchester School, or Manchester liberalism.[8] Jeffrey Auerbach concludes that 'of the ideological links between the exhibition and the Manchester School there can be little doubt'.[9] Free trade was fast becoming a national ideology in Britain.[10] And the Manchester School's staunchest left-leaning ideologues believed that the market interdependence wrought from the worldwide adoption of free trade would bring a panoply of riches: prosperity; industrialization; the devolution of empires; the eradication of hunger by expanding the global food supply and lowering food prices; and the democratization of governments by undermining the political power of militant mercantilist elites. For Manchester liberals, free trade thus offered an intoxicating cure-all for an industrializing world plagued by inefficient markets, aristocratic rule, mercantilist empires, food insecurity, and geopolitical turmoil.

The Crystal Palace provided the ideal forum for tackling multiple pressing left-wing issues at once. Pacifists unsuccessfully sought to ban all weapons from the exhibits and made sure that the year's international peace congress was held simultaneously down the road at London's Exeter Hall. Abolitionists hoped to make the exhibition a testament to the superiority of free-labour products. Karl Marx and Friedrich Engels believed the Festival of Free Trade represented an encouraging capitalist step forward in the progressive march towards socialist revolution. Millenarian Christian evangelicals prayed that the Temple of Peace might also provide a big tent for religious revivalism, uniting all mankind in anticipation of Christ's imminent return. Excepting socialist revolution, the exhibition's more left-leaning pro–free trade architects hoped to knit these strands together to create a more peaceful and less imperial economic cosmopolitan order. As Richard Cobden—the Liberal radical leader of the British free-trade movement and one of the exhibition's organization committee members—promoted it, the event would 'break down the barriers that have separated the people of different nations, and witness the universal republic'.[11]

The hype heralding Hyde Park's mirrored edifice in 1851 reflected the euphoria of the era's economic cosmopolitans, as well as the mounting tensions between these and their economic nationalist counterparts. Their conflict was not only over what constituted the proper path for global economic development and integration, but also over the future course of imperialism and war. Left-wing economic cosmopolitan idealists represented an interdependent world order that promised peace, prosperity, democracy, internationalism, and the devolution of empires. Economic nationalists instead stood for a realist view of geopolitics wherein great power rivalry, militarism, trade wars, and colonialism were considered necessary evils, and the Western imperial nation state the pinnacle of civilization. As explored in the previous chapter, by around 1870, the latter were winning the ideological war. The former, finding themselves on the outside looking in, doubled down on expanding their international grassroots organizing to counteract the imperialism of economic nationalism. Until his death in 1865, Cobden, the 'International Man' and 'Apostle of Free Trade', acted as the economic peace movement's figurehead; hence the frequent use of the term 'Cobdenism' as a synonym for Manchester liberalism thereafter. Cobdenism (and Cobden himself) called for a fundamental overhaul of foreign policy that the wider economic peace movement would also embrace: free trade coupled with non-interventionism, anti-imperialism, disarmament, international arbitration, and an end to war loans. Cobden's own opposition to formal and informal imperialism of all stripes epitomized 'the anti-imperialism of free trade'.[12] Thus from within the belly of the British imperial beast grew a left-wing free-trade tradition dedicated to making wars, poverty, aristocracy, and empires obsolete.

The commercial peace movement spread from Britain to the European continent and the United States in the years surrounding the 1851 Great Exhibition.[13] London hosted the era's first transatlantic peace gathering in 1843, the

General Peace Convention, at which a resolution that free trade was 'one of the best securities for peace' stood out.[14] That same year James Wilson founded the *Economist,* which became the Manchester School's main journalistic mouthpiece amidst their shared effort to overturn the Corn Laws, Britain's protective tariffs on foreign grain. The 1843 peace convention and repeal of the Corn Laws in 1846 sparked a hunger for greater international organization, leading to peace congresses in Brussels (1848), Paris (1849), Frankfurt (1850), and London (1851). The onset of the Long Depression and the global protectionist turn of the 1870s could all too easily overshadow how the economic peace movement was making inroads ever further afield via the era's tools of transport and communication: global steamship lines, transcontinental railways, and transoceanic cables. These new technologies may have facilitated the expansion and consolidation of empires, but they also made the pacifistic ideas of global governance and imperial devolution seem more feasible to liberal radical free traders.[15]

The diffusion of Manchester liberalism played an underappreciated role in making the period between the Franco–Prussian War (1870–1871) and the outbreak of the Great War the 'golden age' of the peace movement and international organization.[16] According to Mark Mazower, 'Cobden's free trade movement was the leading and unquestionably most successful version of radical internationalism to emerge' by the mid-nineteenth century.[17] Over the next century, Cobdenism's popularity led to the creation of numerous left-of-centre grassroots organizations that embraced economic cosmopolitanism as a prerequisite for peace and the devolution of empires.[18] London's Cobden Club, founded by Cobden's friends in 1866 under the mantra 'Free trade, Peace, Goodwill among Nations', remained the unofficial headquarters of the economic peace movement until the Great War, after which several more radical pressure groups in New York, Boston, and Geneva would share the burden. Meanwhile, from around 1910, financial backing from some of the era's leading plutocrats-turned-philanthropists helped the free-trade-and-peace movement stay afloat during the difficult years between the First and Second world wars.

The economic cosmopolitan challenge to the neomercantilist era's imperialism of economic nationalism also gave birth to sophisticated modern liberal radical critiques of imperialism.[19] The most influential came from a panoply of late nineteenth- and early twentieth-century Cobdenite intellectuals—prominent among them Herbert Spencer, Henry George, Vilfredo Pareto, Frédéric Passy, Yves Guyot, J. A. Hobson, Henri Lambert, and Norman Angell—informing a more proactive and radical generation of economic peace workers.[20] The more extreme economic nationalist turn that followed the First World War and the 1929 Wall Street crash only hammered home the view that nations, if left to their own devices, would choose nationalism over internationalism and self-sufficiency over interdependence, perpetuating the militaristic cycle. This realization intensified the common liberal radical belief that only a free-trading world community regulated through supranational governance could bring an end to the economic nationalist causes of imperialism and war—thereby paving a peaceful and prosperous path for global economic development. The positions of Richard Cobden and other mid-nineteenth-century liberal radical opponents of imperialism and war would, in hindsight, appear rather modest when compared to the globalist prescriptions being put forward by their pacifistic interwar torchbearers. The latter would oversee the creation of a more liberal order—their long-sought Pax Economica—in the 1940s from the wreckage of the Great Depression and the Second World War.

Transatlantic Economic Cosmopolitan Confluences: Anti-imperialism, Universal Brotherhood, Antislavery, and Peace, 1846–1870

Globalist fantasies of world federalism, anti-imperialism, antislavery, and peace teased the Victorian left-wing imagination.[21] The transatlantic idea of a congress of nations became ever more popular among liberal radicals from the early 1840s. Their grand universalist plans necessitated some combination of international free trade, cooperation, democratization, arbitration, and imperial devolution. Mercantilist imperialism and aristocratic rule were two big hurdles. Two more were the immoral practice of slavery and the industrializing world's consequent overreliance upon the products of unfree labour. Transatlantic liberal radical economic peace workers and abolitionist radicals therefore formed a natural mid-century alliance to bring their anti-imperial vision of a democratic and interdependent world order to fruition.

This is not to suggest that *all* Victorian-era free traders fell into the antislavery, anti-imperial, and peace camps, nor that *all* antislavery activists were pacifists, anti-imperialists, and free traders. Free-trade imperial policies were well represented in the British Parliament at this time, for example, including from some who were more ambivalent about the consumption of slave-grown products. And in the United States, antebellum Southern plantation owners and politicians of the Jeffersonian free-trade tradition instead supported slavery, imperial expansion, and limiting democracy. These more coercive transatlantic free-market affinities encouraged canny Southern diplomats during the US Civil War (1861–1865) to simultaneously play up their free-trade *bona fides* and threaten to withhold Southern cotton exports in the hopes of manipulating pro–free trade British politicians into recognizing the Confederacy. The Southern gambit garnered some initial British sympathy until the North's antislavery aims became explicit.[22] Conversely, many Anglophobic Whig-Republicans in the antebellum US north-east supported antislavery alongside the American System of protectionism.[23] However, few within any of these camps were invested in the growing international peace movement, and, as discussed in chapter 1, fewer still were opposed to imperial expansion. What follows, therefore, is not their story.

Returning to our economic peace workers, Elihu Burritt, the radical Massachusetts editor of the American Peace Society's *Advocate for Peace*, put forward the mid-century's most popular proposal for a congress of nations, the thirty-thousand-strong League of Universal Brotherhood. With the help of the English Quaker, Anti–Corn Law League (ACLL, 1839–1846) supporter, and abolitionist Joseph Sturge, Burritt's vision became predicated upon a Cobdenite free-trade order.[24] Burritt and Sturge's transatlantic crossings led to a series of international peace congresses between 1848 and 1853, as well as a newfound faith in European federalism to maintain the peace. We might now view with irony the rise of a concerted internationalist effort to eradicate war in 1848, the very year that witnessed a revolutionary growth in nationalisms and nation states. But for many liberal radicals at the time the republican revolutions heralded a democratic peace, European integration, and a corresponding end to aristocratic rule. As Anthony Howe puts it, 'in 1848, free trade enthusiasm swept together with Mazzinian democracy saw the proclamation of a federal free trade United States of Europe'.[25] Burritt, Sturge, and friends embraced the moment by providing much-needed financial backing, political energy, and organizational expertise to the older European and American religious and humanitarian peace societies that had grown out of the Napoleonic wars. The Atlantean burden of mid-century peace coordination thus fell largely upon Anglo-American shoulders.[26]

Richard Cobden, although more sceptical than allies such as Burritt of the utility of supranational state governance, also made explicit the connection between free trade, anti-imperialism, and peace—and the interdependence that would follow in their wake. Cobden had his epiphany in April 1842, a few years into his middle-class ACLL campaign to dismantle Britain's high tariffs on foreign grain. Cobden realized that 'it would be well to try to engraft our Free Trade agitation upon the Peace movement. They are one and the same cause.' Free trade would unite the nations of the world to such a degree that governments would no longer be able 'to plunge their people into wars'. He also argued that free trade would undermine the colonial system.[27] Granting colonies their independence in turn meant that Britain (and by extension rival powers) could substantially cut back on military spending that would otherwise be directed towards imperial defence, thus permitting lower taxation. Four years later, on the eve of the repeal of the Corn Laws, Cobden went even further before his audience in Manchester's jam-packed Free Trade Hall: 'I see in the Free-trade principle that which shall act on the moral world as the principle of gravitation in the universe,—drawing men together, thrusting aside the antagonism of race, and creed, and language, and uniting us in the bonds of eternal peace.' He foresaw a new world order whereby 'the desire and the motive for large and mighty empires; for gigantic armies and great navies [. . .] will die away [. . .] when man becomes one family and freely exchanges the fruits of his labour with his brother man.'[28]

Lord Palmerston's free-trade imperialism as British secretary of state for foreign affairs (1846–1851) and as prime minister (1859–1865) put the nascent British Cobdenite movement's anti-imperial principles to the test. With Henry Richard, the antislavery head of the London Peace Society, Cobden denounced Palmerstonian financial lending and subsequent military interventions to protect the investments of British creditors. He also condemned the imperial entanglements of Britain's 'gentlemanly capitalists'.[29] In 1846, for example, Cobden and his transatlantic disciples supported the low US Walker Tariff in the hope that trade liberalization would mitigate mounting Anglo–American tensions surrounding the disputed Oregon boundary.[30] In 1853, Cobden laid out his opposition to British colonialism in India in *How Wars Are Got Up in India*. The Indian Rebellion of 1857 only reified his belief that British colonialism was a mistake. Those who supported the occupation and coercive enforcement of free trade in India misunderstood 'the full meaning of Free Trade principles! If you talk to our Lancashire friends they argue that unless we occupied India there would be no trade with that country, or that someone else would monopolize it, forgetting that this is the old protectionist theory which they used formerly to ridicule.' On this point Cobden differed somewhat from his ACLL right-hand man, the Quaker pacifist John Bright; while he agreed with Cobden's anti-imperial position, Bright feared the potentially chaotic power vacuum that would result from an immediate British withdrawal from India. But Cobden, Bright, Sturge, and Henry Richard's minority opposition to British intervention in the Crimean War (1853–1856) once again placed them in the crosshairs of Palmerston and his jingoist supporters.[31]

The Manchester School's own—anti-imperial—sights next were turned upon the Second Opium War (1856–1860). The start of the Anglo–Chinese conflict was made more personal because it also represented an act of betrayal of the economic peace cause: the person most responsible for the 1856 bombardment of Canton, the Benthamite liberal John Bowring, had been one of Cobden's most stalwart allies in years past in helping to spread the free-trade gospel to continental Europe, Egypt, Indonesia, and Thailand. Bowring's experiences as consul to Canton (1849–1854) and as governor of Hong Kong (1854–1859), however, had caused him to repudiate Cobden's noninterventionist principles. For an Anglo-Saxonist and utilitarian like Bowring, the Qing Empire's xenophobic refusal to open its markets was evidence of China's barbarity, justifying the use of force in the name of civilization and progress. Bowring's liberal imperial enforcement of free trade as a 'civilizing mission' earned the support of Palmerston himself. But it also earned Cobden's opprobrium, forcing Palmerston to call a snap election in 1857. The election worked against the Manchester liberals, amidst a rising drumbeat for war, and Cobden's non-interventionists were sent packing from the House of Commons.[32] Cobden may have lost the non-interventionist battle, but by taking a principled stance against British formal and informal free-trade imperialism and by framing non-coercive free trade as the antidote to the poisons of nationalism, aristocracy, war, and colonialism, his beliefs and career would give the economic peace movement much to emulate over the next century.

For Manchester liberals, both the devolution of empires and the demise of wars required international trade liberalization. With free trade on the rise in Britain and the United States following, respectively, repeal of the Corn Laws and passage of the low Walker Tariff in 1846, Cobden and his disciples looked next to continental Europe.[33] Up to this point, Cobden had already been laying some of the groundwork with European tours in years past.[34] Concerted mobilization began in earnest in 1847, when *Economist* editor James Wilson met with like-minded reformers in Brussels for the Congrès des économistes, underwritten by the Association belge pour la liberté commerciale (Belgian association for free trade). Burritt, one of the US delegates, thought it was 'the most interesting audience I ever saw. There were men from most all the continental nations, grave, thoughtful, moustachioed men.' Their mission was 'to examine the question of brotherhood among all men', noted the Belgian president of the congress, Charles de Brouckère. Free trade and world peace were consistent themes. Burritt and Henry Richard then worked with French Cobdenite Frédéric Bastiat to hold the next peace congress in Paris in 1849. France's minister of the interior, Alexis de Tocqueville, gave the venture his blessing.[35]

The venue, the Salle Sainte-Cécile, was well suited: the grand hall could seat two thousand. Even so, it was packed to the gills when Victor Hugo, presiding, outlined his vision for a new world order: 'A day will come when bullets and bomb-shells will be replaced by votes, by the universal suffrage of nations, by the venerable arbitration of a great Sovereign Senate, which will be to Europe what the Parliament is to England [. . .]. A day will come when those two immense groups, the United States of America, and the United States of Europe' would trade peacefully with one another, uniting them in eternal friendship.[36] The attendees were to receive a tantalizing glimpse of this new order a decade later when the Anglo–French Treaty of 1860, or Cobden–Chevalier Treaty, ushered in a brief era of European trade liberalization, the likes of which would not be seen again until the post-1945 European Common Market.[37] Economic peace efforts were focused first and foremost on reforming Euro-America.

Slavery remained a major stumbling block to liberal radicals' commercial peace planning. After all, their vision of free trade went hand in hand with democracy, and nothing was less democratic than human bondage. London accordingly played host to the World Anti-Slavery Convention in 1840 and 1843. Their organization, too, was by and large an Anglo-American enterprise. Commercial peace reformers recognized the connection between their fight and that of the antislavery movement from the outset, despite efforts from Southern pro-slavery free traders to derail the growing Anglo-American antislavery alliance. The first general peace convention in 1843 was explicitly designed to follow on the heels of that year's antislavery convention so that the attendees of the first could attend the second.[38] Once again, Cobden emphasized their common cause. He had even suggested in 1841 that the ACLL substitute 'abolition' for 'repeal': '"immediate abolition" [. . .] is stronger language than *total and immediate "repeal"*' because 'it is the old anti-slavery *shibboleth*'.[39] The free-trade-and-peace movement thereby joined itself to the transatlantic antislavery movement.

The confluence of Cobdenism and antislavery spread to the European continent, with long-term consequences for the Spanish Empire. Cobden himself helped get the Spanish free-trade-and-peace movement off the ground. During his 1846 tour of Europe, he warned his Cádiz listeners that their main protectionist stumbling block was Catalonia, whose conservative agricultural and industrial interests were 'afraid of freedom [. . . and] terrified at the mere name of Free Trade'. Why? Because the region was more reliant on the slave-grown resources of Cuba and Puerto Rico and more beholden to aristocratic landed interests. With Cobden and the ACLL's recent British successes in mind, Spanish progressives went to work liberalizing the empire's trade policy during the Liberal Union era (1854–1868). The strongest economic cosmopolitan calls came from Madrid's *economistas*. These professors, engineers, civil servants, and lawyers—led by prominent liberal radical professors-turned-politicians Laureano Figuerola and Gabriel Rodríguez—were disciples of Cobden and the ACLL. They were also abolitionists, and similarly argued that the importance of access to cheap bread for Spain's hungry masses far outweighed that of the profits of the country's aristocratic landowners. Inspired by the ACLL's successes, Spain's *economistas* formed the Sociedad Libre de Economía Política (Free society of political economy; founded in 1857) and the Asociación para la Reforma de los Aranceles de Aduanas (Association for tariff reform; founded in 1859). Upon hearing of Cobden's death in 1865, Figuerola penned a homage to his hero entitled *Cobden, Moralista*. Figuerola and company remained in close contact with London's Cobden Club; Segismundo Moret, Joaquín María Sanromá, Rodríguez, and Figuerola, among others, became honorary members. Cosmopolitan affinities were such that the Asociación even took the Cobden Club's motto as its own: 'Free trade, peace, and goodwill among the Nations'. And Spain's Cobdenites remained vehement opponents of Spanish colonialism and slavery.[40]

Beginning in the late 1840s, Germany's band of Manchester liberals believed the time was ripe for peace, accompanied by a one-two punch of free trade and democratization.[41] Much as in pre–free-trade Britain, Germany suffered under the militant foreign policy dictates of protectionist aristocratic landowners: the Junkers. John Prince Smith, an English-born Prussian citizen, modelled Berlin's Freihandelsverein (Free trade union; founded in 1847) on the ACLL and dedicated much of his political activism to advocating for free trade and attacking German militarism. The Freihandelsverein's founding followed two tours by Cobden, in 1838 and 1847. By the time of the latter, Cobden was welcomed in Germany as a hero. Cobden-themed souvenirs were sold across Germany, and a massive seven-hundred-person banquet was held for him in Hamburg, where his hosts greeted him with a toast: 'To Free Trade, the source of all other freedoms'. Further Cobdenite leagues soon sprouted up in

Frankfurt, Rostock, Stellen, and Hamburg. In 1849, the German free-trade-and-peace movement got more organized under the auspices of the Zentral-bund für Handelsfreiheit (Central union for free trade), which claimed to represent around thirty such local societies. Prince Smith then co-edited the Berlin newspaper *Demokratische Zeitung* with his pro–free trade friend Julius Faucher, who later became Cobden's secretary. When government censors forced the newspaper to close down, Prince Smith reflected on how he had at least been able to bring 'respect for the free trade doctrine to the most extreme left. [. . .] I have demonstrated that the doctrine of economic freedom is more progressive.'[42]

Cobdenism received an even warmer welcome among mid-century Italian economic and political circles. Cobden spent more time in Italy than any-where else on the European continent during his 1847 tour. Roberto Romani notes that the tour marked 'a Cobdenian moment' in which 'Cobden was sur-rounded by the aura of a prophet heralding a new era.'[43] Wherever he went—Rome, Naples, Turin, Milan, Venice, Genoa, Livorno, Perugia, Trieste—he was feted. Guiseppe Montenelli, a professor of commercial law, summed it up best as toastmaster at Cobden's Livorno banquet. 'How many Cobdens are needed to arise in Italy. A Cobden for individual rights, a Cobden for free cit-ies. A Cobden for law codification, standardization of money, weights and measures. A Cobden for a customs union. They will shout "Forward, thus did free trade triumph" in England. [. . .] As you return tell of our struggles begun here [. . .]. Long live Cobden, apostle of civilization.' Soon after Cobden's visit, an Italian commercial league was formed. These Italian free traders supported uniting the disparate Italian states, a position that risked imprisonment in those Italian regions still under Austrian occupation. Austria's secret police duly made sure to keep a close eye on those who attended the banquets honouring Cobden. Among the attendees, Bologna-born economist and statesman Marco Minghetti best embraced Cobden's cosmopolitanism at mid-century. Italy's minister to St. Petersburg wrote to Minghetti in 1863 noting just that affinity, heaping praise on Cobden's plans for global prosperity and peace, and urging Minghetti to call for another European peace congress and 'be the Cob-den of this great idea that can regenerate the world.'[44] Minghetti became one of the Cobden Club's first honorary members soon thereafter.

The French commercial peace movement followed a similar organizational path. Mid-century French economic peace workers drew on a rich Enlighten-ment intellectual tradition, stretching back to physiocrats François Quesnay and Jacques Turgot, and their liberal economic successors such as Jean-Baptiste

Say. In 1845, the liberal radical Frédéric Bastiat undertook the translationg into French of the works of his friend Richard Cobden even as they were both becoming more active in the peace congress movement. Cobden's 1846 French tour led the *Economist* to observe that 'the success of Mr. Cobden and the League [. . .] have really given a new impetus to the serious thinkers and grave public writers of France', and that his 'French imitators' would soon set their sights on vanquishing 'both monarch and monopolists'.[45] Imitation required coordination. Just a few years after the ACLL had been established in Britain, Bastiat and Horace Say, son of Jean-Baptiste, formed the Société d'économie politique in 1842 (rebranded the Société des économistes in 1845). Bastiat edited its journal, *Le Libre Échange* ('Free trade'). Economic pacifism permeated its membership. Joseph Garnier, with Bastiat, founded the Association centrale pour la liberté des échanges (Central association for the freedom of trade) in 1846, after which Garnier penned articles picking apart Friedrich List's critique of 'cosmopolitical economy'. Garnier remained active in the peace movement, becoming an officer of the Société française des amis de la paix (French friends of peace society) following the Franco–Prussian War, and continuing to promote economic pacifism in the *Journal des économistes*. Émile de Girardin, for his part, stood out in connecting free trade with peace at the international congresses of 1849 and 1850.[46]

The French free-trade-and-peace movement's position on colonialism, however, was less clear-cut. Some, such as Paul Leroy-Beaulieu, while anti-war, subscribed to the free-trade imperial ideas of the Saint-Simonians, and so were not entirely opposed to French colonialism. Michel Chevalier, also a Saint-Simonian, never fully endorsed Manchester liberalism and reconciled his support for free trade and peace with French colonialism in Algeria.[47] This set them apart from more left-leaning French critics of empire such as Garnier, Girardin, Bastiat, the 'dean' of the international peace movement Frédéric Passy, and liberal politician Yves Guyot.[48]

The mid-century French Cobdenite story would be incomplete without mentioning the efforts of a twenty-one-year-old Parisian named Edmond Potonié in attendance at Frankfurt's 1850 peace congress. There Potonié, a family friend of Victor Hugo, was introduced to Richard Cobden. It must have been quite the conversation. Potonié spent the next decade attempting to replicate the successes of the ACLL across Europe with financial backing from the middle-class British peace movement. By the 1860s he had also embraced a more cooperative social-democratic approach, which had greater appeal for the continental European working classes and young socialists. The result of

Potonié's internationalist campaign was the Ligue du bien public (League of the public good) and its circular *Cosmopolite*. Launched in the mid-1860s, Potonié's peace and civil liberties league set its main sights on European protectionism and monopolies. Censorship and repression from the French police soon followed, but Potonié continued his grassroots efforts until his death in 1902.[49] His story is illustrative of the continental leftward drift of the economic peace movement as it spread during the latter half of the century.

The Commercial Peace Movement
Gets Organized, 1870–1898

The mid-century Cobdenite vision of European-wide free trade, anti-imperialism, and peace seemed within reach in 1860. Just a decade later, despair displaced optimism. The commercial peace movement became more coordinated to counteract the late-century neomercantilist growth of national consolidation, protectionism, monopolies, and imperial expansion. Europe remained a key part of the playbook. But as Elihu Burritt's mid-century efforts illustrate, beyond Britain, Cobdenite peace workers were most numerous and organized in the United States. The Cobden Club's founding in 1866, in turn, marked the beginning of a new British-led era of economic peace organizing and of new economic theories of anti-imperialism and peace. The late Victorian free-trade-and-peace movement received a much-needed boost from Europe's 'Manchester' liberals. Further reinforcements arrived from more legalistic Cobdenites such as the English labour unionist and Rochdale Cooperative leader Hodgson Pratt, who helped form the International Arbitration and Peace Association (IAPA) in London in 1877, drawing a large number of international free traders into its fold.[50] The growing commercial peace movement, in turn, made good use of the era's imperial transport and communication networks to organize as far afield as Australia, New Zealand, and India by the end of the century.

In the aftermath of the US Civil War, Cobden's US disciples continued mobilizing in coordination with London's Cobden Club. They waged an uphill battle to halt the GOP's protectionist and imperial proclivities in the decades that followed. This first generation of US Cobdenites included an impressive list of antislavery luminaries from Massachusetts and New York, including Senator Charles Sumner, transcendentalist Ralph Waldo Emerson, arch-abolitionist William Lloyd Garrison, the Rev. Henry Ward Beecher, the poet William Cullen Bryant, the statesman Charles Francis Adams Sr., and the economist Edward Atkinson. They formed the American Free Trade League (AFTL) in New York City in 1865, upon which British free traders congratulated it for continuing to fight for freedom after the abolition of slavery. 'Free Trade is the vital element of Free Labour,' as one London free-trade organization wrote to the AFTL. 'Without the former the latter cannot healthfully exist.'[51]

The AFTL spearheaded the postbellum US free-trade-and-peace movement. Renowned poet and editor of the *New York Evening Post* William Cullen Bryant was its inaugural president. Bryant's immediate successor was David Dudley Field, the jurist, peace activist, and brother of fellow American Cobden Club member Cyrus Field, who oversaw the successful laying of the transatlantic cable in 1866. The AFTL's third president, David Ames Wells, was anointed 'the Cobden of America' and was named the Cobden Club's US secretary in the early 1870s to oversee its widening North American propaganda campaign. The AFTL's insignia was a carbon copy of the Cobden Club's. Republican protectionists responded by creating anti-Cobden clubs to counteract the numerous local Cobden clubs sprouting up across the north-east and west.[52]

The relocation from Britain to Toronto of Manchester liberal Goldwin Smith, the former regius professor of modern history at Oxford University, led to more concerted organization between Canadian free traders such as Smith, Erastus Wiman, and Edward Farrer and their US allies. Smith would even flirt with the idea of Canadian–American political union alongside economic integration to bring about hemispheric peace and prosperity. Smith's Commercial Union League in Ontario, the American Commercial Reciprocity League, the AFTL, and New York's International Free Trade Association soon set their pacifistic sights on ameliorating Anglo–American relations through the 1871 Treaty of Washington and North American trade liberalization.[53] For similar reasons, US land reformer, peace advocate, and journalist Henry George threw his growing political weight behind North American commercial union. George believed 'in the international law of God as Cobden called free trade', and joined the Cobden Club in 1881. In his *Protection or Free Trade* (1886), he tied free trade to 'fraternity and peace' to combat the 'spirit of protectionism [...] national enmity and strife'. Liberalizing trade between the United States and Canada was a good first start, thereby making 'the two countries practically one'.[54]

These grassroots investments eventually paid political dividends. US economic cosmopolitans found themselves in positions of more direct political influence during the two Democratic administrations of Grover Cleveland

(1885–1889, 1893–1897). Cleveland, the former reformist governor of New York, surrounded himself with US Cobdenites, including his secretaries of state, war, agriculture, interior, and treasury, as well as Edward Atkinson and David Ames Wells as economic advisors. Together they oversaw a noticeable non-interventionist shift away from Republican imperial machinations. Across the late 1880s, Cleveland's Cobdenites nixed the previous GOP administration's attempts to annex territory in Nicaragua ('America's Egypt', as one Republican pamphleteer called it) and to intervene in the Congo and Samoa. The first Cleveland administration also tried unsuccessfully to lower US tariff rates on multiple occasions while keeping sabre-rattling Republican congressmen from starting a war with Canada over a contentious fisheries dispute. Cleveland's second administration provided more of the same when it immediately thwarted GOP designs on annexing Hawai'i. As Republican senator Henry Cabot Lodge disparaged them in 1895, the Cleveland administrations had 'been successfully Cobdenized, and that is the underlying reason for their policy of retreat'.[55]

Across the pond, British liberals such as the sociologist Herbert Spencer lashed out at the growing British popularity of Benjamin Disraeli's 'new Tory' imperialism (1874–1880) and the neomercantilism of Britain's rivals after 1870. Spencer updated the Cobdenite critique of imperialism and war. For him, neomercantilism was immoral, illustrating 'the profound antagonism' between 'militancy' and 'industrialism'. Militancy represented a protectionist return to barbarism brought on by atavistic landed aristocratic elites, thwarting industrialism's peaceful free-trade march towards prosperity and democracy. British Cobdenites also pushed back against Disraeli's colonialist crackdown in India, arguing instead that far greater prosperity could be had through non-coercive free trade coupled with Indian self-government. With at least a tinge of anti-Semitism, still more of them associated the aristocratic militancy of Disraeli (of Jewish origin) with those financiers of the City of London who backed his investment in the Suez Canal. Such attacks upon the gentlemanly capitalists provided an early glimpse of critiques of 'financial imperialism' that would proliferate by the turn of the century.[56] The Cobden Club remained the administrative hub of the British economic peace movement beyond the end of the century. The evolving working- and middle-class 'cult of Cobden' also played an essential part in laying the progressive groundwork for the New Liberalism and the Liberal–Labour coalition during the Edwardian years.[57]

Not to be outdone, Spain's *economistas* maintained their propaganda campaign for free trade, manhood suffrage, and abolitionism in the years after the

Liberal Union era's end in 1868. The era had sparked a strong protectionist countermovement, a growing conservative alliance of anti-abolitionist agrarians and industrialists seeking to maintain slavery and establish a tariff fortress around Spain and its overseas colonies. Spain's Cobdenites, however, briefly maintained the political upper hand after the 1868 September Revolution. Figuerola was made finance minister and Rodríguez undersecretary of commerce in 1868; Moret became minister of overseas territories in 1870; and Sanromá represented Puerto Rico's Liberal Reformist Party in Congress in 1871. They worked closely with their abolitionist allies in Cuba and Puerto Rico. As Rafael María de Labra, women's suffragist and Spain's abolitionist leader until the 1890s, described it, they were fighting 'against theocracy, monopoly, and dictatorship'. The Moret Law for the gradual abolition of slavery was passed in 1870, leading to emancipation in Puerto Rico in 1873. However, the return to power of the conservative monarchists during the Restoration (1875–1902) for a time marginalized the liberal radical reformers. Abolitionist *economista* Gabriel Rodríguez described the Restoration as a conservative economic nationalist reaction propagated through false patriotism. This protectionist and nationalist trend, he argued, was a European-wide phenomenon. He made this observation in 1881 while reviewing a new collection of Cobden's essays. The time was ripe to publish the collection, Rodríguez concluded, because 'the protectionist reaction seeks to destroy the work of Cobden throughout Europe, while militarism seeks to return us to barbarous epochs'. With slavery abolished in Spain's colonies by the 1880s, the *economistas* pushed on with their free-trade-and-peace efforts against growing protectionist opposition until the turn of the century. Most notably, Moret, as minister of the overseas colonies in 1897, granted autonomy to Cuba and Puerto Rico, and opposed going to war with the United States in 1898.[58]

Although French economic peace workers never embraced non-interventionism or anti-imperialism to the same degree as their British, US, or Spanish counterparts, they were similarly supportive of trade liberalization and critical of militarism, monopolies, and aristocratic elites. Free-trade-and-peace groups such as the Société d'économie politique remained active throughout the latter half of the century, for a time receiving propagandistic reinforcements from the Association pour la défense de la liberté commercial (Association for the defence of free trade, a.k.a. the Free Trade Association, 1878–1881).[59] They remained in close touch with their British counterparts through the Cobden Club. French members of the Cobden Club included the statesman Léon Say (the son of Horace and grandson of Jean-Baptiste),

Frédéric Passy, and Yves Guyot. Passy and Guyot in particular deserve much of the credit for keeping the French free-trade-and-peace movement alive in the latter decades of the century.

Frédéric Passy, nephew of the French Manchester liberal and finance minister Hippolyte Passy, admired Cobden and sought to recreate the ACLL's successes in France. He formed the Ligue internationale et permanente de la paix (International and permanent league for peace) in Paris in 1867. Aimed at European elites, this emphasized free trade, arbitration, and arms reduction as preconditions for world peace. As a member of the Chamber of Deputies throughout the 1880s, Passy advocated for labour rights and disarmament. He also opposed French colonial 'civilizing' designs upon the ancient culture of Indochina (Vietnam). In 1889, he became co-president of the newly formed Interparliamentary Union, whose members emphasized international free trade and arbitration.[60] That same year he also chaired the first Universal Peace Congress. Held in Paris, it marked the beginning of a more concerted coordination between the numerous international peace groups. The Universal Peace Congress itself became a yearly event up until the outbreak of the First World War, and consistently adopted free trade in its yearly platforms. Passy's international peace work earned him the first ever Nobel Peace Prize in 1901, an honour he shared with the founder of the International Committee of the Red Cross, Henri Dunant. By the time of his death in 1912, Passy had well earned his nickname 'the apostle of peace', being numbered among the most influential leaders of the approximately three-hundred-thousand-strong French peace movement.[61]

French journalist and politician Yves Guyot was a generation younger than his peace ally Passy. Drawn to the ideas of Richard Cobden and Herbert Spencer, he was an active French member of the Cobden Club. A peace worker from the 1860s onwards, he fully embraced the Cobdenite critique of aristocracy, protectionism, imperialism, and war. His 1885 book *Lettres sur la politique coloniale* was, according to René Maunier, 'the most violent attack on colonies that has ever been made in France'. A staunch opponent of protectionism, during his brief stint as a cabinet minister Guyot warned against 'the French Corn Laws' and attempted to mollify the protectionist 1892 Méline Tariff. A supporter of labour rights, Guyot also sparred with French socialists on account of their protectionist support for immigration restrictions. In 1893, he even charged them with wanting to imitate the Americans, who 'fortify their frontiers against emigration, just as they protect them against the importation of European goods. [...] They are as short-sighted as unjust in attempting to defend themselves against European and Chinese emigration.' So, too, were the French socialists, who in calling for the expulsion of 1,100,000 foreign workers from France showed themselves to be nationalists of the worst kind. While British Cobdenites aligned themselves against their own government's complicity in the Second Boer War (1899–1902), across the English Channel Guyot was lashing out at Dutch pro-Boer apologists. Upon Passy's demise, Guyot kept the French free-trade-and-peace movement alive through the creation of a new French Cobden club, the Ligue du libre échange (Free trade league; founded in 1911). During the Great War, the league castigated the Allies for not embracing free trade, while praising Woodrow Wilson's Fourteen Points for doing so. A democrat to the end, Guyot railed against the autocratic and autarkic Soviet state and the rise of Italian fascism, until his death in 1928.[62]

The end of the Franco–Prussian War in 1871 witnessed another flurry of German Cobdenite activity and political organization. For a brief time after the conflict, pictures of Cobden were again prominently displayed in Berlin shop windows, and lace handkerchiefs embroidered with Cobden's name were available for purchase. Thanks to the conspiratorial anti-British propaganda work of the nationalistic German Historical School (GHS), however, a decade later the Cobden Club's name was widely scorned, despite German Cobdenite attempts to debunk the conspiracy theories.[63] The journalist, publisher, and consumer co-operativist Eugen Richter led what Bismarck derided as a 'clique of Manchester politicians', within first the Progressive Party and then the Left Liberal Party through the latter decades of the century—a left-wing political alignment that was also forming in Austria at this time.[64] Richter spent much of his long political career speaking out against German protectionism, anti-Semitism, and militarism; on questions of war and peace, like John Prince Smith, his overarching message was consistently 'peace through free trade'. On the question of imperialism, however, Richter was less consistent. In the 1880s, he opposed Germany's formal annexation of overseas territories. But following the German annexation of Kiaochow, China in 1898, he supported keeping it. By 1904, however, he was once again prone to criticizing Germany's 'misconceived colonial policy' from the floor of the Reichstag.[65] In 1881, Spanish Cobdenite Professor Mariano Carreras y Gonzalez highlighted two other prominent German Manchester liberals: the left-liberal publisher Max Wirth and Franz Hermann Schulze-Delitzsch, a co-founder of the German Progressive Party. Cobden Club member Schulze-Delitzsch's anti-monopolistic support for co-operativism helped spread the grassroots German free-trade movement further; his opposition to Ferdinand Lassalle's nationalist brand of socialism, in turn, earned him the disparaging Francophobic moniker 'Herr Bastiat Schulze von Delitzsch'.[66]

Liberal radical English and Danish peace reinforcements landed on German shores in the mid-1880s, and just in time. The country's economic peace workers were finding themselves increasingly outnumbered, outfinanced, and outflanked by the Listian nationalists of the GHS. By this point, Manchester liberalism in Germany had devolved into a minority demesne of Cobdenite socialist internationalists within the Social Democratic Party (SPD: Sozialdemokratische Partei Deutschlands), such as Eduard Bernstein, Karl Kautsky, and August Bebel (see chapter 3), along with a small pacifistic group of non-Marxists such as Eugen Richter, Lujo Brentano, Theodor Barth, and Alfred Fried.[67] Hodgson Pratt, Britain's 'go-between' for London's Interparliamentary Union and economic pacifism, helped breathe new life into the German peace movement following his arrival in the mid-1880s. Pratt helped left-liberal groups like the German People's Party to form peace societies in Stuttgart, Berlin, Darmstadt, and Frankfurt am Main. The arrival of Danish parliamentarian Fredrik Bajer in 1886, in turn, spurred the Frankfurt society to action. There Bajer worked with Franz Wirth, among the city's leading democrats, to found the Frankfurter Friedensverein (Frankfurt peace association) in 1887. The initiative was not well received in nationalist Germany, however. The peace organization's only journalistic support came from a left-liberal newspaper edited by Franz's Manchester liberal brother, Max Wirth. Despite the cool reception from Germany's jingoists, the Friedensverein would count among the most motivated German peace groups until the outbreak of the First World War.[68]

The German economic peace movement became more coordinated at the turn of the century. Cobden Club member Theodor Barth contributed a chapter to Cobden Club secretary Richard Gowing's *Richard Cobden and the Jubilee of Free Trade* in 1896, on the connection between free trade and democracy. Barth next helped organize the 1897 Universal Peace Congress in Hamburg, and remained a strong critic of the imperialism of economic nationalism until his death in 1909. Fellow Cobden Club member Lujo Brentano had attempted to align German labour unions with Cobdenism in the early 1870s, after which he became more interested in German peace work, serving on the executive committee of Munich's 1907 Universal Peace Congress. Alfred Fried's brand of pacifism, which embraced a more scientific approach to international organization and German democracy promotion, was little more than a reiteration of Cobdenism. 'We are everywhere,' Fried observed at the turn of the century. 'We trade everywhere, and we are universally dependent. [...] We have become citizens of the world, true cosmopolitans.' The various regional organizational efforts became national in 1892, when Fried, Barth, Franz Wirth, and Adolf Richter (Eugen's cousin) created the Deutsche Friedensgeselleschaft (German peace society). By 1898, it had five thousand members and fifty-six branches across the country, usually operating in coordination with local Progressive Party members. Both numbers had nearly doubled by 1914, about a third being women. Fried's Cobdenite 'scientific pacifism', his support for the open door and native protections in the colonies, and his democratic opposition to 'Junkerdom' remained popular within the German and international peace movement in the years leading up to the First World War.[69]

Italy's rising tariff walls and consequent trade wars inspired a new wave of Italian commercial peace mobilization from the late 1880s. This led to the formation of Milan's Associazione per la libertà economica (Association for economic freedom) in 1891. Its members included luminaries such as Professor Vilfredo Pareto, another honorary member of the Cobden Club and an avowed anti-militarist, anti-imperialist, pacifist, and critic of Italian elites: a radical combination that eventually got him ostracized from the Italian academy. A Spencerian, Pareto associated protectionism with militarism and aristocracy. His preferred path to peace was through European-wide free trade, as he laid out at the IAPA's first Italian branch congress in 1889. The motion passed with broad support. His anti-militarism landed him an appointment as vice-president of the Comitato fiorentino per la pace (Florentine committee for peace) later that year, whereupon he organized a conference attacking colonialism and war. His pacifism and anti-imperialism also got him working with extreme left-wing Italian radicals both inside and outside Parliament, including Ernesto Teodoro Moneta, the era's leading Italian peace activist. Throughout the 1890s Pareto even flirted with the prospect of a socialist–liberal coalition, inviting Italy's socialists to partner with the free-trade movement.[70]

The late Victorian free-trade-and-peace movement also spread to Belgium, Russia, and Australia. The Belgian movement, for example, picked up pace after playing host to the 1847 Free Trade Congress in Brussels.[71] Brussels's Corr van der Maeren earned the nickname the 'Cobden of Belgium'. In 1872, Charles Lemonnier, the Belgian liberal politician and founder, in Geneva in 1867, of the radical Ligue internationale de la paix et de la liberté (International league for peace and freedom), published Les États-Unis d'Europe, a democratic call for European federation, free trade, and demilitarization. The progressive liberal Auguste Houzeau de Lehaie thereafter took the lead in making sure that free trade maintained its prominent position on the programme of the Universal Peace Congress in 1903, as it had in the previous congresses. The resolution also congratulated 'the Free Trade Associations on their efforts, which cannot but be helpful to the cause of peace, and calls upon all the friends of peace to aid them'.[72] In turn-of-the-century Russia, the anti-militarist Jacques Novicow decried protectionism for causing war, and Jean de Bloch's influential *The Future of War* (1899) preceded Norman Angell's similar Cobdenite critique of war by a decade, earning Bloch the nickname 'Russian Cobden' from liberal British publicist W. T. Stead.[73] Decades of British emigration meant that the free-trade-and-peace movement stretched as far afield as Australia; English émigré Robert Lowe began propagating the pacifistic message of Cobdenism in his Sydney newspaper *Atlas* in the 1850s, and Henry Parkes, Australia's 'Father of Federation', had been converted to Manchester liberalism 'one cold winter's night' by Cobden himself in the early 1860s.[74]

The Cobdenite movement even made modest ideological headway within late nineteenth-century India. The 'Grand Old Man of India' Dadabhai Naoroji represented a rare undercurrent of Manchester liberalism within the Indian nationalist movement. While a Liberal MP in the British House of Commons (1892–1895), he offered a critique of British colonialism in India that called for 'perfect free-trade' between India and Britain for mutual gain instead of the current despotic 'unnatural system' of high taxation, monopolization of Indian capital, and forced military service, all of which kept India in perpetual poverty. In 1900, citing John Bright, he argued that 'if it were British rule [i.e., perfect free trade and self-government] and not un-British rule which governed us England would be benefited ten times more than [under the current] evil system, by which you derive some benefit, but by which we are destroyed'.[75] Naoroji's 1901 book *Poverty and Un-British Rule in India* went furthest in popularizing his 'wealth drain' theory, representing a powerful anti-colonial indictment of British imperialism in India for the turn of the century. 'I like free trade,' he argued; but for it to work for mutual benefit, all countries involved must 'have command over their own resources'. The profits obtained from 'un-British rule' only flowed out of India, never to return. 'Un-British Rule in India', then, was in practice not free trade but neomercantilist exploitation, maintained through the despotic dictates of the British aristocracy and 'powerful' manufacturing interests. Framing British economic imperialism in India as neomercantilism, much as Cobden had done back in the 1850s, for a time allowed Naoroji to square his free-trade ideals with India's growing anti-colonial nationalist movement.[76] But by 1906 he would be putting aside his anti-imperialism of free trade to give his reluctant support to the Swadeshi movement as a temporary means to free-trade ends: 'I am a freetrader, I am a member, and in the Executive Committee of the Cobden Club for 20 years, and yet I say that "Swadeshi" is a forced necessity for India in its un-natural economic muddle.' But he also encouraged the Swadeshi leaders to take inspiration from the grassroots successes of the ACLL to effect political change: in this case, Indian self-government and fiscal autonomy, with 'perfect free trade' and Anglo–Indian prosperity to follow.[77]

'New Liberal' Free-Trade Theories of
Anti-imperialism and Peace, 1898–1918

An explosion of imperial expansion at the turn of the century—the Sino–Japanese War, the scramble for Chinese markets, the US war with Spain, the Second Boer War, the British partition of Bengal, the Russo–Japanese War—drove the international economic peace movement to grassroots retrenchment. The *fin de siècle* neomercantilist escalation of protectionism, militarism, jingoism, and geopolitical conflicts also gave birth to influential anti-imperial theories of free trade from a new generation of liberal radicals, including international disciples of the US liberal radical theorist Henry George. By around 1910, the commercial peace movement became mainstream enough to start to receive financial backing from wealthy industrial benefactors, allowing for greater international peace coordination and promotion before and after the First World War. These New Liberals spearheaded the 'new internationalism' of the early twentieth century.[78]

One new left-wing Cobdenite anti-imperial offshoot that made a big global splash at the turn of the century was what became known in the United States as the 'single tax' movement or Georgism, stemming from the liberal radical theories of US journalist and political economist Henry George. According to Avner Offer, George was 'indubitably a man of the left' and his single tax 'merely an extreme form of Cobden's political creed.'[79] George's ideas crisscrossed imperial boundaries, becoming the leading vein of US free-trade thinking to inspire a new generation of Cobdenites. The positions of George's transnational followers concerning free trade, anti-imperialism, and peace were more radical than those of the more orthodox followers of the Manchester School. George first formulated his single tax theory—which held that a country could derive its entire revenue through a direct tax on the estimated value of land—in his internationally bestselling book *Progress and Poverty* (1879). This single tax on land rent, according to George, would prove to be a panacea of progressive political outcomes. The single tax promised a steady revenue stream for local and federal governments; discouraged land monopolies by incentivizing land development; and eliminated the need for all other forms of direct and indirect taxation, including tariffs. For George and his international disciples, eliminating land monopolies and all other barriers to trade would thus undermine the economic causes of imperialism and war, ushering in a new era of worldwide prosperity and peace.

The single tax's anticipated anti-imperial effects were three pronged. First, developing land to maximum efficiency would expand the global supply of raw materials, undercutting a principal driver of imperial expansion. Second, the single tax would break up the militaristic influence of the landed aristocracy. Third, absolute free trade would eliminate protectionist-inspired market inefficiencies, which were believed to be another key motive behind the imperial search for foreign markets. George, a self-described devotee of British free traders Richard Cobden and Herbert Spencer, considered his land tax proposal a natural outgrowth of the transatlantic free-trade-and-peace tradition. After all, free trade in land had been tied to Cobden's own critique of Britain's landed aristocracy, as George and his transatlantic disciples were keen to point out.[80]

In 1898, amid scathing critiques of Republican president William McKinley's warmongering and autocratic manoeuvrings, the second issue of the newly launched Chicago Georgist publication *The Public* brandished its Cobdenite credentials.[81] US Georgists such as William Lloyd Garrison Jr., Frank Garrison, Mark Twain, Samuel Milliken, Jackson H. Ralston, Herbert Bigelow, and Louis and Alice Post maintained their opposition to US colonialism through *The Public* and through their involvement in the Anti-Imperialist League (AIL).[82] Other Georgist anti-imperialists, such as Massachusetts-born suffragist and abolitionist Susan Look Avery and the legalist anti-war advocate Clarence Darrow, preferred other radical outlets. Avery looked to *The Woman's Journal* to fight US imperialism. And Darrow—at once a socialist, a Tolstoian, a Georgist, and a Spencerian—broadened his earlier opposition to the GOP's monopolistic high tariff policies to include Republican colonialism, always with George's *Progress and Poverty* near at hand.[83]

Even though the single tax remained too radical for some orthodox Cobdenites, the two wings of the economic peace movement remained allies. Their internal differences over fiscal reform stemmed mainly from the fact that the Georgist free-trade position was even more absolute than the Cobdenite doctrine that inspired it. Where orthodox Cobdenites supported indirect taxation through minimal tariffs for revenue purposes only, and so favoured direct taxation to keep tariffs low, George's proposal suggested that all tariffs—and every other form of taxation for that matter—ought to be replaced by a single direct tax on the estimated value of land. Georgists thus expounded a more extreme commitment to free trade. As one correspondent for London's Georgist publication *Land & Liberty* later observed, 'The single tax without Free Trade would be like propelling a boat with the oars all on the one side.'[84] Despite their differences in degree, however, the two Cobdenite camps stood side by side in their common causes of anti-imperialism and peace through the AIL and other transatlantic economic peace organizations created between 1898 and 1919.

Because Georgism represented a radical extension of Manchester liberalism, it found a stronger reception within Britain and its colonies in Australia, Canada, and New Zealand than it did in protectionist America. George himself spent a great deal of time during the 1880s and 1890s travelling between the United States, Great Britain, and the Antipodes in an effort to popularize the single tax, and Britain's New Liberals proved more amenable than his own compatriots to ideas of direct taxation.[85] On the land question, 'the disciples of Henry George make common cause with the disciples of Richard Cobden', noted a 1905 edited volume made up of contributions from leading turn-of-the-century Cobdenites such as Francis Hirst and J. A. Hobson.[86] Jane Cobden Unwin—a daughter of Richard Cobden and active in Britain's turn-of-the-century anti-imperial, Irish home rule, free trade, and women's suffrage movements—was sympathetic to Georgism because she understood the connection between the single tax movement and her father's mid-century push for 'free trade in land', as did British Cobdenites fired up by George's single tax theory. Prominent left-wing British Georgists included George Lansbury and Keir Hardie.[87] The British movement reached its Edwardian zenith in 1909, when Lloyd George's 'People's Budget' included Georgist elements, and the anti-landlord Georgist anthem 'The Land Song' for a time became a rip-roaring Liberal radical rallying cry (Fig. 2.1).

Transatlantic anti-imperial ties between Georgists and orthodox Cobdenites grew stronger through the efforts of AIL officers Lucia and Edwin D. Mead. Lucia—a Boston school teacher, 'a child of the New England antislavery tradition', and a Georgist—opposed US colonialism, navalism, and the Monroe Doctrine.[88] Edwin was a member of the New England Free Trade League

FIGURE 2.1. Henry George pictured alongside Richard Cobden. *The Daily News Land Songs for the People* (1910), cover.

and the American Peace Society (APS), a co-founder of the Twentieth Century Club, and director of Boston's World Peace Foundation (WPF) upon its founding in 1910 by philanthropist Edwin Ginn. Lucia and Edwin Mead's peace internationalist worldviews crystallized following a trip to England in 1901, where they met with British liberal radical J. A. Hobson.[89] Hobson's Cobdenite critiques of the Second Boer War (1899–1902) had a sizeable impact upon their evolving anti-imperial ideology. Lucia described their private meetings with Hobson and other British anti-imperialists as an 'intellectual Thanksgiving.'[90] Soon thereafter, Edwin's Twentieth Century Club in Boston invited Hobson and fellow British anti-imperialist George H. Perris to speak with the members of the New England branch of the AIL in late 1902, just as Hobson's *Imperialism: A Study* was making its transatlantic debut.[91]

In *Imperialism: A Study* (1902) and a further article in 1903, New Liberal J. A. Hobson put forward the era's most influential British anti-imperial critique. As a staunch opponent of Joseph Chamberlain's Tariff Reformers, Hobson showed himself to be a 'born-again cosmopolitan liberal', laying out the guidelines for a 'new moral world' in which 'free trade would reign everywhere and bring with it an element of civilizing cosmopolitanism', as his biographer Peter Cain describes it.[92] Hobson understood the growth of imperialism in the latter part of the century to be directly connected to the Spencerian theory of militancy. Protectionist monopoly interests in the United States and other neomercantilist empires had created inefficient national markets, leading to domestic over-saving and underconsumption. As a result, financiers, in cahoots with industrial monopolists and aristocrats, next turned to formal colonialism to acquire outlets for surplus capital and new sources of raw materials. And behold: the 'scramble for Africa', the divvying up of the China market, and the emergence of a US colonial empire. Hobson's anti-imperial solution was straightforward. It called for the reforming of capitalism, rather than its overthrow. Ousting the militaristic financiers and monopolists from political power through democratic reform would allow industrialism—free trade, efficient markets, prosperity, peaceful competition—to flourish.

Working within this spectrum of New Liberal ideas between Henry George and J. A. Hobson, AIL leaders sprang into action during and after the 1898 US war with Spain. Their anti-imperialism of free trade was put on further display in their post-1898 opposition to the informal and formal economic dimensions of what April Merleaux calls the 'US sugar empire.'[93] Beginning with the 1901 *Downes v. Bidwell* decision, the Republican-friendly US Supreme Court legalized the protectionist framework of the US closed-door empire by allowing the federal government to levy tariffs against the country's own colonies so as to insulate domestic US sugar growers from full competition with the empire's newly acquired sugar-producing colonies. US Cobdenites unsuccessfully fought against this coercive economic nationalist legislation.[94] William Lloyd Garrison Jr., the Georgist treasurer of the Boston-based AFTL and editor of its periodical *Free Trade Broadside* as well as the APS's *Advocate of Peace*, in turn, castigated the hypocrisy of calling for an 'open American door' in China while keeping US doors closed to Chinese immigrants.[95]

Free-trade opposition to US closed-door imperialism grew into an even broader transimperial phenomenon once local critics among the former colonies of the Spanish Empire joined the fray. Cubans and Filipinos were among the loudest in voicing their dissent against US imperialism of economic nationalism. Cuba became an informal US colony after the island gained ostensible independence from Spain in 1898. The question of Cuban–American trade reciprocity soon arose. In 1902, Cuban reciprocity became one of the most hotly contested issues in Congress. Republican imperialists, at odds with both the AIL and anti-expansionists within their own party, wanted to implement protectionist reciprocity as a means of controlling the island's finances and foreign trade. Cuban nationalists instead lobbied Congress for

THE ANTI-IMPERIALISM OF FREE TRADE 77

Cuban–American trade liberalization and greater local autonomy over the island's tariff policy, a position aligned closely with the earlier Cobdenite efforts of Spain's late nineteenth-century *economistas*. To this end, Luis V. de Abad, representing the tobacco interests and 'all the laboring classes' of Cuba, asked the US House Committee on Reciprocity with Cuba for a substantial decrease on the duties on Cuban cigars and raw tobacco. He argued that these protective tariffs were artificially lowering profits and creating unemployment on the island, added to which, 'under the United States tariff it has been impossible for us to go into any foreign market'. Luis V. Placé from Havana, representing a prominent group of liberal Cuban merchants called the Corporaciones Económicas, argued that 'as a Cuban I would like to give the United States free trade. The whole of American products imported into Cuba ought to be free [. . . and] the proper solution of the Cuban problem is virtually free trade with both countries.' In doing so, he also expressed his awareness of the issue's imperial power dynamics: 'I ask for free trade on the understanding it is for you to grant it; we beg.'[96]

The final version of the reciprocity treaty was a far cry from the free-trade version requested by either the AIL or Cuban merchants and independence leaders, as it only ended up providing a twenty per cent discount on US tariff rates. Disillusioned independence leaders such as Juan Gualberto Gómez, head of Cuba's Liberal Party and an ally of José Martí in the Cuban independence movement, came out in opposition to reciprocity in its final form because, according to Mary Speck, the US 'had shown so little commitment to free trade'. Other Cuban nationalists, however, gave their pragmatic backing to the treaty, warning that to do otherwise would risk US annexation. For them the message was clear: Cubans must either embrace US informal imperialism through coercive protectionist reciprocity, or risk formal US colonial rule.[97]

Only a few years later, the side effects of the Republican Party's closed-door imperial policy towards the Philippines were also beginning to show. The US government's protectionist policies had created high prices on basic necessities, harming poverty-stricken Filipino consumers and local businesses.[98] Or as one US Army officer in the Philippines wrote confidentially in 1904, 'Spain, in her palmiest days, never taxed the people out here as they are being taxed now,' and the US Congress was 'doing nothing towards reducing the tariff on the products of the Islands' or 'to give them markets which we took away from them in taking the Islands over'.[99] Filipino nationalist protests soon followed. On 11 July 1908, a large gathering took place in Manila 'to endorse the mass petition for the free entry of Philippine goods to American markets [. . .] prompted by the apparent indifference of the U.S. Senate' to the ill-effects of its colonial protectionist policies. These three hundred Filipino businessmen convened what became the Philippines's first Committee on Free Trade. Its officers included pro-independence advocate Pedro Guevera, future member of the Philippine Congress (1909–1912, 1916–1922) and the nationalist resident commissioner for the Philippines (1923–1936). Another officer was Don Luis Hidalgo, a trade unionist and co-founder of the Chamber of Commerce of the Philippines in 1903. Similar pro–free trade meetings were held across the islands, resulting in the signatures of thousands of supporters.[100]

US commercial peace workers also lent their support. The AIL republished Filipino independence leader Sixto Lopez's 1911 condemnation of the 'absurdly unequal' power of US monopolists over the Philippines economy as 'legal robbery'.[101] And pro-independence sympathizers in the United States such as the Massachusetts journalist Raymond Bridgman and New York Cobden Club member Thomas Mott Osborne at this time began demanding world organization, democracy, and free trade to provide everyone with peace and cheap goods.[102] The GOP's turn-of-the-century protectionist imperial policies garnered opposition not only from the AIL, but also from nationalists in Cuba and the Philippines.

The Georgist wing of the commercial peace movement was also working its way across an ever widening range of transimperial boundaries to include such subscribers as Chinese nationalist leader Sun Yat-Sen and Russian pacifist Leo Tolstoy. In China, German Georgist Ludwig Wilhelm Schrameier had inserted single tax principles into the 1898 Land Order of Kiaochow. The single tax's successful implementation in the German Empire's Chinese colony captured the imagination of Chinese nationalist statesman Sun Yat-Sen, the first president of the Chinese republic (1912) and founding leader of the Kuomintang (1919–1925). Sun had previously encountered George's ideas during his turn-of-the-century political exile in London, and again while in Japan. He found that George's ideas had much in common with Confucian cosmopolitanism. Upon stepping down from his brief tenure as provisional president of China in 1912, Sun told US journalists that he intended 'to devote [himself] to the promotion of the welfare of the Chinese people as a whole. The teachings of your single taxer, Henry George, will be the basis of our program of reform [. . .] and under them we will grow into an industrious, peace-loving, prosperous people.'[103]

Continued free-trade imperialism in China, however, led Sun to walk a challenging tightrope. For a time, he could at once be an avowed Georgist and an officer of Boston's IFTL while also being a critic of the adverse effects of free trade's coercive enforcement in China. He remained an adherent of land reform along Georgist lines, but, much like his contemporary Naoroji in British India, his growing criticisms of European control of China's tariffs eventually led him to support infant industrial policies to resuscitate ancient Chinese industries.[104] Sun's shift to out-and-out protectionism became most visible between 1921 and 1924. In 1921, he yet avoided calls for protectionism and instead requested international financial investment to spur Chinese economic development, accompanied by ending 'the trade war' to 'root out probably the greatest causes of future wars'. By 1924, however, Sun was fed up with continued foreign control of Chinese customs duties and of 'tariff barriers [set up] against home industries for the benefit of foreign goods'. A year before his death, he was demanding protective tariffs for 'home industries'—specifically Chinese textiles—in line with the successful protectionist policies of the United States and Germany.[105]

With less ambiguity, Russia's Count Leo Tolstoy latched onto the single tax in the course of his lifelong search for social justice and world peace. Many of George's publications were translated into Russian by Tolstoy's dear friend S. D. Nikolaev, and Tolstoy helped with their publication and distribution. From the 1890s Tolstoy became an avowed Georgist, believing the single tax 'will usher in an epoch'. George's free-trade through land-reform prescription provided for Tolstoy the economic means to implement his spiritual philosophy and for the dismantling Russian serfdom. Tolstoy's passion for the single tax was passed on to his daughter Tatiana.[106]

The Georgist movement continued its radical internationalist advance. There were only a handful of Georgist delegates at the first International Free Trade Congress, hosted by the Cobden Club in London in 1908. By contrast, at the 1910 congress in Antwerp, of the six hundred delegates, fifty were from the Georgist United Committee for the Taxation of Land Values 'and kindred organisations in Ireland, the United States, Denmark, France, Sweden, Belgium and Switzerland', hinting at the single tax movement's internationalist momentum.[107] Further evidence appeared in Latin America. New York City's Puerto Rican-born Spanish editor of *Scientific American* Antonio Molina helped convert the Italian-born Argentinian reformer Felix Vitale to Georgism in the early 1900s. At the same time, São Paulo's Antonio de Queiros Telles Jr., an officer of the single-tax-dominated International Free Trade League (IFTL) in Boston, was spearheading Brazil's single tax movement. Vitale and Telles joined continental forces to create the Comité Sudamericano para el Impuesto

Unico (South American single tax committee) during the First World War—a conflict that US single taxers claimed was caused by land monopolies.[108] In Denmark, meanwhile, single taxers briefly gained the upper hand after the general election of 1913. In Britain, the inclusion of single tax elements within Lloyd George's 1909 People's Budget owed much to the single tax cohort in Parliament led by Josiah C. Wedgwood. Wedgwood stood at the forefront of the British Liberal radical struggle for the 'taxation of land values', as the single tax was more commonly known in the UK.[109] Less radical than some of his Cobdenite contemporaries on the imperial question, Wedgwood called for reforming British colonial policies along free-trade lines, rather than for dismantling the policies completely. He also put his Georgist reforms into colonial practice. When he found himself sitting on the Northern Nigerian Lands Committee in 1908, he helped replace the land taxation system outlined by Lord Lugard with that of the single tax. His experiences in dealing with British Africa led him to a more radical position by the 1920s, whereupon he came to support Indian and Irish Home Rule, Gandhian non-resistance, and Dominion status for Palestine, India, Ireland, Ceylon, and Burma.[110]

But the growth of Georgism within and beyond the British and US empires owed its greatest debt to the propagandistic efforts of Joseph and Mary Fels, who built upon these transimperial networks following their relocation to London from Philadelphia. Joseph, a wealthy retired US soap manufacturer and officer of the AIL and AFTL, and his wife Mary—a radical suffragist, AIL officer, and peace advocate who eventually became co-editor of the anti-imperial Georgist publication *The Public*—provided the international single tax movement with much-needed financial bolstering at the turn of the century. Georgist reformers in Britain were among the main recipients of the Fels's international largesse, leading to the formation of the United League for the Taxation of Land Values, as well as numerous local chapters scattered throughout the British Empire. The league sought to spread George's single tax policy throughout the British colonies, and thereby break up the land monopolies of the empire's aristocratic elites. Writing from London, Joseph laid this out in an open letter to Andrew Carnegie in 1910, entitled 'Free Trade and the Single Tax vs. Imperialism', arguing that 'if conditions of absolute free trade had prevailed', there would have been no Russo–Japanese war and no need for US control of the Philippines. The unnatural 'need of foreign markets', he continued, 'which is so frequently used as an argument to justify wars of criminal aggression is a "need" that would not be felt if the aggressing nation enforced justice at home' through adoption of the single tax and absolute free trade with the world.[111] As Mary Fels similarly described it in 1916, just before taking part in the transatlantic travails of the Ford Peace Expedition (named after its benefactor Henry Ford), free trade through Georgist land reform would undermine colonialism by dismantling imperial protectionist demands for foreign markets and transportation networks.[112]

Georgism's popularity in Britain was indicative of the New Liberal spirit infusing the Edwardian economic peace movement. Britain's New Liberals— its liberal radicals, Labour socialists, and women's suffragists—rallied around the memory of Richard Cobden and the 'Hungry Forties' in response to Joseph Chamberlain's launching of the Tariff Reform movement for imperial trade preference in 1903.[113] The anti–Boer War Liberal politician Henry Campbell-Bannerman created the pro–free trade League of Peace in 1903, just two years before he found himself serving as British prime minister.[114] Francis W. Hirst could also be spotted marching at the forefront of the New Liberal vanguard. He made a name for himself through his condemnation of the Boer War and financial imperialism, along Hobsonian lines, before marrying Richard Cobden's suffragist great-niece Helena Cobden in 1903. As editor of the *Economist* from 1907 to 1916, Hirst transformed it into Britain's premier anti-militarist and anti-imperialist organ to thwart Chamberlain's Tariff Reformers. Hirst's anti-war stance drew him to the Carnegie Endowment for Peace (CEIP) soon after its founding, but it also placed his *Economist* at loggerheads with Britain's 'gentlemanly capitalists' and, following the outbreak of war in Europe in 1914, with the pro-war interventionists inside and outside Parliament. For commercial peace workers such as Hobson, Bertrand Russell, and Hirst, the *Economist* briefly became the go-to outlet for opposing British intervention, xenophobia, and the 'starvation blockade' against Germany. But Britain's jingoist drumbeat for war soon became deafening; Hirst was dismissed from the *Economist* in July 1916, and with him went his Cobdenite editorial leadership.[115]

New Liberal Norman Angell provided his own pragmatic British Cobdenite argument in *The Great Illusion* (1910). Here he argued that war was bad for business in such an interdependent world marketplace: that even the 'winners' would lose. At this time Angell was still a Cobdenite non-interventionist, and provided a critique of the colonial system that looks to have been cribbed from Adam Smith's *Wealth of Nations*.[116] *The Great Illusion*'s emphasis on economic interdependence and the businessman's pocketbook was meant to entice more conservative industrial, financial, and political circles to the peace cause. In Britain, however, the pacifistic subscribers to 'Norman Angellism' were largely on the left, including socialists within the Independent Labour Party, liberal radicals, and university student peace activists.[117] Thanks to backing from the Garton Foundation, the CEIP, and the WPF, the book was soon translated into twenty-five languages and sold two million copies. *The Great Illusion*'s message took the left wing of Europe and the United States by storm. Groups banded together at meeting halls and universities in Britain, France, Germany, and the United States with *The Great Illusion* as the basis for discussion and affiliation. Hundreds of Norman Angell societies were formed, from Britain and the European continent to California, Australia, and Japan. Norman Angellism reached high into the transatlantic middle and upper classes. International feminist peace activists such as Budapest's Rosika Schwimmer and Chicago's Jane Addams adopted his argument (see chapter 4), as did Christian peace workers such as British Quaker J. W. Graham, George Nasmyth in the USA, and Japan's Abe Isoo (see chapter 5). Belgian lawyer, women's suffragist, and founding president of the International Peace Bureau Henri La Fontaine produced a sequel of sorts, *The Great Solution*, in 1916, which was published by the WPF. La Fontaine called for freedom of access for all international waterways, the internationalization of colonial markets, and the end of 'protective taxes', which, 'more than distances, mountains and oceans, have kept the peoples aloof and given birth to feelings of hatred and anger between the States'.[118] As late as 1937, *The Great Illusion* remained an influential part of international peace culture, inspiring Jean Renoir to write and direct the now classic French pacifist film *La Grande Illusion*.

Two notable differences, however, separated the New Liberalism from that of Cobden's time. One was the degree of the New Liberal faith in the role of regulatory governance at both the national and international level. While some early Victorians such as Elihu Burritt had sought greater supranational oversight, Cobden himself had thought it an act of hubris to believe that Britain or any other state could regulate the world's affairs.[119] By contrast, upon the outbreak of the First World War, in Britain a wide array of liberal radical free-trade-and-peace workers such as Hobson, Hirst, and Angell found themselves working alongside socialist internationalists—Bertrand Russell, H. N. Brailsford, E. D. Morel—to demand a league of nations to oversee a world at peace.[120] By war's end, a preponderance of economic peace humanitarians was persuaded that any such league would also need to govern the world's natural resources so that, as Hobson explained, they could 'be distributed, or rationed, according to the diverse needs, or capacities of enjoyment of the members of this world community' to maximize 'human welfare'.[121]

Concomitant with the New Liberal trust in international institutions was another key difference from classic Cobdenism. Internationalists such as Hobson endorsed something of a paradox that became common within the early twentieth-century anti-imperial imagination: their pacifistic support for supranational governance carved out exceptions to Cobden's earlier clear-cut non-interventionist rules. As Hobson argued, 'some powers of intervention' might need to be 'directed to the welfare of [. . .] backward populations' should they try, in the name of 'national sovereignty', to keep their countries' resources from being developed to the hindrance of 'world prosperity'. Self-determination had its limits; neither colonizers nor colonized should be allowed to shut off access to their markets and resources. For British theorists like Hobson, Britain's more industrially and democratically advanced 'white' settler colonies appeared most ready for international federation—what Duncan Bell describes as 'multilateral imperialism'—as a first step towards a more peaceful, British-led, global community. Elements of this New Liberal multilateral imperialism could be found in subsequent Western intergovernmental 'meddling' to regulate the global distribution of agricultural products and raw materials.[122] Of course, because the New Liberals considered the global scramble for raw materials to be one of the main causes of imperialism and war, they believed themselves to be acting on behalf of anti-imperialism and peace; sovereignty, like nationalism, was part of the problem. Humanitarian arguments in the name of ending slavery were similarly touted to justify early twentieth-century imperial interventions.[123] The tension between anti-imperialist principles and supranational interventionist actions—a problem of 'humanitarian imperialism'—remains a left-wing sticking point to this day.[124]

Such humanitarian interventionist exceptions were also endorsed by less radical opponents of the economic nationalist imperial order. While they demonstrated a similar distaste for the imperialism of economic nationalism, some in this more conservative camp, such as Andrew Carnegie, yet held on to the utilitarian belief that free trade brought 'civilization', and should therefore be imposed, if need be, upon unwilling populations. While these moderates were quick to critique the symbiotic relationship between protectionism, monopolies, and colonial expansion—what Hobson called 'aggressive imperialism'—they also sometimes struggled to envisage an immediate end to colonial rule.[125] In the context of the US empire, for instance, an older generation of Cobdenite anti-imperialists such as Edward Atkinson and David Starr Jordan showed themselves to be amenable to British free-trade imperial

policies, even as they decried US closed-door imperialism.[126] And Andrew
Carnegie, although a turn-of-the-century convert to the idea 'that free trade
carries peace', remained ambiguous regarding the imperial question.[127] Such
endorsements of the imperialism of free trade were, however, rarely ringing
ones. After all, this informal open-door alternative to the 'colonial problem',
which eventually became manifest within the League of Nations mandates
system, was predicated on the understanding that the policy would lead to
economic development, gradual devolution, and independence.[128] As the
Georgist AIL secretary and Philippines independence activist Erving Winslow
argued in a 1917 article replete with references to Hobson, the Cobden Club,
and Henri Lambert, a return to the protectionist status quo ante would only
perpetuate the enslavement and exploitation of colonial subjects, whereas
worldwide free trade would provide 'the backbone' of successful postwar
peace and decolonization.[129]

Pax Economica and the New Liberal Radicals, 1919–1946

In 1918, Henri Lambert laid out the economic causes of the First World War in
his new book *Pax Economica*. 'Tariff restrictions are the worst obstacles to the
advent of peace', proclaimed the Belgian manufacturer and pacifist. Protective
tariffs encouraged economic retaliation, imperial rivalry, and global conflict.
International peace was therefore only possible 'under the conditions of economic justice and security that will result from free trade', Lambert concluded
from his temporary residence in Washington, DC. *Pax Economica* was republished and distributed by the thousand by the International Free Trade League
(IFTL), a newly created Boston peace organization, of which Lambert was a
co-founder and officer.[130] Some of its officers, such as Fanny Garrison Villard
and David Starr Jordan, fell into the orthodox Cobdenite camp. But most, like
IFTL president (and Fanny's Garrison Villard's brother) Frank Wright Garrison and the famed California muckraker Lincoln Steffens, were single taxers.
Lambert and the IFTL were representative of a new interwar radical network
of economic cosmopolitan women and men who condemned protectionism
for precipitating militarism, imperial expansion, and social inequality. Notably,
the network's centre was located in the United States rather than Britain, presaging the wider mid-century Anglo-American realignment whereby the
United States would take up the mantle of free-trade champion.

  A quick perusal of the officer list of the IFTL provides an illuminating win-
dow into the more radical and inclusive political transformation occurring

within the commercial peace movement at the tail end of the Great War. Austrian Julius Meinl II was a strong advocate for the five-day working week, and financed the Viennese pacifist journal *Peace* from 1918. Belgian socialist, senator, and women's suffragist Henri La Fontaine was a delegate at the Versailles Peace Conference and participated in the League of Nations Assembly from 1920 to 1922. The IFTL's British officers were no less prestigious. J. A. Hobson, Josiah Wedgwood, and Francis Hirst require no further introduction.[131] George Lansbury was an interwar socialist leader of the British Labour Party as well as a Georgist, women's suffragist, and peace activist. Female women's suffragists such as Britain's Helena Swanwick, the Netherlands' Aletta Jacobs and Lizzy van Dorp, Norway's Martha Larsen, and Munich's Lida Gustava Heymann were all intimately involved with the women's peace movement (see chapter 4). The French anti-militarist and anarchist Georges Darien was secretary of Paris's Fels-funded single tax league, the Ligue française pour l'impôt unique (French single tax league), and editor of its newspaper *L'Impôt unique*.[132] George Fowlds acted as the left-wing political leader of New Zealand's single tax movement and was a close friend of William Lloyd Garrison Jr. These snapshots highlight how the IFTL's officers included a left-wing roll-call of international radical peace reformers.

These same economic peace workers could barely contain their excitement when the postwar settlement at first seemed to align with their cosmopolitan message. Democratic president Woodrow Wilson (in office 1913–1921), a self-described Manchester liberal with numerous single taxers as advisors, included calls for self-determination and freedom of the seas in his Fourteen Points in 1918, signalling his support.[133] The following year seemed propitious.[134] Lloyd George's former economic adviser George Paish authored *The Economic Interdependence of Nations* on behalf of the League of Nations Society, before undertaking a Cobdenesque free-trade tour of Europe. Herbert Quick, working in the Wilson administration, proposed in 1919 that the world could now be regarded as safe for democracy—as well as the single tax, decolonization, and universal suffrage.[135] Not coincidentally, that same year Berlin's Eighth German Peace Congress resolved to introduce free trade to Germany as both an anti-monopolistic policy and as 'the surest means of bringing about the rapprochement of peoples and of preserving peace'. The Cobden Club's Lujo Brentano joined numerous IFTL members to found the Deutscher Freihandelsbund (German free trade league) in Frankfurt am Main soon thereafter.[136] Austrian economist Joseph Schumpeter put forth his own powerful Cobdenite critique of aristocracy and imperialism in his 1919 essay 'The Sociology of Imperialisms', in which he portrayed imperialism as a monopolistic symptom of atavistic militarism and protectionism—an ailment that only democratic free-trade forces could cure.[137] Georgist Ohio state senator Frederic C. Howe, in turn, condemned US dollar diplomacy (coercive international financial lending) as 'economic imperialism [. . .] the forerunner of force, of conquest, of wars'. His book *The Only Possible Peace* (1919) paid homage to Richard Cobden and John Bright. It argued that the time was ripe to 'challenge the monopoly of the earth, the closed doors, the spheres of influence, the trade preferences' of the imperial powers. Now was the moment to create a 'Pax Economica [. . . :] a peace interested in the development of the world' through 'universal free trade'.[138]

Around this time, the commercial peace movement found new allies among the era's Esperanto movement.[139] A Polish Jewish doctor named L. L. Zamenhof had first unveiled the universalist language in 1887 as a simple, easy-to-learn second language that could unite the world in peace. The linguistic movement promised to eradicate one of the greatest impediments to world trade—the language barrier. Two Japanese advocates described it thus in 1905: 'As world intercourse becomes more incessant with every day, so do the differences between the languages of all the nations make inconvenience and disagreeableness more and more keenly felt'.[140] This economic aspect had become even more explicit by the time of the First World War, in the context of which a number of commercial groups began to view Esperanto as a key component for reconstructing postwar trade.[141] In 1915, for example, the prominent head of a polytechnic school in Germany had promoted the language as the best option for establishing free trade and peace after the war, and similar sentiments were expressed among US, British, Spanish, and Portuguese Esperantists in 1917. In 1921 the French Chamber of Commerce, working with the French group Esperanto et Commerce, called on its counterparts in other nations to embrace Esperanto as the language of international business.[142] The League of Nations even considered adopting Esperanto as its official language the following year, after it received the endorsement of Persia, China, Japan, Bulgaria, and Finland. But the French delegate, representing the wishes of his country's right-wing nationalist government, scuttled the proposal in order to ensure that the French language maintained its duopoly, alongside English, as the League's official medium.[143]

The tragic League fate of Esperanto owed much to its association with left-wing peace politics, hinting at the wider illiberal nationalist fallout from the Versailles Treaty.[144] Within the commercial peace movement, jubilation turned into disillusionment. John Maynard Keynes famously denounced the Versailles Treaty in *The Economic Consequences of the Peace* (1919). The young British economist, drawn to Norman Angellism before the world war, now condemned the punitive and exclusionary policies being perpetuated under the 'abhorrent and detestable' treaty. In keeping with the wider economic peace movement, Keynes called instead for a 'Free Trade Union' encompassing Europe, India, Siberia, Turkey, and Egypt to work towards 'the Peace of the World'.[145] Angell similarly lashed out at the postwar illiberal immorality of protectionism and its close association with 'the phenomenon of Nationalism' at the 1921 International Free Trade Congress in Amsterdam.[146]

The Wilson administration's military interventions in the Caribbean and Mexico, coupled with the coercive mandate-related consequences for 'the score of little countries' stemming from US reluctance to join the League, led some to despair, others to action. Among the former, *The Public* halted publication for good.[147] Louis Post, *The Public's* Georgist founding editor and Woodrow Wilson's assistant secretary of labor, next brought his own political career to an end when he stubbornly opposed Attorney General A. Mitchell Palmer's crackdown on suspected immigrant radicals at the end of Wilson's second term.[148] Post saw in retirement an opportunity to work on his Esperanto.[149] Other economic peace workers instead became more proactive. For example, at this time Fanny Garrison Villard and her son, *The Nation* editor Oswald Garrison Villard, gave their backing to the League of Oppressed Peoples to help fight for worldwide self-determination and an end to imperialism.[150] The new league connected economic peace workers with those favouring the anti-imperialism of economic nationalism, such as Indian nationalist Lala Lajpat Rai and pan-Africanist W.E.B. Du Bois, their NAACP colleague.[151]

Many new liberal radicals showed themselves to be quite comfortable with supranational regulation and state interventionism, as well as working with their socialist internationalist peace allies. In Britain, Fabian socialist Leonard Woolf joined forces with Mary Sheepshanks, George Paish, Norman Angell, J. A. Hobson, Francis Hirst, and Josiah Wedgwood to headline the Fight the Famine Council for Economic Reconstruction in 1920. It called for an end to postwar blockades and 'the fullest use of the machinery of the Co-operative movement' to 'relieve distress in the starving Countries'.[152] At the 1923 single tax conference held in Oxford, Denmark's Signe Bjorner explained how Georgism—or *Retsstaten*, 'the State of Justice and Equity'—had become conjoined with the socialist internationalist co-operative movement.[153] Single taxers lobbied the League-sponsored World Economic Conference at Geneva in 1927 to fight against the false flag of self-sufficiency, 'the antagonism and friction' deriving from economic nationalism, and the colonial search for new markets and raw materials; the League's pledge to world peace was inconsistent unless it embraced Georgist free-trade principles.[154] The Cobden Club–sponsored International Committee to Promote Universal Free Trade (ICPUFT, founded in 1921) witnessed the socialist leaders of the International Co-operative Alliance working alongside non-Marxist organizations such as the International Chambers of Commerce, the Dunford House Association (trustees of Richard Cobden's family home), and the International Federation of League of Nations Unions.[155]

The League of Nations itself remained a popular forum for airing the interwar concerns of left-wing commercial peace workers. The ICPUFT, the international single tax movement, the co-operative movement (see chapter 3), the feminist peace movement (see chapter 4), and the Christian peace movement (see chapter 5) all kept up a steady stream of pro–free trade lobbying throughout the 1920s and 1930s. The 1927 Economic Conference in Geneva called upon the League's Economic Committee to oversee the worldwide regulation and reduction of tariff barriers as peace measures.[156] Japan's economic cosmopolitans also mobilized; the Free Trade Association of Osaka, for instance, was created in January 1928 following the recommendation of the Geneva conference. Further radical reinforcements arrived in Geneva a few years later when the World Youth Congress movement came out in support of free trade, disarmament, and a more proactive and potent League.[157]

The more moderate heads of the CEIP, in turn, continued to provide much-needed financial and logistical support to the interwar free-trade-and-peace movement. In the late 1920s, the Cobden family home, Dunford House, even became the semi-official headquarters of the CEIP's European section. This occurred at the instigation of Jane Cobden Unwin, along with her husband Thomas Fisher Unwin (the publisher, also treasurer of the ICPUFT), and J. A. Hobson, Francis Hirst, and Cobden Club officers George Paish and H. S. Perris.[158]

The international economic peace movement was aghast when the US Republican Party enacted the highly protectionist Hawley-Smoot Tariff of 1930. Their horror was compounded by the timing of the protectionist legislation, arriving on the very heels of the promising resolutions of the 1928 Kellogg-Briand Pact outlawing war.[159] In an open letter to CEIP president Nicholas Murray Butler, Cobden Club treasurer H. S. Perris took Americans to task: 'To limit your armaments whilst you are at the same time raising your tariff walls, is a poor kind of logic; for tariff walls are the frowning-fortresses of economic warfare.' These were not the symbols 'of co-operation and inter-dependence between nations, but of parochialism, of self-sufficiency, of sus-picion and hostility [. . .] born of predatory greed and of the desire to establish remunerative monopoly'.[160]

For 1930s internationalist subscribers to Manchester liberalism, the growth of the Nazi Third Reich and the wider nationalist turn towards more stringent trade and immigration restrictions were all by now clear indicators that an-other world war loomed on the horizon. As the neoliberal LSE economics professor Lionel Robbins described it in his 1939 book *The Economic Causes of War*, 'international liberals and international socialists can surely be at one [. . .] that the coming of national socialism' would merely add to the causes. National Socialism's threat to peace rivalled only that of the 'sinister interests'—militant protectionist elites—in encouraging the widespread embrace of economic autarky, immigration restriction, and trade jealousy. For Robbins and other interwar neoliberal inheritors of Manchester School principles, the remedy was clear: 'Cobdenite liberalism' maintained through regional and world fed-eralism wherein 'independent sovereignty must be limited [. . . for] unless we destroy the sovereign state, the sovereign state will destroy us'.[161] Robbins thereafter represented the UK at the 1944 Bretton Woods Conference, at which various supranational regulatory agencies were created to oversee just such a new economic order.

World federalism also remained a high pacifistic priority for Cordell Hull, Franklin Delano Roosevelt (FDR)'s Democratic secretary of state. Hull's posi-tion made him the new figurehead of the economic peace movement. It also made him the most prominent among the commercial peace workers to attend the 1933 League-sponsored London Economic Conference, which again called for free trade, prosperity, and peace. During his long tenure at the State Depart-ment (1933–1944) Hull well earned his nickname 'the Tennessee Cobden'. Ever since the First World War and his involvement with the AIL, he recollected, 'I embraced the philosophy that I carried throughout my twelve years as Secre-tary of State'. Unhampered trade 'dovetailed with peace; high tariffs, trade bar-riers, and unfair economic competition with war'. Freer trade meant that 'one country would not be deadly jealous of another and the living standards of all countries might rise', thereby creating 'a reasonable chance for lasting peace'.[162] Francis Hirst connected Hull's efforts explicitly to Cobden's a century before. Hirst proclaimed the 1938 Anglo–American trade agreement 'the most impor-tant free (or freer) trade pact' since the 1860 Cobden–Chevalier Treaty.[163] The multilateral trading system that arose in the 1930s and 1940s—Hull's 'tariff revolution', as Alfred Eckes calls it—was explicitly established to foster a more integrated, prosperous, and peaceful world. And it owed much to the past century of economic peace activism.[164]

Hull's State Department wasted little time in implementing its anti-imperialism of free trade. Its 'Good Neighbor Policy' towards Latin America promised to end more than a century of coercive US military interventionism in its hemisphere. Here Hull received help from the director of the Division of Territories and Island Possessions, Ernest Gruening. A leading specialist on Mexican–American relations, Gruening had earlier bulked up his left-wing credentials as an anti-monopoly activist and civil rights reformer in Boston, and then, while managing editor of *The Nation*, as an opponent of Woodrow Wilson's coercive intervention in Haiti. As late as 1933 Gruening was penning editorials entreating FDR to embrace non-interventionism in the region, leading to his appointment within the new Democratic administration. Together, Hull and Gruening fused US anti-imperialism with freer trade and non-interventionism towards Latin America. Topping the list, the US military occupation of Haiti ended in 1934, the same year that many of the coercive elements of the Platt Amendment were abrogated once a new agreement was struck whereby the US government promised not to interfere in Cuban affairs.[165] Hull's anti-imperialism of free trade was also deployed against British imperial trade preference. He and his team saw this as one of the key stumbling blocks to peaceful multilateralism, and worked in vain to dismantle it throughout the 1930s and 1940s.[166]

Trade liberalization accompanied Hull's anti-imperial proclivities to create a 'capitalist peace' to protect both the national and international interest.[167] Passage of the Reciprocal Trade Agreements Act (RTAA, 1934) signalled a seismic shift away from decades of Republican-style protectionism. The latter now took much of the blame for worsening the Great Depression. By 1944, the platforms of both major parties came out in support of the RTAA, hinting at a potential bipartisan shift in favour of freer trade over the intervening decade.[168] Hull's efforts on behalf of supranational organization earned him his other sobriquet, 'Father of the United Nations'. Ill health kept him from representing the United States at the 1945 San Francisco Conference that would give birth to the UN, but he received daily reports either by phone or telegram, and advised the US delegation. Hull's work on behalf of freeing world trade, the Good Neighbor Policy, and the UN earned him a Nobel Peace Prize in 1945.[169]

After Hull's departure in 1944, the US State Department continued to underline the need for economic peace. In *Building a New World Economy* (1946), published in the same year that independence was granted to the Philippines, the State Department outlined the stark choice facing the world: either economic cooperation and peace through freer trade, or protectionism and economic warfare. The State Department therefore endorsed the proposed International Trade Organization (ITO), which aimed to regulate and facilitate the liberalization of the world economy.[170] Will Clayton, like Hull a believer in the pacifying tendencies of trade liberalization, took charge of the State Department's foreign economic policy upon Hull's exit. Through the Marshall Plan, Clayton pushed for European economic integration, alongside the ITO, as prerequisites for effective multilateralism, laying the groundwork for the creation of the European Economic Community in 1957.[171] When the ITO failed to get off the ground, the 1947 General Agreement on Tariffs and Trade (GATT) acted as a substitute, which became the World Trade Organization in 1995. The GATT's unconditional most favoured nation clause immediately contributed to a drastic slashing of tariff rates among its signatories, with the United States leading the way. Although Clayton was the leading US negotiator, today Hull is credited as the GATT's progenitor and, according to Thomas Zeiler, as the person who 'set the standard for the pursuit of market capitalism as a pillar of US trade policy and as a foundation of the process of globalization'.[172] From the embers of the Great Depression and the Second World War, a liberal radical Pax Economica was beginning to take shape.

Conclusion

The economic peace movement that arose in the mid-nineteenth century felt vindicated by the late 1940s. Britain's near century-long national embrace of free-trade ideology not only drove its imperial policies, but also motivated many of its left-leaning critics of imperialism, laying the economic ideological foundations of both the international peace movement and the more open economic order that arose immediately after the Second World War. After a century of grassroots activism, setbacks, and political persecution, the commercial peace movement's liberal radical efforts had finally helped create a new world order that bore the trappings of their Pax Economica.

Illustrating the economic cosmopolitan confluence of peace activism, Cordell Hull's new world order received the notable backing of New York's *Nation* magazine. This occurred under the liberal magazine's interwar editorship of Oswald Garrison Villard, the son of Cobdenite women's peace activist Fanny Garrison Villard and grandson of Boston's famed Manchester liberal abolitionist William Lloyd Garrison. After the First World War, Oswald began reconciling his family's Manchester School beliefs with his growing socialist internationalist sympathies. He threw his continued support behind the Socialist Party of America (SPA)'s six-times presidential nominee Norman Thomas, advocated for the creation of a new third party that combined elements of the SPA platform with those of Manchester liberalism, and endorsed the SPA's internationalist critique of Republican economic nationalism in the early 1930s. His 1947 book *Free Trade: Free World* thereafter supported Hull's and Clayton's trade reforms. The book was published by the Georgist Schalkenbach Foundation and was dedicated 'to those four great apostles of free trade' John Bright, Richard Cobden, William Lloyd Garrison, and Henry George.[173] As will be explored in the next chapter, Oswald Garrison Villard's left-wing political activism was indicative of the growing pacifistic affinities between capitalist liberal radicals and socialist internationalists—the Marx-Manchester free-trade tradition—that had first begun taking shape in 1840s Britain.

3

Marx and Manchester

THE PACIFISTIC EVOLUTION OF
THE SOCIALIST INTERNATIONALIST
FREE-TRADE TRADITION

*In a word, the Free Trade system hastens the Social Revolution. In this
revolutionary sense alone, gentlemen, I am in favor of Free Trade.*

—KARL MARX, 1848[1]

*'No forcible annexation, no punitive indemnities, self-determination of all nations.'
To the famous formula is now added: 'No economic nationalism, no war after
the war.'*

—'SOCIALIST PARTY [OF AMERICA]
CONGRESSIONAL PROGRAM', 1918[2]

FREE TRADE, or *Freihandel*, was a hot-button issue at the German Social
Democratic Party (SPD) Congress held in Stuttgart in 1898, most notably
because of the policy's numerous advocates. SPD leader Karl Kautsky kicked
things off with a resolution denouncing protectionism for counteracting 'international solidarity'. Luise Zietz, a German feminist and head of the SPD
women's movement, seconded Kautsky's call: 'We have to adopt a principled
stance, and that is in favor of free trade and against protective tariffs.' August
Bebel, SPD chairman and longtime pacifist, followed up on Kautsky and Zietz's free-trade endorsements, and the congress adopted a qualified resolution
along these lines. Free trade would receive an even stronger SPD endorsement
in 1900, because 'free international exchange is [...] before all, a working-class

question', German Marxist revisionist Eduard Bernstein explained in a subsequent letter to London's 1908 International Free Trade Congress, which was hosted by the Cobden Club on the heels of that year's Universal Peace Congress.[3] The SPD's efforts were part of a rich socialist internationalist free-trade tradition that began germinating when Friedrich Engels and Karl Marx migrated to Britain in the 1840s, just as the island -nation was embracing free trade as both policy and ideology. As explored in the previous chapter, this same British free-trade embrace was also giving rise to the Manchester School (Manchester liberalism, Cobdenism), an economic ideology that tied international trade liberalization together with cheap food, democratization, antiimperialism, and peace—a cosmopolitan concoction that socialist internationalists increasingly imbibed by the turn of the century.

Recovering the free-trade dimensions of socialist internationalism, and the pacifistic liberal radical influence upon it of Britain's Manchester School, upends the commonly held assumption that socialists the world over have supported nationalism and protectionism in the context of their collectivist opposition to free-market capitalism.[4] Doing so also provides a much-needed prehistory to the growing body of literature on 'socialist globalization'. This scholarship has focused primarily on socialist attempts to deepen regional and global interdependence through market integration and supranational governance amid the Manichean ideological divide of the Cold War.[5] By contrast, earlier attempts have received far less attention, and the role of free trade within the socialist internationalist tradition less still. This chapter therefore traces the evolution of socialist internationalist support for free trade across the century before the Cold War. Much like their liberal radical contemporaries, for many socialist internationalists free trade became closely tied to their peace and anti-imperial activism. As a result, the cosmopolitan subscription to free trade increasingly made for strange bedfellows: liberal radical capitalists, and socialist internationalists seeking a more interdependent and peaceful world order.

The global growth of economic nationalism between the late nineteenth century and the Second World War played a crucial role in aligning the ideological schools of Marx and Manchester. From the 1860s and 1870s, many industrializing capitalist states—most prominent among them the United States, France, and Germany—embraced policies of 'infant industrial' protectionism and went in search of new colonial markets among the underdeveloped regions of Africa, Latin America, and the Asia Pacific (see chapter 1).[6] The close connection between these protectionist and imperial developments helped spark the left-wing growth of socialist theories of imperialism and free-trade-and-peace activism.[7] After the First World War, an even stronger global swing towards economic nationalism and imperial retrenchment encouraged the widespread left-wing socialist internationalist backing of capitalist supranational initiatives such as the League of Nations, and subsequently the United Nations and European Union, in the hope of facilitating freer trade, decolonization, and world peace.[8]

Until now, left-wing socialist internationalist sympathy for free trade and its close association with anti-imperialism and peace in the century before the Cold War had yet to be collectively examined. Such investigation uncovers how this socialist free-trade tradition evolved alongside and drew inspiration from the liberal radicalism of the Manchester School. Of course, as with any intellectual tradition, socialist internationalist support for free trade was not static. Turn-of-the-century Marxist theorists of imperialism began reformulating Karl Marx and Friedrich Engels's mid-nineteenth-century free-trade endorsement. Socialist internationalists during and after the First World War increasingly advocated free trade as a necessary precondition for a more peaceful world order—a left-wing ideological marriage that the Manchester School had so famously wedded together in the 1840s.

Marx, Engels, and the Manchester School

The socialist free-trade tradition began taking shape in the 1840s, just as Britain unilaterally abandoned protectionism following a prolonged grassroots free-trade campaign centred in Manchester. The island nation's political and ideological shift to free trade sparked a brief transatlantic flirtation with trade liberalization.[9] This was due in no small part to the transnational influence and activism of Britain's Manchester School, which asserted that free-trade internationalism brought about a panoply of cheap food, democratization, anti-imperialism, and peace, as explored in the previous chapter. Free trade appealed to the cosmopolitan's ideological and material interests alike by promising to feed the world's poor with cheap food and to undermine the militaristic political influence of atavistic landed elites. This one-two punch would, British free traders like Richard Cobden promised, result in global interdependence, political enfranchisement, prosperity, and geopolitical amity. As a result, Cobden's envisaged interdependent economic order also promised to undermine imperialism and militarism by eliminating 'the desire and the motive for large and mighty empires; for gigantic armies and great navies.'[10]

Cobden's pacifistic free-trade vision found a receptive mid-nineteenth-century transatlantic left-wing audience.

Karl Marx and his close friend and patron Friedrich Engels, based in England from the 1840s onwards, observed this shift from protectionism to free trade in Britain and some of the other Western capitalist states—and they gave it their qualified endorsement.[11] They viewed the turn to free trade as an advancement of the global capitalist project, the dawn of a new epoch of capitalist internationalism. For Marx, free trade was a progressive condition of industrial capitalism, moving it a step closer to socialist revolution. Protectionism, by contrast, was regressive and belonged to the pre- and proto-industrial capitalist era.[12] For Engels, too, free trade was preferable to protectionism, as the former would 'expand as freely and as quickly as possible' the capitalist system and thus hasten the destruction of 'the whole system'.[13] Marx, soon before his relocation to Britain in the 1840s, also presaged subsequent twentieth-century socialist free-trade support for supranational governance. Noting the centuries-long regressive political influence of British protectionist elites, he speculated that 'only by a congress of nations' would free traders be able to surmount national protectionist tendencies.[14] Thus by the time Marx and Engels were headquartered in 'Free Trade England', they had begun to anticipate, as Claudio Katz puts it, 'the present process of globalization' through their 'descriptions of the creation of a world market, economic cosmopolitanism, the universal extension of commercial rules, and the destruction of tariff barriers'.[15]

The mid-century hegemonic rise of Manchester liberalism in Britain informed Marx and Engels's free-trade sympathies. This should not be all that surprising considering that both men spent most of their lives in England from the 1840s onward. Engels himself claimed to have heard the leaders of the Anti–Corn Law League (ACLL, 1839–1846)—Britain's main free-trade pressure group that Cobden spearheaded—'pour forth their Anti-Corn-Law arguments more than a hundred times' following his own arrival in Manchester. He and Marx also predicted that the ACLL's efforts would have the added benefit of bringing down the landed aristocracy, thereby providing a much-needed boon to English tenant farmers.[16] So, too, did Marx and Engels's connecting of protectionism with the rise of monopolies, trusts, and geopolitical tensions contain more than a few of the liberal radical trappings of the Manchester School.

But while Marx and Engels may have shared a similar distaste for protectionism, unlike the Manchester School they did not consider free trade free of sin. Neither man believed that free trade was a true friend of the proletariat.

They assumed that cheaper prices resulting from free trade also meant lower wages for the working man and that the free market's boom–bust economic cycle and overproduction were no boon to workers. But the most important difference between them and the Manchester School lay in where they placed free-trade internationalism within the stages of capitalist development. Marx and Engels considered free trade to be a progressive capitalist step along the path towards eventual socialist revolution, whereas Manchester liberals viewed free trade's universal adoption, and the consequent prosperity and peace that would follow, as the final stage of capitalist development. At the geopolitical level, Marx was more sceptical than later free-trade socialists concerning the Manchester School premise that market interconnectivity derived from trade liberalization would unite the world in a fraternity of nations. Marx also thought the 'squint-eyed set of Manchester humbugs' were hypocritical in condemning war abroad while ignoring the domestic war on workers at home.[17]

Despite these limits to Marx and Engels's free-trade internationalism, they gave it their support. 'We are for Free Trade,' Marx declared in 1847, because the large-scale internationalization of trade across 'the territory of the whole earth' would not only connect the world's markets, but would also help unite the world's proletariat.[18] He also granted that free trade increased productive capital, which would increase the demand for labour and thereby further lay the groundwork for the proletarian revolution: 'It breaks up old nationalities and pushes the antagonism of the proletariat and the bourgeoisie to the extreme point. In a word, the Free Trade system hastens the Social Revolution [. . . so] I am in favor of Free Trade.'[19] While Marx and Engels were sceptical of the idea that free-market capitalism would unite the nations of the world in peaceful fraternity, they were confident that it would unite the world's workers.

Marx and Engels avoided speculating about an ideal socialist trade policy, yet their internationalist vision of the end of the nation state after the socialist revolution had much in common with the free-trade vision of the Manchester School. After all, for Marx and Engels the end of nation states would have meant the end of protectionism between nation states. Manchester School adherents similarly envisaged the gradual decline of the nation state, and with it the elimination of national rivalries and trade barriers.[20] The two intellectual camps therefore overlapped in their predictions of the demise of national boundaries and national rivalries, resulting in worldwide free trade.

The hegemonic influence of the Manchester School in Britain also helps explain why, in the *Communist Manifesto* and elsewhere in the late 1840s, Marx and Engels directed their most scathing critiques against Germany's economic nationalist turn to 'infant industrial' protectionism, rather than against newly minted 'Free Trade England'. Marx charged that, instead of moving capitalism towards socialist revolution, Germany's protectionism was moving it backwards: 'People are thus about to begin in Germany with what people in France and England are about to end. The old corrupt conditions against which these countries are rebelling in theory and which they only bear as one bears chains, is greeted in Germany as the dawn of a beautiful future.' Marx singled out the protectionist theories of Friedrich List in particular, while also broadly condemning German protectionism and its manipulative call to patriotism for allowing the bourgeoisie to '*exploit his fellow-countrymen*'.[21] Marx emphasized that protectionism 'forcibly' abbreviated 'the transition from medieval to the modern mode of production', and, if allowed to progress naturally, would soon be replaced by free trade as the next stage of capitalist development. Engels shared Marx's criticisms of German protectionism.[22]

Marx and Engels, again sounding very much like their Manchester School contemporaries, considered protectionism harmful to the international system and the prime suspect for creating monopolies and trusts. As early as 1842, seven years before he moved to London, Marx began decrying protectionism as 'the *organization of a state of war* in time of peace, a state of war which, aimed in the first place against foreign countries, necessarily turns in its implementation against the country which organizes it'.[23] Engels, though initially more sympathetic to List's arguments, soon came around to Marx's position, and argued well into the 1880s that the creation of monopolies and trusts provided 'the surest sign that protection has done its work and is changing its character'. He denounced protectionism for being

> at best an endless screw, and you never know when you have done with it. By protecting one industry, you directly or indirectly hurt all others, and have therefore to protect them too. By so doing you again damage the industry that you first protected, and have to compensate it [...] and so on ad infinitum.

The necessary turn to free trade was 'immensely more difficult' and necessitated a 'fight'. Germany had perverted this order, leading to the rise of trusts and landed monopolies.[24] Marx and Engels thus gave their pragmatic socialist endorsement to the productivity and internationalism that capitalist free trade created, in anticipation of the eventual global proletarian revolution it would help foster.[25] Their socialist focus on the stages of capitalist trade policy from the late 1840s onward received further attention from turn-of-the-century Marxist theorists, owing to the wider cosmopolitan influence of Manchester liberal theories of imperialism within international left-wing political circles.[26]

Free Trade and Socialist Theories of Imperialism

Marx and Engels had undertaken much of their theorizing about the stages of capitalism during an era marked by a transatlantic turn to trade liberalization and the growing popularity of the Manchester School.[27] But this short-lived mid-nineteenth-century freer trade trend underwent a sharp reversal in the latter half of the nineteenth century. As explored in chapter 1, the American System of protectionism became the preferred policy for developing nations such as the United States, Germany, France, Russia, and Japan as the century closed, due in large part to a surge in industrialization and national consolidation, coupled with the onset of a series of global economic depressions between 1873 and 1896. The List-inspired German Historical School (GHS), for example, took over the German imperial government and universities in the 1870s and 1880s to counteract the spread of *Manchestertum* (the German epithet for the Manchester School).[28] Similarly, in the United States, the Republican Party rebranded itself after 1865 as the party of economic nationalism and steered US foreign trade policy along its protectionist course until the 1930s. Even among Britain's own settler colonies, protectionist policies became entrenched by the turn of the century. While free trade kept its hold upon Britain, economic nationalism gripped the imperial world, as did the monopolistic rise of trusts and cartels and a new wave of Western colonialism in Africa, Latin America, and Asia. For turn-of-the-century socialist theorists of imperialism such as Kōtoku Shūsui, Rudolf Hilferding, Vladimir Lenin, Karl Kautsky, and Eduard Bernstein, these protectionist, monopolistic, and imperial trends were interrelated. They accordingly honed their theories of imperialism from within this evolving Marxist free-trade tradition, and updated it to account for the turbulent, protectionist, and militaristic world order.[29] They critiqued protectionism for being a root cause of monopoly capitalism and imperialism—much like their contemporary non-Marxist liberal radical theorists—while at the same time inverting Marx and Engels's stages of capitalist trade development.

Japanese socialist internationalist and anarchist Kōtoku Shūsui became disillusioned with the Meiji Restoration's turn-of-the-century embrace of imperialism and protectionism, inspiring him to write his anti-imperial tract

Imperialism: Monster of the Twentieth Century (1901). The book started what biographer Robert Tierney describes as 'a cosmopolitan and democratic anti-imperialist movement in Japan'. Kōtoku was the first in Japan to undertake translations of *The Communist Manifesto* as well as of the pacifistic writings of Russian Georgist Leo Tolstoy. Preceding Hobson's similarly titled book by a year, the substance of Kōtoku's *Imperialism* aligned more closely with Hobson than Lenin, whereas his support for socialist revolution was more in tune with Lenin. Like Hobson, Kōtoku understood imperialism mainly as a formal policy of territorial acquisition wrought from the machinations of atavistic military officers, nationalists, industrialists, and financiers in a mistaken belief that new colonial markets were needed as outlets for the overproduction of surplus capital. Also more like Hobson, he encouraged the curbing of Japanese imperialism and jingoism through emulation of the liberal radicalism of the 'Little Englanders'. While opposed to the coercive free-trade treaties forced upon Japan as well as British interventions in Africa, Kōtoku heaped praised upon Britain's policy of free trade, withholding explicit criticism of its rule in India. He opposed the Russo–Japanese War through his radical pacifist newspaper *Heimin* (1903–1905), landing him a short stint in a Japanese prison in 1905. Upon his release, he spent a year in exile in California. In San Francisco he worked on his English while he fomented socialist sentiment among Japanese Americans, lectured in support of universal suffrage, dipped into Emma Goldman's anarchist magazine *Mother Earth*, and spoke out against US racist immigration policies and Jim Crow. His support for more violent left-wing socialist and anarchist action in Japan thereafter led to his execution for high treason in 1911.[30]

Austria's Rudolf Hilferding, like Marx and Engels, favoured free trade over protectionism. In *Finance Capital* (1910), Hilferding wrote that undoubtedly 'free trade would amalgamate the whole world market into a single economic territory. Free trade would also ensure the highest possible labour productivity and the most rational international division of labour.'[31] He also granted that protectionism, not free trade, went hand in hand with imperialism.[32] But he broke from Marx and Engels in portraying protectionism as a progressive rather than a regressive developmental stage of capitalism: a successor to the mid-century free-trade epoch rather than its antecedent. According to Hilferding, protectionism had created the monopolies, the market inefficiencies, the disparities of wealth between rich and poor, and the friction between the imperial powers that were now paving the way towards the proletarian revolution. The protectionist rise of finance capital and the resulting imperial rivalries were now seen as an inevitable step forward in the stages of capitalism. In other words, by making protectionism the successor to free trade, turn-of-the-century revolutionary theorists of imperialism such as Hilferding could claim that the twin international rise of protectionism and financial monopolies was the latest, or even the highest, stage of capitalism. Hilferding could also claim that the need of these same protectionist nations to export surplus capital to new markets and to obtain raw materials naturally led to imperial capitalist conflict. His progressive placement of protectionism within the capitalist stages was thus a critical point of departure for his and subsequent Marxist theories of imperialism. Hilferding's inversion of Marx and Engels's capitalist stages—free trade preceding rather than succeeding protectionism—and his theory of the cartel tariff thereafter reappeared in the work of Russian theorist Vladimir Lenin.

Lenin's evolving imperial theory leaned upon Marx, Engels, and Hilferding, as well as 'new' Manchester liberal J. A. Hobson. Like Marx and Engels, Lenin had at first identified free trade as the next progressive stage of capitalism, but came around to the stage theory of Hilferding.[33] By 1895, he was demanding that 'Russian Marxists must stand for free trade, since the reactionary character of protection, which retards the country's economic developments, [...] serves the interests [...] of a handful of all-powerful magnates [...] and since free trade means accelerating the process that yields the means of deliverance from capitalism.'[34] But by 1916, with the world's empires at war, this free-trade progression fell by the wayside; Lenin now asserted that the rest of the industrializing world, 'sheltering themselves with "protective" tariffs', had undermined Britain's more peaceful free-trade policies. And he famously proclaimed the present protectionist monopoly stage to be capitalism's last.[35] Lenin's theory of imperialism was an explicit combination of Marx and Manchester. While Lenin admitted to borrowing heavily from Hilferding, he also acknowledged his intellectual debt to J. A. Hobson, whose *Imperialism: A Study* (1902) condemned the protectionist international system for creating the market inefficiencies that led to the financial imperial search for raw materials and new markets for surplus capital. The overlap between the theories was such that it has been dubbed 'the Hobson-Lenin thesis'.[36]

The free-trade sympathies of German socialist imperial theorist and SPD leader Karl Kautsky went even further in combining Manchester liberalism with Marxism. Kautsky's support for free trade remained remarkably consistent, and was tied closely to his antipathy towards German protectionism and colonialism.[37] His time spent in London from 1885 to 1890 proved formative, leading to a close relationship with Friedrich Engels alongside an intellectual infatuation with the Manchester School.[38] His association of 'industrial capitalism' with free trade, peace, and progress and protectionism with pre-industrialism and militarism reflected the theories of non-Marxist contemporaries such as Hobson, Norman Angell, and Joseph Schumpeter.[39]

Around the same time as Hobson was penning *Imperialism*, Kautsky was drawing similar inspiration from what he perceived as the decline of Manchester liberalism in Britain, resulting in the outbreak of the Second Boer War (1899–1902). In 1900, Kautsky wrote that 'Manchester ideals' were being 'pushed into the background by Imperialism' thereby increasing 'the power of militarism'. And like Hobson, he observed how colonialism after 1870 followed from the search for new markets as outlets for surplus goods and capital resulting from inefficient protectionist policies. 'The higher the tariff barriers between individual capitalist states grow, the more each of them feels the need to assure itself of a market which no one can exclude them from, and to gain supplies of raw material which no one can cut off', sparking an 'arms race' that 'must grow ever greater' and making 'the danger of a world war come ever nearer'. In his 1914 article 'Ultra-imperialism', Kautsky associated free trade with peace and industrial capitalism, and contrasted them with the connection between protectionism, cartels, financial capitalism, and the consequent need to export surplus capital—'the principal roots of imperialism' that had 're-placed free trade'.[40] Kautsky therefore roundly condemned colonialism de-rived from protectionism.[41] His Marx-Manchester ideology also informed his belief that European trade liberalization could only maintain peace through supranational governance. He argued that a free-trading 'United States of Europe' would 'ban the spectre of war'.[42] Kautsky's support for free trade, supranational governance, European integration, and peace—positions scholars more commonly associate with interwar 'neoliberal' intellectuals—continued to influence the SPD in the interwar years and beyond.[43]

Eduard Bernstein, an SPD spokesman on foreign policy and taxation issues in the German Reichstag from 1902 to 1928, epitomized even more than Kautsky the confluence of *Manchestertum* and Marxism in Germany.[44] Bernstein's formative years of exile in London (1888–1901) placed him at the centre of turn-of-the-century Marxist and Manchester School radicalism. This time in England, rubbing shoulders with Kautsky, Engels, and the Fabians, as well as Cobdenites such as Hobson, had a profound effect upon his later socialist free-trade internationalism.[45] Manfred Steger states, indeed, that Bernstein fell under the influence 'of both Engels and the British free-trade tradition'.[46] Like Kautsky, Bernstein was consistent in his support for free trade over the course of his socialist political career. He believed free trade to be not only progressive, but also good for both the proletariat and the bourgeoisie. Also, like Kautsky (and Marx), Bernstein condemned List-inspired 'infant industrial' protectionism for creating geopolitical tensions and for being reactionary and atavistic, a throwback to the era of mercantilism and a stumbling block to modernization. His critique of militarism—for which he blamed jingoism, nationalism, protectionism, and the undue influence of arms manufacturers on German policymaking—owed much to the influence of the later Engels. Much like Kautsky, Bernstein's critique had much in common with those of Hobson and Schumpeter, as did his belief that free trade and industrialism were the foundation stones of a peaceful economic order, such that R. A. Fletcher posits that Bernstein was 'not only fundamentally more British than German but also thoroughly imbued with the values of Cobdenite radicalism'.[47] Bernstein's Marx-Manchester free-trade-and-peace beliefs would find wide-ranging left-wing subscribers among early twentieth-century socialist internationalists.[48]

The Marx-Manchester Tradition vs. the Marx-List Tradition, 1880–1918

Socialist commercial peace activism grew substantially between the turn of the century and the end of the First World War, emanating from Britain to Argentina, Germany, and the USA. The economic peace movement's socialist internationalist popularity grew during this period to counteract the contemporaneous Western growth of protectionism, monopolies, and colonial expansion. The era also saw the rise of a competing Marx-List tradition among socialist nationalists in Britain, the USA, Germany, the Soviet Union, India, and China, who were more concerned with 'socialism in one country', as Stalin's regime would later describe it. Within Euro-America, Marx-List nationalist adherents tended to support militarism, immigration restrictions, monopolies, and imperialism, providing a stark contrast to the Marx-Manchester internationalist supporters of free trade, anti-imperialism, and peace.

The Marx-Manchester tradition took root within turn-of-the-century Britain, where free trade evolved into a cause, and Richard Cobden became a popular hero, among the working class. Socialist leaders of the British trade union movement and the Independent Labour Party (ILP) remained supportive of the Manchester School's belief that free trade mollified geopolitical conflict, owing to the decades-long relationship between the nation's working class and Liberal radicals.[49] 'The ILP's internationalism', Paul Bridgen observes, 'was influenced more by the nineteenth-century liberal internationalist campaigns of Cobden and Gladstone than by the anti-national internationalism of socialism.'[50] The growing influence of the liberal radical land reform theories of Henry George provided another avenue for Marx-Manchester collaboration. As Peter d'Alroy Jones describes it, George became 'godfather of the British socialist revival' of the late nineteenth century, despite not being a socialist himself.[51] On the land question, a 1905 British volume observed, 'the Liberal tradition and the Socialist movement converge.'[52]

The growing hemispheric might of the US following its imperial acquisitions in the Caribbean and the Asia-Pacific in 1898 helped kindle Marx-Manchester mobilization in Argentina. Manchester liberalism was a mainstay of Argentine university economics curricula thanks to the enduring influence of the British education system among Argentine elites. Reliant as Argentina was on British finance, the South American nation earned the unofficial designation of 'sixth Dominion' within the British Empire. By 1910, the more radical Manchester School philosophy of Henry George was also becoming more popular among Argentine liberal intellectuals.[53] Within the space of ten years, the secretary-general of the University of Buenos Aires, Mauricio Nierenstein, supported the translation of Henry George's work into Spanish, and Andrés Máspero Castro helped found the Liga Argentina por el Impuesto Único (Argentine single tax league) and became president of the Reformist Party.[54] Marxism instead made its way into Argentine intellectual circles thanks largely to Juan B. Justo, who undertook the first complete Spanish translation of Marx's Das Kapital in 1898. In Buenos Aires, he formed the Argentine Socialist Party in 1896 and modelled its reformist platform on that of the Bernstein wing of the SPD. Justo became a potent force in both the Argentine Parliament and socialist internationalism for decades to come. His activism in the latter field included consumer co-operativism, frequent travels through Europe and the United States, and participating in the international socialist congresses in Copenhagen (1910) and Bern and Amsterdam (1919). Left-wing economic cosmopolitan affinities, including a common enemy in Argentina's conservative 'large land-owning oligarchy', led Justo to co-found the Liga Argentina por el Impuesto Único in 1916. By 1920, his moderate land socialization policies were receiving the endorsement of Georgists in Britain; added to which, he was a vociferous defender of free trade and its connection to peace. He was even known to take socialist internationalists such as Rosa Luxemburg to task for not supporting free trade and anti-colonialism.[55] The efforts of Argentine activists such as Justo gave credence to the assertion of the US protectionist journal *American Economist* in 1918 that 'all Socialists are both Free-Traders and Single Taxers'.[56]

German socialist internationalists, imbued with their own Marx-Manchester-inspired notions, appear to have been even more proactive than their British and Argentine counterparts in their opposition to Germany's protectionist imperial government. By 1879, a unified German state had embraced an economic nationalist programme of infant industrial protectionism along lines first laid out by Friedrich List in the 1840s, which Marx had previously condemned as retrograde within the capitalist stages of development. From the 1890s, opposition SPD leaders such as Engels, Kautsky, Bernstein, Zietz, and Bebel began advocating instead for free trade in their struggle against the avowedly anti-*Manchestertum* protectionist policies of the GHS and Wilhelm II's imperial government.[57] As in Edwardian Britain, albeit with less success, the German socialist fight for free trade promised to provide cheap food for the working class and to undermine the power of the landed elite (the Junkers), the nation's foremost imperial protectionists. As a result, by 1902 the SPD found itself allied with the country's sidelined liberal progressives. 'The link between them', George Lichtheim notes, 'was of course free trade.'[58]

Germany's Marx-Manchester free traders were thereafter instrumental in shaping the free-trade-and-peace programmes of the international socialist congresses in Copenhagen (1910) and Basel (1912). Both programmes foreshadowed Woodrow Wilson's subsequent Fourteen Points, including a call for 'no economic war after the war[, . . .] freedom of the seas[, . . .] and the most rapid possible extension of the policy of free trade in the colonies as well as in the home land'. At the 1912 Basel congress, Bebel and Kautsky received support from Bebel's new SPD co-chairman, Hugo Haase, who observed that 'economic interdependence constitutes a force that restricts belligerent agitators'. Bernstein, in turn, called for a 'protest against protectionism, a demonstration in favor of peace, freedom, and free trade'.[59] Just a month into the First World War, Kautsky accordingly laid out three principles for socialist internationalists to support in any peace negotiations that exemplified the evolving Marx-Manchester tradition: '(1) The freedom of subject races of nationalities, (2) Steps towards disarmament, and (3) Steps towards world-wide free trade.' As one US socialist observed with regard to this last proposal, Kautsky's vision was of 'a world-wide economic *interdependence* of nations that would soon bring it about that wars would be neither economically desirable nor economically feasible'.[60]

Kautsky's left-wing cosmopolitan vision bore an uncanny likeness to that laid out just a few years earlier by Manchester School journalist Norman Angell, who had argued that war was economically futile owing to the era's unprecedented global market interdependence, in his internationally bestselling book *The Great Illusion* (1910). The similarity between Kautsky and Angell's arguments was doubtless more than coincidental. In 1913 German pacifists had made sure to distribute two thousand German translations of Angell's book (*Illusion, Die Falsche Rechnung*), as well as forty thousand fifteen-page pamphlets containing its key arguments, in advance of the author's acclaimed—to nationalists, notorious—speaking tour of German universities sponsored by the Carnegie Endowment for International Peace.[61]

Before the Great War, the Marx-Manchester amalgamation of free trade and peace was also manifesting itself in Hungary, the USA, and the Second International (1889–1916). Karl Polanyi's non-violent, anti–land monopoly, pro-democratic Radical Bourgeois Party in Hungary, for example, reflected Marx-Manchester principles.[62] In the USA, Charles Edward Russell, the famed Georgist muckraking journalist, anti-monopolist, anti-imperialist, and co-founder of the NAACP, ran as the Socialist candidate for governor of New York in 1910 and 1912, New York City mayor in 1913, and the US Senate in 1914. And the left-wing internationalist wing of the Second International remained dedicated to free trade and free migration.[63]

As the world war progressed, more and more left-wing international peace activists, Marxist and non-Marxist alike, envisaged a peaceful, economically interdependent postwar world. The 1916 Socialist Peace Conference held at The Hague—which included delegates from Spain, the United States, Denmark, Sweden, Argentina, and Holland—adopted resolutions 'condemning an economic war after the war and favoring free trade and freedom of the seas.'[64] And the mixture of Manchester liberal and Marxist attendees of the First American Conference for Democracy and Peace in 1917 at New York's Madison Square Garden drew attention to how their shared belief in free trade and peace had brought them together. Morris Hillquit, the international secretary of the Socialist Party of America (SPA), reported on the endorsement of worldwide 'freedom of commerce' by the conference's Committee on Peace. 'We are trading in a world market. Economically and commercially, it is one,' and yet people had tried 'to parcel out this world into rigid nations or countries with rigid boundary lines, separated from each other by various and conflicting treaties and customs, duties and other artificial restrictions' that ultimately led to world war.[65]

Such activism became a groundswell between 1917 and 1918, owing in large part to Wilson's Manchester School-inspired Fourteen Points and the newly announced peace programme of the Soviet government. In Britain, the 1917 National Labour Conference held in Manchester gave its socialist backing to Woodrow Wilson's 'international league for peace', and passed its own resolution demanding 'free trade for every country'.[66] The following year, Max Eastman, with his sister Crystal Eastman, began co-editing the US communist magazine *The Liberator*. Max, 'as an international socialist, welcomed Wilson's "Program of the World's Peace"', including its support for 'renouncing economic war on Germany' and 'free-trade and the principle of the open door everywhere'.[67] In early 1918, the National Executive Council of the SPA issued a 'Memorial' to Wilson, giving its unreserved anti-imperial endorsement to 'the peace program of the Russian Socialist government', which included a call for freedom of the seas and 'full equality of trade conditions among all nations', and asked Wilson to take part in the Russian–Central Powers peace conference.[68] The SPA's 1918 *Congressional Program* similarly echoed the Soviet government's peace programme, while adding 'to the famous formula [. . .] "No economic nationalism, no war after the war."'[69] Lacking the context of the Marx-Manchester free-trade tradition, such international socialist support for Wilson's Manchester liberal economic vision might seem striking. After all, there was no love lost between US socialist peace activists and the Wilson administration, which had persecuted, censored, and even jailed them during the war.[70] And yet their shared internationalist vision of a postwar world of free trade and peace allowed them to transcend their mutual antagonism.

Socialist free-trade-and-peace activism increasingly became a matter of international collaboration. With radical socialist academic Scott Nearing presiding, Harlem's 1918 National Conference of Labor, Socialist, and Radical Movements developed a peace programme demanding self-determination, disarmament, freedom of the seas, free migration, and that 'free trade should prevail'. The programme was then sent to Germany, Italy, France, and England for 'approval and support'.[71] Nearing, an officer of the radical left-wing Boston-based peace organization the International Free Trade League (IFTL), also made sure to send a copy of the Harlem programme to IFTL president Frank Wright Garrison, a grandson of Boston's mid-nineteenth-century arch-abolitionist Cobdenite William Lloyd Garrison. Frank shared his family's radical progressive predisposition on social and economic issues. A fervent non-Marxist disciple of Henry George and Richard Cobden, Frank nevertheless gave Nearing's socialist programme his blessing because 'economic freedom heads the list and is thoroughly sound and uncompromising'.[72] Just half a year later in London, similar socialist motions were made at the Inter-Allied Labour Conference. The conference roundly condemned, first, 'the colonial policy of capitalist Governments'; second, 'economic aggression, whether by protective tariffs or capitalist trusts or monopolies'; and third, 'the alliance between the Military Imperialists and the Fiscal Protectionists in any country whatsoever' as a 'grave menace to peace' and to the prosperity of the working class.[73] Frank Garrison happily noted in 1919 how in Britain and in the United States 'the Socialists and the followers of Cobden have been thrown together' in defence of free trade and against monopoly.[74] The evolving Marx-Manchester tradition, however, did not maintain a complete monopoly on late nineteenth- and early twentieth-century socialist thought.

Although less prominent at this time, an antagonistic Marx-List tradition was evolving as well. German-American protectionist theorist Friedrich List had argued in his influential book *The National System of Political Economy* (1841; see chapter 1) that Western developing nations' infant industries required a combination of colonialism and protectionism to catch up to the more advanced British; universal free trade ought to occur only once worldwide developmental parity was achieved at some undefined point down the road. List's protectionist theory was a critique of British free-trade imperialism. But it also issued a protectionist call for colonial expansion among industrializing states like Germany and the United States, which List believed needed captive protectionist markets to acquire raw materials and to invest their surplus capital.[75]

Despite Marx's own strong criticisms of List's theories, some more nationalistic socialists ended up drawing on his ideas to bolster their nations' protectionist imperial policies. When Britain adopted free trade in the 1840s, for example, numerous nationally focused French socialists disavowed free trade owing both to the long-standing rivalry between the two countries and to the growing influence of List's Anglophobic theories within French politics.[76] In turn-of-the-century Britain, Fabian socialists such as George Bernard Shaw were throwing their support behind protectionism and British imperial expansion.[77] Although a free-trade utopian in the 1880s while under the influence of Henry George's single tax theory, by 1904 Shaw sought to counter the British socialist predilection for free trade by insisting that British socialism should be 'ultra-Protectionist' and required imperial federation to obtain social reform. The Fabian Society's majority report, authored by Shaw, endorsed Joseph Chamberlain's Tariff Reform movement, leading some more left-leaning Fabians to resign in protest.[78] British *Clarion* socialists, even more than Fabians like Shaw, viewed foreign trade as a zero-sum game. By 1910 the *Clarion* socialists began running a strong pro-Tariff Reform campaign assailing 'The Liberal-Free Trade-Labour Party'.[79] The Anglo-Saxonist social democratic leader H. M. Hyndman vociferously condemned the anti-war 'extreme capitalist Free Trade bigots and hangers-on', calling rather for stringent commercial war against Germany and its allies, coupled with trade preference for Britain's 'white' settler colonies, all of which aligned with his decades-long advocacy for imperial federation and his antipathy towards 'sham Free Trade'.[80] In Germany, meanwhile, attempts were also made to wed List's ideas to the SPD. Along Listian and Lassallian lines, the SPD's minority cohort of Marxist protectionists such as Paul Lensch gave their nationalistic stamp of approval to German imperial expansion.[81] And in the United States, during the First World War, the socialist and pro-war nationalist William Walling took to the editorial pages of the *New York Times* to level charges of sedition against Henri Lambert and the US economic peace movement for their extreme pacifism.[82]

In quite different economic imperial circumstances, some leading early twentieth-century anti-colonial nationalists also began turning to a combination of Marx and List for inspiration in the United States, India, Ireland, and China. W.E.B. Du Bois perhaps best encapsulated the era's left-wing Marx-List tradition. As explored in chapter 1, Du Bois became steeped in the Listian tradition of the GHS during his university studies in 1890s Berlin. The GHS helped shape his desire for a separate, economically self-sufficient Black America, as well as his subsequent pan-African developmental vision, to counteract the violent political and economic discrimination of a white supremacist global capitalist system. Following a visit to Soviet Russia in 1926, Du Bois also increasingly began drawing upon Marxism in thinking about race and Pan-Africanism, the latter of which also contributed to his initial support for Japan's pan-Asian imperialism in the early 1930s. His ideological trajectory illustrates an early variant of the Marx-List tradition, albeit one that leaned more heavily upon List than Marx.[83]

List was also more attractive than Marx among early twentieth-century nationalists in India, Ireland, and China because these colonial regions suffered under the yoke of British free-trade imperialism. Whereas the British 'white' settler colonies had been granted fiscal autonomy, these colonized spaces were forced to keep tariffs low to the detriment of their own industrial development (see chapter 1). As a result, whereas socialist nationalists in France, Germany, and Britain embraced List's protectionist call to colonize and exploit undeveloped states, List's Indian Swadeshi and Irish nationalist disciples focused narrowly upon his critique of British free-trade imperialism. An ideological confluence between Marx and List began manifesting itself within the early twentieth-century Swadeshi movement.[84] In Ireland, Arthur Griffith's 1905 nationalistic enunciation of his Listian anti-colonial vision for Sinn Féin to develop Irish infant industries received support from some Irish socialists; for them, the policy was seen as an essential step for furthering capitalist development, and thus hastening the socialist revolutionary endgame. Others, however, like Griffith's Irish republican and Marxist revolutionary friend James Connolly, waxed far less enthusiastic. For Connolly, socialism and Irish nationalism needed to be entwined, but Griffith was instead tying Irish nationalism to capitalism. Connolly, writing from his New York City apartment in 1909, publicly rebuked Griffith's nationalism for its capitalistic and materialistic embrace of List. 'Socialists have no sympathy [for Griffith's] adoption of the doctrines of Frederick List,' Connolly declared.[85]

The choice between List and Marx was made even more stark in early twentieth-century China. When Ma Yinchu—future president of Peking University—returned to China in 1922 following his university studies in the United States, he gave a speech in Peking (Beijing), 'Doctrines of Marx and List: Which Is Fit for China?' His answer was clear: List's, because of China's long-standing exploitation at the hands of European imperial powers, which continued to force open the nation's markets. Without tariff autonomy and industrialization, 'China would forever remain a supplier of raw materials and a consumer of manufactured goods', he argued.[86] China's combining of Listian industrial development with Marxism would, however, only substantively occur after Mao's rise to power in 1949.

The Marx-List tradition's association with early twentieth-century anti-colonial spaces within the United States, Ireland, India, and China was tenuous, but these examples provide a glimpse of what was to come in the latter half of the century. The confluence of List and Marx would resonate in a much bigger way after 1945 among nationalists throughout the Global South. In the decades immediately following the First World War, however, advocacy of the Marx-List tradition yet remained the exception to what was fast becoming the Marx-Manchester rule.

Marx-Manchester Free-Trade Internationalism and Supranational Regulation, 1919–1946

Interwar Europe became a breeding ground for left-wing socialist free-trade-and-peace activity, to be maintained and regulated, its proponents argued, through a league of nations. Even such socialist luminaries as Albert Einstein were becoming quite explicit in their association of free trade with world peace.[87] In order to create a more peaceful geopolitical order, the socialist parties of France, Germany, Austria, Britain, and Hungary came out in support of international freedom of the seas and freedom of trade in 1919. That year's International Socialist Congress in Berne also endorsed these pacifistic free-trade positions, coupled with 'the Socialist ideal of a League of Nations' endowed with the power to regulate inter-state trade and to control 'world thoroughfares' and 'the production and distribution of foodstuffs and raw materials throughout the world'.[88] And the Marx-Manchester association of protectionist monopolies with the imperial search for new markets and natural resources meant that no contradiction was seen in calling for universal free trade alongside supranational regulation and distribution of raw materials. All were deemed necessary to undermine the economic foundations of colonialism, militarism, and war.

Boston feminist Crystal Eastman and her brother Max played a key part in entwining the US socialist, free trade, and peace movements through their Marxist magazine *The Liberator*. Crystal Eastman took the opportunity as co-editor to spread the word about Boston's newly formed IFTL (like Nearing, she was an IFTL officer), placing a full-page advert immediately after the front-page visage of Lenin in the *Liberator*'s January 1919 issue. By clearly Cobdenite lines of argument, the advert made sure to stress the connection between free trade and peace. Free trade was the 'only secure foundation' for the League of Nations. The free-trade panacea would also end the colonial question, protect small nations, end militarism, provide cheap goods, lower the cost of living, create global prosperity, and establish permanent peace. 'International Free Trade' therefore must be 'incorporated in the Peace Treaty as repeatedly recommended by (1) President Wilson, (2) the British Labor Party, (3) the German Reichstag, (4) the Russian People's Government, and (5) Socialists everywhere.'[89]

The Western embargo of the new Soviet government from 1919 to 1921 also became a hot-button issue for left-wing socialist free traders. IFTL officer Ludwig Martens, the Soviet government's official representative to the United States between 1917 and 1921, with the assistance of Santeri Nuorteva—a Finnish Marxist politician, journalist, and fellow IFTL officer—worked hard to obtain US loans and end the embargo from their Soviet Bureau offices in New York. Under the suspicious watch of the US government, their organization's Marxist publication *Soviet Russia* began propagandizing how normalization of trade would make 'a real peace' and alleviate the mass starvation of eastern Europe.[90]

Socialist free traders in interwar Britain wielded considerable influence in national and international politics and were among the country's leading left-wing defenders of Manchester liberalism. While some heterodox British socialists supported protectionism and imperialism, the Labour Party itself remained a melting pot of socialist and Manchester liberal economic ideas. As Frank Trentmann notes, Labour inherited the Liberal radical 'belief that trade promoted the brotherhood of man by breaking down the walls of insular prejudice and chauvinism associated with protectionist imperialism': a 'socialist-radical dualism'. Leading Manchester liberal internationalists, including Norman Angell, J. A. Hobson, H. N. Brailsford, and Bertrand Russell, had associated themselves more strongly with progressive social reform during the Edwardian period—New Liberalism—helping to pave the way for Labour's postwar popularity.[91] Owing in no small part to this confluence of 'new' Manchester liberalism with Labour socialism, opposition to protectionism remained a key facet of British socialist peace activism well into the 1930s and 1940s. The first position the Labour Party laid out in its 1923 manifesto was an indictment of protectionism 'and the whole conception of economic relations underlying it'.[92] Following the National Government's abandonment of free trade for imperial preference in 1932, Labour's 1934 publication *For Socialism and Peace* attacked 'the disastrous economic nationalism of the present age by working for an all-round lowering of tariffs' through 'a system of planned international exchange'. In 1937, Labour supported a blanket open-door policy across colonial Africa under the auspices of the newly formed League of Nations Committee on Raw Materials. Labour's support for a domestic planned economy in the early 1940s, in turn, remained coupled with a call for a supranational body that would oversee a new era of multilateral free-trade agreements and international control of raw materials.[93]

More and more international socialist organizations in continental Europe also began giving their pacifistic free-trade blessing to supranational governance. The Labour and Socialist International (LSI), the more inclusive rival of the Comintern, looked for a middle way between Marxism and liberal radicalism in its search for peace.[94] Revitalized in 1923, the LSI called for 'permanent peace', supported the League of Nations, condemned capitalist imperialism, and demanded that 'labour must also fight against protectionism and in favour of free trade' and the free movement of people. The socialist International Federation of Trade Unions (IFTU, 1919–1945), an avowed peace organization based in Amsterdam with close ties to the LSI, likewise endorsed universal free trade and the liberal internationalist vision embodied in the League of Nations.[95]

The Marx-Manchester peace movement received an interwar boost from the resurgent international co-operative movement, which advocated for an economic 'third way' situated between individualism and collectivism, and between liberal reform and socialist revolution. The international co-operative movement had come a long way from its modest origins in 1840s Rochdale, located in what is now Greater Manchester, a town where Cobdenite roots went deep.[96] By the 1920s, the movement's umbrella organization, the International Co-operative Alliance (ICA), rivalled the international trade union movement as the interwar world's largest transnational non-governmental organization.[97] World peace was a stated goal from the ICA's 1895 founding.[98] The ICA's peaceful economic vision was a social democratic one focused upon a grassroots, not-for-profit, working-class version of free trade that would empower the world's consumers and local producers alike. To accomplish this and to undermine international trusts and cartels, co-operative free trade also called for supranational control over the global distribution of food and raw materials through the League of Nations.[99] By replacing capitalist competition with peaceful co-operation, the ICA believed it had devised the most effective anti-imperial vision for a free trade world order.

The predominant interwar international co-operative movement embodied the Marx-Manchester ideological paradigm in its grassroots efforts to promote worldwide prosperity and peace through co-operative free trade. The Women's Co-operative Guild (WCG, 1893), a feminist peace organization that maintained close ties to Britain's ILP, had given its formal endorsement to free trade by the turn of the century, pointing its members to the free-trade activism of socialist workers in Germany for inspiration.[100] The ICA, in turn, endorsed peace and world federalism in 1913 in the hope of stopping the world war before it began.[101] At war's end, the ICA drew up a memorandum to send to the Paris Peace Conference that connected peace with a League of Nations that embraced co-operative free trade.[102] The international co-operative movement remained prominent within the interwar peace movement, keeping up its League lobbying campaign on behalf of its particular brand of Marx-Manchester free trade.[103]

By the end of the 1920s, however, rifts had begun to develop between the international co-operative movement's more moderate socialist majority and the more radical representatives of the Soviet co-operatives, who instead saw co-operativism as a path towards socialist revolution.[104] The Soviet representatives expressed their disappointment that the ICA had failed to explicitly endorse the principle of class struggle. They also criticized ICA leaders for continuing to seek co-operative free-trade-and-peace reforms through the liberal capitalist League of Nations. The Soviet delegates instead argued that, as Katarina Friberg puts it, 'only the "United States of the Soviet Republics" could achieve real free trade'.[105] For Soviet co-operativist advocates of 'real free trade', the term itself was being transformed to mean an economic policy to be practised only between socialist planned economies, rather than between all the world's producers and consumers as advocated by the era's Marx-Manchester co-operative disciples.

The world economic crisis of the 1930s and the consequent global turn to economic autarky, nationalism, and imperial consolidation only reaffirmed the Marx-Manchester tradition for its socialist internationalist subscribers. They continued to connect protectionism with imperialism and militarism, and free-trade internationalism with peace. The SPD's Rudolf Hilferding, recently removed from his position as Germany's finance minister, wrote in 1931 in favour of international co-operation under the auspices of the League's International Labour Organisation in order to substitute the 'chaos wrought by economic nationalism with a well-planned order' of global exchange.[106] Even as Britain itself was abandoning its long-held free-trade orthodoxy for imperial trade preference and the Soviet Union was becoming ever more closed off, the Executive Committee of the Comintern explained at its 1932 meeting in Moscow that it knew where to lay the brunt of the blame: 'The fierce struggle the imperialists are waging for markets and colonies, the tariff wars and the race for armaments, have already led to the immediate danger of a new imperialist world war.'[107] A similar refrain was heard from the 2,196 socialists from India, China, Japan, the Balkans, South America, the United States, and western Europe who attended the World Congress Against War in Amsterdam in 1932, claiming to represent thirty thousand organizations and thirty million workers of the world. Its manifesto blamed the protectionist measures 'adopted under the pressure of the economic crisis' for deepening that crisis and for rendering 'inevitable the transformation of economic rivalry into armed conflict'.[108] The international co-operative movement also continued mobilizing on behalf of free trade and peace throughout the 1930s.[109]

Owing to the growth of economic nationalism across the globe, socialist internationalist supporters of free trade found themselves increasingly at odds not only with the capitalist powers of the West, but also with the ostracized Soviet East, as its foreign trade became ever more autarkic under Stalin's autocratic 'socialism in one country' prescription.[110] Kautsky, for example, denounced the Soviet monopoly of foreign trade, arguing that the latest economic nationalist upward swing was contributing to the growth of fascism.[111] In contrast to the Soviet Union, socialist internationalist left-wingers in Germany and France sought instead to toe the free-trade-and-peace line, including supporting liberal capitalist supranational organizations to oversee its regulation. Germany's SPD and the French Socialist Party became, according to Brian Shaev, "the largest political forces in their countries committed to liberalising international trade".[112] And in 1943, while the Second World War raged, the French Socialist Party became adamant in calling for a 'United States of Europe' as a necessary first step towards a 'United States of the World', empowered with the ability to regulate and monitor customs tariffs.[113]

Just a year before, however, Vienna-born Marxist intellectual Franz Borkenau had criticized the pervasive left-wing Marx-Manchester vision of a global economic order of supranational governance, free trade, and peace. In *Socialism: National or International* (1942), written from London, he argued that internationalism was 'not socialist but a liberal ideal, borrowed by socialists from the liberals of their age'. Marx himself had 'carried the convictions and the prejudices of the liberal age into the labour movement. It is now necessary to say that the Marxists were as ready to carry into the labour movement the convictions and the prejudices of the bourgeoisie of a later day.' For Borkenau, the Marx-Manchester panacea of a new economic order based upon 'international free trade and international planning, absolute self-determination of nations and federal union to the exclusion of all sovereignties' was a pipedream. He also discounted the 'Hobson-Hilferding-Lenin' theory of imperialism; its association of protectionist monopoly capitalism with imperial expansion was but 'more proof of the overwhelming influence of liberalism upon early socialism'. Socialist 'neo-liberal utopians, of the Federal Union type' were similarly mistaken in seeking to devise an equitable and democratic 'second, "more efficient" edition of the League of Nations' for governing in a new age of free trade and peace. Soviet Russia's embrace of economic nationalism, the worldwide turn to fascism and autarky after the Great Depression, the unequal levels of global economic development, and worldwide racial conflict all proved such 'utopian' socialist internationalist dreams delusional.[114]

Yet just such a Marx-Manchester planned supranational vision of free trade and peace prevailed among US socialist internationalists in the 1930s and 1940s. Under the political and intellectual leadership of Norman Thomas and Scott Nearing, US socialists renewed their Marx-Manchester commitments in response to the Great Depression and continued Republican protectionism. Thomas—a prominent interwar pacifist, anti-imperialist, and six times the SPA's presidential nominee between 1928 and 1948—believed that the only way to end war was to reform the world economic system through a combination of Cobdenism, international socialism, co-operativism, and supranational regulation of food and raw materials.[115] Under his leadership, the SPA made sure to single out the GOP's protectionist 1930 Hawley-Smoot Tariff, calling it 'the most monstrous tariff legislation in the history of the country. [. . .] It has, in effect, declared economic war against the rest of the world and served to aggravate the instability of world economy and world trade.'[116] Nearing took to task not only US protectionism, but also the European turn to autarky and fascism. 'Theory denies the possibility of economically self-sufficient twentieth century nations. But fascists are not concerned with theory [. . . ;] they propose to make autarchy work.'[117] Western Europe, he argued, 'builds the frontiers of each nation every higher, with tariffs, subsidies, quotas, immigration prohibitions. [. . .] The pursuit of this autarchic goal is driving West Europe steadily toward' economic sectionalism, militarism, and geopolitical conflict.[118] The SPA's advocacy of free trade remained a key ingredient in its peace programme well into the postwar years, as it was too for various other socialist parties in Europe seeking regional and international economic interdependence as a prerequisite for peace.[119]

Conclusion

What would become a widespread early to mid-twentieth-century socialist internationalist belief that free trade was a requirement for world peace originated in 1840s Britain, in the heyday of Manchester liberalism. Building on Marx and Engels's qualified mid-nineteenth-century endorsement of free trade, socialist internationalists thereafter borrowed from, inspired, and at times even worked alongside liberal radical disciples of the Manchester School, owing to their shared left-wing desire to overturn the militaristic economic nationalist world order that prevailed over the late nineteenth and early twentieth centuries. By the interwar years, and into the 1940s, they also shared a belief that supranational governance was necessary to regulate and maintain a freer, more peaceful, and interdependent global marketplace: a vision for a more equitable and ethical international economic order that informed the post-1945 globalization projects of the capitalist West, the socialist East, and the Global South.[120]

On the eve of the Cold War, socialist internationalists continued to draw upon a free-trade tradition that shared a common pacifistic heritage with the

Manchester School's mid-twentieth-century liberal radical heirs. As a result, both camps supported the shaping of a new economic cosmopolitan order. However, whether the peace and prosperity deriving from worldwide free trade was in itself the desired end—as it was for Manchester School capitalists such as Cordell Hull—or whether it was seen as the next progressive step towards a socialist Pax Economica remained the essential point of divergence. Meanwhile, the Marx-Manchester tradition would also help shape the early twentieth-century feminist peace movement.

4

Free-Trade Feminism

THE INTERNATIONAL FEMINIST FIGHT FOR FREE TRADE, ANTI-IMPERIALISM, AND PEACE

Our members [of the Women's Peace Society] are devoted to the principle of Free-Trade and assert the right of every human to buy in the cheapest market and to sell in the dearest, and regard the constant infringement of this right as a chief cause of friction between nations. Richard Cobden [...] saw clearly the intimate connection between Free-Trade and Peace.

—FANNY GARRISON VILLARD (USA), 1921[1]

Remember that in the Women's International League [for Peace and Freedom] we are believers in free trade.

—EVA MACNAGHTEN (BRITAIN), 1924[2]

JANE ADDAMS MADE landfall in Holland in early July 1919. The prominent fifty-eight-year-old Chicago social reformer, suffragist, pacifist, and anti-imperialist had undertaken the transatlantic ocean voyage at the request of London's Society of Friends. The Christian organization wanted her to bear witness to the destructive aftermath of the First World War in Europe. Upon arrival, Addams's most pressing concern was the famine afflicting millions of Europe's children. Addams and her two travelling companions began their overland journey to Berlin by car, courtesy of the Red Cross, which was also focusing its attentions upon Europe's hungry children.[3] Their trek marked the beginning of what would become a multi-year European humanitarian mission of a new left-leaning feminist organization: the Women's International League for Peace and Freedom (WILPF).[4]

Addams, in her role as WILPF's inaugural president, had her first of many encounters with Europe's malnourished children during a stopover in the northern French city of Lille. Inside a local school, she watched as a physician examined them by the hundred. 'Stripped to the waist', the children looked more like 'a line of moving skeletons; their little shoulder blades stuck straight out, the vertebrae were all perfectly distinct as were their ribs, and their bony arms hung limply at their sides'. Adding to the macabre ambience, an eerie quiet hung over the impromptu emergency room; the French doctor on duty, having lost his voice as a side effect of wartime shellshock, 'whispered his instructions to the children as he applied his stethoscope and the children, thinking it was some sort of game, all whispered back to him'. Addams encountered similarly graphic scenes in Zurich and throughout Germany.[5] The mission's findings reinforced her belief that, while the war may have ended, securing the peace had only just begun.

Addams led a follow-up WILPF humanitarian mission during the scorching summer of 1921, this time to south-eastern Europe, where she again encountered mass hunger. 'Food resources which were produced in Europe itself and should have been available for instant use', she wrote, 'were prevented from satisfying the desperate human needs.' Why? Because 'a covert war was being carried on by the use of import duties and protective tariffs', which the war's food blockades had legitimized. These small European states, seeking self-preservation, mistakenly 'imitated the great Allies with their protectionist policies, with their colonial monopolies and preferences'. To Addams, such suffering in the name of 'hypernationalism' only amplified the need for a new international system of 'free labor and exchange'. The postwar world faced a stark choice: either 'freedom of international commerce or international conflict of increasing severity'. To meet world food demands, her envisaged free-trade economic order would also require supranational regulation of global transportation lines to counter 'the ambition of rival nations'. She called her cosmopolitan vision 'Pax Economica'.[6]

Addams, the head of the interwar international women's peace movement, rode upon the crest of feminism's first wave that crashed upon the shores of the industrializing world in the mid-nineteenth century.[7] First-wave feminists tended to see themselves as the mothers of the world, believing that women's active participation in politics would curb or counter men's predilection for nationalism and war, and their activity became an indelible component of the 'new internationalism' of the early twentieth century.[8] Widespread feminist involvement in international peace and political emancipation movements was in part an outgrowth of the mid-nineteenth-century antislavery movement, particularly within the radical Garrisonian abolitionist wing. This radical confluence further solidified in the turn-of-the-century transatlantic women's suffrage and anti-imperialist movements, to become what Harriet Alonso has described as 'the suffragist wing' of the international peace movement from the First World War onwards.[9] The intersection of first-wave feminism and these other internationalist left-wing reform movements has received due scrutiny.[10] By contrast, scant attention has been paid to the part played by left-wing economic ideology that helped tie them all together—free trade. Recovering the feminist free-trade tradition expands our understanding of feminists' contributions to the foundations of International Relations theory, as well as their role in creating a more liberal economic order in the 1940s.[11]

As Jane Addams's 1921 European diagnosis outlined above illustrates, the economic cosmopolitan vision of first-wave feminist peace internationalists was crucial to shaping their understanding of what was ailing the global capitalist system, and how they sought to heal it. These predominantly Western, middle-class, white women believed that protectionism—and its ensuing trade wars and geopolitical conflicts—laid the economic foundations for imperialism, war, and hunger. Free trade instead promised a panacea of cheap food, political emancipation, prosperity, anti-imperialism, and peace. Even more than their male peace allies, feminist peace activists emphasized free trade's association with plentiful food, democratization, and social justice. For one thing, the free market's ability to break up the monopolistic power of male landed elites would create a more conducive political environment for the expansion of women's suffrage. For another, free trade's dual promise of peace and cheap food meant putting an end to the violence, poverty, and starvation of women and children that invariably followed in the wake of the era's frequent trade wars, embargoes, and military conflicts. And yet these economic cosmopolitan ideas behind first-wave feminist peace activism are to be noted for their near absence from the historiography.[12]

Stretching from the Victorian world of Harriet Martineau and Florence Nightingale to the interwar networks of the international women's peace movement, feminist free-trade activism was quite often a Marx-Manchester commingling of liberal radicalism, democratic socialism, and grassroots cooperativism. In the context of this left-wing economic cosmopolitan melting pot, free trade naturally became the economic ideological bedrock for interwar feminist peace and anti-imperial activism;[13] And the feminists' transnational efforts eventually became entwined with Democratic US secretary of state Cordell Hull's mid-twentieth-century designs for creating a more peaceful and integrated economic order: a new US-led system of international trade liberalization regulated through supranational governance and institutions.[14]

Transatlantic Feminists against Protectionism, 1846–1898

Free trade and feminism first met within the mid-nineteenth-century transatlantic antislavery movement. The freeing of world trade and the empowerment of women were, for some of the more radical abolitionists of both sexes, seen as necessary next steps towards reaching their goal of universal emancipation, culminating in the eradication of world hunger, aristocracy, militarism, and imperialism.[15] This cosmopolitan cocktail proved critical in shaping the free-trade vision of nineteenth- and twentieth-century feminist peace internationalists.

As discussed in previous chapters, the radical left-wing free-trade ideology of transatlantic abolitionist reformers and women's suffragists that arose in the 1830s and 1840s became known at the time as the 'Manchester School' or 'Cobdenism': the former because much of the early activity of the movement was centred in Manchester, England, and the latter because the doctrine was famously espoused by Richard Cobden, Victorian England's apostle of free trade, who led the overthrow of the British protectionist system as leader of the Anti–Corn Law League (ACLL, 1839–1846).[16] Cobden and the ACLL first set their sights locally upon Britain's aristocratic landowners, who for too long had profited from tariffs on foreign grain even though this meant higher bread prices for hungry British consumers. Upon winning their 'cheap loaf' in 1846 with the overturning of the Corn Laws, Cobdenites turned their sights abroad. Building upon the international dimensions of Adam Smith's and David Ricardo's trade theories, Cobden and his followers believed that a universal policy of free trade would ultimately bring about domestic prosperity, political emancipation, and world peace.

Cobden and his disciples would accordingly number among the mid-nineteenth-century leaders of the transatlantic abolitionist and peace movements, both of which fast became associated too with women's suffrage. Cobden himself was a supporter of women's rights, as was his wife Kate Cobden, ACLL allies such as Elizabeth Pease Nichol, and prominent US Cobdenite abolitionists such as William Lloyd Garrison and Henry Ward Beecher.[17] In the 1840s, Kate Cobden and other women of the ACLL staged wildly popular

free-trade bazaars, which gave direct and indirect encouragement to US abolitionists, while also raising much-needed funds for the ACLL.[18] Owing to this
ideological intersection, some of the mid- to late nineteenth century's leading
feminist reformers became committed to free trade as a necessary step towards
universal suffrage, social justice, decolonization, and peace. By the time of the
First World War, international feminist peace activists were speculating that
free trade's promise of cheap food could even, with proper supranational oversight, eradicate world hunger.

Harriet Martineau was Britain's most renowned mid-nineteenth-century
feminist advocate of free trade, abolitionism, and peace. In her popular *Illustra-
tions of Political Economy* (1832–34), she crafted fables to universalize the economic cosmopolitan teachings of classical political economy and, as with her
story 'Demerara', to argue that free trade would undermine slavery. She explored this emancipatory motif of free trade further in her 1845 novel *Dawn
Island*, a homage to the ACLL that she unveiled at that year's free-trade bazaar
held in London's Covent Garden theatre. Her book portrayed free trade as a
God-given and natural state for all humankind, but with a specifically feminine
slant through its emphasis upon the underappreciated value of women's
labour. As Ayşe Çelikkol puts it, in *Dawn Island* free trade became 'a pregnant
woman in touch with nature and at peace with the rest of humankind, a figure
capable of reconciling the pursuit of individual freedom to trade with the long-
ing for interpersonal connection.'[19]

Martineau, like many of her fellow abolitionist contemporaries, considered
protectionism to be a form of economic slavery because it created unfree markets for the world's consumers and undemocratically supported aristocratic
landed elites. US slavery in the South and protectionism in the North were also
a concern. As a frequent traveller and commentator on American affairs, Martineau was quick to condemn the antislavery Republican Party's protectionist
1861 Morrill Tariff. Following the outbreak of the US Civil War later that year,
she worried that 'this insane protective policy' of the North would so antago-
nize Europeans that they would side with the free-trading South. 'European
sympathy', she wrote in the *Standard*, 'which ought to be wholly with the North
in your present conflict, is impaired by the spectacle of the fiscal tyranny.'[20]
More broadly, she condemned protectionism as an 'injustice and unkindness
to foreign peoples' and a 'vicious aristocratic principle' in which 'every working-
man [. . .] is injured for the illicit benefit of wealthier classes.'[21]

Martineau's economic cosmopolitanism also helped shape her criticisms
of the exploitative colonial economic policies then practised by the European

powers. For her, much as for her mid-nineteenth-century Cobdenite male counterparts, free trade in its purest form was antithetical to the exploitative colonialism of the mercantilist empires as well as British gunboat diplomacy in China. Regarding the latter, like Richard Cobden, she criticized British free-trade imperialism for coercively prising open Chinese markets.[22] 'Our troubles with China are thickening at this day,' she argued. 'How much of the virtue of free-trade itself may be lost when it is introduced through a process of wrong and violence?'[23]

But also like some of her mid-century left-leaning contemporaries, Martineau's opposition to imperialism had its limits. She endorsed free-trade imperial maternalism in British colonial spaces such as India and Ireland. *Dawn Island* portrayed free trade as a Western civilizing mission that would raise the non-Western world from both poverty and barbarism. And while she condemned the mercantilist colonialism of the European empires, she adopted an informal imperial position with regard to Britain in India that was reminiscent of her liberal imperialist contemporary John Stuart Mill, who argued that the British were duty-bound to 'civilize' India through benign despotic governance.[24] In *British Rule in India* (1857), Martineau called for letting India and the rest of the British Empire's colonies trade freely with the world, but she never went so far as to call for an end to British colonial rule there. She instead argued that the British should 'demand, and legislate for, commercial freedom of the people of India'. For her, free trade in India and other underdeveloped areas brought 'civilization', and thus must be embraced to eradicate 'barbarism' through the development of canals, railways, steamships, and the telegraph: all of which, in her view, went hand in hand with free trade.[25] In 1863, she even looked approvingly on the coercive enforcement of free trade in Ireland, because it was providing the colony, for so long dependent upon homegrown potatoes for sustenance, with newfound food security through the 'free importation of grain and meal'.[26] Martineau's free-trade imperial maternalism towards colonies deemed less civilized would reappear among international feminist peace activists in subsequent decades, but would noticeably diminish following the First World War.[27]

Florence Nightingale also contributed to the Victorian commingling of feminism and free trade in Britain. Her oft-studied establishment of a nursing profession for women had placed her among the forerunners of modern feminism.[28] Her advocacy of free-trade internationalism is less recognized. Like Martineau, Nightingale gave her strong support to overturning the Corn Laws in 1846.[29] In 1871, she called upon Liberal prime minister William Gladstone to make free trade a requirement in the Australian colonies in exchange for continued naval protection from the empire.[30] And in 1885, at her own insistence, Nightingale became the first official female member of London's Cobden Club, which Richard Cobden's friends and disciples had founded in 1866 to spread his free-trade-and-peace gospel to the furthest reaches of the globe.[31]

Also like Martineau, Nightingale's subscription to free-trade cosmopolitanism coloured her maternalistic views on British colonial policy in India, as well as her opposition to aristocratic monopolization of Indian lands. She believed that Richard Cobden had lit 'a fire in the world which has never been put out', and she prayed that the slash-and-burn of free trade might cultivate land reform in India and thus undermine the monopoly of the country's aristocratic landlords.[32] But far from demanding an end to British imperial rule in India, she advocated 'the "United Empire of Great Britain and Ireland, the Colonies and India". God bless the empire!' She was also quite critical, however, of British colonial misrule of famine-stricken India. Combining her interests in both public health and free trade, amid the Indian famine of 1878 she urged the colonial government to provide India with 'cheap water communication to bring her wheat and corn and cotton to her ports, and so ship it over the world, [such that] she might be the richest instead of the poorest of countries'.[33]

Late Victorian British pacifism evolved alongside that of Cobdenism and feminism. This evolution, Hilary Browne observes, 'inevitably affected pacifist feminism as it began to emerge in the 1870s and 1880s'.[34] Although lacking Martineau's and Nightingale's degree of fame, Caroline Ashurst Biggs, Lydia Becker, and Monica Mangan also came of age in the mid-nineteenth-century commercial peace movement. Biggs's *Englishwoman's Review*, and Becker's *Women's Suffrage Journal*, founded in 1866 and 1870 respectively, splashed Cobdenite radicalism across their pages for years thereafter. Both organs came out against imperial conflicts such as the Franco–Prussian War (1870–1871) and the First Anglo–Boer War (1880–1881), although never with a full-fledged critique of imperialism. Monica Mangan, the inaugural secretary of the International Arbitration and Peace Association's Women's Committee in 1887, took the opportunity to lay out the Cobdenite way towards world peace in 1892 before her marriage to Hodgson Pratt and motherhood caused her to withdraw from the pacifistic limelight.[35] Within the left wing of Victorian British politics, free trade was forming a triarchy alongside feminism and peace. The feminist application of the anti-imperialism of free trade, however, remained inconsistent.

Across the Atlantic, the growing role of women as abolitionists, peace activists, and consumers informed feminist free-trade activism from the late nineteenth century, just as the tariff issue came to dominate the US political arena. Following the emancipation of US slaves in 1865, the politico-ideological conflict between economic cosmopolitanism and economic nationalism took centre stage. In 1866, women's suffragist, Irish Home Rule supporter, and abolitionist Elizabeth Cady Stanton of New York accordingly made her controversial bid for Congress with the following creed: 'free speech, free press, free men, and free trade—the cardinal points of democracy'.[36] A decade later, she associated free trade and peace squarely with women's suffrage. The peaceful principle of free trade, she argued, needed also to be applied to political enfranchisement: 'the cry of "peace" is mockery [. . .] with 20,000,000 women in chains'.[37] She nevertheless held back from full-throated opposition to US imperialism after war broke out with the Spanish Empire in 1898, a further, transatlantic, illustration of the limits to the anti-imperialism of free trade among Victorian-era feminists.

With a more radical Marx-Manchester edge, a twenty-nine-year-old feminist from Pennsylvania named Florence Kelley joined the US battle between free traders and protectionists in the late 1880s; and as a socialist internationalist she sided squarely with the free traders in what became known as the Great Debate. The Great Debate over US trade policy reached fever pitch during the 1888 presidential election, pitting the Cobdenite Democratic incumbent Grover Cleveland against the protectionist Republican challenger Benjamin Harrison. As the November election neared—and with the help of her friend Friedrich Engels, by then in his late sixties—the daughter of Pennsylvania's arch-protectionist Republican congressman William 'Pig Iron' Kelley oversaw the publication of the first English-language translation of Karl Marx's 1848 'Speech on the Question of Free Trade'. She did so to give socialistic support to Grover Cleveland's re-election campaign, which was focused on reining in the GOP's expansionist protectionist programme. She also had rebellious familial motivations for doing so, 'wishing the pamphlet unmistakable on the protectionist question because the Republican protectionist press which is all at my father's beck and call will forthwith proclaim the fact that the daughter of the Apostle of Protection has come out in a pamphlet proving Free Trade rank Socialism and getting Marx himself as an authority'.[38] Kelley would continue to support free trade as a precondition for a new more peaceful and anti-imperial economic order in the decades to come, as well as promoting ethical consumerism. In 1891, she helped found the National Consumers' League (NCL). Inspired by the British Consumers' League (founded in 1887), the NCL encouraged the purchase of goods that did not rely upon the exploitation of women's and child labour, presaging the ethical consumerism of the post-1945 Fair Trade movement (see chapter 6).[39]

By the end of the nineteenth century the growing recognition of women as consumers and as producers of domesticity gave US free-trade feminism a further boost. From controlling household purse-strings to establishing arm-chair travel clubs, white middle-class women became central to what Kristin Hoganson calls a 'consumers' imperium': a consumer culture that relied upon 'the informal empire of U.S. commercial power, and the secondhand empire of European imperialism through shopping for trifles and savories.'[40] Thorstein Veblen's *Theory of the Leisure Class* (1899) numbered among the first of many publications to take seriously women's purchasing power, at the same time that US women increasingly began expressing their unwillingness to pay artificially high prices for tariff-protected goods. This added yet another political strand to feminist free-trade advocacy—what Rhodri Jeffreys-Jones describes as 'the feminization of consumption.'[41]

Free-Trade Feminism's Anti-imperial Evolution, 1898–1913

Economic cosmopolitan ranks were swelled by numerous early twentieth-century feminist peace internationalists who opposed continued Western colonialism, from the 'scramble for Africa', to the coercive prying open of Chinese markets, to the US occupation of the Philippines. The feminist fight for free trade, anti-imperialism, peace, and social justice, from this economic ideological perspective, can be seen as part of a larger grassroots struggle to overthrow the illiberal imperial order. They blamed the economic nationalist policies of the imperial powers for creating so many of the world's social injustices; for fomenting imperial rivalry; for exacerbating geopolitical tensions; and, by the time of the First World War, for laying the economic foundations of global military conflict. Leading international women's suffragists would accordingly establish a variety of progressive international peace organizations promoting women's empowerment, free trade, food security, and anti-imperialism. Their efforts would also engender right-wing opposition from anti-feminist supporters of protectionism, imperialism, and militarism.

Broadly speaking, the anti-imperial radicalism of the mostly middle-class white women's suffrage movement remained tempered by a racialized world-view common at the turn of the century. The suffragists' racial blinkers were often to constrain their anti-imperial vision and the racial inclusivity of their organizations, for much of the early twentieth century. Some even toed the imperial line, hoping that doing so would legitimate the women's suffrage movement in the eyes of male political elites. Elizabeth Cady Stanton and Susan B. Anthony, for example, both at first supported the turn-of-the-century US imperial project in the Philippines on the racialized basis of the 'civilizing mission': for them 'universal sisterhood' effectively meant 'Anglo-Saxon sisterhood'. Leaders of pro-suffrage organizations such as the International Council of Women, the International Woman Suffrage Alliance, the Woman's Christian Temperance Union, WILPF, and the Young Women's Christian Association (YWCA), in turn, struggled internally with both the imperial question and racial inclusivity.[42] Muddying the issue further is that it is not always clear whether the common first-wave feminist acquiescence in the racialized imperial order demonstrated approval, or merely an inability to conceive of a world that transcended it; for even 'imperial suffragists' such as Stanton and Anthony opposed empire when it was shown to hinder the expansion of women's suffrage.[43]

The Cobdenite left-wing of the transatlantic women's suffrage movement stood out because its subscribers tended to buck this racialized pro-imperial trend. Feminist free traders numbered among the leaders of both the early twentieth-century anti-imperialist and the civil rights movements. In the United States, for example, anti-imperialists Fanny Garrison Villard, Florence Kelley, Jane Addams, and Ellen Winsor joined up with male Cobdenite anti-imperialist counterparts Oswald Garrison Villard, Clarence Darrow, Thomas Mott Osborne, and Moorfield Storey to help create the National Association for the Advancement of Colored People (NAACP) in 1909. British free-trade feminists, including Kate and Richard Cobden's daughters, contemporaneously mobilized against Edwardian British colonialism while also working on behalf of aboriginal rights.

The more radical left-wing of the burgeoning women's peace movement at the turn of the century was suffused with the Manchester liberal doctrine. In 1898, German feminist Luise Zietz, head of the Social Democratic Party (SPD)'s women's movement, argued for free trade at the party conference in Stuttgart. Much like that of Florence Kelley in the United States, Zietz's was a Marxist variant of Manchester liberalism—the Marx-Manchester tradition discussed in the previous chapter—that the SPD leadership would adhere to for years to come because they believed that free trade would support German democratization and the country's hungry working class, unite the world's workers, and help curb geopolitical strife.[44] Austrian peace worker Baroness Bertha von Suttner, who in 1905 became the first woman to be awarded the Nobel Peace Prize, was a prominent advocate of women's rights, free trade, and

Women's Free Trade Demonstration,

Under the auspices of the
WOMEN'S CO-OPERATIVE GUILD,
will be held in the

Free Trade Hall, Manchester,
- - ON - -

WEDNESDAY, NOV. 11th, 1903.

SPEAKERS:

Miss ALISON GARLAND (Women's Free Trade Union).
Mr. ERNEST BECKETT, M.P. (Unionist Free Food League).
Mr. ALFRED EMMOTT, M.P. (Vice-President Free Trade Union).
Miss BERTHA MASON (President, Lancashire Union B.W.T.A.).

Mr. PHILIP SNOWDEN (Labour Candidate for Blackburn).
Miss TUCKWELL (Women's Trade Union League).
Mrs. BOOTH (North-Western Sectional Council W.C.G.).
Mrs. COBDEN UNWIN.
Mrs. JOHN WINBOLT (Weaver, Stockport).

Chair to be taken at 7-30 p.m. by Mrs. BURY (Vice-President W.C.G.).

SUPPORTED BY

CENTRAL COMMITTEE AND NORTH-WESTERN SECTIONAL COUNCIL W.C.G., Mr. J. C. GRAY (General Secretary of the Co-operative Union), Mr. SHILLITO (Chairman of the Co-operative Wholesale Society), Miss ASHTON, Mrs. BEXLEY, Mrs. ALFRED BOOTH (Liverpool), Mrs. STUART BROWN (Liverpool), Miss BULLEY (President of the Manchester Women's Trades Council), Mrs. SYLEA, Mrs. BRIGHT CLARK, Mrs. CROMPTON (Rivington), Mrs. R. E. DOWSON, Miss I. O. FORD (Leeds), THE MAYORESS OF HEYWOOD, Mrs. HARKER, Lady BEATRICE KEMP, Lady MATHER, Miss DURSTALL, Mrs. REDFORD, Dr. MARGARET BELL, Mrs. SCHWANN, Mrs. THOMASSON (Bolton), Mrs. HANSON (Ex-Mayoress of Oldham), and many others.

Numbered and Reserved seat 2/6

Doors open at 6-30. Reserved Seats (in Gallery), 1s. The rest of the Hall, FREE.

Applications for Bills and Tickets (Reserved and Free) should be made to Miss LLEWELYN DAVIES (General Secretary, W.C.G.), Kirkby Lonsdale; Miss BAMFORD, "Co-operative News" Office, Long Millgate, Manchester; and the Local Secretary.

[over]

Free Trade brings Cheap Food.

Bread and Meat cost more in Protectionist Germany and France than in Free Trade England.

Free Trade makes the Housewife's money go furthest.

£1 of groceries in Free Trade England costs £1 6s. in Protectionist France.

Protection does NOT bring High Wages.

In Free Trade England wages are higher by one-fourth than in Protectionist France and by one-third than in Protectionist Germany.

Protection does NOT bring Constant Employment.

Protectionist Germany has been going through a severe commercial depression, with many workers unemployed and much distress.

The Largest Workers' Party in the World supports Free Trade.

In Protectionist Germany the Workers are fighting for Free Trade.

FIGURE 4.1. Leaflet, *Women's Free Trade Demonstration* (Manchester: Women's Co-operative Guild, 1903), Jane Cobden Unwin Papers, Box 6, Folder DM 851, 'Miscellaneous 1901–1911'. Courtesy of University of Bristol Library, Special Collections.

limiting national sovereignty to defend peace and human rights. Upon arriving on US shores in 1904, she referred to the officials who 'rummaged' through her belongings as 'the vandals of the tariff'. And while attending the 1908 London free-trade congress, she described it as being 'just like the peace congress', with 'peace and good will' overseeing the proceedings.[45] Feminist free traders across the English Channel were paying close attention. By the turn of the century, the first explicitly women's free-trade-and-peace organization, the Women's Co-operative Guild (1883–1921), was looking to Zietz's SPD for inspiration (Fig. 4.1).[46]

In turn-of-the-century Britain, Richard Cobden's friends and family continued to champion his liberal radical causes long after his death in 1865. Within the Marx-Manchester tradition, Annie Cobden invoked her father's memory in 1904, the centenary of his birth, to argue for socialist land nationalization to strike the final blow to Britain's 'feudal class', and penned the 1906 Independent Labour Party pamphlet *Richard Cobden and the Land of the People*. She also landed herself in jail that same year, thanks to her suffragette militancy; upon her release, she went on a US lecture tour to fire up its suffrage movement.[47] Richard Cobden's great-niece Helena, orphaned at age eleven, was brought into the progressive Cobden family fold. She attended her first Cobden Club meeting in 1893 when she was twelve, accompanied by her cousins Jane and Ellen. Alongside her anti-imperialist cousins, at the age of twenty Helena also got involved in the pro-Boer South Africa Conciliation Committee, and threw herself into the British women's suffrage movement. Helena and her husband Francis Hirst, British Cobdenite editor of the *Economist* from 1907 to 1916, worked in vain to keep Britain from going to war with Germany in 1914. The two thereafter oversaw the maintaining the Cobden family residence of Dunford House as their home base for carrying on the free-trade-and-peace cause.[48]

Kate and Richard's daughter Jane Cobden was notable for her involvement across the range of British women's suffrage, anti-imperialism, abolitionism, aboriginal rights, and free trade. In 1879 she formed a local free-trade club in Heyshot, not far from the family home in Dunford. In 1883 she and Helen Priestman Bright Clark, daughter of her father's ally John Bright, campaigned to include women's suffrage in the parliamentary Reform Bill of that year. Jane then controversially ran as a Progressive candidate for the London County Council in 1889. She and her sisters Maggie and Nellie were outspoken in advocating for Irish independence from the 1880s. Jane also took a lead role in opposing the Second Boer War (1899–1902) as head of the women's department of the Stop the War Committee, working alongside Emily Hobhouse and Josephine Butler, daughter of prominent ACLL campaigner and antislavery activist John Grey.[49] Jane Cobden's uncompromising opposition to South African segregationist policies got her ousted from the executive committee of the Anti-Slavery and Aborigines' Protection Society in 1917. She also assumed her father's free-trade anti-imperial mantle in her opposition to the imperial protectionist Tariff Reform movement (1903–1913) (see chapter 1).[50] Her publications, *The Hungry Forties: Life Under the Bread Tax* (1904) and *The Land Hunger: Life Under Monopoly* (1913), were in keeping with her father's radical cosmopolitan vision in arguing for a free market to make food affordable and land accessible.[51]

Transcending the 'Cobden sisterhood', by the time of the First World War Britain had become a hotbed of feminist commercial peace activism, as more and more women's suffragists demanded free trade to further their cause.[52] Prominent among them were Emily M. Leaf, Catherine Marshall, Eva Mac-naghten, W. Gladys Rinder, Ethil Snowden, Mary Sheepshanks, Helena M. Swanwick, and the leaders of the Women's Co-operative Guild.[53] From 1919 the British Section of WILPF provided an even wider umbrella to unite the various wings of the British suffrage movement owing to their shared belief in the pacifistic and emancipatory effects of economic liberalism on the world stage.[54]

Britain's turn-of-the-century confluence of women's suffragism with the Liberal–Labour politics of economic cosmopolitanism, anti-imperialism, and peace, in turn, often found its reverse image within the right-wing British anti-suffrage movement. Women 'antis', as they were sometimes dubbed, were mostly from wealthy elite families, and aligned themselves with Conservative policies of protectionism and imperial consolidation.[55] Australian-born Mrs. Humphry Ward, a popular novelist and member of the prominent intellectual Arnold family, was an early leader of the English anti-suffrage movement. An opponent of Irish Home Rule, according to biographer John Sutherland she also 'happily embraced Tariff Reform, and the quirky pro-imperialism that was part of the package'.[56] Another 'anti', Ethel Tawse Jollie, was married to Rhodesia's first administrator, Archibald Ross Colquhoun, and the two travelled the globe during their posting in Rhodesia, before settling into London and Edwardian British imperial politics. Jollie became a staunch defender of the 'natural order' of social and gender inequalities, and fought for strengthening the British Empire through emigration, imperial defence, imperial federation, and Tariff Reform. She was also active in the National Service League, which advocated compulsory military service; the Imperial Maritime League; the Women's Unionist and Tariff Reform Association; and the Royal Colonial Institute, where in 1914 she succeeded her husband as editor of its journal, *United Empire*.[57]

Lady Mary Maxse was a notable 'anti', protectionist, and imperialist. She was married to the military officer Sir Frederick Ivor Maxse, who had been stationed in Egypt and South Africa at the turn of the century and became a divisional commander in the First World War. Mary Maxse lived with Ivor in South Africa during his stint in the Second Boer War (1899–1901), but for the most part was based in London, where she became a promoter of Tory imperial politics, especially Tariff Reform. Joseph Chamberlain was even godfather to her second son, Fred. Chamberlain himself was keen to enlist her early on into the Tariff Reform fight. At Chamberlain's request, she joined the women's branch of the Tariff Reform League in 1904, whereupon she travelled the

country, held meetings, and made numerous speeches on behalf of the movement. In 1905, she became the chair of the Women's Unionist and Tariff Reform Association. She thereafter kept busy during the first months of the First
World War in pursuing her campaign for Tariff Reform alongside fighting
against the country's radical suffragette movement.[58]

The patriotic fervour brought on by the First World War provided upper-
and middle-class white Conservative women with the opportunity to tout
imperial consumerism for many years to come. During the war, the Women's
Patriotic League (founded in 1908) shifted from promoting home defence for
children to promoting imperial consumption. From the 1920s to the 1930s,
Conservative women thereafter maintained a grassroots 'Buy British Empire'
protectionist movement advocating imperial consumerism. The Women's
Unionist Organisation, which by 1928 could claim a million Conservative
housewives as members, spearheaded the interwar effort. According to Frank
Trentmann, they 'were the footsoldiers of the movement, organizing Empire
cake competitions, canvassing shopkeepers to stock and label Empire goods,
and promoting "surprise Empire boxes" [. . . :] a hands-on imperial consumer
politics, the Conservative middle-class counterpart to cooperative culture'.
They promoted the Empire Shopping Week and empire-made teas to children,
and even distributed recipes for empire-made foods such as banana jelly—
which called for bananas from Jamaica and South African glacé cherries—and
'imperial Christmas pudding', the Conservative counter to the free traders'
'cheap loaf'.[59] British left-wing feminist free traders thus faced a growing right-
wing opposition from anti-suffragist proponents of imperial Tariff Reform.

The First World War and the
Transnational Growth of Free-Trade Feminism

While British free-trade feminists were encountering early twentieth-century
pushback from anti-suffragist imperial protectionists, the feminist free-trade-
and-peace movement was picking up steam across the Atlantic from within
the US anti-imperialist movement. During and immediately after the Great
War, the movement expanded rapidly across Europe and across the Pacific
Ocean. National and international organizations such as the Woman's Peace
Party (WPP, founded in 1915) and the Women's Peace Society (WPS, 1919) in
the USA and WILPF, headquartered in Geneva, became central organizations
within the interwar commercial peace movement.

In the United States, first-wave feminist leaders such as Jane Addams, Alice Thatcher Post, Fanny Garrison Villard, and Lucia Ames Mead adapted their anti-imperial activism into an all-out assault on militarism and war. They first established themselves as officers of the Anti-Imperialist League (AIL, 1898–1920), a predominantly Cobdenite organization (see chapter 2).[60] These women played key roles in carrying forward and updating the legacy of abolitionism, free trade, and peace activism for the twentieth century. Fanny Garrison Villard—Cobdenite abolitionist William Lloyd Garrison's daughter—along with fellow women's suffragists Elinor Byrns, Crystal Eastman, and Madeline Doty, helped found the Woman's Peace Party of New York State in 1914, with trade liberalization among the planks of its platform. The organization was set up following visits from Austro-Hungarian suffragist Rosika Schwimmer and British suffragist Emmeline Pethick-Lawrence.[61] A year later the national WPP was created, with the New York branch its most radical. Headed by Garrison Villard, Addams, Grace Hoffman White, and Georgist editor Alice Post, the WPP became the suffragist arm of the US peace movement during the First World War, owing to the continued marginalization of women within the older US peace organizations and the WPP's contention that equal participation of women in politics was necessary to guarantee world peace.[62]

The women's free-trade-and-peace movement expanded rapidly during and immediately after the First World War, despite frequent attacks from the conservative press and the public, and despite censorship and persecution from governments. Almost overnight, Jane Addams went from being America's darling to one of its most dangerous subversives. The first International Congress of Women was convened at The Hague in Spring 1915, where it urged 'in all countries that there shall be liberty of commerce', freedom of the seas, and the open door.[63] The 1918 congressional programme of the Woman's Peace Party of New York State made a similar case for 'why a League of Nations must be based on free markets and free seas'.[64] Not finding the New York peace organization's endorsement of free trade and non-resistance radical enough, in 1919 Byrns and Garrison Villard formed the WPS. Its motto was, 'Immediate and universal disarmament. Abolition of mob violence. *Free trade, the world over.*' (Fig. 4.2).[65]

The WPS's dedication to free trade remained unequivocal until the society's dissolution in the early 1930s following the death of Fanny Garrison Villard. Its stated aims made clear that protectionism was a principal cause of imperialism and war. 'Why? Because where Free Trade is restricted, nations fight one

Women's Peace Society

The underlying principle of this Society is a belief in the sacredness and inviolability of human life under all circumstances

Officers

Chairman
Mrs. HENRY VILLARD
525 Park Avenue, New York

Vice-Chairman
ELINOR BYRNS
KATHERINE DEVEREUX BLAKE

Treasurer
Miss MARY ABBOTT
29 East 29th Street, New York

Secretary
Mrs. WM. C. HARRIS
1588 East 19th Street, Brooklyn, N.Y.

Immediate and universal disarmament.
Abolition of mob violence.
Free trade, the world over.

Non-resistance is not a state of passivity. On the contrary, it is a state of activity, ever fighting the good fight of faith, ever foremost to assail unjust power, ever struggling for liberty, equality, fraternity, in no national sense, but in a world-wide spirit. It is passive only in this sense,—that it will not return evil for evil, nor give blow for blow, nor resort to murderous weapons for protection or defense.

WILLIAM LLOYD GARRISON.

525 Park Ave., New York City, Nov. 18, 1920.

FIGURE 4.2. WPS letterhead, 18 November 1920. Swarthmore College Peace Collection (McCabe Library, Swarthmore, PA), WPS Papers, Box 1, 'Literature'.

another in order to gain railroads or ports, spheres of influence, trade concessions, new markets, and exclusive right to undeveloped territory.' Protectionism—be it preferential trade, boycotts, or blockades—was 'a fountain source of hatred, greed, and false patriotism. Without question it prevents the spread of human brotherhood upon which all civilization and peace must rest.'[66] The Cobdenite message was clear.

The international women's free-trade-and-peace movement received a bigger boost in 1919 with the creation of WILPF, whereupon the WPP became WILPF's US Section and the WPS a friendly rival. AIL officer Jane Addams, a 'Free Trader by conviction', was elected WILPF's first international president, with another American, Wellesley College economist Emily Green Balch, becoming its first international secretary at its headquarters in Geneva.[67] From its inception, WILPF endorsed the call for 'liberty of commerce' as first enunciated at the 1915 Hague conference, making free trade an explicit programme for the international organization and its national sections for years to come.[68] At the 1921 congress in Vienna, the British Section's Emily M. Leaf moved a resolution for 'Freedom of Trade and Communications', which called on all national sections to 'urge on their Governments a Free Trade policy and the pressing need for International Co-operation'. Catherine Marshall also spoke in favour, noting 'that [John Maynard] Keynes and other Liberals in England looked to this Congress to support them in their fight for Free Trade between nations'. The French Section went further still, calling for 'the abolition of all

Trade Boycotts' to be added to the resolution, which was seconded by the
Danish Section. Fanny Garrison Villard, representing the WPS at the conference, took the opportunity to reiterate that she and the other WPS members
associated with WILPF 'are devoted to the principle of Free-Trade' along the
pacifistic lines laid out by Richard Cobden.[69] In advance of Garrison Villard's
attendance, the WPS's Sara Bard Field—a US single tax advocate, suffragist,
lawyer, and poet—had even sent out an appeal to all the Vienna delegates to
encourage, first, explicit adoption of 'the principle of non-resistance' as laid out
by Gandhi and William Lloyd Garrison; second, universal disarmament; and
third, 'absolute free trade and freedom of trade opportunities the world over'.[70]

The WPS's dedication to free trade as a prerequisite for peace remained
prominent. Slogans such as 'Trade Barriers Lead to War—abolish them' and
'Cooperation pays better than Competition. Let's try it between Nations' pep-
pered the November 1921 Disarmament Parade in New York City, organized
by the WPS and the Women's Peace Union.[71] And as the decade ended, the
programming of the WPS's 'Radio Time' on local New York stations featured
Annie E. Gray, the executive secretary, discussing 'Free Trade as an adjunct to
World Peace' (Fig. 4.3).

At this time, the WPS also noted with unconcealed delight that US protectionists had taken notice that 'two out of three women have a grudge
against the tariff', owing to its ill effects upon consumer prices, with Gray adding that the WPS hoped 'the "grudge" will grow into a unanimous vote for Free
Trade'.[72] The leaflet continued to be republished and mass distributed and so,
too, would Gray continue to hammer home the society's Cobdenite message
as editor of the WPS's monthly newsletters until the society was disbanded in
the early 1930s.

Of course, US conservative nationalists also took notice of the women's
peace internationalists—and took aim. Against the backdrop of the first 'Red
Scare', conservatives began associating any endorsement of internationalism,
free trade, or peace with Bolshevism. The War Department itself was also
prone to spying on the US women's peace movement's activities and correspondence. Militarist nationalist women's groups such as the American War
Mothers, the Daughters of the American Revolution (DAR), and the Women's
Relief Auxiliary cultivated a symbiotic alliance with the War Department; together they hounded the women's peace movement throughout the 1920s, and
submitted reports on the 'ultra-pacifists' to government intelligence officers.
These anti-radical and anti-internationalist women's groups also took to propaganda and disruptive protests of the various women's peace conferences. Their

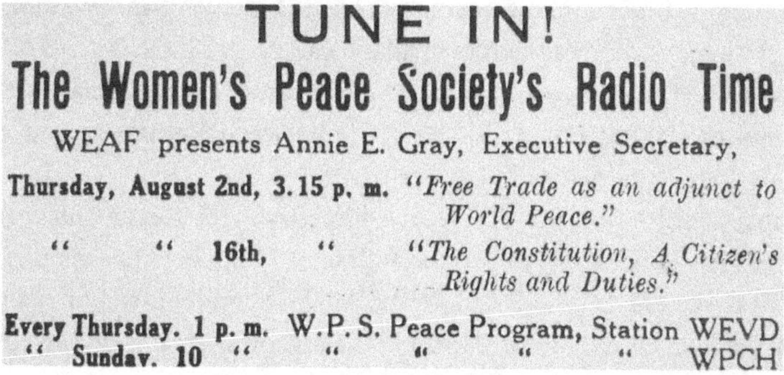

TUNE IN!
The Women's Peace Society's Radio Time

WEAF presents Annie E. Gray, Executive Secretary,

Thursday, August 2nd, 3.15 p. m. *"Free Trade as an adjunct to World Peace."*

"   "   **16th,**   "   *"The Constitution, A Citizen's Rights and Duties."*

Every Thursday. 1 p. m. W.P.S. Peace Program, Station WEVD
"   **Sunday. 10** "   "   "   "   "   WPCH

FIGURE 4.3. 'Tune in! The Women's Peace Society's Radio Time', *Newsletter Published by the Women's Peace Society* 2 (Aug. 1928), 3. Swarthmore College Peace Collection (McCabe Library, Swarthmore, PA), WPS Papers, 'Newsletters/Photography', Box 1.

efforts against pacifism and radicalism culminated in a coalition in 1927: the Women's Patriotic Conference on National Defense. The organization would continue to meet annually well into the Cold War years.[73] From 1946 onwards, groups such as the DAR also maintained their opposition to 'any plan for world government involving world citizenship, universal currency, free trade, and the dominance of the United States by any other nation'.[74]

WILPF's economic cosmopolitanism remained central to its interwar peace activism as local sections witnessed nation after nation embrace economic autarky. In 1924 Lucie Dejardine of the Belgian Section put forward the establishment free trade and a 'United States of Europe' under the auspices of the League of Nations.[75] At WILPF's 1926 congress in Dublin, representatives of the sections from Canada, Czechoslovakia, France, Germany, Hungary, the Netherlands, Norway, and Japan all once again endorsed free trade as a prerequisite for peace.[76] Emmy Freundlich, head of WILPF's Austrian Section, thereafter gave a fiery speech to the mostly male attendees of the 1927 Geneva Economic Conference, in which she warned that 'barbed-wire entanglements have given place to new frontiers in the form of high customs tariffs, which imprison goods and men'. The Netherlands's Lizzy van Dorp similarly called upon the conference delegates to deliver the world 'from the nightmare of customs duties'.[77] Inspired by the 1928 Kellogg–Briand Pact renouncing war, the British Section's Mary Sheepshanks condemned postwar industrial protectionism and economic autarky for starting 'a ruinous system of putting high tariffs' on raw materials and food, and the German Section made a point of reaffirming WILPF's commitment to free trade.[78] The WPS instead took more direct action, sending out letters to all US candidates for state and national offices to ask them where they stood on three issues: the renunciation of war, international arbitration, and 'Free Trade between Nations as a means of bringing about International Cooperation.'[79]

In 1931, WILPF and the WPS received free-trade reinforcements from the International Alliance of Women for Suffrage and Equal Citizenship (IAW). At its Peace Conference in Belgrade, the Alliance condemned 'the old methods of commercial and financial rivalry'. The organization also gave its support to the League of Nations's call for economic interdependence and European union to end the 'menace to world peace'.[80]

Free trade maintained through supranational institutions such as the League of Nations and European union became key to the economic programmes of international feminist peace organizations for years to come.[81] Advocacy for universal free trade remained a crucial cosmopolitan implement in the interwar women's peace movement's toolkit. It would also become the cornerstone of the movement's economic critique of the military-imperial order.

Fighting Hunger, War, and Colonialism: the Interwar Feminist Anti-imperialism of Free Trade

In seeking to understand the causes of the First World War and to avoid a sequel, interwar feminist peace activists developed sophisticated free-trade critiques of colonial economic policies. While having much in common with the critiques of their male anti-imperial contemporaries such as J. A. Hobson, feminists placed greater emphasis upon child hunger and women's empowerment. Recognizing the perennial and militaristic power of nationalism on the world stage, WILPF's economic cosmopolitan vision for a new anti-imperial order also made sure to include a demand for supranational governance to maintain it.

The radical New York wing of the WPP provided a preliminary enunciation in 1918 of what would effectively become WILPF's position on the imperial question. The New York wing connected neomercantilism to the imperial search for new colonies as sources for raw materials and markets for surplus goods and capital, imperial rivalry and conflict being, in its view, the inevitable results. The WPP insisted, as the remedy, on 'the open door', which would 'remove the advantage which makes colonies desirable, and strike at a root cause of war'. Its proposal drew explicitly upon two anti-imperial theorists. One was Johan Hansson, a Swedish follower of 'Turgot, Cobden, and Henry George'. In 1914, following a trek around the globe, he had outlined his theory in a paper given to Mary Fels, the era's most active Georgist feminist. Hansson envisaged a supranational mandatory system over the colonial world. He argued that through Western-governed policies of free trade, industrialization, and democratization, the colonial world would begin to take on self-governing responsibilities, culminating in full-fledged sovereignty and representation within a 'world federation'. The other theorist was Emily Greene Balch. She offered a challenge to the paternalistic racism and Anglo-Saxonism of the 'white man's burden' thesis by promoting, as Melinda Plastas describes it, 'a vision of a new world steeped in a racially sensitive humanist mutuality'.[82]

WILPF's own call for supranational oversight was first laid out in detail at its 1924 meeting in Washington, at which world hunger remained of paramount humanitarian concern. Andrée Jouve outlined how the French Section had established the Help for the Children of Europe Committee in 1919 to assist the starving children of Germany, Austria, and Hungary. WILPF's humanitarian relief efforts were then expanded to the children of famine-ridden Soviet Russia in 1921. But despite their efforts, in Germany 'unhappy women' were yet 'falling dead of hunger in the streets, and children were going to school unfed'. As a result, Lucie Dejardine of the Belgian Section supported establishing free trade and a 'United States of Europe' under the auspices of the League of Nations. The Executive Committee also called for a new League of Peoples that expressly prohibited the 'use of hunger blockades or any blockade as a means of pressure on a nation rebellious to the new order, for it is the innocent who always pay with their misery and death', as was the present case in Ukraine and Russia. The economic section of the proposed league would also oversee the global distribution of food 'to keep the peoples from the famine and want which still afflict some of the populations of Europe, Africa, Asia, etc.'[83]

Ending the policies of food sanctions and blockades through supranational regulation were part of WILPF's broader humanitarian programme for an anti-imperial free-trade order. W. Gladys Rinder drew attention to the British Section's efforts to thwart the recent attempt to establish a system of imperial trade preference throughout the British Empire, and called on 'every National Section' of WILPF to work towards abolishing tariffs in order to establish 'the New Order we all desire'.[84] Emily Balch followed this up with a condemnation of the symbiotic relationship between economic nationalism, profit seeking, colonialism, and militarism. The nationalistic 'economic alliance between governments and business' was the primary culprit for 'the whole structure of protective tariffs, of preferential arrangements in colonial policies', and of providing protection to a nation's investors and bankers in foreign countries. These policies were preventing 'any true international order in the world. [. . .] Mars is the God of the countries which fear interdependence, and work to become commercially self-sufficing. Mars is the God of passports, and the God of tariffs, and the God of concessions.' Balch called for nothing less than a sweeping reform of the global economic order: 'international supervision and administration in economic matters' through the League; 'international control of international waterways [. . .] and absolute freedom of navigation of the ocean itself, as demanded in the famous Fourteen Points'; stabilization of the global financial system; a 'more definite arrangement for international succor in cases of famine'; and 'international allotment, or regulated distribution, of scarce raw materials or supplies'. This last, she qualified, would prove unnecessary 'if we had permanent peace and complete free trade'.[85] Balch's was a truly cosmopolitan vision of a free-market world devoid of national borders and race hatred, albeit one that could never itself entirely transcend the era's racialized structures and suppositions.[86]

By the time of its 1926 Dublin congress, WILPF, now claiming fifty thousand members across forty nations, laid out a detailed call for worldwide political and economic decolonization.[87] The organization called for international control of financial companies involved in colonial exploitation, for a gradual move towards independence in all colonies, and for international organization of 'exploitation of the natural resources of the colonies' that would not 'defraud the natives'; it also labelled the League of Nations mandates system merely 'a new method of colonization'; and) denounced the commonly held idea of white superiority among the colonial powers.[88]

WILPF's left-wing politics had come a long way from Martineau and Nightingale's rather rosy Victorian view of British free-trade imperialism. In contrast to the common feminist acquiescence in Anglo-Saxonist racial hierarchies and colonialism before the First World War, WILPF was now demanding free trade, decolonization, and racial justice maintained through supranational governance. While the organization as a whole never completely distanced itself from the era's ideas of racial hierarchies, its more progressive anti-imperial theorists understood economic imperialism as both a formal and informal policy 'of acquiring great undeveloped territories or commercial concessions in backward countries, and exploiting them, not in the interest of the native inhabitants'. They identified an acceleration of this policy between 1880 and the outbreak of the First World War, and its perpetuation in the years since. 'Tropical and semi-tropical possessions have not provided outlets for surplus populations [. . . ;] neither do these countries [. . .] provide substantial markets for manufactured goods'; the economic advantage was doubtful, but the hostility such exploitation aroused between the colonizer and colonized was palpable. Perpetuation of the colonial project stemmed largely from a desire for 'prestige', imperial rivalry, and 'wire-pulling of financial and commercial companies'.[89]

According to WILPF, the interwar growth of nationalism and protectionism among the imperial powers only served to abet military conflict across the globe. 'The aggressive nationalism of the new post-war States in Europe shows itself in the setting up of high tariff-walls, an economic policy closely akin to the policy of the "self-sufficing Empire" of the imperialists, and will soon sow similar seeds of war.' Numbering among the most dangerous factors of the current age of economic imperialism was 'the protectionist policy adopted by the majority of States in Europe and America, the British Dominions and India'. The policy 'throws each Nation back on its own resources, and is inspired by the effort to be self-supporting and to acquire territories that will make it self-supporting'. The policy also exacerbated geopolitical tensions by raising 'animosity, fear and envy between States, each being afraid of being cut off from markets and raw materials'.[90]

At the 1926 Dublin congress, WILPF's sophisticated remedy for curbing informal economic imperialism entailed a multipronged combination of supranational governance through the League, the outlawing of 'native' military service and forced labour, and support for free trade. Trace elements of the racist 'civilizing mission' remained, however, and the remedy took little account of what colonial subjects themselves might have wanted: 'In the struggle for markets equality of conditions makes for safety'; and so the League needed to be empowered to 'insist on the "open door" in all tropical colonies, on the non-militarisation of natives, on abolition of all forms of forced labour, and on an international rationing of raw materials. [. . .] International economic control and equality of rights in economic opportunities in undeveloped territories are a real need of civilisation.' Britain instead looked more and more likely to 'adopt a Protectionist and exclusive policy', which Mary Sheepshanks warned was a clear and present danger to the world order. 'Trade and commerce should be free and not limited or "protected" by force'; economic isolationism was both 'impracticable' and 'unthinkable'.[91]

At the same congress, Emily Balch enunciated her nuanced awareness and criticism of Western informal economic imperialism. She was also in tune with the wider transatlantic anti-imperialist movement. While a professor at Wellesley College in 1902, for example, she had invited J. A. Hobson to speak, and the two of them had co-organized a conference on socialism seven years later.[92] Her writings in support of internationalism, anti-racism, free immigration, and anti-imperialism had long been included among the recommended readings of the women's peace movement, alongside the male Cobdenite treatises of Hobson, H. N. Brailsford, and Norman Angell. Her peace work during the First World War had even cost her her job at Wellesley. At the fourth WILPF congress, held at Howard University in Washington, DC, Balch presaged today's Fair Trade movement when she criticized any embrace of globalized trade while lacking 'any sense of community of indebtedness, or an sense of personal relation to the coolie who picked the tea leaves or the Australian bushman, if that's the proper name, who took care of its sheep'.[93] In Dublin, Balch called for a non-coercive programme of free trade and supranational governance to give underdeveloped states a leg up. The best solution to the problem was 'regulation without control'. The open-door principle was an 'important step in the right direction and has wider bearings than may appear on the surface. It takes away a motive for international quarrels over colonial booty.' While the road ahead was a difficult one, 'we can be content with no less ambitious program' than one that requires working with underdeveloped states in 'such a way as to be useful to them and favorable to their development [...] without forcing our control upon them'.[94] In Balch's vision for a new economic order, the anti-imperialism of free trade would curb economic imperialism, promote democracy, and uplift less developed decolonizing economies.[95]

The Japanese Section's Tano Jodai similarly cautioned at the 1926 congress that her country was trending towards the European model of economic imperialism. The island nation's dependence upon international trade had made it all too quick to copy the continental European imperial model of securing markets abroad while 'more or less disregarding their interests and welfare [...]. Japan is only imitating the European school of business in the Far East.' American imperial expansion into the Asia-Pacific region and its exclusionary Asian immigration policy, Jodai continued, were only compounding the problem and further souring relations with Japan.[96]

The Dublin congress concluded its extensive critique of colonial and economic imperialism with a final powerful yet pragmatic resolution in favour of free trade, peace, decolonization, and supranational governance. WILPF was opposed to 'every kind of Imperialism, Colonial and Economic' and 'opposed in principle to the possession of colonies and holding of mandates'. However, 'in view of the fact that colonies do exist', the organization's proposal was for substantial revisions to the mandate system, along the lines laid out above. Regarding economic imperialism, WILPF's foremost provision was 'that preferential tariffs, custom barriers and all measures tending to impede the free exchange of goods and free intercourse between countries, should be abolished'. A pan-European customs union would provide 'the first step towards the attainment of Free Trade in all countries and Continents'. And to guarantee worldwide food security, WILPF also called for 'the international control of the distribution of raw material and food, according to the needs of the peoples and not the profit of the entrepreneurs'. This was to be administered by a League of Nations international economic council 'including a large representation of workers and consumers of both sexes'.[97]

But WILPF's anti-imperial support for free trade was increasingly being put to the test by the global growth of economic nationalism among anti-colonial movements during this period, from the Swadeshi Movement in India (see chapter 1) to President Lázaro Cárdenas's oil nationalization programme in Mexico. By the late 1930s, while some within WILPF argued that temporary exceptions should be made for these in their economic nationalist efforts to wrest control of their natural resources from Western powers, others worried that doing so contradicted WILPF's cosmopolitan vision and would only heighten geopolitical conflict. Internal tensions between WILPF headquarters and some national sections became irreconcilable. In the case of Mexico, upon the outbreak of war in Europe in 1939, WILPF was unable to salvage its Mexico Section.[98]

The Free-Trade Ideologies of Feminist Peace Activism

The international feminist peace movement's association of free trade with cheap food, political empowerment, humanitarianism, anti-imperialism, and peace illustrates the permeation of a handful of ideological strands of Cobdenism by the time of the First World War. The most prominent were international co-operativism, Henry Georgism, and Norman Angellism. Despite some cosmetic differences of means, all shared similar Manchester liberal ends: a peaceful, food-secure, democratic, interdependent world tied together through free trade and supranational governance.

International co-operativism provided the women's peace movement with a transnational, grassroots, consumer-oriented 'third way' between socialist revolution and Manchester liberalism (see chapter 3). Co-operativism's 'open tent' grassroots approach to organization allowed for one of the earliest feminist efforts to mobilize on behalf of free trade, peace, and social justice. As Austria's Emmy Freundlich—one of Europe's leading feminists involved in the early twentieth-century international co-operative movement—described it, co-operative women strove 'for ourselves, freedom and the right to responsible action and the development of our personalities; for our children, a higher social order and economic system which will abolish want and misery; for the world, peace among nations and common activities for the welfare of mankind'.[99]

Women's co-operativism expanded rapidly across Europe in the wake of the First World War. The Marx-Manchester movement ambitiously connected women's empowerment, free trade, the free movement of people, and peace through nonprofit co-operative enterprise. At WILPF's 1926 congress, Austrian co-operativist and WPS member Yella Hertzka castigated the 'great international financiers of the world' as 'the real power behind the throne in every country'. She called instead for expansion of the international co-operative movement to stimulate 'good will between nations'.[100] In 1929, Freundlich warned that Europe's 'perpetual tariff wars constitute a perpetual danger of war' along lines she had previously laid out at the 1927 World Economic Conference. She called, alongside free trade, for the free movement of people under the auspices of the League of Nations's International Labour Organisation. Without labourers' ability to find work wherever they could, countries with 'chronic unemployment [. . .] like overheated boilers, which must get air [. . .] will try to do so through war, especially colonial wars'. Trusts and cartels only added to the problem by fostering 'violent disputes' in their efforts to obtain protectionist legislation from governments in order to increase profits. Her call to action was simple. First, 'women must everywhere support the efforts of the League of Nations to lower the tariff walls'. Second, women needed to become more involved in the international co-operative movement to undermine the profit-seeking influence of the world's monopolistic cartels.[101]

Following the onset of the Great Depression, the International Co-operative Women's Guild reaffirmed its commitment to peace through economic cosmopolitanism. At its 1930 conference in Vienna, the Guild declared that 'the working women of all countries, house-wives and mothers' must further 'cooperative enterprise nationally and internationally so that a system of cooperative economy may permanently prevent war'.[102] As late as 1943, the co-operative women's movement continued to support a 'congress of nations, free trade', and 'immediate postwar planning'.[103] From the late nineteenth to the mid-twentieth century, the international women's co-operative movement thus worked to create a more peaceful world order based upon the 'third way' cosmopolitan principles of non-profit exchange, free trade, free migration, and supranational economic governance.

The radical 'single tax' idea of US political economist Henry George provided another Cobdenite economic ideological strand within the feminist peace movement from the turn of the century (see chapter 2). Georgists argued that placing a tax on the estimated value of land would break up land monopolies and undermine the political power of militant aristocratic elites. The theory was first enunciated in George's internationally popular *Progress and Poverty* (1879), which drew direct inspiration from Richard Cobden and Herbert Spencer. According to Georgists, governments would be able to derive all their necessary revenue from a single tax on land values. Tariffs and other forms of indirect taxation would be made redundant, ushering in a new age of unfettered free trade, prosperity, political enfranchisement, and peace.

Thanks to the single tax's potential for reforming the economic nationalist order, as well as the Georgist movement's strong support for women's empowerment, George's pacifistic ideas had spread through the growing transnational network of women's suffragists by the turn of the century. As C. B. Fillerbown pitched it to the Massachusetts Woman's Suffrage Association in 1897, the single tax was 'the one missing ingredient to the woman's suffrage alchemy, the yeast that will compel the loaf to rise whether the loaf wants to rise or not'. The Women's National Single Tax League was created the following year, after which the association of the two movements only grew stronger. Arthur Young, in his detailed Progressive Era study of the American single tax movement, went so far as to state in 1916 that 'there is scarcely a single taxer who is not an ardent advocate of woman suffrage'.[104]

Mary Fels, working alongside her husband Joseph, a wealthy retired Pennsylvania soap manufacturer, gave the single tax movement a substantial financial and propagandistic boost at the turn of the century following their relocation from Philadelphia to London. Mary herself was a radical US suffragist, an officer of the AIL, and a peace worker. Just before setting off on the Ford Peace Expedition in 1916, she explained how absolute free trade through the single tax would curb imperial demands for foreign markets and transportation networks wrought from protective tariffs—thereby eliminating the economic roots of colonialism.[105] She would eventually take over as editor of the Chicago-based anti-imperial Georgist publication *The Public*.

Georgist feminist reformers in Britain and across the globe received much-needed financial support from Mary Fels and her husband. In Britain, their largesse led to the formation of the United Committee for the Taxation of Land Values, as well as numerous local chapters across the British Empire to break up the land monopolies controlled by the colonies' aristocratic elites. With the Fels's added financial bolstering, various leading women's suffragists across the globe thus zealously took to George's pacifistic single tax idea, owing to its straightforward prescription for breaking up land monopolies, eliminating tariffs, and its promise of a new economic order of absolute free trade, political equality, prosperity, and peace.

The Felses financing included helping to fund the creation of the single tax colony of Arden, Delaware, founded in 1900. There Georgist resident Elizabeth Magie patented the board game *The Landlord's Game* in 1904 (Fig. 4.4) to help educate others about the evils of land monopolies. One of her neighbours, the socialist professor Scott Nearing (see Chapter 3), fell in love with it and used it as a teaching tool with his students at the University of Pennsylvania. *The Landlord's Game* was repackaged in the 1930s to become the world's bestselling board game, *Monopoly*. Few today are aware that the board game's radical roots stretch back to a rather forgotten Georgist women's suffragist in the turn-of-the-century economic peace movement.[106]

The single tax movement's alliance with the international women's peace movement expanded rapidly from the turn of the century. Alongside Mary Fels, Alice Thatcher Post played a notable part in this convergence, as a prominent feminist, peace activist, civil rights reformer, and a leader of the US single tax movement. She co-edited the popular Georgist publication *The Public*, first with her husband Louis Post and then with Mary Fels once Louis joined Woodrow Wilson's cabinet as assistant secretary of labor. Alice was also a member of the New York peace organization the American Free Trade League (AFTL) and the Ford Peace Expedition, co-founder of the WPP, an officer of the AIL, and an Esperanto enthusiast.[107] Massachusetts peace worker Mary Ware Dennett, a niece of Lucia Ames Mead, was an officer of both the AFTL and the IFTL, and prone to connecting Georgism with women's suffrage.[108] Nova Scotia-born suffragist Christine Ross Barker helped spread the single tax movement to Canada. She was the inaugural president of the Women's Henry George League of Manhattan upon its founding in 1904. She afterwards returned to Canada, where she took a lead role in the Canadian Section of WILPF and in creating the Women's Peace Union of the Western Hemisphere, which worked closely with the WPS in New York. She remained a prominent Georgist in Toronto throughout the interwar years.[109] Like Dennett, she was a founding officer of the Boston-based IFTL, a predominantly Georgist

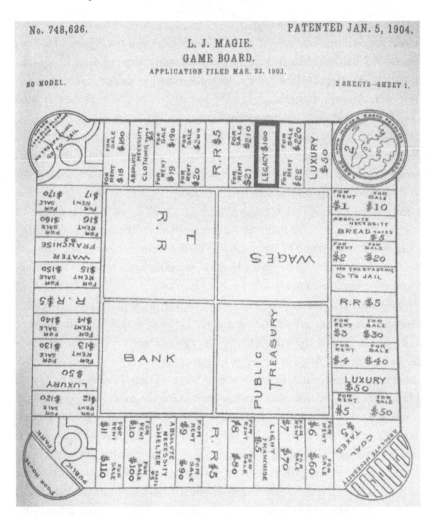

FIGURE 4.4. Lizzie Magie's original patent drawing for her board game, *The Landlord's Game*, 5 January 1904.

organization (see chapter 2).[110] Anna Angela George de Mill, meanwhile, Henry George's daughter, was active on both sides of the Atlantic as a member of WILPF as well as an officer of London's International Union for Land Value Taxation and Free Trade. As late as 1937, in a speech before that year's Henry George Congress, de Mill argued that 'to destroy the seeds of war there must be [. . .] freedom of trade in production [. . .] free trade between nations', and 'freedom for labor and capital'.[111]

The commingling of Georgism and feminist peace activism transcended transatlantic Anglo-American circles. Denmark's Georgist feminist Hedevig Sonne Hald drew a clear association between land monopolies and war at the 1929 WILPF congress: 'The damage, brought about by Protectionism, *the monopoly of trade* is emphasized, lately [. . .] but still more fatal is *the monopoly of land*.' Hald's pacifistic Georgist sentiment was shared, she noted, by such international luminaries as Ellen Key, Leo Tolstoy, Herbert Spencer, and Sun Yat Sen (see chapter 2).[112] Russia's Tatiana Sukhotin-Tolstoy, the eldest daughter of Leo Tolstoy, was, like her father, a single tax and peace advocate, and worked to expand the movement globally.[113] And in *Quest for Peace as I Have Known It in Australia* (1949), Melbourne IFTL and WILPF officer Eleanore M. Moore explained why Melbourne's Free Trade and Land Values League was so involved in the Australian women's peace movement, 'not only as a co-operator, but as believing that its own policy is integral to the attainment of international peace.'[114]

The early twentieth-century Cobdenite ideology then famously called 'Norman Angellism' after British journalist Norman Angell for a time rivalled the influence of co-operativism and Henry Georgism within the women's peace movement. Angell's fame and influence followed the publication of his international bestselling book *The Great Illusion* (1910), which argued along Manchester School lines that businessmen should be inherently predisposed towards peace because the world's markets were so interconnected and interdependent that war would create nothing but economic loss to the world. It was both a pragmatic appeal to the businessman's bottom line, and a pacifistic endorsement of international trade liberalization. It was also a pessimistic appeal, as Angell and other peace internationalists sought unsuccessfully to redirect the turn-of-the-century global turn towards economic nationalism, imperial rivalry, and militarism (see chapter 2).[115]

The strong connection between Norman Angellism and the women's peace movement was far from accidental. Peace activist Julius Moritzen, in his 1911 treatise on the US peace movement, made the case that women, as the 'peaceful sex', could be a powerful pacifistic force. 'But as a force for international peace they are negative unless they have specific instruction. They must be set to [. . .] reading Norman Angell's *Great Illusion*.' Once so instructed, he argued, they could 'be of very great service in informing their own busy husbands and brothers who may not have time to discuss international ethics, history, and politics.'[116] In the USA, Angell soon found himself a spokesperson for the Boston-based World Peace Foundation (WPF) and the New York-based

Carnegie Endowment for International Peace (CEIP), founded, respectively, in 1909 and 1910. Leaders of the women's peace movement often worked in coordination with these two well financed US-based peace organizations, and similarly took to Norman Angellism. Poet and psychologist Anna Sturges Duryea even lectured about Norman Angellism on behalf of the WPF, and headed its women's department in order to bring more women's suffragists into the Angellite fold.[117] Fanny Garrison Villard also took to Norman Angellism. Like her brothers, she was instilled with her father's passionate defence of free trade, peace, abolitionism, civil rights, and women's suffrage. But unlike her brothers, who gravitated to the single tax, Fanny stuck to Cobdenite orthodoxy and the more pragmatic appeal of Norman Angellism.[118]

Angell himself was a supporter of women's suffrage and a co-worker of British feminist peace activists through his work with the Union for Democratic Control. At the instigation of Fanny Garrison Villard, in the course of Angell's frequent US visits he became a speaker at WPP and WPS engagements; his letters to the WPP leadership were reprinted in their propaganda materials; his articles appeared in *Jus Sufragii*, the publication of the International Woman Suffrage Alliance; and the WPP leadership recommended his work to educate its members on issues of international political economy, along with the writings of other radical free-trade-and-peace activists such as the turn-of-the-century Cobdenite J. A. Hobson, who had helped inspire the anti-imperial activism of Lucia Ames Mead (see chapter 2).[119]

Budapest's Rosika Schwimmer best embodied the direct transatlantic influence of Norman Angellism on the women's peace movement.[120] Schwimmer became a leading light of the European feminist movement upon founding the Hungarian Feminist Association in the late 1890s. In 1913 she became an officer of the International Woman Suffrage Alliance, after which she played a key role in the creation of the WPP in 1915 and WILPF in 1919. Following the publication of *The Great Illusion* in 1910, Schwimmer began to study what she referred to as the 'Norman Angell theory'. She even forced her way into an all-male Norman Angell summer school in England in 1914 by promising 'to do as much as possible to spread the idea, in writing and speaking' during her upcoming US tour on behalf of international women's rights and world peace.[121] In Angellite fashion, shortly after her arrival in America, Schwimmer met with the automobile manufacturer Henry Ford in Detroit in November 1915. Ford apparently found persuasive Schwimmer's argument that war was bad for business; he agreed to fund what became known as the Ford Peace Ship Expedition of December 1915, followed by the Neutral Mediation Conference in Stockholm in February 1916. By 1920, Ford was demanding that the United States 'open the tariff doors' as a boon to business and to humanity.[122]

Like Georgism, Norman Angellism reached across the Pacific to the women's peace movement in Australia. Melbourne's Sisterhood of International Peace included in its 1917–1918 syllabus a discussion entitled 'What About Norman Angell Now?' And Melbourne IFTL and WILPF officer Eleanore M. Moore gave lectures across the continent on Norman Angellism.[123]

Jane Addams, the leader of the interwar women's peace movement, influenced Norman Angell, and vice versa. She and Angell corresponded with one another, and Angell was awarded the Nobel Peace Prize in 1934 thanks in part to Addams's support. Addams had been developing her own views on the subject for some time, as illustrated in her 1906 book *Newer Ideals of Peace*. However, Addams's subsequent writings and interviews illuminate Angell's influence on her changing *international* economic outlook. For example, in a 1913 *Ladies Home Journal* article, 'Peace on Earth', Addams weighed in on the international aspects of commerce and peace by highlighting that 'perhaps the most striking manifestation among our own contemporaries is the international outlook resulting from "a world market" and the ever increasing interdependence of commercial relations'. She had noted this recently when 'a leading citizen in Chicago' had told her that 'his business interests in Russia had never recovered from the profound disturbance caused by the war with Japan, and that conservative business men could no longer stand for such stupendous folly; although nothing would have astounded this man more than to have been told that he was reflecting the attitude of the Pacivists [*sic*]'. Indeed, 'his very words suggested the theme of Norman Angell's recent book, with its powerful presentation of the folly and illusion of war'.[124] And following her 1921 visit to the starving masses imprisoned behind eastern European high tariff walls, she observed that 'the situation [...] seemed to bear out completely Norman Angell's theory of the futility of war'.[125] Armed with the pacifistic ideologies of Cobdenism, Addams led the interwar feminist fight for a new free-trade order.

Cordell Hull and the Feminist Pax Economica

The women's peace movement reified their support for free trade amidst the global embrace of economic nationalism, trade wars, and imperial consolidation following the onset of the Great Depression. And they found a new ally in Cordell Hull, Democratic president Franklin Roosevelt's secretary of state. Hull shared the feminist peace movement's belief that free trade created a more peaceful economic order, and that protectionism created conflict. This alliance between the women's peace movement and Hull's State Department culminated in the creation of a more liberal trading system after the Second World War, their Pax Economica.

Jane Addams, in her long-held role as international president of WILPF, continued to argue for free trade as a prerequisite for world peace along Cobdenite lines until her death in 1935. During an NBC radio interview in 1932, for example, she was asked to elaborate on the feminist peace movement's free-trade advocacy. She argued that 'we believe [. . .] that unrestricted intercourse between nations must in the long run make for better understanding and good will [. . .] and the freedom of trade intercourse is essential to national prosperity'.[126] Around the time Addams was giving her NBC radio interview, the movement received a bolstering from the National League of Women Voters (NLWV). This added support brought Addams's envisaged new international economic order—her Pax Economica—closer to reality once the women's peace movement allied with Cordell Hull.

Thanks largely to US Georgist and suffragist Carrie Chapman Catt, the more moderate NLWV aligned itself with the free-trade principles of the international women's peace movement. In 1922, the NLWV established the Department on International Cooperation to Prevent War, based around expanding the regulatory powers of both the League of Nations and the US federal government to establish and maintain free trade as a means of fostering domestic prosperity and world peace. Throughout the interwar years, the NLWV advocated for economic integration and cooperation as a means of curbing protectionism, colonial monopolization of raw materials, and ensuing global conflict—'imperialistic mercantilism', as the NLWV's Beatrice Pitney Lamb described it. On behalf of the department, Lamb outlined how 'economic nationalism has come to be so much a part of the atmosphere we breathe that it is usually accepted by most people without challenge'. But if 'world-wide economic competition were kept free of nationalist sentiment [. . .] if it were regulated by joint international action', there was 'every reason why it should strengthen rather than disturb the peace of the world', ushering in a new world order based upon the principles of 'economic internationalism'.[127] From the early 1940s, arms limitation and cooperation through the United Nations (UN) were added to the department's pacifistic arsenal. According to Carole Stanford Bucy, the NLWV worked 'hand-in-hand with the state department' in campaigning for the UN even as the NLWV gained greater representation in the halls of Congress.[128]

WILPF and the various women's organizations stayed hard at work to stem the militarist tide through a reformation of the 1930s economic nationalist order. In 1936, their ranks swelled still further with the addition of the National Federation of Business and Professional Women's Clubs. In the pages of the federation's publication *Independent Woman*, Lucy Goldsmith and Marie Deems outlined the 'Trade Channels to Peace'. Goldsmith, a former New York City export manager, foreign trade consultant, and trade adviser to the prime minister of Spain, became the director of the World Trade League of the United States. Deems, a successful entrepreneur, in turn, could claim an impressive international background that included university studies at the Sarbonne, London, and Weisbaden, and a journalistic career with the pro–free trade *New York World*. In their *Independent Woman* article, Goldsmith and Deems highlighted how the current 'situation' in Germany owed much to the 'rising wave of economic nationalism', as well as why women should oppose the GOP's 1936 platform calling for the dismantling of Hull's trade liberalization reforms: 'The sooner women acquaint themselves with the mechanism of the world wheel of commerce the sooner can we avoid the ambushes of destructive warfare and promote the cause of peace on a solid economic basis.'[129]

The following year witnessed another flurry of feminist activism on behalf of a new world order devoid of economic warfare and economic imperialism. WILPF called for a new international organization for world peace to replace the League of Nations, and doubled down on its opposition to economic imperialism. While some WILPF members such as the British Section's Mosa Anderson expressed continued support for the civilizing mission of the mandates system so long as it was governed by the 'open door', the US Section announced its opposition to all forms of economic imperialism. It condemned 'the struggle to control foreign markets and raw materials and to maintain profits upon foreign investments' as 'the basic reason for modern conflict'. It called for an anti-lynching bill; a relaxation of immigration restrictions; the extension of the Good Neighbor policy to China, Japan, and Russia; the halting of US 'financial domination of Caribbean and Central American countries and of Liberia'; Japan to end its control of Chinese tariffs; and creation of the foundations for 'real peace' by ending economic wars 'waged through selfish and short-sighted tariffs, monetary measures and debt policies and through unchecked competition'. Its solution also sought to raise the standard of living for the world's workers alongside 'the steady and gradual elimination of all tariff barriers' via Hull's reciprocal trade agreements, and 'the creation of international export and import boards' to regulate global trade in raw goods and materials.[130]

Rosika Schwimmer and Lola Maverick Lloyd put forward a comparable proposal, published concurrently in the 1937 pamphlet *Chaos, War, or a New World Order?*, which was updated and republished in 1938 and in 1942. Schwimmer and Lloyd—a co-founder of the WPP and married to the son of the radical US single taxer and anti-monopoly muckraker Henry Demarest Lloyd—first and foremost called for a 'Federation of Nations' organized economically through a planned industrial policy to re-employ 'the millions liberated by the abandonment of the war system'; regulation of global raw materials to undermine the 'excuse' for empire; a supranational arbitration board to settle trade disputes between member states; 'international control of traffic between states'; 'regulation of world finance and to evolve a uniform monetary system'; and 'the abolition of all tariffs and customs and the establishment of free trade between all nations'.[131] Free trade regulated through supranational governance thus remained a common theme within the women's peace movement on the eve of the Second World War.

The looming spectre of world war in 1939 also led WILPF's Executive Committee to call an emergency meeting to demand a new league of nations. This new league would guarantee equal access to the world's raw materials, 'just regulation of production and distribution in the interests of the consumer', racial equality, free migration and care for refugees, disarmament, and 'the removal of trade barriers'.[132] WILPF's annual meeting in Washington, DC the following week contained an 'American Foreign Policy' symposium. Among the headliners was peace activist Clark Eichelberger, who would help draft the first charter of the United Nations in 1944–45.[133] The women's peace movement continued to support Hull's tariff revolution through the Citizens' Committee for Reciprocal World Trade (CCRWT, founded in 1948), despite congressional GOP attempts to silence them. California's Republican B. W. Gearhart unsuccessfully sought to dismiss the CCRWT's efforts in the House of Representatives, stating, 'I can't see that any useful purpose would be served by listening to spokesmen for a bunch of ladies' sewing societies reading statements prepared by the State Department.'[134] Despite such opposition, with the Second World War winding down, the long-standing left-wing feminist vision for a liberal international economic order regulated through a more potent and inclusive supranational organization was starting to become reality.

Conclusion

The economic cosmopolitan vision of feminist peace actors and organizations from the Victorian era to the Second World War was driven by the belief that universal free trade, facilitated through planned supranational governance, was crucial to obtaining a more just and peaceful world, free from want. The relationship between feminism, free trade, peace, and anti-imperialism evolved. Feminist free traders became more aware of informal economic imperialism, and more opposed to it, from the turn of the twentieth century onwards. Whereas the Victorian feminist free-trade activism of Harriet Martineau and Florence Nightingale turned a blind eye—and sometimes even a supportive wink—to its coercive implementation in places such as India, feminist free traders increasingly advocated non-coercive economic cosmopolitan reforms in order to devolve imperial systems rather than perpetuate them. By the outbreak of the Second World War, however, this free-trade endorsement would sometimes place the international feminist peace organizations at loggerheads with those anti-colonial nationalists across the Global South who instead embraced economic nationalism in order to develop domestic industries and undermine Western colonialism.

This chapter thus provides a new transnational history connecting free-trade ideas with the international feminist vision for peace from the mid-nineteenth to the mid-twentieth century. It uncovers how an earlier era of feminist peace internationalists envisaged their ideal global economic order: one of universal free trade, political equality, abolitionism, decolonization, and peace to be maintained through supranational institutions such as the League of Nations and the United Nations. But the century-long feminist fight for free trade and peace was not just a secular one. It also owed much to the pacifistic efforts of what is today the world's largest Christian feminist organization, the YWCA. As the next chapter explores, by the mid-twentieth century the YWCA numbered as one among many left-wing Christian organizations working towards a more peaceful, free trade world.

5

Free Trade, Fraternity, and Federation

THE ECONOMIC COSMOPOLITANISM
OF CHRISTIAN PACIFISM

Free trade is a Divine Law [...] according to the Divine Order of things, men should fraternize and exchange their goods and thus further Peace and Goodwill on Earth.

—RICHARD COBDEN, C. 1841[1]

National autarchy and international imperialism are alike condemned. [...] Economic nationalism, no less than political nationalism, has bedeviled the relations of nations.

—LISTON POPE, 1941[2]

THE YOUNG WOMEN'S CHRISTIAN ASSOCIATION (YWCA), which today claims to be the world's largest ecumenical feminist organization, began moving further left on foreign policy after the First World War.[3] Its US branch led the way. Upon the creation of the League of Nations in 1920, the YWCA USA's white middle- and upper-class leadership got behind progressive demands for supranational governance to help curtail the prevailing illiberal nationalist impulse. The YWCA USA next became an outright peace group in 1922 when it included within its charter a demand for the outlawing of war. Coming to an official position over the connection between war and global trade, however, proved more complicated; the organization spent over a decade studying the relationship between tariffs and international conflict. Finally, in 1936, a consensus was reached. Amid a worsening economic depression, mounting trade wars, and shrinking supply chains, the YWCA USA came out in support of free trade as a prerequisite for world peace.

The YWCA immediately began working to undermine the military-economic nationalist world order. In 1937 the organization helped launch the New York-based National Peace Conference's Campaign for World Economic Cooperation. The campaign endorsed the liberal trade reforms of Democratic secretary of state Cordell Hull, with added support from the liberal ecumenical organization the United Council of Church Women and its magazine *Church Woman*.[4] Through pamphleteering, congressional lobbying, and letter-writing campaigns, the YWCA continued to throw its nongovernmental weight behind maintaining Hull's Reciprocal Trade Agreements Act (RTAA, signed into law in 1934) and the General Agreement on Tariffs and Trade (GATT, established in 1947). In other words, owing to the illiberal geopolitical fallout from the First World War and the Great Depression, the YWCA transformed itself into an economic peace organization. Its interwar rebirth as a pacifistic pro–free trade organization was by no means the outcome of an immaculate conception. As explored in the previous chapter, the YWCA's move had already been undertaken by other feminist peace organizations. Furthermore, the YWCA's endorsement of free trade as a prerequisite to peace in the 1930s was in keeping with a century of left-wing Christian economic cosmopolitanism.

Tracing the role of left-wing Protestants and Catholics within the commercial peace movement from the mid-nineteenth to the mid-twentieth century uncovers a treasure trove of Christian contributions to international relations and economic thought.[5] It also sheds much needed economic ideological light upon Christianity's ambiguous, even contradictory, place within that century of imperial globalization.[6] Like free trade, Christianity motivated imperial as well as anti-imperial actions.[7] Also like free trade, Christianity was a cause of war as well as promising its cure.[8] This chapter seeks to help clarify this ambiguity by recovering the history of those left-wing Christian internationalists who opposed economic nationalism, imperialism, and war. They instead desired a new economic order as, they felt, God had intended it: an interdependent, peaceful, and equitable global order to be derived from free trade, fraternity, and federation.[9]

Left-wing Christian economic cosmopolitans held leadership positions within the mid-nineteenth-century transatlantic peace movement. They viewed their commercial peace work as 'a religious covenant or moral crusade', as Richard Francis Spall puts it.[10] F.S.L. Lyons has similarly pinpointed the early transatlantic marriage between evangelical pacifism and free trade to the 1830s and 1840s. According to Lyons, the struggling early nineteenth-century Christian movement needed reinforcements for its peace crusade, and, lo and behold, a powerful ally 'appeared—the Free Trade movement'.[11] In Britain, this confluence occurred amidst the fight to repeal the protectionist Corn Laws, often in concert with the more radical elements of the transatlantic antislavery movement. The two main Liberal radical leaders of the Anti–Corn Law League (ACLL, 1839–1846), John Bright—a devout Quaker and antislavery activist—and Richard Cobden—an opponent of slavery who believed that international free trade was part of God's plan—helped solidify the alliance between the older Christian peace organizations and the burgeoning mid-century economic peace movement.[12]

The left-wing evolution and diffusion of the Christian commercial peace movement was pronounced. Victorian-era leaders came to oppose slavery as well as imperialism in both its formal and informal manifestations. While the movement remained grounded within Anglo-American networks, Christian free-trade-and-peace missionaries made landfall as far afield as Japan by the early twentieth century. By the time of the First World War, they numbered among the vanguard of left-leaning internationalists who recognized what Andrew Preston describes as 'the emergence of a new global community' that promised 'peace through mutual dependence'.[13] The illiberalism of the 1930s, in turn, drove a more radical generation of Christian economic cosmopolitans—liberal radicals, socialists, and feminists—to peace and anti-imperial activism. By the time of the Second World War, left-wing Protestant and Catholic economic peace workers were fighting for free trade, fraternity, non-interventionism, decolonization, social justice, and world federation as preconditions for their Christian Pax Economica.

Christian Pacifism and Manchester Liberalism: an Arranged Marriage, 1846–1898

Our story begins one last time in mid-nineteenth-century Britain. This was an era when numerous evangelical Christians reconciled themselves to British imperial expansion so long as it brought with it the 'civilizing' missionary bounties of antislavery, religious converts, and global market interdependence. The abolitionist impulse, for example, caused some zealous missionaries to turn their attention by the 1840s to ending the African slave trade. As a result, Christian missionaries such as David Livingstone found themselves acting as informal imperial emissaries of Britain's newfound free-trade ideology; the spread of British commercial networks became conjoined with the civilizing missions of Christianity and antislavery.[14] Nor did Benthamite Unitarian peace worker John Bowring find any contradiction in proclaiming in 1841 that 'Jesus Christ is Free Trade and Free Trade is Jesus Christ' only to then coercively prise open the China market (see chapter 2).[15] Thanks to Bowring's free-trade imperial efforts, the 1842 Treaty of Nanjing promised new markets for Manchester manufacturers—and new converts to Christianity.

Many Anglo-American evangelicals may have disapproved of the violent means by which China had been opened to the West, and many may have decried the immoral traffic in opium that followed, but many also understood the spiritual profits to be gleaned from working within British imperial networks. As Brian Stanley describes it, 'Providentialist theology enabled the missionary lobby to welcome the outcome of a war fought in the cause of free trade—a war whose morality they had consistently condemned.'[16] Antislavery missionaries also implicitly supported British colonialism in India when they argued that Indian lands ought to be used for growing cotton and sugar rather than opium in order to wean Britons from their dependence on the US and Cuban slave economies.[17] Livingstone made a similar case to his British free-trade audiences with respect to developing Zambezi free-grown cotton as a replacement for US slave-grown cotton. Livingstone's free-trade imperial designs on Central Africa were thereafter replicated in India following the 1857 'mutiny'.[18] The late 1850s thus represented the high point of a British 'Christian imperialism of free trade'.[19]

As Emily Conroy-Krutz shows, many nineteenth-century US evangelical missionaries allied with their British counterparts amid their shared search for 'sacred purpose in commercial and imperial expansion'.[20] John Bowring's civilizational defence was even shared by a minority of US liberals such as the ageing statesman John Quincy Adams, who saw the First Opium War (1839–1842) as an antislavery police action.[21] The next generation of US missionaries was more critical of the illegitimate British opium traffic in China, believing that the money could have been better spent on legitimate US goods. Yet, as Ian Tyrrell highlights, by the turn of the century many such enterprising US Christian capitalist missionaries yet viewed 'free trade and moral improvement' as 'mutually reinforcing', even if this meant participating in informal imperialism in China.[22]

But what about those left-wing Christian radicals who opposed such coercive formal and informal imperial initiatives? The answer requires a closer look at the growing relationship between Richard Cobden's inner circle of non-interventionist free traders and those Protestant millenarians who supported the mid-century anti-imperial, peace, and antislavery movements.[23]

This left-wing Protestant marriage was contracted against the backdrop of the First Opium War. In 1840, Birmingham Evangelical Quaker, ACLL supporter, and antislavery activist Joseph Sturge called on all his fellow British Christians to condemn the 'wholesale carnage' wrought from the war.[24] Cobden himself decried the war in China alongside the Corn Laws, whereas free trade in its natural non-coercive form was for him 'a Divine Law: if it were not, the world would have been differently created'.[25] In 1842, he wrote privately to a friend in Lancashire, the Quaker cotton merchant and ACLL ally Henry Ashworth, that the Quaker peace movement should be conjoined with the free-trade movement because 'they are one and the same cause'.[26] The ACLL's own circular thereafter increasingly included propaganda connecting Christianity with free trade and peace:

> Free trade, like religion has doctrines of peace,
> Universal and God's vital air;
> And throned o'er doomed evil, he hails its increase,
> While his enemies only despair.[27]

Throughout the 1830s and 1840s, British abolitionist free-trade firebrand George Thompson proved particularly adept at appealing to the Christian sensibilities of his transatlantic male and female audiences and, according to Simon Morgan, 'made the greatest contribution to making the Corn Laws a moral question'.[28] Manchester liberalism also revived what Sarah Crabtree describes as the Society of Friends's deep-rooted Enlightenment-era 'cosmopolitan sensibility' as 'citizens of the world', which had been on the decline following the Napoleonic wars and the subsequent nationalist demands trending across Europe.[29]

With the likes of Sturge and Thompson as ACLL missionaries, Cobden's proposed arranged marriage between the free-trade movement and the Christian peace movement fed the era's Protestant millenarian spirit on both sides of the Atlantic. Lancashire Methodist and cotton miller David Whitehead joined the ACLL in 1842 because he believed that free trade 'would tend very much towards establishing universal peace: and hasten on the "millennium"'.[30] And Massachusetts Congregationalist minister Artemis Bullard, brother-in-law of abolitionist the Reverend Henry Ward Beecher, augured at the 1850 Frankfurt Peace Congress that the day was coming when the scriptural prophecy would be fulfilled, 'when nations should beat their swords into ploughshares, and their spears into pruning hooks'. What transformative events heralded the advent of Bullard's new Christian millennium? 'The union of nations in commerce, the intercourse in travelling and visiting, encouraged by steam navigation and railroads, were hastening the day. Distant people were brought together as we are, as brothers instead of enemies.'[31] The early Victorian marriage between free trade and Christian pacifism helped 'missionary cosmopolitanism' evolve into what Winter Werner describes as a growing belief that 'everyone, despite seemingly irreconcilable differences, would eventually end up wanting constitutional government, free trade, and Protestant Christianity'. For an increasing number of evangelicals, 'Commerce and Christianity' had become inextricable.[32]

The 1851 Great Exhibition provided another Anglo-American sanctuary for preaching the Christian peace message and for renewing vows to economic cosmopolitanism. William Forster's pronouncement that the 'Temple of Peace' heralded a new spiritual revival emanating from England to all parts of the world through modern technological advancements and free trade expressed a sentiment by then held by many of his fellow Congregationalists.[33] Unitarian minister Thomas Marshall shared Forster's enthusiasm that the Great Exhibition was 'the glorious result of Free-Trade legislation'. Marshall quoted Acts 17:26—'And hath made of one blood all nations of men for to dwell on all the face of the earth'—as evidence that trade liberalization, coupled with Protestantism, would make the world more prosperous and more peaceful.[34] Consummation of the marriage was such at the Great Exhibition that Marx wrote to Engels that Britain had been overrun by the 'cosmopolitan-philanthrophic-commercial hymns of peace'.[35]

American Unitarian Elihu Burritt illustrated how the Christian cosmopolitan belief in free trade, peace, and anti-imperialism had become an Anglo-American holy trinity by the time of the Great Exhibition.[36] Christian peace workers such as Burritt believed that the 1851 Peace Congress—convened simultaneously with the Exhibition at Exeter Hall, just two miles down the road—represented the flip side of the same cosmopolitan coin. The twin London events were signs of Burritt's brotherhood of men.[37] As Martin Ceadel portrays it, Burritt's 'universal brotherhood' was 'a Christian-humanist variant of Cobdenite liberalism' that lifted the left-wing Unitarian spirit.[38] As editor of *Advocate of Peace*, in 1846 Burritt had begun republishing correspondence from his fellow British 'friends of peace' in a new section, 'Universal Brotherhood'. Notable among these were letters from the liberal radical journalist and playwright Douglas Jerrold, who had written to Burritt from Oxford to condemn Britain's recent violent imperial aggrandizements at the expense of India and China, actions that should 'sicken [any] true Christian'. Jerrold, who would go on to christen the 1851 Great Exhibition the 'Crystal Palace' in the pages of *Punch*, also feared that war might soon break out between the United States and Britain over the Oregon boundary dispute. Yet he also held out hope that 'free trade principles' would go far in bringing about peace, and nothing less than 'the political and religious regeneration of the world'.[39] Burritt expressed similar sentiments to Manchester ACLL leaders: that the overturning of the Corn Laws represented the 'Commercial Harbinger of the Millennium'.[40]

Burritt's US Christian Cobdenite message grew stronger in the years that followed. He incorporated an unequivocal call for free trade in 1863. The 'ordained' modern-day interdependence of humankind naturally stirred 'the appetite for peace[...;] friendly commerce between different countries [...] is a condition provided and established in the very anatomy of the globe [... and] perfectly *Free Trade* is the only condition provided for in the constitution of nature'. Commerce was 'vindicating its prerogative and mission of *universality.* [...] Commerce has no country but the world, no patriotism but an earnest interest in the well-being of all the nations'.[41] Burritt has even been credited with doing more than Cobden himself to join the British free-trade movement with Christian pacifism.[42]

The Reverend Joshua Leavitt took a different approach from Burritt's brotherhood by placing greater emphasis on the connections between the antislavery movement, Christian principles, and free trade. The Massachusetts-born Congregationalist minister, founder of the antislavery Liberty Party, and editor of both the New York abolitionist periodical *The Emancipator* and the evangelical newspaper *The New York Evangelist*, sought a resolution condemning the Corn Laws at London's 1840 World Anti-Slavery Convention. Their repeal, he argued, would enable Britain to import free-grown wheat from the US north-west as an alternative to slave-grown cotton and tobacco from the south. Following one of Joseph Sturge's US visits, Leavitt discovered that Cobden's ACLL ally John Bright, and other British manufacturers, were keen to move away from their dependence on southern slave-grown cotton, reaffirming Leavitt's belief that free-grown US wheat from the west could provide greater Anglo-American prosperity and amity following repeal of the Corn Laws. In 1842, Leavitt therefore entreated the US Congress to lobby the British in favour of repeal. He brought a similar case to the 1843 London antislavery convention, before undertaking an ACLL lecture tour with Cobden and Bright. Upon returning to the United States, Leavitt founded anti-Corn Law organizations across the US north-east and west to keep up the grassroots pressure.[43]

Leavitt's efforts overlapped with the Quaker-led transatlantic Free Produce movement. This consisted of a small but dedicated group of Black and white abolitionists and peace workers who advocated for more ethical consumer practices, including the boycotting of slave-grown goods. Among its Quaker leaders was Sarah Pugh of Philadelphia, an officer of the American Free Produce Association and an aunt of the feminist free-trade socialist Florence Kelley (see chapter 4). As Julie Holcomb argues, 'the boycott was indeed a Quaker movement'. But it also transcended Quakerism. Philadelphia's Richard Allen—a former slave and founder of the first national Black church, the Bethel African Methodist Episcopal Church—viewed the boycott as a practical means to enhance the economic power of the freed Black community within the United States.[44] And as Bronwen Everill explores, the movement became even more international once it aligned itself with the 'legitimate commerce' movement, which sought to incentivize West African slave traders to shift instead to commodity production.[45]

Few Cobdenites, however, could fully accept the Free Produce movement's reliance upon the boycott. Cobden himself argued that prohibition was counterproductive and wasteful: better in the longer term to show that free labour was more efficient than slave labour. Boston's William Lloyd Garrison, 'a free trader to an illimitable extent' who would go on to become one of the first honorary (non-due paying) members of London's Cobden Club, became openly hostile to the Free Produce movement. He had grown sceptical of the efficacy of a boycott deterring slave owners, because he believed that they were driven more by the lust for power than by greed. But some transatlantic Cobdenites such as Joseph Sturge reconciled themselves to the boycott; they noted that while barring slave-produced goods might temporarily raise the price of slave-grown products, this would be offset by shifting consumer spending to free-grown products. Businesses relying upon the products of slave labour would either fail or would turn to free labour to circumvent the boycott.[46] Owing to a lack of antislavery cohesion, the Free Produce movement began petering out by the mid-1850s. But it provided an important mid-century precedent for subsequent ethical consumer movements. When coupled with the efforts of Leavitt, it also illustrated how, although they did not always agree on the means, these Christian reformers shared the same left-wing belief: that freeing men from human bondage and freeing trade were both necessary for obtaining their envisaged peaceful, democratic, and Christian world federation.

The late nineteenth-century Anglo-American economic peace movement continued to hammer home the connections between Christianity, free trade, peace, and antislavery, even after US slavery's end in 1865. The Reverend Joshua Leavitt and other US Cobdenites formed the American Free Trade League (AFTL) in New York City immediately after the US Civil War. The motto of the AFTL's news organ *The League* (named after the ACLL's circular) was a quotation from Cobden: 'Free trade: the international common law of the Almighty'. The Reverend Henry Ward Beecher, famed US abolitionist and another of the country's first honorary members of the Cobden Club, went on tours on behalf of the AFTL to lecture on how protectionism was anti-Christian. 'I reject the doctrine of "Protection", as opposed not only to the principles of liberty but to the essential principles of Christianity,' he thundered before his sympathetic audience, the New York Free Trade Club, one evening in November 1883. 'The fundamental doctrine of Christianity is that all men are brethren. The fundamental doctrine of protectionism is that all men are *not* brethren.'[47] British Quaker, abolitionist, and ACLL leader John Bright had long connected Christian principles with the Manchester School, and worked to spread the free-trade gospel to the United States in the early 1880s.[48] By then in his seventies, he was made an honorary member of the Boston Free Trade Club at this time, and penned the introduction to the 1884 republication of M. M. Trumbull's popular *The American Lesson of the Free Trade Struggle in England*, prophesying for America that much as 'the shackles have been struck from the limbs of the slave', so 'they cannot remain to fetter the freedom of your industries'.[49] The Christian commercial peace work of Leavitt, Beecher, and Bright helped infuse the postbellum US free-trade movement with the rhetoric of antislavery.[50]

Quaker Irish nationalists also played their part. Dublin printer R. D. Webb drew upon his Quaker heritage to explain his antislavery and anti-colonial views. He and his Quaker family had been intimately involved with the mid-nineteenth-century Irish, British, and US abolitionist movements, as well as the anti–Corn Law movement through Daniel O'Connell, Harriet Martineau, and John Bright. Webb and his fellow Dublin Garrisonian abolitionists also supported women's suffrage and opposed the East India Company's monopolization of trade in China and in India, as well as the opium traffic that bound the two together. The Dublin abolitionists instead advocated non-coercive free trade. Their efforts in the 1840s led to the creation of the Dublin British India Committee and the Hibernian Peace Society. R. D. Webb himself also coordinated US Black abolitionist Frederick Douglass's 1845 Irish lecture tour. Webb's son Alfred became a prominent Irish Home Rule advocate in the British Parliament, and a close friend and parliamentary ally of Indian nationalist leader Dadabhai Naoroji (see chapter 2). Alfred Webb was quite explicit in connecting his cosmopolitan Quaker upbringing with his late-Victorian support for Irish and Indian self-rule. The connection was such that he would serve as president of the Indian National Congress in 1894.[51]

By the late 1880s and early 1890s the economic peace movement controversially began extending its reach in the United States and Ireland to those of the Catholic faith, thanks to the pacifistic disciples of the US political philosopher Henry George. Georgism thus proved instrumental in drawing Irish-American Catholic peace workers into the wider commercial peace network. Leading left-wing Catholic peace workers in the United States became drawn to George's turn-of-the-century single tax movement, which advocated for a tax on the estimated value of land to provide a government's entire revenue, negating the need for tariffs (see chapter 2). George's outspoken support for Irish land reform and home rule earned him a devoted following among radical Irish Catholic nationalists in Chicago and New York City, propelling him to run as New York's labour/single tax mayoral candidate in 1886.[52] Chicago's prominent Catholic lawyer, women's suffragist, and civil rights activist Edward Osgood Brown was one such Georgist disciple, and moved in the same anti-imperial and anti-war circles as fellow Chicagoans Clarence Darrow, Henry Demarest Lloyd, Jenkin Lloyd Jones, and Jane Addams. Brown would later become an outspoken supporter of Philippine independence, the League of Nations, and the outlawing of war as an officer of both the AFTL and the AIL. But Brown's Georgist credentials at first landed him in hot holy water with Pope Leo XIII in the early 1890s. A far worse fate befell his radical Irish nationalist friend, New York's Father Edward McGlynn. McGlynn was excommunicated for his Georgist beliefs, and then ordered to travel to Rome to explain his adherence to this brand of economic liberalism, social justice, and peace.[53]

Pope Leo XIII's *Rerum novarum*—published in 1891 as a blueprint for Catholic social thought and as a moralistic critique of capitalism's social inequalities—seemingly left little room for the single tax. However, George himself penned a hundred-page open letter to Leo to make the case that the two positions were compatible: that the principle of the single tax was 'a conforming of human regulations to the will of God', whereas protectionism 'sanctifies national hatreds' and 'inculcates a universal war of hostile tariffs' and was thus 'opposed to Christianity'.[54] George's letter appears to have mollified Leo. Papal policy from 1892 was more amenable to the single tax movement, and the papal delegate in Washington, Archbishop Francesco Satolli, duly lifted the excommunication on McGlynn.

Catholic co-operativism in Ireland provided another left-wing path for some Irish Catholic reformers to toe the line between capitalist individualism and socialist collectivism. Co-operativism's consumer-oriented non-profit approach to free trade (see chapter 3) worked particularly well when coupled with Irish land reform, usually situated somewhere between Henry George's single tax proposals and the socialist land nationalization policies of the Land League (founded in 1879). Irish Catholic support for these Marx-Manchester economic reforms was tied in part to a desire to develop the British colony's agricultural technologies and to democratize the Irish economy. It was also meant to establish social, economic, and industrial peace in the British colony, which was increasingly riven by nationalist demands for Home Rule.[55] During the First World War, however, the nascent Irish Catholic co-operative movement became subsumed within the Listian anti-colonial nationalist project of Arthur Griffith's Sinn Féin (see chapter 1).[56]

Griffith was far from the only Christian reformer to embrace economic nationalism by the turn of the century, foreshadowing the mounting tensions between Christian cosmopolitanism and Christian nationalism on both sides of the Atlantic. Some Christian nationalist realists took to the strong state activism of the German-American System of protectionism (see chapter 1). In the United States, for example, the Massachusetts-born Presbyterian Reverend Calvin Colton, an influential Whig anti-abolitionist, wrote a series of pamphlets between 1843 and 1844 in support of Henry Clay's presidential run and Clay's American System. Colton followed this up in 1846 with *The Rights of Labor*, a stirring defence of high tariffs and their compatibility with slavery, as well as a scathing indictment of the repeal of the Corn Laws as a smokescreen for British free-trade imperialism.[57] Dorothy Ross has instead emphasized the influence of the GHS upon US Christian Socialist nationalist supporters of a more activist and protectionist state from the late 1870s.[58] In February 1884, Iowa's Republican congressman John A. Kasson, in turn, took aim at Richard Cobden's connection of free trade and Christianity in a speech before the Brooklyn Revenue Reform Club entitled 'Free Trade Not the International Law of the Almighty'.[59] Kasson would go on to become one of the leading architects of the Republican Party's expansionist economic programme of

'Protection and Reciprocity' from 1890, and would oversee a series of bilateral trade agreements under subsequent Republican imperial administrations.[60] At the turn of the century, the protectionist news organ *The American Economist* yet made a forceful case that 'it is the Christian example which Protection has taught to foreign nations of their duty to their own people [. . . :] "God helps those who help themselves."'[61]

Christian nationalism proved even stronger in early twentieth-century Germany. Most German evangelical church leaders got caught up in the nationalist euphoria of the First World War and the existential atheistic threat posed by the 1917 October Revolution. The influential Catholic Zentrum Party (founded in 1870), for example, had already become supportive of high tariffs as a show of solidarity with German conservative nationalists, alienating left-leaning Protestant and Catholic workers involved with Christian unions.[62] This nationalism and conservatism was exacerbated at the war's end, leading to what John Conway describes as 'a retreat to the bastion of national conservative values' now that the atheistic Soviets stood at Germany's doorstep. This trend only continued under the Nazi Party's 'dynamic rise of nationalist and racist extremism' and its persecution of pacifism alongside Judaism and Marxism. As a result, Germany's left-wing Christian internationalists never had much room to manoeuvre on behalf of anti-militarism, trade liberalization, or world peace.[63] The German example also highlights why, from the Christian cosmopolitan perspective, nationalism—whether political, religious, racial, or economic—often bore the brunt of the blame for perpetuating imperialism and war at the turn of the century.

The New Christian Radicals: Henry Georgism, Norman Angellism, Socialist Internationalism, and Christian Anti-imperialism, 1898–1934

The nationalism, militarism, and colonialism in the years surrounding the 1898 US war with Spain and the First World War renewed the left-wing Christian cosmopolitan's anti-imperialist creed. The spread of Henry George's single tax movement played its part here. Russian peace worker Leo Tolstoy went so far as to describe George's single tax theory as 'the culmination of Christianity— the City of God on earth [. . .,] the reign of the Prince of Peace,' and numerous Christian socialists in Britain subscribed to the single tax.[64] So, too, did the pacifistic popularity of Norman Angell's *The Great Illusion* (1910), known at the time as 'Norman Angellism', help draw more Christians into the commercial peace fold in Britain, the United States, and Japan owing to its apolitical argument that war was futile for all involved owing to the era's unprecedented economic interdependence. The Marx-Manchester socialist internationalist free-trade tradition also left its imprint via the co-operative movement. The illiberal 'isms' that grew in the wake of the First World War and the Great Depression—fascism, Nazism, colonialism, protectionism—only strengthened the Christian cosmopolitan resolve that economic interdependence and international fraternity must underpin a peaceful world order.

The US war with Spain in 1898 and the acquisition of a US colonial empire in the Caribbean and Pacific spurred Christian commercial peace workers in the United States into anti-imperial action. Under the left-wing editorship of Unitarian clergyman Jenkin Lloyd Jones, the Chicago-based weekly *Unity* became ever more outspoken against imperialism, war, and the economic nationalist policies that produced them. Jones had spent much of his adult life working on behalf of abolitionism, women's suffrage, temperance, labour rights, and democracy. Upon the war's outbreak in 1898, he also became dedicated to international peace. He went about joining as many peace organizations as he could find. Unsated, he started forming his own, co-founding the Church Peace Union (CPU), the National Arbitration and Peace Congress, and the Chicago Peace Society.[65] During the First World War, he next joined the People's Council of America for Democracy and Peace. This single-tax-dominated anti-war organization, headed by the likes of Daniel Kiefer and Mary Ware Dennett, also invited socialist internationalists into its ranks, including Emily Balch, Crystal Eastman, Scott Nearing, and Norman Thomas.[66]

Even as Lloyd Jones was radicalizing the pacifistic pages of *Unity*, Benjamin Trueblood, a Quaker and long-time spokesman for the American Peace Society and editor of its journal *Advocate of Peace*, connected Christian principles with a united world at peace in *The Federation of the World* (1899). The volume consisted of two lectures that Trueblood had recently given at Medville Theological School in Pennsylvania. 'Christian Society', he argued, had 'created a new sense of human worth [...,] undermined tyranny and slavery [...,] developed democracy [..., and] the world-wide commercial interchanges of our day', which required 'brotherly cooperation.' A 'new world race', world federation, one universal language, and economic interdependence would make colonialism obsolete and 'war impossible.'[67]

Episcopal economic peace workers also kept a close critical eye on how the Republican imperial government in Washington would treat its newly acquired colonies. As a result, the early GOP decision to levy tariffs on goods going into and out of the Philippines gave US and Filipino free-trade critics of Republican closed-door imperialism another ally: the Episcopal Church's Charles H. Brent. This progressive Canadian-born Episcopalian bishop of the Philippine Islands and early advocate of ecumenism attacked the so-called 'splits' tax, which placed a one hundred per cent surtax on cheap, low-quality textiles from Britain. Enacted following the lobbying efforts of the US cotton textile industry, its purpose was to encourage Filipino consumption of US-made textiles. But it resulted in pushing already poor Filipinos further into poverty by forcing them to purchase the more expensive US cotton fabrics. The Anti-Imperialist League (AIL) and many US Episcopal bishops seconded Brent's moralistic free-trade call. By contrast, the protectionist publication of the US cotton textile industry, *Textile World Record*, imperialistically defended the tax by deeming it 'a trifling detail' that helped alleviate the burdensome US guardianship over those 'brown men in the Philippines' unable to govern themselves.[68]

Following the publication of English journalist Norman Angell's Cobdenite-inspired *The Great Illusion* in 1910 (see chapter 2), many leaders within the Christian peace movement became drawn to the pragmatic apolitical allures of Norman Angellism. In Britain, the Quaker peace worker J. W. Graham got involved with the Liberal Party and the Manchester Norman Angell League. At a 1913 Quaker peace conference he urged the Society of Friends to join forces with Norman Angell's disciples, the leaders of the 'new pacifism'.[69] So, too, did the Quaker theologian William E. Wilson, who argued in 1914 that Christian pacifism and Norman Angellism were compatible.[70] That same year, *The Great Illusion* also informed Presbyterian minister Richard Roberts's vision for founding the Fellowship of Reconciliation (FOR) in Cambridge: a transatlantic connection that he brought with him to his subsequent ministry positions in New York City (1917), Montreal (1922), and Toronto (1927).[71] Bethlehem, Pennsylvania's John Sayre drew upon similar Angellite inspiration when he helped establish the American FOR in 1915 and its news organ, *The World Tomorrow: A Journal Looking Toward a Christian World*, in 1918.[72] Angell gained another key left-wing Christian disciple in Ohio-born George Nasmyth, who would become a prominent religious leader within the commercial peace movement until his untimely death in 1920. And *The Great Illusion*'s arguments were again resurrected during the Second World War even in the most provincial of Australian settings; as late as March 1943, at the Conference House of Berwick, Victoria, a small town near Melbourne, the Anglican Bible

Class Union held a conference on non-violence with Norman Angellism the topic of discussion.[73]

Early twentieth-century Japanese pacifists working within YMCA transimperial networks borrowed liberally from a combination of Christian socialism, Georgism, and Norman Angellism. Christian pacifist Abe Isoo, for example, believed that salvation rested in reconciling left-wing economics with Christianity. He drew upon Christian socialism and the ideas of Japanese Protestant pacifist Niijima Jo, Henry George, and Norman Angell for inspiration. Abe's studies at Hartford Theological Seminary in Connecticut in the early 1890s had also led to his intellectual discovery of Edward Bellamy and Leo Tolstoy. While editor of *Rikugo Zasshi* (Cosmos), the journal of the Tokyo Unitarian Association and the Young Men's Christian Association (YMCA) in Japan, Abe opposed the Russo–Japanese War (1904–1905). In 1912, he published his Japanese translation of Angell's *The Great Illusion*. Abe continued to oppose Japanese militarism throughout the interwar years as a leader of Shakai Minshuto (the Socialist People's Party), prompting a right-wing extremist attempt to assassinate him in 1938.[74]

By the end of the First World War, US followers of the 'social gospel' were 'in the midst of taking a sharp leftward turn', as Andrew Preston puts it. Christian economic cosmopolitans were also working alongside their more secular counterparts, such as the Woman's Peace Party and the World Peace Foundation (WPF).[75] The movement's interwar expansion owed much to the efforts of Toyohiko Kagawa, Kirby Page, Sherwood Eddy, Norman Thomas, Parker Moon, Reinhold Niebuhr, and John Herman Randall, as well as organizations like the Federal Council of Churches (FCC, founded in 1908), the YMCA, the FOR, the World Alliance for Promoting International Friendship through the Churches (the Alliance), the World Council of Churches (WCC), and the Catholic Association for International Peace (CAIP). And much like their interwar secular economic peace allies, they shifted further left in response to the economic nationalist disorder of the 1930s. The growing popularity of economic autarky, authoritarianism, and nationalism drove more and more Christian pacifists under the big tent of economic cosmopolitanism owing to its left-wing promise of peace, prosperity, fraternity, and social justice. Tariff walls were even likened to the walls of Jericho, requiring divine intervention to bring them down (Fig. 5.1).

Following the Great War, Japan's Toyohiko Kagawa found himself drawn to the pacifism of Leo Tolstoy, universal suffrage, the FCC, and the international co-operative movement. After Presbyterian missionaries converted the

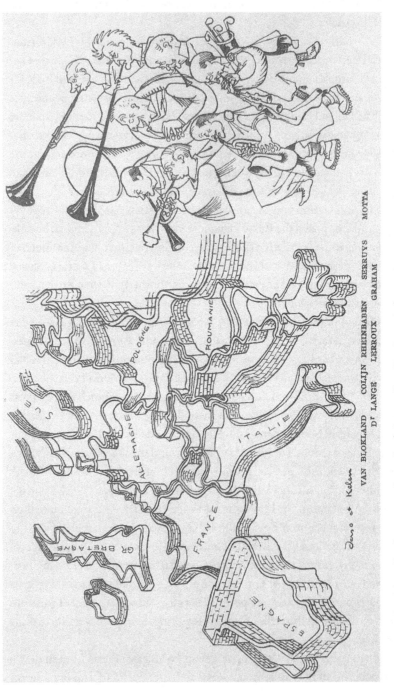

FIGURE 5.1. *Les Murailles douanières de Jéricho* (The tariff walls of Jericho), in Alois Derso and Emery Kelen, *Le Testament de Genève* (Paris: G. Lang, 1931), 30.

teenage Kagawa to Christianity, he got his start as a street preacher before studying at Princeton between 1914 and 1917. Upon his return to Japan, he became more involved with the international peace and co-operative movements. He helped create and lead the National Anti-War League of Japan in 1928. He also preached to welcoming US mainline Protestant audiences in 1936 about how 'the causes of war are largely economic', and all could be cured through the 'co-operative ideal'. The FCC, an interdenominational ecumenical organization that backed Roosevelt's New Deal, sponsored Kagawa's six-month lecture tour of a hundred and fifty US cities to preach the pacifistic free-trade ideas of the international co-operative movement. Kagawa's anti-war activism also led to his arrest in Japan in 1940. Undeterred, this Japanese representative of the Marx-Manchester tradition next co-founded the International Peace Society in Tokyo in 1945, after which he threw himself into the World Federation movement.[76]

In 1920s New York City, as Michael Thompson illustrates, liberal Protestantism was becoming more closely aligned with left-wing radical anti-imperialism thanks in no small part to Kirby Page and Sherwood Eddy.[77] Like many of the nation's liberal Protestants, the FCC, the CPU, and YMCA leadership, including Page and Eddy, had become caught up in the patriotic fervour of the First World War. They now sought to do penance. Democratic president Woodrow Wilson, an avowed disciple of Manchester liberalism and son of the famous Presbyterian theologian Joseph Ruggles Wilson Sr., in turn breathed new life into their progressive millenarian mission of creating a peaceful and interdependent world order in the wake of his Fourteen Points speech in 1918.[78] Page, working alongside Eddy, was instrumental in connecting liberal organizations such as the YMCA and the FCC with the Quakers' more radical American FOR and the Socialist Party of America (SPA). From YMCA headquarters in New York City, Page and Eddy oversaw mass pamphleteering campaigns on behalf of Russian recognition and Filipino independence. In *The Abolition of War* (1924), Page laid the lion's share of the blame for colonialism and war upon the 'economic imperialism' of the 'industrially advanced nations [...] securing control of the raw materials [...] and markets in backward nations' since the 1870s. He criticized economic blockades for being 'as deadly as war' and harmful to neutrals as well as belligerents. He also noted with approval that the League of Nations was moving away from the economic boycott as a 'means of enforcing its decisions'.[79]

In *Imperialism and Nationalism* (1925), Page showed that he well understood imperialism's formal political and informal economic manifestations.

The industrializing powers were ratcheting up their economic nationalist policies and their imperial search for raw materials and new outlets for surplus capital. Turkey's economic woes, for example, had only been 'aggravated and intensified by extreme nationalism' by way of 'drastic tariff regulations' and 'heavy taxation'. He also took 'dollar diplomacy' in Latin America—a US policy of providing loans with coercive strings attached—to task. In the case of El Salvador, he criticized a US loan of $6 million because it was to be repaid principally from customs duties, making El Salvador's tariffs a permanent fixture. Drawing directly upon British 'New Liberal' J. A. Hobson's *Imperialism: A Study* (1902), Page concluded that 'international commerce and international finance [. . .] desperately need regulation' at the international level, and that 'the whole question of the distribution of the raw materials of the earth deserves serious and immediate attention [. . .] as does also the extraordinarily vital question of tariffs'. 'The old theory of the absolute sovereignty of the nation needs to be abandoned', he continued, to establish 'permanent peace and justice throughout the earth'.[80] The following year, Page once again referenced Hobson alongside the New Testament to lay out his vision for a 'Christian Economic Order' centred upon social justice, industrial democracy, equality for women, and universal brotherhood. Page had also recently created the Fellowship for a Christian Social Order, which tarred racism, autocracy, and 'monopoly of natural resources for private gain' as 'unchristian'.[81]

Page had big shoes to fill at the *World Tomorrow* in 1926, when he succeeded Christian socialist Norman Thomas as editor of the radical Protestant journal. On Thomas's editorial watch, the FOR-funded monthly news organ had already taken a clearly left-wing Christian stance in support of a wide array of issues, including women's suffrage and anti-lynching. The popularity of Jamaican-born Marcus Garvey's Universal Negro Improvement Association and Black Star Steamship Line in the early 1920s had been deemed 'profoundly significant of the growing discontent of the Negro against the arrogant overlordship of the white man'.[82] Thomas had even thumbed his editorial nose at US censors at a time of growing anti-communist crackdowns when, although denouncing its violent implementation, he gave the Bolshevik Revolution his cautious endorsement.[83]

Under Thomas's and then Page's editorship, the *World Tomorrow* also continued to give its pacifistic backing to economic cosmopolitanism. As the Great War wound down, the *World Tomorrow*'s support for free trade and anti-imperialism was extended to Woodrow Wilson's Fourteen Points and a League of Nations. Norman Angell worked closely with Thomas, and the *Nation's*

Cobdenite editor Oswald Garrison Villard (son of Fanny Garrison Villard) also served on the *World Tomorrow*'s editorial board.[84] Belgian peace activist Henri Lambert splashed his endorsement for free trade and the League of Nations across its pages, a position that was echoed by the CPU, the FCC, and New York's newly formed National Committee on the Churches and the Moral Aims of the War.[85] The journal's adverts contained many from the Co-operative League of America and the International Free Trade League (IFTL), including plugs for Lambert's 'book of the hour', *Pax Economica* (1918).[86] US feminist economic peace advocates Jane Addams and Florence Kelley acted as judges for the *World Tomorrow*'s essay prize on 'The League of Nations: Its Practicability and Its Need'. German abolitionist, women's suffragist, and peace worker Lida Gustava Heymann called for free trade between France and Germany as a first step towards 'a Pan Europe'.[87] And German Communist Youth Movement member Kurt Klaeber echoed Heymann's call for the dismantling of tariff walls.[88]

As some of these examples suggest, the League loomed large in the *World Tomorrow*'s interwar internationalist imaginings about ending imperialism, war, and hunger through free trade, fraternity, and federation. The editorial board, speaking on behalf of the FOR to the journal's five thousand subscribers in January 1919, weighed in with a special issue focused on the universalism of Christianity and the paramountcy of ending imperialism and war through the League. If a League of Nations was to 'express the faith of Jesus', it needed to act democratically as international arbiter; it ought not to 'interfere with internal developments in any country', and 'especially must it acknowledge the right of all nations to self-determination, and insure for all economic fairplay and freedom from discriminating tariffs'.[89] The editors saw new 'opportunities to save hundreds of thousands of lives from starvation in countries hitherto closed to aid by the war. [. . .] Out of this international cooperation in feeding the hungry, as Miss Jane Addams has suggested, may grow a real federation of peoples'.[90] IFTL officer and socialist internationalist Scott Nearing was more sceptical, deriding the League Constitution for ignoring 'economic factors entirely'. As a result of this omission, he predicted, 'commercial and financial rivalries will breed wars in the future as they have in the past'. With more optimism, Episcopal bishop, socialist, and pacifist Paul Jones believed that the way was clear for the League to develop 'along the lines of a real Christian world brotherhood' that included 'a program of complete free trade'.[91]

The twin issues of freeing world commerce and European federation remained high on the *World Tomorrow*'s peace agenda. In the October 1920 issue, disciples of Henry George deplored the class warfare and anti-democratic tendencies of the US protectionist system.[92] John Maynard Keynes's call for 'a free trade union of the European states' was 'perfectly adapted for the potion of peace and good will. [...] Self-determination of peoples must carry with it the removal of economic barriers if it is to be a blessing.'[93] Another threat to peace was 'exclusive nationalism with its tariffs and strategic frontiers', whereas 'true internationalism' was 'opposed to imperialism, political and economic'.[94] Christian spirituality was proclaimed a natural ally of the international co-operative movement.[95] Republican congressman Joseph Fordney's proposed raising of US tariff rates in 1921 was 'positively scandalous', a boon to 'big business. [...] The worker is almost always worse off under a system of tariffs.'[96] The Republican protectionist plan to 'lace a tax on food' while 'most of the world can't produce enough to keep from starving' only exacerbated the crisis.[97]

The World Tomorrow's transatlantic Marx-Manchester connections—a blending of socialist internationalism with liberal radicalism—were often explicit. Unitarian public school teacher Jessie Wallace Hughan—women's suffragist, Georgist, secretary of the War Resisters League, and the 1920 Socialist candidate for lieutenant-governor of New York City—took to the pages of the World Tomorrow in 1920 to give her endorsement to Eugene V. Debs as US president. At the same time she expressed her 'admiration' of the British Labour Party for aiding 'in the development of British democracy, along with Magna Carta, the Bill of Rights, and the Cobden Club'.[98] J. A. Hobson, now affiliated with the Labour Party and democratic socialism, provided a stirring defence of free trade and free speech in a 1922 article.[99] As the British Congregational clergyman the Reverend Albert D. Belden summed it up, 'Christian internationalism' needed to join hands with socialist internationalism to remake 'a largely unsocialized civilization riven by competitive industry and divided by tariff walls', both to save democracy and to cure 'the poison of imperialism'.[100]

The World Tomorrow showed off its radical anti-imperial credentials against the British, Japanese, and US empires. Amid the editors' condemnation of the British 1919 Amritsar massacre, and support for self-government for India, they took time out to note with approval 'the remarkable development of the co-operative movement'.[101] Norman Thomas himself advocated for Irish independence in his article 'England, Ireland and America', a clear homage to Richard Cobden's 1835 pamphlet of the same title. Thomas followed this up with strident demands to be 'done with all imperialisms which by their ruthless coercion make impossible the real unity of free peoples. [...] It is this essential unity of the human race which warrants American interest in Ireland, India, Armenia, and all the rest. By the same token our treatment of the Negroes is emphatically of concern.'[102] Gandhi's non-violent fight for democracy in India also received Thomas's unreserved seal of approval, and he opened the journal's pages to Gandhi's anti-colonial sentiments.[103]

The Meiji Empire also came in for censure. An anonymous Japanese source for the *World Tomorrow* reported on how Japan's 'whole autocracy is inextricably bound up with great masses of capital, exploitation at home and abroad, and a subsidized foreign trade that makes millionaires, but sucks the lifeblood of the nation through its high prices at home'. And yet, the author observed, it was not Japan's imperial ambitions, but US racism, that motivated the newest round of anti-Japanese laws.[104] Prominent commercial peace worker and Stanford University president David Starr Jordan sought to dampen US anti-Japanese sentiment and immigration restrictions, while conceding 'that some Japanese, educated in Germany, have adopted Prussian ideals and have hoped to work them out by the use of the army'.[105]

United States imperialism received most of the *World Tomorrow*'s opprobrium. The journal found the USA guilty of having established 'a colonial empire in the Caribbean regions' of Nicaragua, Guatemala, Honduras, Costa Rica, Santo Domingo, and Haiti. US colonial rule was replete with civil rights violations, autocratic governance, and allegations of torture. 'The Navy Department is ruling three republics without their consent primarily in the interests of their American creditors.' Was there really no other 'way of helping to educate "backward" people without subjecting them to flagrant economic and political imperialism'?[106] A foreign policy of non-interventionism was instead advocated to counteract financial imperial interests in the Caribbean, China, Soviet Russia, and Mexico.[107] From 1926, under Page's editorship the *World Tomorrow* took even sharper aim at US nationalism, imperialism, and militarism for contravening Jesus's teachings.

Page soon obtained editorial assistance from Reinhold Niebuhr, who yet had an important ecumenical part to play within the interwar economic peace movement. Niebuhr was made associate editor of the *World Tomorrow* in 1928, soon after his relocation to New York City, his teaching appointment at Union Theological Seminary, and his joining the FOR. Then came the stock market crash of October 1929, driving Niebuhr further to the Christian socialist left. The crash also nudged him closer to the SPA's commercial peace champion Norman Thomas, who stayed on at the *World Tomorrow* as a member of its editorial board.[108]

Understanding the evolution of the Marx-Manchester tradition aids in understanding how and why Niebuhr continued his attack on the militant and nationalist interwar economic order.[109] He castigated the US high-tariff system throughout the 1930s for contributing to the era's trade wars, militarism, and nationalism.[110] With Sherwood Eddy, he co-organized the Delta Cooperative Farm and helped with unionization efforts in Mississippi. As the 1930s ended and the horrors of Nazism and Soviet totalitarianism became better known, however, Niebuhr moved away from pacifism and Marxism and towards liberal realism. His backing for military interventionism during the Second World War and the Cold War severed any remaining ties to the Christian peace movement and Norman Thomas's SPA—but he maintained his Christian realist support for economic justice, civil rights, democratic socialism, and freer markets.[111]

As Toyohiko Kagawa's activism suggests, the left-wing Christian peace movement's broader engagement with the international co-operative movement provided another Marx-Manchester connection. Christian Socialists began working with the co-operative movement as early as the 1850s. This occurred shortly after the co-operative enterprise was initiated in the town of Rochdale as a socialist internationalist alternative to the Manchester School's 'cult of *laissez faire*'.[112] The Christian co-operative movement made continental European inroads by the 1890s.[113] By around 1950, radical working-class missionaries within the Anglican Church had even began paternalistically implementing co-operative principles in Papua New Guinea and among Australia's Aborigines and Torres Strait Islander communities.[114]

In the years surrounding the First World War, the ecumenical World Alliance for Promoting International Friendship through the Churches (the Alliance) also outlined its Christian economic cosmopolitan vision for a new anti-imperial world order from its headquarters in New York. At its most popular, the Alliance had national councils in as many as thirty countries, its US and British councils being the most active. Its leaders kept in touch with secular organizations such as Boston's WPF; Edwin Mead in fact had a hand in the creation of both the WPF and the Alliance.[115] The Alliance vowed that cooperation would replace competition. Christian internationalism would supersede 'selfish nationalism' through 'the familyhood of nations, the limitation of sovereignty', and equal access to global resources.[116] The past half-century had shown that the 'spirit of selfishness' was everywhere on display: from the colonial partition of Africa and its 'heartless disregard of the interests of native populations', to US 'dealings with American Indians', to British exploitation of

Peruvian rubber resources, to the two Opium Wars. International cooperation, the Alliance argued, entailed not only world governance but also 'control of world economic conditions'; economic war would become 'needless' if 'all tariff walls [were] taken down'.[117]

Free trade, social justice, and world federation remained foundational to the Alliance's interwar peace work. Around the time that Norman Thomas's *World Tomorrow* was beginning to throw its support behind women's suffrage, women leaders were also being welcomed into the Alliance's American Council.[118] In 1920, the Alliance's International Committee picked Ohio's George Nasmyth to be its 'world organizer'. He was chosen owing to his dedication to world federation and his vast European network cultivated through his earlier involvement with Norman Angellism, the Cosmopolitan Clubs, and the International Student Movement—an impressive peace career cut tragically short by a deadly typhus infection in September 1920.[119] Sidney Gulick, as secretary of both the Alliance and the FCC's Commission on International Justice and Goodwill, then helped to carry on Nasmyth's work. Gulick, too, emphasized free trade, racial equality, international arbitration, and supranational organization.[120]

The Great Depression, and the subsequent worldwide ratcheting up of political and economic nationalism, worried the Alliance. In 1932, it organized the International Goodwill Congress in New York City around the theme 'World Understanding and Economic Justice'. The Great War itself took the brunt of the blame for the economic depression, exacerbated by worldwide land speculation, 'the rise of ultra-nationalism', and 'excessive tariffs'. The following year's League-sponsored World Economic Conference raised the hope that international cooperation might yet replace the rampant growth of militarism, trade wars, and imperialism.[121] A year later, the Alliance elaborated on its critique of political and economic nationalism. Intolerance and 'racial pride' had degenerated 'into extreme nationalism', which had manifested itself universally out of a frantic attempt of governments 'to save themselves'. But what disasters would this 'obsession' lead to? 'Extreme economic nationalism is more than a barrier to the exchange of goods, the maintenance of financial stability, and the free intercourse of men. It is an incitement to imperialism, conquest and war. It is itself a subtle and insidious form of war'. The report of the Alliance's Recommendations Committee—which included Presbyterian Jane Addams and Catholic commercial peace worker and Columbia University political scientist Parker Moon—concluded with a ray of hope. It called for the renewal of its 'faith in the possibility of wider and more effective international cooperation.'[122] But hope gave way again to despair in the 1934 report, focused on the theme 'International Cooperation vs. Isolation'. The committee reminded its members that 'the world is one' and that 'the task of promoting international friendship is essentially a religious task'. And the onus also fell upon the United States to work through the League because 'peace can be assured' only 'through adequate world organization'. It also reiterated its opposition to the economic manifestations of 'extreme nationalism'.[123]

The Chicago ecumenical *Christian Century* became another outlet for the economic peace movement following the Great War. Under the ownership of mainline Protestant Disciples of Christ minister and Christian socialist Charles Clayton Morrison, the periodical condemned Japanese imperial designs upon China in 1919, and encouraged instead 'a reciprocal free-trade policy' that would allow for 'equitable and friendly interchange of commodities' and democracy.[124] A couple years later it declared that if the church was 'faithful to its Christian mission', the question of tariffs would be decided by 'what is best for the one family of mankind', and that 'immigration shall be unrestricted'.[125] In a July 1923 issue, Kirby Page could at once recognize that 'the economic life of Europe is being strangled by tariff barriers and custom walls' and exacerbating geopolitical tensions, while at the same time carving out an exception for the anti-imperialism of economic nationalism (see chapter 1); Gandhi and the Swadeshi movement in India had 'revealed the enormous power of boycott and non-cooperation. [. . .] This policy could be used with great power against an aggressive nation.'[126]

New York City Baptist clergyman John Herman Randall joined the interwar Christian commercial peace movement in the late 1920s as editor of the Unitarian magazine *World Unity* (1927–1935). The magazine's debut followed a series of World Unity Conferences held in 1926 across the north-eastern United States, Montreal, and Toronto. In terms of its commercial peace message, Randall's magazine proselytized from beginning to end. Its issues were replete with such luminaries as Lucia Ames Mead, Edwin Mead, Norman Angell, Jane Addams, Fannie Fern Andrews, David Starr Jordan, and Parker Moon. As laid out by Randall in its inaugural 1927 issues, *World Unity* levelled its strongest criticisms against nationalism, class conflict, and economic imperialism. The anti-colonial movements in Turkey, Egypt, India, Persia, Afghanistan, the Philippines, Latin America, and China all demonstrated that the era of the Western imperial search for 'markets and raw materials' was 'breaking down before our very eyes, and gradually giving way to a new spirit that recognizes the equality of all peoples and seeks to create unity and understanding between them rather than disunity and strife.'[127] The railway, telegraph, telephone, and radio 'have made of this world a tiny whispering gallery. Space has been annihilated. [...] When aerial travel is once practically established—and it will be at no distant date—what then will become of national boundaries, of custom tolls, of tariffs, and even of the distinctions of languages?' New York was now 'a suburb of China. [...] We are all living today in one community.' Drawing on Norman Angell's work, Randall also noted that the world was 'fast becoming an economic unit [...]. We have all become mutually dependent and interdependent one upon the other.'[128] The magazine halted publication in 1935, at which point the people behind it created the World Federation Committee to continue *World Unity*'s fight for a more interdependent, democratic, peaceful, anti-racist, and just global community.

Interwar Catholic peace workers also moved further to the free-trade left. Washington, DC's CAIP, founded in 1927, aligned itself with the wider economic peace movement following the onset of the Great Depression. In 1930 the CAIP's Reverend Parker T. Moon highlighted how war resulted from 'the failure of mankind to obey the laws of God'. Moon emphasized a series of political and economic causes of modern war. First was the very nature of 'contemporary imperialism': the industrial powers' scramble for markets invariably created geopolitical enmity, as exemplified by the Boer War (1899–1902) and the Russo–Japanese War (1904–1905), as well as violent responses from the colonized themselves. Second, in the previous century, 'immoderate territorial nationalism' led 'German-speaking people' into three wars and the United States into a war with Mexico. Third were the 'economic causes of enmity'. In Cobdenite fashion, topping Moon's list here were war loans, 'monopolistic controls of raw materials', 'pleas for a policy of national self-sufficiency', immigration restrictions, and 'tariffs and trade barriers'. These last, Moon explained, had led to a series of international trade wars such as the Franco–Italian tariff war of 1888–1899, the Russo–German tariff war of 1893, and the German–Spanish tariff war of 1894. These trade wars culminated in the nationalist-inspired conflict between Austria-Hungary and Serbia; the Great War, Moon contended, 'was in part caused, or at least aggravated, by Austro-Hungarian tariff barriers to Serbian exports'. Moreover, from the 1880s tariffs had created 'one of the leading arguments used by European statesmen to justify imperialist conquests' out of an 'alleged need of colonial markets to compensate for the barring of foreign markets by high protective tariffs'. Moon concluded that Christians who loved 'peace and justice' must come to terms with the 'proper relations between industrial empires and undeveloped

territories' and 'the wisest arrangements regarding raw materials, tariffs, reparations and international debts'.[129]

Similar economic cosmopolitan criticisms of high tariff walls, monopolization of raw materials, and immigration restrictions abounded in the CAIP's
1931 Europe Committee report calling for Euro-American comity as the first
step towards 'the unity of the Kingdom of Christ' and a more just and chari-
table world order.[130] The CAIP's Economic Relations Committee soon began
publishing entire pamphlets dedicated to the subject, such as the Reverend
Thomas F. Divine's *Tariffs and World Peace* (1933). This pamphlet drew inspiration from Pope Pius XI's warning against 'the ultimate consequences of this
Individualistic spirit in economic affairs [. . . ,] economic nationalism or even
economic imperialism [. . . ,] and detestable internationalism or international
imperialism in foreign affairs, which holds that where a man's fortune is, there is
his country'. Divine posited that the world had entered 'the age of economics',
wherein economic nationalism was the primary driver of imperial expansion
and war. Protectionism in the 1930s equated to prohibition; 'it is Neo-
Mercantilistic in stamp and design, a part of the driftwood of the old Mercantilistic doctrine'. The present predicament was the culmination of 'the blind
fury of unbridled nationalism that swept over postwar Europe [. . .]. Tariff
walls rose higher and higher along the political boundaries of the new Europe,
old nations aiming at an economic self-sufficiency that would prevent a repeti-
tion of the indignities suffered in the World War, new ones adding to this
motive a desire to protect their infant industries'. All told, it created geopolitical conflict by exacerbating tariff wars, long-standing race hatred, and imperial
trade preference. By contrast, trade liberalization, in 'recognition of the Divine
Will that all share the goods of this world on equitable terms', offered up the
promise of worldwide prosperity and peace.[131]

Under Moon's chairmanship, the CAIP continued to work on behalf of
economic interdependence, equitable distribution of natural resources and
food, freedom of migration, democratization, disarmament, decolonization,
and supranational governance. Its new world order would require direction
from the International Labor Office, the League, and, subsequently, the United
Nations. During the Second World War the organization gave its unequivocal
support to European and world federalism. It also maintained its belief that the
triumph of free trade 'would relieve the struggle for raw materials' and migration so that 'colonies would no longer be sought for exploitation'. Nationalism
remained the greatest hurdle, and so 'limitation of sovereignty must be a basic
principle' of whatever organization arose to replace the League of Nations.[132]

Blueprints for a new ecumenical Protestant economic order were drawn up at the 1937 Oxford Conference, which also launched the WCC as an anti-war organization. The conference was responding to the illiberal policies of Germany, Italy, the Soviet Union, and Japan, and to the wider problems of nationalism and sovereignty. The conference was fraught with great differences between its realist and absolute pacifist factions, mounting tensions between continental European and Anglo-American Protestantism, and a lack of consensus surrounding world federation.[133] Nevertheless, the delegates were able to agree on the blueprints of a new Christian order wherein 'the principle of justice', guided by a love for one's neighbours, would counteract coercion. The conference chided secular nineteenth-century liberalism for cultivating nationalism at the expense of universalism. Proceedings began with a report on 'The Church and the Economic Order', which lauded 'free enterprise' for spurring industrialization and overcoming the problem of 'the natural scarcity of economic resources'. It had, what was more, 'for the first time in history [...] brought all parts of the world into interdependence with each other and [...] made the idea of the unity of mankind a fact of common experience'. The promise of social justice, however, had not followed in its wake. Instead, echoing Hobson and Lenin, the report noted how mid-nineteenth-century 'free trade and free competition' had been replaced by 'protectionist measures' and 'a monopolistic stage' of capitalism that had only been 'accelerated and accentuated' by the Great War. But the delegates at Oxford, including Reinhold Niebuhr, remained hopeful that plenty could replace poverty, and that industrial democracy, racial harmony, and economic justice could supplant financial tyranny, racial discrimination, and economic inequality. The solution lay in some combination of Christian social democracy and economic co-operativism, an internationalist answer that the US delegates took back home, where, as Michael Thompson describes, it 'became fused with the new American internationalism' of the late 1930s and 1940s.[134]

The United Nations, Cordell Hull, and a Christian Pax Economica, 1934–1946

Leading left-wing Christian economic peace workers such as Walter Van Kirk, and organizations such as the FCC, the Alliance, the CPU, and the Commission of the Churches for International Friendship and Social Responsibility, believed that the liberal transformation of US foreign policy under FDR's secretary of state Cordell Hull (1933–1944), the 'Tennessee Cobden', portended a more peaceful age. And never was it more needed. Fascism, economic nationalism, and militarism were on the rise in Japan and Europe. Colonial expansion accompanied these 'isms', from the Japanese invasions of Manchuria (1931) and mainland China (1937) to Italy's invasion of Ethiopia (1935) and Nazi Germany's advance into Poland (1939) (see chapter 1). Against this illiberal geopolitical backdrop, the ecumenical alliance with the US State Department only grew stronger as the left-wing Christian youth peace movement, especially the YMCA and the YWCA, became more involved. Hull's support for US leadership within whatever replaced the League of Nations eventually earned him another epithet, 'Father of the United Nations', as well as a Nobel Peace Prize in 1945. Finally, the world's most powerful economy had someone at the helm of the State Department who shared these peace workers' Christian belief that both freer trade and supranational governance to maintain it would secure a more peaceful, prosperous, and fraternal economic order. An ideological commitment to the pacifying effects of free trade thus played a key role in wedding Christian and US internationalism by the time of the Second World War and the promise of a Christian Pax Economica.[135]

The fascism and colonialism of the 1930s created new crises for the Christian commercial peace movement. Not least, it softened some hardline stances against military interventionism. The YMCA's Sherwood Eddy, for instance, responded to the 1935 Italian occupation of Ethiopia with a call for supranational police action through the League, and even Norman Thomas began questioning his long-standing adherence to nonviolence. By the end of the Second World War, Reinhold Niebuhr had abandoned the Christian peace movement altogether. But despite—or perhaps because of—these big global challenges, economic cosmopolitanism yet remained a key instrument in the left-wing Christian toolkit.[136]

New York Methodist Episcopal minister Walter W. Van Kirk and the FCC were among the first within the Christian movement to give Cordell Hull's liberal economic reformation their blessing. In *Religion Renounces War* (1934), Van Kirk condemned 'economic imperialism' for violently carving up the world, erecting high tariff walls, and exploiting the resources of 'backward countries'. He blamed 'economic isolationism' for laying 'the seeds of war', and noted that both the Northern Baptist Convention and the US branch of the Alliance supported freer trade. The FCC, in turn, gave its backing to Hull's RTAA, which was designed to liberalize US trade by strengthening presidential powers over foreign economic policy.[137]

The Alliance became even more pointed in its support for Hull's foreign economic reforms between 1936 and 1937. Economic justice was needed to complement racial justice, and in 1936 the Alliance called upon Democratic president Franklin Roosevelt, following the launch of his liberal New Deal reforms at home, to convene a world conference to tackle matters of 'tariffs, trade regulations, stabilization of currencies, colonies and mandates, outlets for excess populations, access to raw materials and other essentials of life, in a spirit which subordinates national advantage to the common good'.[138] In 1937, the same year as the Oxford Conference, and in which FOR executive secretary Harold Fey opposed economic sanctions against Japan, the Alliance became more explicit; it joined the FCC in endorsing Hull's 'promoting reciprocal trade agreements with other nations'. The FCC also recommended 'full cooperation with the World Economic Cooperation Campaign under the direction of the National Peace Conference', the YWCA-backed campaign discussed at the beginning of this chapter.[139]

The outbreak of war in Europe in 1939 instilled a new sense of urgency. In 1941 the Alliance joined up with the CPU to publish *Religious Proposals for World Order*. They concluded that an effective world government required a 'fundamental reconstruction of international economic relations. [...] National autarchy and international imperialism are alike condemned.' US church leaders concluded that 'economic nationalism, no less than political nationalism, has bedeviled the relations of nations'. Private monopolization of industries needed to be broken up. The world had 'become a single economic unit', requiring world organization. 'Embargoes, trade restrictions (such as quotas and tariffs), currency restrictions, and the like [must be] abolished, [and] all nations must have equal access to raw materials and to markets, subject to the supervision of some supra-national authority.' The 'principal objective' for colonies must be 'eventual self-government'.[140]

The Christian cosmopolitan message of free trade was contagious. Methodists associated with John Foster Dulles's Commission on a Just and Durable Peace convened in Chicago in May 1941 to discuss postwar planning.[141] Prominent issues included national sovereignty and economic nationalism. According to the journal *Methodist Woman*, among the conclusions were 'that unlimited sovereignty as now practiced is outmoded' and that world government was inevitable. Regional federations, such as European union, were first steps to world federation. The meeting also concluded that the diminution of economic sovereignty would foster 'a free flow of goods between nations, equal access to necessary raw materials, [and] free access to markets'. The New Deal and co-operatives were also promoted. Whilst realists and pacifists were at loggerheads over the war, they were able to find some common ground when devising a postwar economic peace.[142]

In 1942 the Commission of the Churches for International Friendship and Social Responsibility, under the chairmanship of the archbishop of Canterbury, published *Social Justice and Economic Reconstruction*. The divisions of the world stemmed from 'divine creation and divine providence. [...] The true principle of human society is a unity which is yet a diversity'; hence 'the phenomena of race and nationhood'. However, 'the prosperity of the whole human family depends upon the degree to which the total resources of the earth can be made available for the needs of all [...;] all nations are economically interdependent'. To create a peaceful world, mankind required 'a common moral purpose [...] to direct the world's economic and political systems'. Nations must subordinate themselves to world government, 'a true world order' with the power to create laws and 'the means of enforcing it'. Economic justice necessitated economic freedom. 'Excessive self-sufficiency' must be prevented, and 'the weaker states' protected from 'the tyrannous aggression' of stronger states; 'the resources of the world' must be used justly 'for the good of all and the proper development of the several national economies' that 'have been continually threated by the existence of powerful financial interests'; 'the human rights of the inhabitants of the colonial territories must be safeguarded and in particular their inalienable right to govern themselves should be recognized and the way prepared as speedily as possible for its realization'; relations between Soviet Russia and the West must be normalized; and 'any fancied superiority of the white to the coloured races' must be eliminated. Such was the great mission for economic and social justice lying before the church, because 'the world order we seek is one that has foundations and its builder and maker is God'.[143]

Peace-minded Christian youth were all too aware of the promises and perils of the new era of globalization, providing what Ian Tyrrell describes as 'a major contribution to the emergence of a Christian internationalism in the 1930s'.[144] The Christian student movement similarly placed the brunt of the blame for the deglobalization and global inequity that followed the onset of the Great Depression upon political and economic nationalism.[145] In 1931 the Christian Student Association Movement began outlining its new Christian economic order. It criticized the anti-democratic US maintenance of a high tariff for being 'contrary to all economic authority'. The movement declared that a new political party was needed that emphasized international consumer co-operativism, 'world-mindedness', 'the social ownership of public utilities, natural resources, and the basic industries', and 'abolition of tariff duties'.[146] Amidst another world war, in 1940 the American FOR's Youth Committee Against War demanded the 'elimination of restriction on world trade' and free migration for refugees, in coordination with 'world peace, labor, and cooperative movements'.[147] 'Communities of every color and climate, at every level of social development, have been drawn by the network of trade into a world economy,' observed Richard Fagley in *To Build a Better World: International Problems for Religious Young People* (1941). The perils of unregulated interdependence had been on full display over the past twenty years:

> An Austrian bank fails in May, touching off a depression that hits the United States in October. Gandhi starts a boycott of cotton goods in India and cotton workers in England are thrown on the dole. American Congress passes a new law for buying silver and Chinese coolies starve for lack of silver money. The 'living space' of each nation in our time is the rest of the world, for world economy means interdependence.

'Religious youth' needed to 'stand should to shoulder around the earth. [...] An international mind [...] is essential to the solution.' Yes, the world had 'grown together, like the suburbs of a great city, but without the formation of police and fire departments. As a result, lawlessness and anarchy stalk the streets.' Only world governance could maintain peace harvested from interdependence.[148]

The YMCA early on had established itself as a key international organization for the coordination of modern Christian youth activist networks after its founding in London in the 1840s. It had grown out of an 1844 London meeting consisting of a handful of Anglican, Baptist, Congregationalist, and Methodist leaders seeking a new cooperative organization. As YMCA peace worker Sherwood Eddy described it, the 'founders believed in organization as much as did the widening commerce of world trade'.[149] Following the 1851 Great Exhibition, the first US offshoot was formed in Boston, and the movement also made inroads in western Europe, Canada, India, Australia, and New Zealand around this time. But Henri Dunant, the secretary of YMCA Geneva, would turn it into a global movement when he helped organize the inaugural YMCA World Conference in Paris in 1855. Over the next century, the YMCA would gradually reorient its remit to include world peace.

Thanks largely to Eddy's early twentieth-century efforts as secretary, the YMCA USA became a more explicitly radical left-wing anti-war organization.[150] It also became more closely aligned with the wider economic peace movement.

In the early 1910s the YMCA began working with secular peace movement leaders like Norman Angell.[151] These links were such that, in 1919, the Republican
Publicity Association viewed with alarm the YMCA's promotion of pro–free
trade texts in its night school classes.[152] Dunford House, Richard Cobden's
family home in England, in turn was gifted by the family to the YMCA in 1952.
And as late as 1953, Georgist ideas were included in local YMCA curricula.[153]
And, of course, the YMCA supported Cordell Hull's trade reforms.

But the most crucial economic cosmopolitan addition to the interwar youth
Christian peace movement came from the YWCA USA (founded in 1858). As
outlined at the beginning of this chapter, its official embrace of free trade occurred just as Cordell Hull began liberalizing US foreign trade policy in the
mid-1930s. This cosmopolitan confluence led to a direct line of communication
between the Christian commercial peace movement and the US State Department. The story of when and how this relationship between the YWCA and
Hull's State Department developed is a remarkable one—and it might as well
have been taken straight from Norman Angell's *The Great Illusion*.

The YWCA's Angellite political manoeuvring was initiated between 1935 and
1936 by Swiss-born Clara Guthrie d'Arcis, treasurer of the YWCA's Disarmament
Committee and president of the Geneva-based Union mondiale de la femme
pour la concorde internationale (Women's world union for international harmony). She and Henrietta Roelofs, the vice-chair of the National Committee
on the Cause and Cure for War (NCCCW), developed the aptly entitled 'Plan
for Bringing Economic Forces into Co-operation with the Women's Peace
Movement'.[154] Their plan was to persuade export-oriented organizations such
as the American Manufacturers' Export Association that it was in their financial
interest to support the international women's peace movement.

After receiving a copy of the YWCA's new economic peace plan, the vice-
president of General Motors wrote back to d'Arcis, letting her know that he was
going to bring her organization's initiative to the attention of his close friend
Cordell Hull because 'he is literally consumed with a desire for continued
peace, both morally and as the only possible restorative to world trade and our
own domestic prosperity'. FDR's secretary of state was

> surely the best ally you have in the world today. He is an idealist who believes
> in peace for its own sake, but he is also a realist who is striving earnestly to
> make peace possible by breaking down the barriers to world trade—the
> vicious implements of economic warfare—by a program of direct political
> action which is sound philosophically and feasible in practice.

The move would necessitate joining forces: 'If I can get Secretary Hull to endorse the laudable work you are doing in your field to educate the public to the utter hopelessness of war, I would say that you ought, for your own part, to stand for the principles Mr Hull stands for.'[155]

So it came to pass. Led by the YWCA, the NCCCW maintained a decades-long pamphleteering and congressional lobbying campaign on behalf of international trade liberalization and supranational institutions such as the United Nations (UN) and the General Agreement on Tariffs and Trade (GATT, established in 1947) to facilitate it.[156] By 1940, numerous other left-wing Christian peace organizations were following the YWCA's lead, including the American Friends Service Committee, the American Unitarian Association, the American Youth Congress, the CPU, the Council for Social Action of the Congregational and Christian Churches, the CAIP, the General Conference Commission on World Peace of the Methodist Episcopal Church, and the Alliance.[157]

At the end of the Second World War, ecumenical influence over US foreign policy reached its zenith once world federation had become a top priority. The promise of supranational organization raised Christian internationalist hopes for a more peaceful world federation, giving rise to the World Order movement in 1942. With left-wing women's groups at the vanguard, the movement rivalled the interwar mass mobilization on behalf of Prohibition.[158]

Left-wing Christian advocates of world federation and free trade thereafter made a sizeable contribution to the creation of the UN. The CAIP gave its support to the 1944 Dumbarton Oaks agreements supporting a new international organization to replace the League of Nations. In contrast to US conservative evangelicals, who opposed human rights and world organization, after much internal debate the World Order movement duly gave its blessing to the 1945 San Francisco Conference of the United Nations Organization.[159] Walter Van Kirk, now a member of the Council on Foreign Relations, next led a conference delegation to the San Francisco Conference on behalf of the FCC.[160] He would continue to advocate for the advancement of 'the cause of peace and justice' through UN technical assistance and food aid for the underdeveloped world.[161]

Brooklyn's Hamilton Holt stood out among the Christian cosmopolitans participating in the San Francisco Conference. He had already established himself within the early twentieth-century international peace, world federation, and social justice movements. He was the publisher and editor of the liberal New York magazine *The Independent*. He was also an advocate for immigrant and Black civil rights, co-founding the National Association for the

Advancement of Colored People in 1909. In 1910, through the New York Peace Society, he helped found the World Federation League, and he and David Starr Jordan joined forces to persuade Andrew Carnegie to send Norman Angell to Germany 'in the cause of peace'.[162] Holt served as president of New York's CPU, as a founding member of the Alliance, and as an officer of the League to Enforce Peace (founded in 1915). He served on an advisory committee of the Women's Peace Party during the First World War to explore the feasibility of world federation; and he was thereafter executive director of the Woodrow Wilson Foundation to support international peace, a lecturer for the WPF, and author of the 1916 article 'A Declaration of Interdependence'.[163] In 1923, the protectionist news organ the *American Economist* described Holt's name as being 'synonymous with Free-Trade'.[164] Holt's secular and ecumenical peace pedigree provided him with a vast network of contacts to call upon in 1940 to help devise a more durable and substantive supranational organization. He then invited international speakers to New York to tackle the problem of world peace, with support for Cordell Hull's reciprocal trade agreements high on the agenda, followed by Holt's own participation in the 1945 San Francisco Conference. With some degree of self-congratulation, he called the establishment of the UN 'the greatest milestone in international political progress' since the US Constitution.[165] World federation and supranational governance looked poised to oversee the birth of a Christian Pax Economica.

Conclusion

Liberal radicals in Britain and the United States explicitly married the free-trade movement to the Christian peace movement in the 1830s and 1840s. The connection between free trade, antislavery, and peace became stronger at an evangelical millenarian moment that marvelled at the promise of the era's new tools of globalization on behalf of world fraternity. Subsequently, in response to the illiberal fallout from the First World War and the Great Depression, the Christian peace movement's interwar left-wing attachment to free trade intensified, as did its support for supranational governance to maintain it. The movement's criticisms of nationalism also became sharper. Along the way, it allied itself with other radical social justice initiatives, including abolitionism, women's suffrage, world federalism, and civil rights. Although centred within Anglo-American networks, the movement reached as far afield as Japan. Along the way, the Christian commercial peace movement drew ecumenical inspiration from numerous Cobdenite traditions, including Georgism, Norman Angellism, and co-operativism, by the turn of the twentieth century.

These efforts culminated in the 1940s, when Christian economic peace workers maintained their support for Cordell Hull's trade liberalization initiatives, from the RTAA to the GATT. They also backed the creation of the UN and its goals of free trade, economic and social justice, universal human rights, and world peace. Nationalism remained the biggest obstacle, leading to worried speculation that national sovereignty yet remained too powerful within the UN framework. Even so, 1946 marked, as the World's YWCA put it, the dawning of a new 'world order which shall make possible peace with justice'.[166] After a century of left-wing Christians' grassroots activism on behalf of free trade, fraternity, and federation, their ecumenical Pax Economica appeared to have finally arrived.

6

Pax Economica vs. Pax Americana

THE LEFT-WING FREE-TRADE
FIGHT AGAINST NEOCOLONIALISM,
NEOMERCANTILISM, AND
NEOLIBERALISM, 1945–2022

*At mid-century, a farsighted generation of leaders acted on the bitter lessons of
protectionism, devastating depression and war. They embraced the revolutionary
idea that freedom—free democracies, free markets, the free flow of ideas, the free
movement of people—would be the surest route to the greatest prosperity for all [...,]
that growing economic interdependence would lead to greater peace among nations.
[... T]hey have been proven spectacularly right.*

—DEMOCRATIC US PRESIDENT BILL CLINTON, WORLD TRADE
ORGANIZATION CONVENTION, GENEVA, 18 MAY 1998[1]

*Cobden would have roared with laughter at the idea [of Brexit]; before getting very
angry at the false choice between nationalism and internationalism, worse at the
crass epithet coined by a prime minister [Theresa May] not fit to wipe the boots of
Peel or Gladstone, that those whose affinities do not stop at the white cliffs of Dover
are to be maligned as 'citizens of nowhere'.*

—SIMON SCHAMA, *FINANCIAL TIMES*, 28 FEBRUARY 2019[2]

YOU MIGHT RECALL that our story began with *Strike Up the Band*, the Gershwins' late-1920s musical satire about a high tariff on cheese leading to a US war
with Switzerland. You might also recall that the reboot a couple of years later
switched the cheese tariff for one on chocolate. It's therefore rather fitting that
our story now closes with a story about trade and chocolate. Only this time

it's not about tariffs, but about their lack—at the airport. If you've ever flown, you've probably also strolled through an airport duty-free shop. You might even have purchased something from its perfume-laden tax-free counters. What you might not know is that this experience is a post-1945 outgrowth of the left-wing fight for free trade, anti-imperialism, and peace.

'Duty free' as we know it today was the brainchild of an Irish anti-colonial visionary named Brendan O'Regan. The man who in the 1970s and 1980s would go on to help spearhead the Irish peace movement through the Irish Commission for Justice and Peace, Co-operation North, the Centre for International Co-operation, and the Irish Peace Institute, O'Regan got his start as a caterer at Shannon Airport in Ireland in the 1940s. As Europe's westernmost airport, Shannon became the primary mid-century stopover for passengers making the transatlantic journey. O'Regan thought, 'Why not take advantage of the traffic, and make the airport a discounted one-stop shop, too?' Duty free allowed international consumers to circumvent international trade barriers, popularizing domestic products such as Irish whiskey around the globe and spurring his nation's industrial growth.

To be sure, for O'Regan duty free was both a profit maker and a nationalistic economic recipe. But it was also an anti-colonial and a peace project. As he saw it, Ireland found itself in an even worse situation than the rest of postwar Europe owing to the island's legacy of formal British colonial exploitation, which had artificially stunted Irish industrial development. British-controlled Northern Ireland was also riven by mounting tensions between Protestants and Catholics. O'Regan speculated that offering duty-free goods could address both these pressing issues at once by bringing in tourism, boosting industries, creating jobs, and incentivizing peaceful economic exchange with Northern Ireland. Nor was O'Regan's anti-imperialism of free trade designed solely for Ireland. If duty free could work there, it could work anywhere. He specifically eyed the decolonizing world. 'Particularly in Third World situations,' O'Regan believed, 'the Shannon Zone should be duplicated.' He therefore cast an aspirational anti-colonial eye towards exporting the idea as a peaceful path towards economic independence and cooperation. It caught on. In 1972, the UN even began funding multi-week training courses at Shannon Airport to educate other nations on how they might set up their own duty-free zones, among them Sri Lanka, Taiwan, China, Indonesia, Mexico, Columbia, Egypt, Ghana, and Nigeria.[3]

Let's return to chocolate. Aside from Irish whiskey, Shannon Airport's other early duty-free smash hit came from an at the time middle-ranking Swiss chocolatier called Toblerone. The triangular-shaped chocolate's addition to Shannon's duty-free shelves back then has since become a household name for sweet-tooths across the globe. While taxes on Swiss chocolate once sparked a farcical fictional war in the Gershwins' 1920s USA, tax-free Swiss chocolate now helped cultivate a new cooperative era of decolonization, prosperity, and peace in real-world 1950s Ireland.[4]

O'Regan's anti-imperialism of free trade at the airport, Swiss chocolate included, fitted comfortably within the wider economic cosmopolitan moment.[5] His scheme joined others in the century-long left-wing fight for free trade, anti-imperialism, and peace undertaken by the liberal radicals, socialist internationalists, feminists, and Christian peace workers that has been explored in previous chapters. Thanks to the movement's grassroots efforts, during and immediately after the Second World War, the Western powers seemed ready for peace through interdependence. Led by the United States, a concerted effort was undertaken to avoid returning to the economic nationalist status quo that had long prevailed over the imperial order and that had deepened the Great Depression. This more liberal economic order required regulation and governance through new supranational bodies such as the United Nations (UN), the International Monetary Fund (IMF), the World Bank, and the General Agreement on Tariffs and Trade (GATT). Multilateralism and international development were baked into what became the Bretton Woods system (1944–1971).[6] Left-leaning supporters of a free-trade Pax Economica also called for the dismantling of the European empires. The commercial peace movement's mid-century champion, Franklin Delano Roosevelt's secretary of state Cordell Hull, whom Martin Daunton describes as 'Richard Cobden reincarnated', is widely regarding as the pacifistic programme's progenitor. Decolonization and Western advocacy for freer trade and multilateralism now seemed poised to supplant the protectionism of the previous era of imperial globalization.[7]

Yet within just a few years of the launching of these same pacifistic trade liberalization initiatives, the world again found itself on the verge of global war. By the end of the 1940s, multilateralism was floundering as the great powers settled onto a permanent Cold War footing. The turn away from multilateralism included a growing chorus of US policymakers, who started to identify their envisaged postwar Pax Americana more with the projection of US military might than with economic cooperation.[8] At the same time, the surviving imperial powers also remained reluctant to part with their colonies, leading to violent clashes with anti-colonial nationalists. The liberal radicals, socialists, feminists, and Christians who led the commercial peace movement once more found themselves on the outside looking in.

The main culprits for this illiberal turn of events were three ideological 'isms'—neocolonialism, neomercantilism, and neoliberalism—that wove their way through the hyper-militarized tapestries of the Cold War and decolonization. To anti-colonial nationalists, Western domination of the new supranational governance organizations looked like old-school economic imperialism dressed up in new clothes: what became known as neocolonialism. Anti-colonial nationalists fought back against neocolonialism, culminating in the UN's Conference on Trade and Development (UNCTAD), established in 1964. Continued collaboration between the developing world led in 1974 to the un-veiling of the anti-colonialists' alternative global economic vision, the New International Economic Order (NIEO), to counteract continued Western discrimination. Historians have long emphasized how Western, US-led neocolonialism was a new form of free-trade imperialism—what New Left revisionists call 'open door imperialism.'[9] And yet, while free-trade imperialism was at times included in the critique, a closer look at the early UNCTAD and NIEO proceedings of the 1960s and 1970s illuminates how the Third World remained far more critical still of the protectionist policies of the neocolonial powers—as a neomercantilist carry-over from the imperialism of economic nationalism. The 1962 US embargo on Cuba became the poster child of the Cold War's coercive implementation of economic nationalism. The commercial peace movement's main condemnations of Western trade practices grew to echo the Third World's anti-neomercantilist refrain. From these left-wing perspectives, the neomercantilist continuities between the post-1945 trade regime and the century that preceded it are striking.

The free-trade-and-peace movement adapted its grassroots strategies in response to the increasingly militant and exploitative post-1945 geopolitical landscape. From the 1970s, this included the growing influence of Western neoliberalism, which the commercial peace movement had unknowingly helped facilitate through its century-long efforts. The organizations spearheading the left-wing movement, such as the Socialist Party of America (SPA), the Young Women's Christian Association (YWCA), the Women's International League for Peace and Freedom (WILPF), and the World Council of Churches (WCC), were at first supportive of the liberal multilateral initiatives that Cordell Hull helped set up in the late 1940s, including the Reciprocal Trade Agreements Act (RTAA), the proposed International Trade Organization (ITO), and its replacement, the GATT. Working more closely with less radical but better funded peace bodies such as the Carnegie Endowment for International Peace (CEIP), the economic peace movement set up big-tent lobbying groups like the Citizens' Committee for Reciprocal World Trade (CCRWT, founded in 1948) to better facilitate and defend its Pax Economica from neomercantilist forces. But from around 1970, the increasing popularity of anti-democratic free-trade ideas and policies among conservative political elites—the growth, that is, of neoliberalism—forced the left-wing movement to seek out alternative grassroots pathways. Its 'alter-globalization' vision sought to reconcile the movement's long-standing desire for economic interdependence with the decolonizing world's demands for economic sovereignty.[10] Left-wing alter-globalization accordingly embraced the ethical and equitable economic ideals of the international co-operative movement and the burgeoning Fair Trade movement, whose hallmark we now find stamped on coffee bags and bars of chocolate.

Closing Doors: Neocolonialism, Neomercantilism, and the Anti-imperialism of Economic Nationalism, 1946–1970

Just as the commercial peace workers believed they finally had Pax Economica in their grasp in the late 1940s, it slipped through their fingers. The divisiveness of the Cold War—be it in terms of the capitalist West versus the socialist East, the First World versus the Second and Third Worlds, the Global North versus the Global South, or the neocolonial world versus the decolonizing world— meant that global economic cooperation became a big ask. As in the century before, economic nationalism as both an imperial and anti-imperial policy remained a geopolitical force to be reckoned with.

Decolonization and neocolonialism created massive impediments to peaceful postwar multilateralism. The developing world's desire to 'catch up' with the West often came with requests for preferential treatment and infant-industrial protectionism. Some of the loudest calls came from Latin America.[11] As Mexican finance minister Ramón Beteta Quintana put it in November 1947 during the ITO negotiations,

We recognize the convenience of international economic cooperation, but we still must reject any plan to suppress all protective tariffs, because that would mean the economic destruction of the weak nations while entrenching the commercial supremacy of the stronger countries.[12]

The growing popularity across the developing world of protectionist American System-style policies, implemented as a bulwark against the looming threat of Western neocolonialism, fitted but awkwardly within the West's newfound multilateral freer-trade vision; added to which, the European imperial powers remained reluctant to grant their colonies formal independence. Economic dominance and military oppression came to be understood by many as two ends of the same stick. The 1950s and 1960s witnessed violent acts of repression as the Western powers sought to halt democratic nationalist movements across the decolonizing world.[13] This included the administrators of the British Empire, who tenaciously held on to imperial preference with the Dominions until Britain joined the European Economic Community (EEC) in 1973.[14]

Cold War divisiveness further inhibited peaceful globalism. The Soviet approach to interdependence, or 'socialist globalization', was quite often at loggerheads with that of the capitalist West. The Soviet Union's anti-Western paranoia, planned economy, and monopolistic bilateral approach to trade expansion all deserve their share of the neomercantilist blame. While the Soviet Empire's communist leaders decried their exclusion from Western capitalist markets, they had no intention of opening their own up to everyone else. Soviet trade with developing nations never exceeded thirteen per cent, and trade with communist allies through the Council for Mutual Economic Assistance, or Comecon, grew at an even slower rate than Soviet trade with the West. Ideological rifts between the Soviets and Chinese from the 1950s—the Sino–Soviet split—further fractured socialist globalization. The Soviet internationalist vision for the socialist world was indeed a constrained one.[15]

The US government's paranoid anti-communist blinkers, in turn, blinded it to its own sizeable contributions to the multilateralism deficit. Neocolonial policies further restricted the anti-communist tunnel vision. US policymakers of both major parties began to suspect left-leaning anti-colonial nationalists of being Soviet agents in disguise, resulting in numerous US military interventions in the 1950s and 1960s, including the Korean War and France's colonial conflict in Vietnam. US interventionism was often accompanied by the covert toppling of democratic left-wing governments across the Third World. US policymakers were also inconsistent in their defence of trade liberalization. At times, US governments coercively encouraged allies to lower their barriers to trade, reflecting British free-trade imperial policies from the previous century. At others, they coercively discouraged allies from trading with the Soviet sphere, a neomercantilist hangover from the GOP's imperialism of economic nationalism.[16]

From 1945 to 1948, Harry Truman's Democratic administration pushed the ITO as the main mechanism for a new era of freer trade and peace against wide-ranging opposition. Republican protectionist forces in Congress pushed back against this proposed multilateral trade initiative.[17] So, too, did British right-wing defenders of imperial trade preference. Numerous left-wing Latin American states also sought exceptions for the Global South and the enshrinement of the principles of anti-imperialism. The developing world's nationalistic demands for temporary protectionism within the ITO charter even made paranoid conservative defenders of 'free enterprise' see red. One such was Philip Cortney, a member of both the National Association of Manufacturers' International Relations Committee and the neoliberal Mont Pèlerin Society (founded in 1947). Cortney predicted that if economic nationalist exceptions for the Global South were enshrined within the ITO charter, 'we shall drift into Communism and finally to war'.[18]

Cortney's observations illustrate a profound shift starting to take place within conservative US economic ideology and policymaking. During the GOP-dominated era of the first 'Red Scare' of the early 1920s, free-trade internationalism had been akin to Bolshevism in the eyes of Republican economic nationalists. Just over two decades later, economic nationalist movements across the Global South were now perceived as paving the way for Marxist revolution.

The GOP's paranoid style of politics only intensified. The advent of a Pax Americana that favoured military might over multilateralism created a nightmare scenario for left-wing proponents of Pax Economica.[19] Cold War containment doomed dreams of global cooperation. Following the outbreak of the Korean War in June 1950, US military assistance superseded trade aid, and unilateralism trumped multilateralism. Cold War national security concerns soon prompted US support for the French war against anti-colonial nationalist insurgents in Vietnam. For one thing, successive presidential administrations claimed, Vietnam contained valuable raw materials and trade opportunities for US Cold War allies in Asia. For another, US policymakers believed that if Vietnam were lost to Ho Chi Minh's Marxist insurgency, the rest of Asia would follow. What remained of liberal US policymakers' ambitions for cooperation with the Third World became casualties of the US war in Vietnam.[20] Containing the spread of communism through economic power also transformed US multinational corporations into Cold War agents of the national security apparatus, with tragic consequences for labour protection, consumer rights, and democracy promotion in the Third World. Left-wing visions of multilateralism, decolonization, prosperity, human rights, development, and peace were stymied by security-driven demands for an expanded US military presence abroad, with adverse results for Third World sovereignty and economic development.[21]

The initial postwar retreat from multilateralism happened swiftly. The newly launched multilateral institutions of the Bretton Woods system—the IMF, World Bank, the GATT—were unable to halt it. As early as 1948, trade between western and eastern Europe fell to a third of prewar levels, and the Soviets exacerbated the downward trend with a blockade of Berlin. The following year, the US government passed the Export Control Act, embargoing a wide array of goods that could aid the Soviet Union. By the mid-1950s, the US State Department had expanded the Western trade embargo to encompass the entire Soviet sphere. The creation of the EEC in 1957, in turn, signalled that regional approaches to trade liberalization were becoming more politically palatable, not least because of their versatility; they could be sold domestically as free-trade initiatives to some, protectionist blocs to others. US free-market designs on integrating Japan into the Bretton Woods system, in turn, included breaking up Japanese cartels and aristocratic land monopolies, but also allowed for discrimination against Western imports to boost Japanese manufacturing. As Thomas Zeiler puts it, 'the Cold War itself froze in its tracks the development of a truly open multilateral world economy', and much as in Europe, US attempts to 'reintegrate Asia' often meant that guns 'supplanted butter as the driving force of regional policies'. Owing to the Cold War and the lobbying of US protectionist interests, the GATT itself thereafter increasingly 'reflected protectionist demands [...;] mercantilist instincts tempered the free market'.[22]

The United States' own neomercantilist legacy of wielding protectionist policies to coerce its neighbours and punish its rivals—its closed-door imperialism—remained prominent after 1945. As outlined above, Western paranoia at Marxism's spread led to the economic isolation of the socialist East from the capitalist West, accompanied by US military bases and covert actions. Following one of the latter against Fidel Castro, from 1962 the Cuban embargo became the most vivid example of US closed-door imperialism, an economic imperial policy that has remained a fixture long after the collapse of the Soviet Union and the ending of the Cold War. US neocolonialist and neomercantilist policies towards the Third World helped spark a more revolutionary anti-imperial response.[23]

The movement away from the peaceful vision of multilateralism in the United States had its countermovement in decolonization. The anti-imperialism of economic nationalism—employing protectionism as a shield against the neocolonial policies of the Global North—became more popular throughout the decolonizing world following Indian independence in 1947. As explored in chapter 1, early twentieth-century Irish, Indian, Egyptian, and pan-Africanist advocacy of protectionism had represented rare anti-colonial variants upon the American System's imperial rule. But after 1945 the American System model became ever more popular with the developmental economic policies of decolonizing states. Global South political and intellectual leaders redrafted the ideas of Friedrich List and the American System as economic blueprints for the decolonizing world.[24] Economic nationalism became a requirement to counteract the West's neomercantilism—what in 1958 Swedish economist Gunnar Myrdal referred to as 'a protective "rich men's club"'.[25]

Developing states increasingly looked to Friedrich List for guidance. They also conveniently overlooked his arguments against industrialization in the 'tropical countries' and his arguments for Euro-American colonialism.[26] As historian Theodore von Laue observed in 1969, 'among List's recent disciples we may count Sukarno and Nkrumah, as well as Mao'.[27] List's biographer W. O. Henderson portrays him as a 'prophet of the ambitions of all underdeveloped countries'.[28] And as Leonard Gomes notes, 'whether they are conscious of the fact or not, development economists the world over owe a great debt to the memory of Friedrich List'.[29] Heterodox economist Ha-Joon Chang has similarly drawn upon List to advocate protectionism for the developing world in his popular 2002 book *Kicking Away the Ladder*, the title of which paraphrases a famous line from List's *National System of Political Economy* (1841).[30]

India had a Listian head start over much of the decolonizing world. Once Swadeshi became codified in the Bombay Plan of 1944 and then enacted following independence in 1947, it evolved from a grassroots anti-colonial Listian nationalist project to a government-endorsed developmentalist one. Swadeshi's nationalist leaders now preferred big modern industrialization projects funded by Indian-owned capital to the Gandhian-style emphasis upon traditional homespun *khadi*. What began as a movement of protests, boycotts, exhibitions, newspapers, and lanternslide shows at the turn of the century was now a full-blown national policy of protective tariffs and economic planning. From the 1950s, economic autarky and import-substitution industrialization policies (ISI) supplanted Swadeshi's earlier grassroots practices.[31] The rest of the decolonizing world took note.

With Swadeshi India as trailblazer, post-1945 Western neocolonialism sparked a widespread anti-colonial economic nationalist double movement.

In 1965, for example, just eight years after Ghana obtained independence from Britain, President Kwame Nkrumah famously lambasted the West's imperialistic abuse of the new postwar supranational institutions and agreements. The World Bank, the IMF, and the GATT all perpetuated Western dominance, he argued in his Marxist-Leninist-inspired book *Neo-colonialism: The Last Stage of Imperialism* (1965). Economic nationalist policies meant to ensure Ghanaian economic sovereignty followed. The Ghanaian flag's 'Black Star' emblem became a symbol of political and economic freedom for Pan-Africanists such as W.E.B. Du Bois of the United States and Trinidadian George Padmore, both of whom had settled in Ghana. Du Bois, a student of the Listian German Historical School (GHS) during his graduate years in Berlin, and Padmore helped inform Nkrumah's pan-Africanist vision. But Nkrumah, a university student in the United States in the 1930s, also borrowed from Jamaican-born pan-Africanist Marcus Garvey. The Black Star had been the name of Garvey's earlier Black-owned steamship line, which had sought to create a pan-African trading system separate from that of the white supremacist West. And much as early twentieth-century Indian nationalists had turned traditionally made *khadi* cloth into a symbol of swadeshism, Nkrumah transformed luxurious and colorful *kente* cloth into the dress code of Ghanaian nationalism, which Black Americans have since adapted as a symbol of their own Africanity.[32] Third World approaches to economic development after 1945 adapted and updated the older anti-colonial tradition of the American System described above in chapter 1.

From the perspective of the left-wing free-trade-and-peace movement, the Cold War's Manichaean militarism helped keep economic nationalism alive and well, as did the protectionist demands of the decolonizing world. Amid the paranoid politics of the Cold War, the neocolonial West stifled trade with the Soviet East while coercing the developing world into throwing open its markets. The Soviet Empire compounded the problem with its planned economy of state monopolies, protectionism, and bilateral trade, which limited socialist globalization and trade with the West. The anti-colonial world's Listian nationalist desire for economic independence created a further stumbling block for multilateralism, as did the violent Western attempts to halt the advance of socialism and to hold on to colonies by clamping down on left-wing nationalist movements. All combined, the Cold War, decolonization, neocolonialism, and neomercantilism thwarted post-1945 left-wing free-trade plans for global cooperation and peace.

The Anti-imperialism of Free Trade, 1946–1970

The Cold War resurgence of economic nationalism may have undercut post-1945 left-wing globalist plans for Pax Economica, but they also kept the commercial peace movement motivated, albeit with new leadership. The British wing of the movement was by now a shell of its former self. Britain's centenary celebration of the repeal of the Corn Laws in 1946 paled in comparison to the galas and jubilees that had marked the centenary of Richard Cobden's birth in 1904. During the interwar years, the Labour Party's support for free trade had become lukewarm at best, showing a strong preference to work only with fellow adopters of the welfare state; added to which, the anti-imperialism of former liberal radical leading lights such as Norman Angell had weakened as they became more hawkish and defensive of the British Empire in the 1930s in response to the right-wing threats posed by Japanese, Italian, and Nazi imperialism.[33] The Cobden Club, for so long the hub of the international economic peace movement, had evolved into an old men's club of dwindling numbers. Now headquartered in New York, Washington, DC, and Geneva instead of London, the commercial peace movement's socialists, feminists, and Christians continued to coordinate with liberal radical champions in the United States such as Cordell Hull. The movement's postwar leaders also sought an end to Western imperialism and exhibited more sympathy for anti-colonial nationalist demands for temporary protectionism than had existed before the Second World War. The free-trade-and-peace movement even became more accepting of the Cold War-era preference for regionalism over globalism, beginning with the economic integration of western Europe. Economic peace workers would soon find new grassroots allies following the left-wing revitalization of international co-operativism, followed by the rise of the Fair Trade movement from around 1970.

Cold War neocolonialism and neomercantilism ensured that collaboration between the commercial peace movement and Cordell Hull continued well after his tenure at the State Department ended in 1944. In March 1948, a year after the creation of the GATT, Hull was made honorary chair of the nonpartisan Citizens' Committee for Reciprocal World Trade (CCRWT), co-founded by the YWCA USA and other US peace organizations. As the CCRWT acknowledged in an open letter to the Senate Finance Committee in June 1948, its membership also included a broad cross-section of US industrial, banking, consumer, veteran, labour, farm, and church groups. This provided a strong political foundation for a trade-fuelled peace. 'For that matter, the responsible leaders of both major parties and of the Socialist Party publicly support the reciprocal trade agreements principle', thereby putting 'the rest of the world on notice that the United States is holding undeviatingly to its course toward world recovery and world peace.' Alger Hiss, chairman of the CCRWT executive committee, was particularly proactive in thwarting Republican attempts to undo Hull's tariff revolution.[34] The Carnegie Endowment for International Peace (CEIP), in turn, helped launch the non-profit and non-partisan World Trade Foundation of America (WTFA) in the mid-1940s, which was tasked with educating Americans about how reliant they were on global supply chains. The WTFA was part of a multipronged CEIP campaign to overcome Republican protectionist stonewalling and to ensure the 'United Nations peace structure'. Liberalization of US and world trade were in the 'long-term interests of the American people' and for the advancement of 'world recovery, stability and peace'.[35]

The YWCA's leadership within the CCRWT was but one way that the women's peace movement maintained its fight for the trade liberalization initiatives begun under Cordell Hull. Owing to the close relationship between the YWCA, the US business community, and the State Department, the YWCA and other women's empowerment organizations lent Hull and his state department successors their continued backing. In the late 1940s the YWCA published 'Filling the World's Market Basket' in *Public Affairs*, emphasizing the peace and prosperity to be derived from international trade liberalization.[36] Their free-trade efforts would claim more success after 1947, when the first negotiation round of the GATT ended with the twenty-three participating countries slashing import tariff rates. The United States led the way, lowering its tariffs on average by thirty-five per cent. For decades to come, the YWCA, WILPF, the American Association of University Women (AAUW), the National League of Women Voters (NLWV), the National Women's Trade Union League of America, the Women's Action Committee for Lasting Peace, WILPF, and the United Council of Church Women (UCCW) continued to back the RTAA, which strengthened presidential trade negotiation powers and the GATT. These groups also supported unsuccessful supranational freer-trade initiatives such as the ITO in the mid- to late 1940s and the Organization for Trade Cooperation in 1955. The stark choice before them was clear: 'trade cooperation or trade warfare'.[37]

The US feminist peace movement's support for the GATT extended well into the 1970s. The movement, both secular and ecumenical, maintained its connection to the White House and State Department in support of freeing

US and world trade. The NLWV continued to associate free trade with peace amid the Cold War and decolonization, believing that open markets were an essential means of aiding global economic development and halting the spread of communism, as well as keeping prices low for consumers.[38] In 1972 the YWCA—along with the AAUW, the NLWV, the National Council of Jewish Women (NCJW), and the National Council of Negro Women (NCNW)—next founded the Consumer Education Council on World Trade (CECWT). The CECWT lobbied in support of the Nixon administration's Trade Reform Act of 1973, arguing to the Senate Finance Committee that protectionism was against the consumer's interests and that 'it therefore behooves the American consumers to become vigorous advocates of a freer trade policy. [...] Considering that the American consumer is the one most likely to be affected adversely by trade barriers, and from the potential trade wars which such barriers are prone to generate, this seems to be assigning the consumer a very low priority.'[39] As late as 1974, the AAUW, Church Women United (CWU), the NLWV, the NCJW, and the NCNW joined with the YWCA to lend their political weight to the continuation of the GATT. Their free-trade humanitarianism also extended to condemning the US trade embargoes of Vietnam and Cuba.[40]

The YWCA's Cold War commercial peace crusade also highlights how left-wing Christian cosmopolitans maintained their century-long alliance with their secular counterparts to liberalize the global economic order as God had intended. Together they emphasized the USA's moral obligation to become permanently engaged with the new supranational organizations tasked with regulating the new multilateral order and other nations. Their left-wing communion would continue to lobby for their preferred policies in the two decades that followed the Second World War.[41] Hull's trade reforms remained a top priority. In 1948, for example, under the umbrella of the CCRWT, these further Christian organizations gave their pacifistic endorsement to maintaining the RTAA: the Methodist Church's Women's Division; the Presbyterian Church in the USA; the UCCW; the CAIP; the Church Peace Union; the Council for Social Action of the Congregational Christian Churches; the Federal Council of the Churches of Christ in America (FCC); and the Friends' Peace Committee.[42]

These groups increasingly identified Western economic imperialism as a paramount threat to world peace. In the 1950s and 1960s, left-wing Christian globalists therefore became more strident in their opposition to Western neocolonialism. Their radical demands emphasized universal human rights, democratization, anti-racism, free trade, and aid to the developing world.[43] In the early 1960s the National Council of the Churches of Christ in the USA coordinated with CWU, the United Christian Youth Movement, the YWCA, and the YMCA to undertake a national education campaign. The campaign emphasized international cooperation through the UN, opposition to the Vietnam war, foreign aid, and 'more constructive trade policies [. . .] to the improvement of life for nations and peoples around the world'. The WCC's Commission of the Churches on International Affairs similarly endorsed UNCTAD's 1964 resolutions regarding international trade and cooperation, while praising the GATT's 'new attention' towards expanding trade with and between 'developing countries'.[44]

By the end of the 1960s, the wider left-wing Protestant community was becoming more and more disillusioned with Western global market leadership, not least its dereliction of duty towards the world's poorest.[45] In 1968 J. M. Lochman, as chair of the WCC's World Economic and Social Development Section, demanded that more aid be given to the Third World. 'We must stop pillaging the developing countries,' he argued. 'We are still doing so today through the so-called free world market, which is increasing from year to year the gap between the prices at which these countries sell and the prices they have to pay for what they buy.' His critique reminds us of the disjunction people like him saw between the West's peaceful trade rhetoric and Western trade's coerciveness in practice. His solution entailed a reorganization of global markets to create price stability, limit speculation, and transfer resources more equitably to the developing world. It was a vision of a more just global free market: 'The essential thing is to transform the system of international trading and to purchase the agricultural or industrial products of the countries in the third world wherever they can produce more cheaply than the industrialized countries.'[46]

Lochman's reference here to 'the so-called free world market' pointed to how Western neomercantilism, rather than free-trade imperialism, remained the main sticking point. 'The rich countries surround themselves with protective tariffs and quotas', Lochman noted, 'so as to prevent exports from the third world entering their countries.' That argument aligned with economic critiques of Pax Americana from the Third World. S. L. Parmar of the United Church of Northern India, another member of the World Economic and Social Development Section, similarly chastised 'the growing tendency towards neo-isolationism', neocolonialism, and neomercantilism. The WCC ended up decrying how 'in several developing nations ruling groups monopolize the produce of their economy and allow foreign resources to aid and abet them in such action'. The WCC also called for an end to the US economic blockade against Cuba, and the creation of new 'supra-national structures' to stabilize the global economy and to 'increase multilateral aid programmes' and regional economic integration 'as steps toward a wider international community'. The WCC thus put forward a strong critique of Western neocolonialism and neo-mercantilism by arguing instead for a new supranational regulatory regime that maintained open markets in the Global North alongside temporary pro-tectionism and wealth transfer for the Global South to 'contribute to peace [. . .] towards the goal of one world community'.[47]

Elements of the Marx-Manchester tradition also survived after 1945, as so-cialist internationalist proponents of freer trade began to reconcile themselves to the infant industrial demands of the Global South while coming to grips with the divisions wrought by Cold War geopolitics. Contesting the unequal trading system through economic cooperation became a common refrain at conferences of the communist World Peace Council (WPC, founded in 1949) and the non-aligned International Confederation for Disarmament and Peace (ICDP, founded in 1963), as did opposing the US embargo of Cuba after 1962. The SPA gave its pacifistic endorsement to various US-led postwar trade lib-eralization projects, which remained a key ingredient of its peace programme well into the Cold War.[48] In 1948 the SPA laid out its plan for postwar peace. The plan included support for world governance through the UN; for decolo-nization; for 'world-wide outlawry of trade barriers'; and for 'world planning [. . .] to meet the needs of world, not national, markets' through the UN Food and Agriculture Organization and the ITO.[49] As late as 1952 the SPA yet main-tained that, to establish world peace, 'our interdependent world [. . .] has no room for isolation or economic nationalism', and that the UN's regulatory powers needed to be strengthened to better foster freer trade worldwide.[50] Such socialistic ideas informed labour groups' assessments of the state of world trade. The 1953 Trades Union Congress, which also included delegates from the Soviet Union and China, 'declared itself' for world peace and free trade. The thirty-fifth Australian Trade Union Congress in Brisbane in 1959 unanimously endorsed resolutions in support of socialism, 'international peace and free trade with all countries'.[51] The West German Social Democratic Party (SPD)'s 1959 Godesberg programme, in turn, curtailed the power of monopolies, protected private property, provided aid for the developing world to distribute wealth more equitably, opposed nuclear weapons, and called for free trade as a requirement for world peace.[52] As sociologist Stephanie Mudge argues, Western left-wing parties were finding a third way between the welfare state and the free market.[53] As they did so, they emphasized their left-wing vision of globalization, even as they tempered it to the hard realities of the Cold War and the nationalistic demands of the welfare state.

The 'third way' grassroots socialist internationalism of co-operativism became a staple of US foreign economic policy between the 1940s and 1960s. Under US auspices, co-operativism, too, reconciled itself to Cold War realities in its pacifistic efforts to counteract food insecurity and the revolutionary spread of communist collectivism. The European co-operative movement found itself destitute after the Second World War, opening the way for new US leadership. The US co-operative movement began at home before moving abroad. By 1960, nearly a quarter of US families were associated with a co-operative. Co-operatives had come about as close as they ever would to the US political mainstream, such that at the 1961 National Conference on International Economic and Social Development in Washington DC, Democratic president John F. Kennedy himself delivered the keynote speech. This was followed by that of Democratic senator Hubert Humphrey. A member of the Senate Foreign Relations Committee, Humphrey argued that the co-operative way was the American way. For him, co-operativism needed to be exported to Latin America, Africa, the Middle East, and Asia alongside military aid, financial investment, and free trade in order to defeat communism and famine. Such 'a mobilization meeting for peace' was the 'only way [. . .] to save this area of the world from collectivism'. His vision was shaped by the Cold War, but also by a vision of peaceful cooperation: 'They answer the Communist collective. This is the "democratic cooperative". And everybody knows it. [. . .] America must never become a dominator—it must become a cooperator.' Humphrey made sure to insert a global call for co-operative development in the 1961 Foreign Assistance Act's section on the 'vital role of free enterprise'. Heads of the US co-operative movement were made advisors to the United States Agency for International Development (USAID) through the 1960s with the goal of establishing forty thousand co-operatives in fifty-three nations. Amid the ideological contest of the Cold War, however, promoting peace soon took a back seat relative to promoting profits, despite attempts to place the Peace Corps within the State Department's International Cooperation Administration. Between the 1970s and 1980s the US co-operative movement lost its moralistic momentum, as multinational corporations gained the upper hand in US and supranational trade negotiations.[54]

As they reconciled themselves to the divisiveness of the Cold War, many left-leaning European political leaders and peace activists began substituting regionalism for globalism. For them, regional economic integration became the entering wedge for a new era of free trade and cooperation. As touched upon in preceding chapters, liberal radical, socialist internationalist, feminist, and Christian peace workers had been fighting for European integration as a peace project for a very long time indeed—since the mid-nineteenth century. The sentiment had not waned. As discussed in chapter 2, thanks to Cordell Hull's State Department protégé Will Clayton, funds from the Marshall Plan got regional integration rolling in 1948 with the formation of the Organization for European Economic Co-operation (OEEC), replaced by the Organization for Economic Co-operation and Development (OECD) in 1961. Throughout the 1950s, the West German SPD, the French Socialist Party, and other leading European socialist internationalists favoured pan-European trade liberalization to foster a more peaceful and prosperous continent. As French foreign minister Robert Schuman described it in 1950, 'world peace' required 'a united Europe'. Governed under 'a common High Authority' that reported to the UN, such a union would thwart the 'restrictive practices' of 'international cartels' by fusing European markets together.[55] Their combined efforts led to the creation of the European Coal and Steel Community in 1951 and the European Economic Community (EEC) in 1957, which Britain joined in 1973.[56] In response to Third World demands, between 1971 and 1975 the EEC also became the first to allow manufactured products from all G77 countries tariff-free access without requiring reciprocity.[57] The 1975 Helsinki Final Act, in turn, not only recognized the principle of universal human rights—it also provided a pacifistic reaffirmation of European integration.[58]

Integrating Europe was by no means the sole demesne of the Left. The EEC became a peace project that numerous European right-wing supporters of freer markets also got behind. Unsurprisingly, British liberals were ready to join a common European market in 1946.[59] What is surprising is that Britain would join the EEC in 1973 under a Conservative government, foreshadowing free trade's rightward drift within British politics under Margaret Thatcher's Tory leadership. Right-wing neoliberals such as the Austrian Friedrich Hayek also weighed in, just as he and other neoliberal intellectuals were becoming a more organized 'thought collective' via the Mont Pèlerin Society.[60] Hayek argued that European states needed to surrender certain national economic powers to a supranational federative body. Doing so would undermine national monopolies and national socialisms, and thereby create a peaceful European 'liberal economic regime' fostered through free trade. Hayek also recognized that socialist free-trade internationalists had much in common with capitalist advocates of Manchester liberalism, owing to their shared desire to overturn the military-economic nationalist world order that had prevailed over the late nineteenth and early twentieth centuries.[61] European integration therefore heralded a new era of regional prosperity and peace that both left-wing and right-wing free traders could get behind. But for non-members in the Soviet and developing worlds, the EEC instead represented a powerful trade bloc from which they were often excluded. In reality, the EEC was a bit of both.

The advent of the grassroots left-wing Fair Trade movement in Britain around 1970 gave the commercial peace movement much-needed neo-Cobdenite reinforcements to combat the emerging triumvirate of neocolonialism, neomercantilism, and neoliberalism. Fair Traders wanted to make the world trading system more moral and equitable through consumer activism. They encouraged the purchase of ethically sourced products and sought an end to world hunger. What is signified by 'fair trade' here therefore is not to be confused with the right-wing protectionist meaning of the term, which had been in popular parlance since the 1870s as shorthand for tit-for-tat tariff retaliation, as touched upon in chapter 1. The post-1945 Fair Trade movement, which by the late 1970s included more and more left-wing mainline Protestant and feminist organizations, also often relied on boycotts should an imported product be suspected of relying on exploitative labour or environmentally damaging practices.[62] If this all sounds familiar, so it should: the Fair Trade movement was an ideological heir, however unwittingly, of the mid-nineteenth-century Quaker-led Free Produce movement in which economic peace workers such as Joseph Sturge took part (see chapter 5), as well as the ethical efforts of the feminist peace movement such as US Marxist feminist Florence Kelley's turn-of-the-century National Consumers' League (NCL) and WILPF from the 1920s (see chapter 4).[63]

The left-wing Fair Trade vision upheld key aspects of the anti-imperial free-trade tradition. Grassroots activists in Britain published its manifesto, the Haslemere Declaration, in 1968. The declaration called upon the Global North to eliminate all quotas, subsidies, and tariffs, and to follow its own GATT-required rules of liberalization to support Global South economic development. But Fair Trade was about more than just Third World economic development, opening Western markets to the Global South, and ethical consumerism. From the outset, Fair Trade was also an explicit anti-colonial and peace movement. The Haslemere Group's first publications included *The United States and Bolivia: A Case of Neocolonialism* (1969), published in the year that the group held its first peace conference, 'Poverty is Violence', in London.[64] Left-wing

Fair Trade stood for ethical trade liberalization, economic development, anti-colonialism, and peace.

The siting of Fair Trade's headquarters and first peace conference went against the grain. By 1945, New York City, Washington, DC, and Geneva had displaced London as the hubs of the free-trade-and-peace movement, a reflection of how advocates of Pax Economica accommodated themselves to Pax Americana's displacement of Pax Britannica. For a time, an ailing Cordell Hull remained its most prominent liberal radical representative. Christian, feminist, and socialist free traders worked with him and gave their support to the capitalist supranational initiatives that he helped create, such as the RTAA and the GATT. But Cold War geopolitics upset the Pax Economica chessboard, even as Third World demands for economic sovereignty and market access grew louder. The commercial peace movement found new allies in their anti-imperial fight against neocolonialism and neomercantilism through trade liberalization, decolonization, and regional integration projects such as the EEC. The protectionist side effects of the Cold War and decolonization thus sparked a renewal of left-wing grassroots activism among transnational networks of liberal radicals, feminists, Christians, socialists, international co-operativists, and Fair Traders. By 1970, however, the grassroots successes and failures of the left-wing free-trade-and-peace movement had unwittingly opened the door for right-wing 'neoliberal' free-trade ideas and policies that showed little sympathy for Third World demands.

Doors Reopened? Neoliberalism vs. the NIEO, 1970–1989

The growing popularity of neoliberalism in the 1970s and 1980s among Euro-American conservative politicians effectively ostracized free trade's left-wing supporters from the very supranational institutions and structures they had helped create. The death of Bretton Woods and the birth pangs of floating exchange rates in the early 1970s caused a global recession and demands for a new economic order from both left and right. Republican president Richard Nixon's dismantling of Bretton Woods's fixed monetary exchange rates brought with it severe inflation and unemployment, or 'stagflation', causing demand for goods from the developing world to fall and the costs of imports to skyrocket. The crisis worsened following the 1973 Yom Kippur War between Egypt and Israel, whereupon the Organization of the Petroleum Exporting Countries cartel ratcheted up global oil prices, including punitive embargoes against what Mexican foreign minister Emilio Rabasa described as the 'monopolistic countries' in the West that had supported Israel.[65] But the global economic crisis also provided new opportunities. On the Left, the developing world and the economic peace movement saw a path towards establishing a more equitable trade system, even as hot-button issues such as nuclear non-proliferation and universal human rights competed for the attention of the wider international peace movement.[66] The commercial peace movement was more and more open to the demands of the Global South. Through UNCTAD, the NIEO, the G77, and the Non-Aligned Movement, the Third World sought to rebalance the rules of trade in its favour, to protect sovereign control over its countries' raw materials, and to demand that the First World practise what it preached by freeing its markets. On the Right, Bretton Woods's demise made way for freeing trade through supranational governance along neoliberal lines. The First World, warming to the free-market ideas of right-wing neoliberal intellectuals, wanted to open the doors of trade by making markets more profitable and less democratic, sovereignty and Third World exceptions be damned. The Nixon administration's détente with the anti-democratic communist regime in China following the Sino–Soviet split also opened up new market opportunities.

The economic peace movement may have unintentionally helped pave the way for neoliberalism's right-wing ascendancy, but they should not be conflated with one another. Granted, right-wing intellectuals like Friedrich Hayek drew from the same Manchester liberal wellspring as the commercial peace movement, and saw many of the same globalist postcolonial opportunities stemming from decolonization. Similar to left-wing economic peace workers, neoliberals such as Hayek supported supranational oversight and a diminution of national sovereignty to enforce it. And like their left-wing counterparts, most European neoliberals (a label they initially gave to themselves) supported regional integration initiatives such as the EEC and continued to connect free trade with prosperity and peace.

But ideological affinities diverged when it came to the role of the welfare state, temporary protectionist exemptions for the Third World, labour protections, and democracy promotion. Unlike the left-wing commercial peace movement, neoliberals like Hayek of the Geneva School and the Chicago School's Milton Friedman were deeply critical of the welfare state, anti-colonial nationalism, and trade unions.[67] Neoliberals even gave their backing to authoritarian human-rights abusing regimes so long as they shared their free-market interests, as in the cases of Augusto Pinochet's Chile (1973–1990) and apartheid South Africa.[68] For such neoliberals, democracy was no longer seen as an accompaniment to worldwide free trade, but as an impediment.[69]

The neoliberals of the 1970s and 1980s also abandoned another key precept of Manchester liberalism: military non-interventionism. In the United States, the non-interventionism that Cordell Hull brought back into vogue in the 1930s and early 1940s was replaced by the late 1960s and early 1970s with a growing bipartisan willingness to support military interventions and to prop up compliant authoritarian regimes if it meant that the spectres of communism, protectionism, and anti-colonial nationalism were held at bay. The Cold War sowed distrust, pushing neoliberals further to the right, and hindering their ability to find common cosmopolitan ground with the left-wing economic peace movement, as did, too, their opposition to the NIEO. In sum, right-wing neoliberals such as Hayek advocated for what Quinn Slobodian calls 'militant globalism', in contrast to the pacifistic globalism of left-wing economic cosmopolitans.[70]

Neoliberals were proving particularly adroit in challenging the Christian wing of the economic peace movement by the 1970s. Such a Christian economic ideological realignment had already happened in West Germany. In 1949 the ordoliberal advocate of European free-trade federation Wilhelm Röpke had turned the Christian Democratic Party to support for what Samuel Moyn describes as 'a hybrid Christian-neoliberal welfare state'.[71] A similar right-wing Christian transformation was taking place within the United States. In 1950 George S. Benson, president of Arkansas's Harding College (which was associated with the right-wing Church of Christ) launched his 'Freedom Forums'. They were designed, as Gene Zubovich puts it, to 'rally for free enterprise'. As Darren Dochuk has uncovered, Benson's 'cult of free enterprise' was such that 'free enterprise economics grew into a pastime for the entire family to enjoy' in places like Orange County, California in the mid-1950s. From then onwards, Protestant free-enterprise cold-warriors such as Reinhold Niebuhr's 'Christian realists' continued to chip away at the peace-minded mainline Protestant Left, particularly the pacifistic WCC. Niebuhr's internationalist cold-warriors also garnered conservative nationalist rivals from Billy Graham's new evangelical journal *Christianity Today*. The journal—born in the mid-1950s from what William Inboden describes as 'a quintessentially American amalgam of conservative theology and free-market economics, of denominational fissures and evangelical unity'—was prone to attacking US foreign aid, the anti-nuclear movement, and the UN's Universal Declaration of Human Rights. The pro–free trade CAIP also lurched to the right, transforming itself into an anti-communist supporter of US containment and 'just war'. By 1970, when 'fair trade' was becoming the catchphrase of the Christian and secular Left, 'free enterprise' was becoming more associated with the white 'New Christian Right'. Under this new programme of right-wing proselytizing, free trade's connection to world peace was notable for its absence. The 1970s witnessed a new era of free-market propaganda targeting conservative Christian evangelicals, contributing to the left-wing ecumenical free-trade-and-peace movement's decline.[72]

The neoliberal ascendancy of Ronald Reagan from 1981 represented a new Republican epoch, as the party aligned itself more closely with Christian right-wing defenders of free enterprise. Conservative evangelical Jerry Falwell, a long-time admirer of Milton Friedman's work, became a crucial ally who believed that 'the free-enterprise system is clearly outlined [. . .] in the Bible'. He also opposed divestment and sanctions against apartheid South Africa, and disparaged anti-apartheid activists. As Bethany Moreton puts it, 'although free-market economic theories captured the hearts and minds of elite policy-makers in the later twentieth century, the animating spirit of Christian free enterprise shaped the outcome'.[73]

With his conservative evangelical partners, Reagan began dismantling what little remained of the New Deal and Hull's anti-imperialism of free trade. His administration slashed government jobs, cut taxes, deregulated the US market, and dragged its feet when pressured to implement economic sanctions against apartheid South Africa. He also saw no contradiction in decrying Big Government even as he massively expanded US military spending and the carceral state. Nor did Reagan the cold-warrior have any qualms about propping up dictators and intervening militarily to defend perceived threats to the expansion of free enterprise.[74]

A neoliberal revolution was also taking place across the pond during the 1970s and 1980s, where Friedrich Hayek acted as both advisor and muse to British Tory politician Margaret Thatcher. As practically her first act as Conservative leader, in a meeting in 1975 Thatcher 'reached into her briefcase and took out a book. It was Friedrich von Hayek's *The Constitution of Liberty*. Interrupting [the speaker], she held the book up for all of us to see. "This", she said sternly, "is what we believe," and banged Hayek down on the table.'[75] In 1982, Hayek himself encouraged her to look to the successful economic reforms of Pinochet's Chile as a guide for reforming Britain.[76] She apparently listened, and followed up her war in the Falklands with a violent crackdown on striking British miners, mass deregulation, privatization of the public sector, and reluctance to join the international anti-apartheid sanctions regime against South Africa.

While neoliberals—the Geneva School, the Chicago School, the Christian Right, Reagan, and Thatcher—rallied around free enterprise and grew distrustful of democracy, human rights, and national sovereignty, Third World visionaries instead sought to create a more equitable economic order that sanctified sovereign rights. This left-wing economic vision of the decolonizing world—the NIEO—innovatively combined elements of the anti-imperialism of free trade and the anti-imperialism of economic nationalism. The NIEO called upon the neocolonial powers to make their markets freer. At the same time, it called for distributive and social justice for the developing world through a combination of preferential trade, wealth transfer, infant industrial protectionism, and welfare state reforms.[77] Formally created in 1974, the NIEO arose following years of debate surrounding trade liberalization within the ITO and the GATT in the late 1940s and UNCTAD from 1964.

UNCTAD's interwar origin story in Argentina owed an intellectual debt to the previous century's GHS and the American System of protectionism. Following the First World War, Alejandro Bunge, a professor at the National University of La Plata and a grandson of the former Prussian consul-general Karl August Bunge von Reinessend und von Renschenbusch, bucked the prevailing pro–free trade trend among Argentine economists and socialists. As Edgar Dosman recounts, Bunge instead concluded that the imposed economic isolation of the war had worked to Argentina's benefit by stimulating the growth of the nation's infant industries and agricultural production. Autarky, he argued, needed to be cultivated to lower Argentina's dependence upon the USA and Britain. Bunge, trained in German universities, made his case in part by drawing upon the American System's leading intellectual lights: Henry Carey, Friedrich List, and the GHS.[78]

In 1920, Bunge acquired a new research assistant, an aspiring twenty-year-old economist named Raúl Prebisch. Bunge's advocacy for a German-style customs union between Argentina, Uruguay, Paraguay, Bolivia, and Chile intrigued Prebisch. But while he found Bunge's heterodox advocacy of the American System for Latin America refreshing in a field dominated by neoclassical theory, he was not yet a convert. Prebisch, whose father Albin had emigrated to Argentina from Germany in the late nineteenth century, soon hit it off better with Alejandro's brother, the sociologist Augusto Bunge, a key player within the Argentine Socialist Party (PSA: Partido Socialista Argentino). Under Augusto's tutelage, Prebisch briefly joined the PSA, and endorsed its various free-trade and Georgist land reform initiatives.[79] In line with the prevailing Marx-Manchester policies of the interwar PSA, Prebisch remained a free trader until the early 1930s.

The economic fallout from the Great Depression and the protectionist retrenchment among the leading industrial powers—including Britain, far and away Argentina's biggest export market—led Prebisch to believe that only a more activist Argentine state could further its development and expand its trade relationships. Among the consequences of the depression were decreasing global prices for raw materials and increases for industrial goods, a catastrophic combination for underdeveloped, export-reliant states such as Argentina. Britain's embrace of imperial trade preference in 1932 in turn signalled the end of British support for multilateralism, and the possible closure of Argentina's biggest export market.

Cap in hand, Prebisch joined the Argentine delegation tasked with negotiating a bilateral trade agreement with a neomercantilist British government. The British demanded big concessions from their erstwhile Argentine counterparts, dangling over their heads like the sword of Damocles the threat of cutting off Argentine access to British markets. The unequal power dynamics on display were seared into Prebisch's memory; he returned to Argentina with a vision that was now more in line with Alejandro Bunge's Listian technocracy.[80] Prebisch got down to work devising Argentina's Economic Recovery Plan in 1933, which included a variety of protectionist measures designed to discourage imports, including raising tariffs to promote ISI and subsidizing a new highway system to undercut the British-monopolized railway system. The American System-style reforms were sold as temporary emergency measures in a mostly unsuccessful attempt to placate the pro–free trade PSA. The thirty-three-year-old economist next set about establishing a national central bank, followed by subsidies for Argentina's struggling agricultural exporters. The leading industrial powers, meanwhile, resorted to beggar-thy-neighbour protectionism, effectively closing off their markets to export-reliant agrarian economies such as Argentina's.[81]

Prebisch was therefore understandably sceptical when the United States and its Western allies started overhauling the global economic system in the late 1940s. From Prebisch's Latin American perspective, the GATT's trade liberalization programme appeared to have been designed with Western industrial powers foremost in mind, with little thought for the world's many underdeveloped agrarian-oriented economies. His scepticism only grew after the Democratic Truman administration supported the Cuban dictatorship of Fulgencia Batista in 1952, which broke with the non-interventionist promises of Hull's Good Neighbor policy. Adding salt to the wounds, two years later Dwight Eisenhower's Republican administration gave the green light to a CIA-backed coup against Guatemalan president Jacobo Arbenz Guzman. Prebisch's frequent roundtables in Santiago, Chile, in turn, gave voice to a powerful ideological alternative to that offered by Western neoclassical orthodoxy for Latin American industrialization. As Dosman puts it, Prebisch couched the Santiago gatherings in terms of a 'war of ideas', wherein Latin American nations needed to 'regain their intellectual autonomy and shake off the dead hand of US and European theorists. [. . .] Their version of the international division of labour and the "laws" of comparative advantage condemned Brazil and Latin America to remain suppliers of commodities under declining terms of trade.' Latin America needed to industrialize, but Prebisch's 'indigenous theory of development' did not mean self-sufficiency or a Soviet-style planned economy; rather, it called for an activist state that fostered foreign investment, subsidies, protective tariffs, ISI, and trade expansion.[82] Despite proclaiming an ideological break from Euro-American economics, Prebisch was effectively demanding American System policies for Latin America. And yet Argentina's adaptation of the American System was mistaken by many hotheaded US cold-warriors for a Soviet-style planned economy.

Third World economic nationalism thereafter contained a sharp anti-colonial edge in the postwar era of decolonization. Protectionism came to be seen as a safeguard against Western neocolonialism by the time UNCTAD was established in 1964, with Prebisch its inaugural secretary general.

UNCTAD's initial 1964 meeting in Geneva was the city's highlight of the year. About four thousand delegates representing over a hundred countries, media outlets, and international organizations filled Geneva's hotels to overflowing. More impressive still (and troubling for the developed nations), the developing countries showed up as a coherent caucus, the G77. Che Guevara himself made quite an entrance in his tailor-made pinstripe suit. But an even greater aura of anticipation filled the Palais des Nations when it came to Prebisch's new economic order. Prebisch's introductory remarks to the thousands in attendance brought them to their feet, a ringing endorsement for his promise to tackle global inequality. He even got an official message of support from the World Bank and an acknowledgment from Eric Wyndham-White, the British economist then running the GATT, that the two programmes were not in conflict or competition.

Wyndham-White's conciliatory response hints at the potential for shared space between UNCTAD and GATT at this moment. This was precisely the sort of North–South cooperation that the commercial peace movement was hoping to see: a Pax Economica that was truly global in scale and sympathetic to Third World demands. And it was a conciliatory refrain that left-wing supporters would return to time and again. As late as 1979, for example, the

French-Egyptian Marxist economist Samir Amin observed in his defence of the NIEO that 'this programme is perfectly in conformity with the principles defended by the liberal West. It places the highest ever priority on the object of intensified links of world economic interdependence.'[83]

But the airy promise of North–South rapprochement was quickly brought crashing back to earth owing to the intransigence of Pax Americana's representatives at the 1964 conference. US undersecretary George Ball criticized Prebisch and UNCTAD's idealistic message. He then announced that the US government would not support Prebisch's request for $20 billion in trade or financial concessions from the West unless the request for preferential treatment for Third World industrial exports was abandoned. Gridlock ensued. Delegates began joking in the hallways that for the world's developed nations the acronym UNCTAD stood for 'Under No Circumstances Take Any Decisions.'[84] The developmental road ahead of Prebisch and his successors suddenly looked a lot bumpier.

But the willingness of the G77 to work together also made the idea of a new economic order focused on the demands of the developing world seem more feasible following the global financial shocks of the early 1970s, paving the way for the NIEO. The UN General Assembly convened its first ever special session dedicated to economics in 1974. Then, on 1 May 1974, the General Assembly adopted a Declaration on the Establishment of the NIEO, despite reservations from the USA. UNCTAD was designated the forum for hashing out the details.

A closer look at the G77 debates within UNCTAD and the NIEO uncovers an oft-overlooked offshoot of the anti-imperialism of free trade. Che Guevara enunciated UNCTAD's Marx-Manchester ideological inheritance at its first gathering in 1964. He railed against the neomercantilism, embargoes, blockades, and other forms of 'trade discrimination practised by the imperialist metropolitan countries against the socialist countries'. Why? Because these neocolonial economic policies were 'a danger to world trade and world peace. This conference must also establish in plain terms the rights of all peoples to unrestricted freedom of trade.'[85] Guevara's radical critique of Western neocolonialism and his tying of freer trade to world peace were just the tip of the iceberg. Albania's trade minister, Kiço Ngjela, similarly targeted 'the selfish and neo-colonialist policy of exploitation carried out by the imperialist powers, first and foremost by American imperialism. All discrimination, blockades and artificial restrictions on foreign trade must be liquidated.' According to Ngjela, such Western neocolonialism stretched from the US embargo of Cuba to the tariff discrimination of the European Common Market. A similar, albeit less polemical, refrain appeared in UNCTAD secretary-general Raúl Prebisch's report, 'Towards a New Trade Policy for Development', which singled out the protectionist policies of western Europe and the United States on agricultural products as principal stumbling blocks. UNCTAD's continued support for trade liberalization and South–South cooperation through programmes such as its Economic Cooperation among Developing Countries represented a new phase of post-1945 socialist globalization, encompassing the Soviet and non-aligned world as well as nations within the US Cold War orbit.[86] Elements of the century-old Marx-Manchester tradition thus remained visible within UNCTAD.

Aspects of the Marx-Manchester legacy were next carried over into the NIEO. This remained dedicated to multilateralism alongside eradication of 'the remaining vestiges of alien and colonial domination, foreign occupation, racial discrimination, apartheid and neo-colonialism in all its forms'.[87] High on the NIEO's 'Programme of Action' was 'improved access to markets in developed countries through the progressive removal of tariff and non-tariff barriers and of restrictive business practices', coupled with regional economic integration.[88] Its 'Charter of Economic Rights and Duties of States', spear-headed by Mexican president Luis Echeverría, called for 'increasing expansion and liberalization of world trade' to maintain 'international peace' and 'friendly relations among nations', starting with the removal of discriminatory tariffs among 'developed countries'.[89] The NIEO's emphasis upon economic integration, non-interventionism, supranational governance, and freer trade in the Global North bore the stamp of the Marx-Manchester free-trade tradition.

However, the NIEO's left-wing freer-trade endorsement was coupled with calls for more sovereignty and protectionist exemptions to allow the developing world to catch up. The NIEO's anti-imperialism of economic nationalism emphasized a return of state control over natural resources to counteract the neocolonial influence of the Western powers. Whereas the previous century of economic peace work had emphasized supranational regulation of raw materials and their worldwide distribution to undermine one of the main causes of colonialism, the NIEO wanted more sovereignty over national resources, not less. The protectionist emphasis also extended to other key policies. The NIEO requested price controls, preferential trade arrangements, technology transfer, wealth redistribution, and access to non-coercive foreign financial assistance. These aspects reflected elements of the Marx-List tradition discussed in chapter 3, which set NIEO advocates further apart from their neoliberal contemporaries, as did the NIEO's stronger emphasis on social jus-tice, democratization, and public ownership of the means of production.

The NIEO's ideologies created an economic ideological Gordian knot, by enunciating simultaneously aspects of the anti-imperialism of free trade and of the anti-imperialism of economic nationalism. Its support for economic interdependence as a prerequisite for peace and justice contained elements of the Marx-Manchester tradition. Its protectionist prescription for the decolo-nizing world, however, placed it within a longer legacy of anti-imperial activ-ism that had formerly been grounded within the late nineteenth- and early twentieth-century anti-colonial spaces of the British Empire. Considering that Argentina had fallen within the orbit of Britain's informal free-trade empire by the mid-nineteenth century, Prebisch's own contributions to the creation of UNCTAD and the NIEO are quite fitting.[90] We can also see within the Global South's critiques of neocolonialism outlined above that the West's imperialism of economic nationalism was much more of a concern to the NIEO than was the imperialism of free trade. It was a concern that was broadly shared by the left-wing commercial peace movement, but not by right-wing neoliberals, who viewed the NIEO's economic nationalist demands for the Global South as the greater threat.

From around 1970, globalists on both the Left and the Right were prepared to open new doors to trade, but with very different priorities in mind. Left-wing economic peace workers reinvested in their free-trade grassroots and warmed to UNCTAD-NIEO anti-colonial calls for freer trade for the Global North and temporary protectionism for the Global South. Right-wing neo-liberal intellectuals and politicians similarly supported free enterprise, in-tegration, and supranational governance, but were instead suspicious of sovereignty, democracy, anti-colonial nationalism, and non-interventionism. The right-wing reforms of Ronald Reagan and Margaret Thatcher laid the groundwork for the neoliberal free-trade regime that would arise at the Cold War's end. During the 1970s and 1980s, the US and UK governments brazenly cosied up to authoritarian regimes willing to accept the free enterprise system and to violently quash left-wing nationalist challengers. Crushing debt also laid waste to many developing states that had little choice but to take loans from the Western-controlled IMF and World Bank. As a result, by the early 1980s the NIEO found its negotiating position severely weakened. This em-boldened Reagan and Thatcher, long-time fans of Hayek and Friedman, to reject the NIEO's demands, paving the way for the post–Cold War neolib-eral order.[91]

The Rise and Fall of the Neoliberal Order, 1989–2016

The collapse of the Soviet Union made globalism great again. The Berlin Wall's dismantling in 1989 became emblematic of a new age of openness as Western neoliberalism began to displace socialist globalization.[92] Neoliberal integration at a regional and global scale had seemingly replaced the divisiveness of the Cold War. The European Union (EU) came into being in 1993. The North American Free Trade Agreement (NAFTA) came into effect in 1994. The World Trade Organization (WTO) was launched in 1995. The cosmopolitan imagination ran wild. 'Instead of containment or détente,' the German philosopher Thomas Pogge noted in 1992, 'political scientists are discussing grand pictures: the end of history, or the inevitable proliferation and mutual pacifism of democracies. And politicians are speaking of a new world order.'[93] Globalist soothsayers augured that the end of the nation state was at hand: that national sovereignty would soon be subordinated to supranational governance, and global citizenship would displace national tribalism.[94] The world's markets appeared open for neoliberal business. 'By the end of the twentieth century,' Slobodian observes, 'it was a common belief that free-market ideology had conquered the world.'[95] Free enterprise displaced the welfare state as the economic handmaiden of human rights. But while the world was perhaps becoming more humane, it was also becoming more unequal, as the developing world fell deeper into debt.[96] The swift rise of the oligarchs in post-Soviet Russia, in turn, aptly illustrated that neoliberalism did not travel hand in glove with democracy. The gradual erosion of democracy in Latin America, Europe, and the United States in the decades since provide further evidence.[97] The ending of the Cold War indeed opened up former Soviet markets previously off limits to the capitalist West and offered up a new era of bipartisan, US-led multilateralism, the 'Washington Consensus'. But this neoliberal order—this new era of the Pax Americana—fell far short of the ethical, equitable, and regulatory requirements that left-wing economic peace workers sought.

The tripartite rhetoric of free trade, democracy, and peace nevertheless became bipartisan US mainstays of the neoliberal order. Republican George H. W. Bush praised all three in his 1991 State of the Union address during his push for what would become NAFTA. That same year, he awarded ninety-two-year-old Friedrich Hayek a Presidential Medal of Freedom, noting 'how magnificent it must be for him to witness his ideas validated before the eyes of the world.'[98] The conservative strain of peace through free trade glossed over its most glaring contradictions and inconsistencies, even as it became a bipartisan refrain.

'Democracy and free trade go hand in hand,' Democratic president Bill Clinton similarly noted in 1994, when NAFTA came into force. He next backed the creation of the WTO to replace the GATT as the clearinghouse for global trade disputes. The 'Washington Consensus' was by now firmly entrenched.[99] Clinton's championing of free trade and supranational economic governance even led economist Alfred Eckes to opine in 1995 that Clinton represented 'Cobden's Pyrrhic victory', the ill-fated triumph of Cobdenism in the USA.[100] Clinton's Republican successor, George W. Bush, in turn called the signing of the Central American Free Trade Agreement in 2005 'a commitment of freedom-loving nations to advance peace and prosperity throughout the Western hemisphere', and similarly backed the massive Trans-Pacific Partnership (TPP), as would Democratic president Barack Obama after him.[101]

Such bipartisan free-trade-and-peace rhetoric may have contained echoes of Manchester liberalism, but their foreign policy track records told a different story. These presidents were not neo-Cobdenites dedicated to non-interventionism, democracy, and peace: far from it. For example, the Cuban embargo—that seemingly perpetual enshrinement of US closed-door imperialism—remained official policy throughout the neoliberal era. George H. W. Bush and Bill Clinton's debilitating economic sanctions against Iraq following the first Gulf War (1990–1991) wreaked havoc upon Iraqi civilians; UNICEF estimated that upwards of half a million Iraqi children under the age of five died as a result. Bipartisan US policy towards Haiti during the neoliberal era, sandwiched between two US invasions of Iraq, provides yet another case study in the anti-democratic interventionism of the neoliberal state. Beginning in 1991, George H. W. Bush and subsequently Bill Clinton secretly backed the right-wing paramilitaries responsible for overthrowing the democratically elected left-wing president of Haiti, Jean-Bertrand Aristide. The military junta's leader responsible for the coup, Emmanuel Constant, had been a CIA asset. After years of turning away Haitian refugees seeking asylum from the brutal Constant regime, Clinton only returned Aristide to power in 1995 once the latter promised to practise economic austerity as laid out by the World Bank and the IMF. Constant, responsible for the murder of thousands of Haitian pro-democracy activists, was thereafter allowed to live freely in New York City. George W. Bush would once again tacitly back the overthrow of liberation theologian Aristide in 2004 not long after Aristide requested $21 billion in reparations from France. The reparations harkened back to the debts accrued following Haitian independence two centuries prior. In 2022 the *New York Times* reported how the French ambassador to Haiti at the time of the

2004 coup had admitted that the United States 'had effectively orchestrated "a coup" against Mr. Aristide', partly in response to his request for reparations.[102] These examples, far from exhaustive, are only meant to highlight the post-1989 bipartisan neoliberal penchant for coercive interventionism and the superficiality of the Washington Consensus's stated belief in the power of free trade to promote peace and democracy.

Rather than fostering peace, moreover, the neoliberal era brought endless US war.[103] After 1989, the projection of US military power reigned supreme. Both major political parties oversaw a host of military interventions large and small, culminating in the bipartisan-backed US invasions of Afghanistan and Iraq following the terrorist attacks of 11 September 2001. The invasion of Afghanistan in late 2001 would stretch on to become the USA's longest war. George W. Bush next misled the US public into supporting the invasion of Iraq in 2003 on the false premise that Saddam Hussein had been behind '9/11', coupled with the belief that democracy could best be exported at the barrel of a gun. The Bush administration's neoliberal preference for free enterprise also meant that the rebuilding of Iraq fell largely to private US companies.[104]

Neoliberal imperialism received plenty of left-wing opposition in the 1990s and after, but the free-trade advocacy of the Washington Consensus muddied the ideological waters for what remained of the economic peace movement. Neoliberals had effectively co-opted free trade as a neocolonial tool. This left free trade's left-wing proponents in a difficult bind, which echoed a sentiment of British Marx-Manchester peace worker Bertrand Russell from a century earlier: 'It seems to be the fate of idealists to obtain what they have struggled for in a form which destroys their ideals.'[105] Then came the Great Recession of 2008–2009, a side effect of financial market deregulations begun during Bill Clinton's presidency. The recession fomented a populist rebellion against the Washington Consensus from both the Left and the Right in the respective guises of the Occupy Wall Street and the Tea Party movements. By 2016, the beginning of the end of the neoliberal order was at hand.[106]

Our Neomercantilist Moment, 2016–2022

Remnants of the 150-year-long left-wing economic peace movement are all around us. They are on display at the airport duty-free shop, or when picking up a copy of the *Economist* at the news stand. They can be found in pacifistic regional integration projects such as the EU. They can be glimpsed within global integration initiatives maintained through the OECD and the WTO. They live on in peace organizations such as the CEIP and WILPF. They underpin the moralistic economic cosmopolitan visions of Fair Trade and international co-operativism. They provide the ideological foundations of capitalist peace theory and of the world's remaining single-tax colonies. They are represented on Duol-ingo, where you can brush up on your Esperanto. They are even tucked away in attics and closets, as with the world's most popular board game *Monopoly*.

Whereas neoliberalism disassociated its brand of free trade from democ-racy promotion, what remains of the economic peace movement has done the opposite.[107] Since the 1990s, for example, WILPF has been quite clear in its opposition to neoliberal free-trade agreements, which, the organization argues, have been used to erode sovereignty, racial equality, labour and environmental rights, and democracy. As WILPF Boston's Valentine Moghadam explained in 2017, 'neoliberal capitalist globalization' may have 'liberalized markets and free trade' for the benefit of 'some countries and populations within them, but they have also driven out small businesses, undercut domestic producers, and pro-moted "the race to the bottom"'. Fair Trade remains WILPF's preferred choice for peaceful and equitable global economic interdependence. At the same time, WILPF and other women's peace organizations continue to oppose the imperialism of economic nationalism, not least the US embargo of Cuba.[108] The socialist WPC, amid its 'struggle for peace and democracy', similarly con-tinues to oppose the Cuban blockade, as do left-wing Protestant peace organizations.[109] Still other mainline Protestants today call for expanding global economic governance to guide trade liberalization along a more equitable and ethical path.[110] The director of Carnegie Europe, Rosa Balfour, in turn, blames ongoing troubles with China, Russian imperialism, and US economic nation-alism for destabilizing the long-standing transatlantic partnership between the US and the EU.[111]

As these left-leaning liberal radical, feminist, socialist, and Christian peace organizations illustrate, the free-trade-and-peace movement is down but not entirely out. The airport duty-free shop remains a global phenomenon, as does the co-operative movement, although the former has undergone its own neoliberal reformation, and neither is commonly associated with peace nowadays.[112] The Fair Trade movement also maintains an international pres-ence. While today's Fair Trade movement might oppose contemporary free-trade agreements between more advanced economies and the developing world, it does so because the agreements tend to be weak on protections for labour, the environment, and the consumer, not because Fair Traders are opposed to trade liberalization per se. For its supporters, the Fair Trade movement offers an alter-globalization—what Paul Adler refers to as 'fair globalization': an alternative to the neoliberal regime of trade liberalization that prioritizes corporate profits over human rights. Fair globalization instead emphasizes consumer, environmental, and labour rights, maintained through ethically driven regulation of world trade that draws upon a longer anti-monopoly tradition.[113] The movement also encourages consumers to pay more for ethically sourced goods and services, providing an indirect subsidy to 'the rest' to equalize trade and power imbalances with the West. Drawing upon its mid-twentieth-century liberal radical roots, the neoliberal WTO launched its Trade for Peace programme in 2018. The illiberal geopolitical fallout from Britain's dislocation from the EU, the growth of European right-wing nationalist parties, and Russia's annexation of Crimea and invasion of Ukraine have, however counterintuitively, helped reinforce the left-wing pacifistic rationale for a more interdependent Europe.[114] Last but not least, the long-sought dream of pan-African economic union is now becoming a reality. With the neoliberal endorsement of the World Bank and the WTO's Trade for Peace programme, since 2021 fifty-four African nations have begun integrating in the name of prosperity, anti-colonialism, women's empowerment, and peace through the African Continental Free Trade Area.[115]

But these free-trade-and-peace initiatives are not concerted, nor are they pervasive within what little remains of today's international left-wing peace movement. This is partly a result of the hawkish right-wing neoliberal championing of free markets over the past half century, which has contributed to free trade's political and ideological disassociation from anti-imperialism and peace. Opposition to neoliberalism has encouraged the anti-war Left to seek a new foreign policy agenda bereft of any vestiges of liberal internationalism. As a result, outside what remains of the commercial peace movement, many on the Left today, such as Sam Moyn, remain far more sceptical of the pacifistic dividends to be gleaned from US-led multilateralism. Others still, like Aziz Rana, envisage 'a genuinely anti-imperial alternative' social democratic order that is divorced from US-style free market capitalism.[116] In Europe, far-Left intellectuals such as German socialist theorist Wolfgang Streeck have gone further in expressing their antipathy towards free markets and open borders; Streeck has even given Brexit his blessing, seeing it as the beginning of the end of the EU's neoliberal empire project.[117] Where for so long economic cosmopolitanism and regional integration were precepts of the international peace movement that bridged the divide between moderates and the far Left, they are now more often treated as the right-wing weapons of neocolonialism and neoliberalism.

But must a Pax Economica be in opposition to a Pax Americana, Pax Europa, or Pax Atlantica?[118] Not according to the leaders of the commercial peace movement explored here. For them, the pacifistic leadership of the United States and Europe was considered essential for obtaining their democratic, equitable, non-interventionist, and interdependent economic order between the 1840s and today. And for a fleeting moment in the late 1940s, things even seemed to be going their way. In response to the Cold War penchant for neocolonialism and neomercantilism, the commercial peace movement next warmed to the anti-colonial leadership of the Global South through UNCTAD and the NIEO. This book's left-wing globalists would recommend for today a new supranational governing structure that included a triumvirate of the United States, Europe, and the Global South. They'd also recommend that if regulatory bodies such as the WTO are no longer fit for purpose in defending democracy, social justice, and peace alongside free markets, then they should either be reformed or replaced entirely. But they would not abandon their dream of an interdependent world at peace. They would also be amenable to working with more moderate capitalist allies to bring these pacifistic reforms to fruition.

It remains to be seen whether the mounting left-wing opposition to economic cosmopolitanism will continue now that, in recent years, the legacies and continuities of neomercantilism have become so pronounced. Granted, some neomercantilist elements were on display well before the post-2016 turn against the neoliberal order. Economic sanctions, sanctified in the interwar years, had already become the punitive weapons of first resort in world affairs during the neoliberal era.[119] And the ongoing US embargo of Cuba highlights how the imperialism of economic nationalism has remained a coercive tool of US foreign policy for over half a century. But the 2016 Brexit referendum and Republican president Donald Trump's 'America First' foreign policy have brought a new neomercantilist order into existence. Trump's brand of America First economics included trade wars with the nation's main trading partners, pulling the USA out of the TPP, scrapping NAFTA, and working to dismantle the WTO from within. Democratic president Joe Biden has maintained and even expanded upon many of his Republican predecessor's economic nationalist policies, hinting at a new protectionist Washington Consensus for the twenty-first century. Brexit, in turn, has created barriers to trade and geopolitical tensions with Britain's largest trading partner, the EU, threatening the very fabric of the European peace project.[120] Numerous nationalist governments across the globe have, in due course, followed the Anglo-American neomercantilist assault on neoliberal multilateralism.[121] These attacks have only been exacerbated by the Covid pandemic, China's regional expansionist designs, and Russia's nationalist imperialism in Ukraine. Russian export embargoes on natural gas to Europe, the loss of Ukrainian wheat from global markets, and crippling Western economic sanctions against Russia have further haemorrhaged global supply chains and worsened world food and energy insecurity. The neoliberal order has been placed on notice. Today's nascent economic nationalist order—punctuated by trade wars, sanctions, imperial interventions, and impotent supranational oversight—bears all the neomercantilist hallmarks that the commercial peace movement had fought against for the past 150 years.

The history of the left-wing fight for free trade, anti-imperialism, and peace challenges what appears to be a growing economic nationalist partnership between the far Left and the far Right. It does so by recovering a radical economic cosmopolitan tradition that for so long created alliances between peace-minded liberal reformers and leftist revolutionaries. Rediscovery of the economic peace movement's radical history arrives as left-wing internationalists search for a new foreign policy to combat both neoliberalism and a new twenty-first-century protectionist order. Our current neomercantilist moment, should it continue, might spell the beginning of the end of the post–Cold War neoliberal regime. But neoliberalism's demise might also open the door once again to left-wing globalist dreams of Pax Economica.

NOTES

Acknowledgements

1. Marc-William Palen, 'Economic Nationalism in an Imperial Age, 1846–1946', in Aviel Roshwald, Matthew D'Auria, and Cathie Carmichael, eds, *The Cambridge History of Nationhood and Nationalism*, 2 vols (Cambridge: Cambridge University Press, 2023), 2: 538–58; Palen, 'Marx and Manchester: The Evolution of the Socialist Internationalist Free-Trade Tradition, c. 1846–1946', *International History Review* 43 (March 2021): 381–98; Palen, 'British Free Trade and the Feminist Vision for Peace, c. 1846–1946', in David Thackeray, Richard Toye, and Andrew Thompson, eds, *Imagining Britain's Economic Future, c. 1800–1975: Trade, Consumerism, and Global Markets* (London: Palgrave MacMillan, 2018), 115–31; Palen, 'The Imperialism of Economic Nationalism, 1890–1913', *Diplomatic History* 39 (Jan. 2015): 157–85; Palen, 'Pandemic Protectionism: Revisiting the 1918 "Spanish" Flu in the Era of COVID-19', *Diplomatic History* 45 (June 2021): 571–79; Palen, 'The Transimperial Roots of American Anti-imperialism: The Transatlantic Radicalism of Free Trade, 1846–1920', in Jay Sexton and Kristin Hoganson, eds, *Crossing Empires: Taking US History into Transimperial Terrain* (Durham, NC: Duke University Press, 2020), 159–82.

Introduction

1. 'Strike Up the Band', *Variety* 88 (7 Sept. 1927), 54.

2. 'Theaters: Strike Up the Band', *Christian Science Monitor* (26 Dec. 1929), 12.

3. Marc-William Palen, 'Pandemic Protectionism: Revisiting the 1918 "Spanish" Flu in the Era of COVID-19', *Diplomatic History* 45 (June 2021): 571–79.

4. G. John Ikenberry, *A World Safe for Democracy: Liberal Internationalism and the Crises of Global Order* (New Haven: Yale University Press, 2020).

5. Duncan Bell and Srdjan Vucetic, 'Brexit, CANZUK, and the Legacy of Empire', *British Journal of Politics and International Relations* 21 (2019): 367–82.

6. See, among others, David Harvey, *A Brief History of Neoliberalism* (Oxford: Oxford University Press, 2005); Philip Mirowski and Dieter Plehwe, eds, *The Road from Mont Pèlerin: The Making of the Neoliberal Thought Collective* (Cambridge, MA: Harvard University Press, 2009); Ben Jackson, 'At the Origins of Neo-Liberalism: The Free Economy and the Strong State, 1930–1947', *Historical Journal* 53 (March 2010): 129–51; Jamie Peck, *Constructions of Neoliberal Reason* (Oxford: Oxford University Press, 2010); Angus Burgin, *The Great Persuasion: Reinventing Free Markets Since the Depression* (Cambridge, MA: Harvard University Press, 2012); Daniel Stedman Jones, *Masters of the Universe: Hayek, Friedman, and the Birth of Neoliberal Politics* (Princeton:

Princeton University Press, 2012); Edward Nik-Khah and Robert Van Horn, 'The Ascendancy of Chicago Neoliberalism', in Kean Birch, Simon Springer, and Julie MacLeavy, eds, *The Handbook of Neoliberalism* (London: Routledge, 2016), 27–38; Quinn Slobodian, *Globalists: The End of Empire and the Birth of Neoliberalism* (Cambridge, MA: Harvard University Press, 2018); Gary Gerstle, *The Rise and Fall of the Neoliberal Order: America and the World in the Free Market Era* (Oxford: Oxford University Press, 2022); Jamie Martin, *The Meddlers: Sovereignty, Empire, and the Birth of Global Economic Governance* (Cambridge, MA: Harvard University Press, 2022); Clara E. Mattei, *The Capital Order: How Economists Invented Austerity and Paved the Way to Fascism* (Chicago: University of Chicago Press, 2022).

7. Glenda Sluga, *Internationalism in the Age of Nationalism* (Philadelphia: University of Pennsylvania Press, 2013), 43–44; Martin H. Geyer and Johannes Paulmann, eds, *The Mechanics of Internationalism: Culture, Society, and Politics from the 1840s to the First World War* (Oxford: Oxford University Press, 2001), 2, 24; Anthony Howe, 'Free Trade and Global Order: The Rise and Fall of a Victorian Vision', in Duncan Bell, ed., *Victorian Visions of Global Order: Empire and International Relations in Nineteenth-Century Political Thought* (Cambridge: Cambridge University Press, 2007), 26–46 at 35–36; Walter D. Mignolo, 'The Many Faces of Cosmo-polis: Border Thinking and Critical Cosmopolitanism', *Public Culture* 12 (2000): 721–48; David Weinstein, 'Consequentialist Cosmopolitanism', in Bell, *Victorian Visions*, 267–90.

8. Eric Helleiner, *The Neomercantilists: A Global Intellectual History* (Ithaca, NY: Cornell University Press, 2021).

9. See, for instance, Caroline Elkins, *Legacy of Violence: A History of the British Empire* (New York: Penguin, 2022); Jennifer Pitts, *A Turn to Empire: The Rise of Imperial Liberalism in Britain and France* (Princeton: Princeton University Press, 2005); Uday Singh Mehta, *Liberalism and Empire: Study in Nineteenth-Century British Liberal Thought* (Chicago: University of Chicago Press, 1999); Karuna Mantena, 'The Crisis of Liberal Imperialism', in Bell, *Victorian Visions*, 113–35; Bernard Semmel, *The Liberal Ideal and the Demons of Empire: Theories of Imperialism from Adam Smith to Lenin* (Baltimore: Johns Hopkins University Press, 1993); Onur Ince, *Colonial Capitalism and the Dilemmas of Liberalism* (Oxford: Oxford University Press, 2018); Jens-Uwe Guettel, *German Expansionism, Imperial Liberalism and the United States, 1776–1945* (Cambridge: Cambridge University Press, 2012); Matthew P. Fitzpatrick, *Liberal Imperialism in Germany: Expansion and Nationalism, 1848–1884* (New York: Berghahn, 2008).

10. Stephen Howe, *Anticolonialism in British Politics*, 30. See also Edmund Fawcett, *Liberalism: The Life of an Idea* (Princeton: Princeton University Press, 2018), 202–6; Gregory Claeys, 'The "Left" and the Critique of Empire c. 1865–1900: Three Roots of Humanitarian Foreign Policy', in Bell, *Victorian Visions*, 239–40.

11. Tara Zahra, *Against the World: Anti-Globalism and Mass Politics Between the World Wars* (New York: W. W. Norton, 2023), 2.

12. Helen Bosanquet, *Free Trade and Peace in the Nineteenth Century* (London: Williams and Norgate, 1924), 74.

13. Merle Curti, *Peace or War: The American Struggle 1636–1936* (New York: W. W. Norton, 1936), 307–8; Gorham Bert Munson, 'The Sterility of Pacifist Economics', *The Christian Century* 56 (19 April 1939), 513; John K. Nelson, *The Peace Prophets: American Pacifist Thought, 1919–1941* (Chapel Hill: University of North Carolina Press, 1967), 60–63.

14. See, for example, Mark Mazower, *Governing the World: The History of an Idea, 1815 to the Present* (New York: Penguin, 2012), 31–48; Ikenberry, *World Safe for Democracy*, 79–88.

15. *International Free Trader* 2 (June 1919), 3.

16. Sluga, *Internationalism*, 42.

17. Semmel, *Liberal Ideal*; Douglas Irwin, *Against the Tide: An Intellectual History of Free Trade* (Princeton: Princeton University Press, 1998); Stella Ghervas, *Conquering Peace: From the Enlightenment to the European Union* (Cambridge, MA: Harvard University Press, 2021); Jacob Soll, *Free Market: The History of an Idea* (New York: Basic Books, 2022).

18. On the liberal concept of 'economic cosmopolitanism', see also James D. Ingram, *Radical Cosmopolitics* (New York: Columbia University Press, 2015), 35–36.

19. On 'transimperialism', see especially Kristin L. Hoganson and Jay Sexton's 'Introduction' in their edited volume *Crossing Empires: Taking US History into Transimperial Terrain* (Durham, NC: Duke University Press, 2020), 1–22.

20. A. G. Hopkins, *American Empire: A Global History* (Princeton: Princeton University Press, 2018), 18.

21. On Eurocentric cosmopolitanism, see especially Inés Valdez, *Transnational Cosmopolitanism: Kant, Du Bois, and Justice as a Political Craft* (Cambridge: Cambridge University Press, 2019).

22. Duncan Bell, *Dreamworlds of Race: Empire and the Utopian Destiny of Anglo-America* (Princeton: Princeton University Press, 2020), ch. 7; Ikenberry, *World Safe for Democracy*, 73; Frank Trentmann, 'After the Nation-State: Citizenship, Empire and Global Coordination in the New Internationalism, 1914–1930', in Kevin Grant, Philippa Levine, and Frank Trentmann, eds, *Beyond Sovereignty: Britain, Empire and Transnationalism, c. 1880–1950* (London: Palgrave Macmillan, 2007), 34–53.

23. Susan Pederson, *The Guardians: The League of Nations and the Crisis of Empire* (Oxford: Oxford University Press, 2015), ch. 8; Ikenberry, *World Safe for Democracy*, 74.

24. Ozay Mehmet, *Westernizing the Third World: The Eurocentricity of Economic Development* (London: Routledge, 1999).

25. This common use of Western economic methods to undermine Western imperialism has since come under fire. For instance, anti-colonial nationalists in Kenya have, since the 1980s, criticized this earlier generation of nationalist leaders that came of age in this era of imperial globalization for relying upon Western education and Western-style developmental policy prescriptions. Corrie Decker and Elisabeth McMahon, *The Idea of Development in Africa: A History* (Cambridge: Cambridge University Press, 2020), ch. 4.

26. Christopher L. Hill, 'Conceptual Universalization in the Transnational Nineteenth Century', in Samuel Moyn and Andrew Sartori, eds, *Global Intellectual History* (New York: Columbia University Press, 2013), 134–58. This also included early twentieth-century India. See Aashish Velkar, '*Swadeshi* Capitalism in Colonial Bombay', *Historical Journal* 64 (Sept. 2021): 1009–34 at 1012.

27. Glenda Sluga and Patricia Clavin, 'Rethinking the History of Internationalism', in Glenda Sluga and Patricia Clavin, eds, *Internationalisms: A Twentieth Century History* (Cambridge: Cambridge University Press, 2016), 3–14 at 3–4.

28. See, for example, the influential work of W. A. Williams and the Wisconsin School; Gary Gerstle, 'The Protean Character of American Liberalism', *American Historical Review* 99 (Oct. 1994): 1043–73 at 1046–47; Gerstle, *Rise and Fall*, 75–83; Clinton Rossiter, *Conservatism*

in America (New York: Knopf, 1955); Dorothy Ross, 'Socialism and American Liberalism: Academic Social Thought in the 1880's', *Perspectives in American History* 11 (1977–78): 5–79.

29. For notable exceptions, see Patrick J. McDonald, *The Invisible Hand of Peace: Capitalism, the War Machine, and International Relations Theory* (Cambridge: Cambridge University Press, 2009); Niels P. Petersson, 'The Promise and Threat of Free Trade in a Globalizing Economy: A European Perspective', in Thomas Hippler and Miloš Vec, eds, *Paradoxes of Peace in Nineteenth Century Europe* (Oxford: Oxford University Press, 2015), 92–110; Thomas W. Zeiler, *Capitalist Peace: A History of American Free-Trade Internationalism* (Oxford: Oxford University Press, 2022).

30. David Armitage, *Foundations of Modern International Thought* (Cambridge: Cambridge University Press, 2012), 45. See also Glenda Sluga, 'Turning International: *Foundations of Modern International Thought* and New Paradigms for Intellectual History', *History of European Ideas* 41 (2015): 103–15.

Chapter 1. The Imperialism of Economic Nationalism

1. Friedrich List, *The National System of Political Economy*, trans. by Sampson S. Lloyd (London: Longmans, Green and Co., 1885 [1841]), 216–17 (emphasis in original).

2. Sydney Sherwood, *Tendencies in American Economic Thought* (Baltimore: Johns Hopkins University Press, 1897), 12 (emphasis in original).

3. Scott C. James and David A. Lake, 'The Second Face of Hegemony: Britain's Repeal of the Corn Laws and the American Walker Tariff of 1846', *International Organization* 43 (Winter 1989): 1–29.

4. *Manchester Times*, 17 January 1846.

5. C. P. Kindleberger, 'The Rise of Free Trade in Western Europe, 1820–1875', *Journal of Economic History* 35 (March 1975): 20–55; Cornelius Torp, *The Challenges of Globalization: Economy and Politics in Germany, 1860–1914* (New York: Berghahn, 2014), ch. 2.

6. Jeffrey G. Williamson and Kevin H. O'Rourke, *Globalization and History: The Evolution of a Nineteenth-Century Atlantic Economy* (Cambridge, MA: MIT Press, 1999), ch. 3.

7. A. G. Hopkins, *American Empire: A Global History* (Princeton: Princeton University Press, 2018), 7; Marc-William Palen, 'The Imperialism of Economic Nationalism', *Diplomatic History* 39 (Jan. 2015): 157–85.

8. Marc-William Palen, 'Empire by Imitation? US Economic Imperialism in a British World System, c. 1846–1946', in Martin Thomas and Andrew Thompson, eds, *The Oxford Handbook of the Ends of Empire* (Oxford: Oxford University Press, 2018), 195–211.

9. A. G. Hopkins, 'The United States, 1783–1861: Britain's Honorary Dominion?' *Britain and the World* 4 (Sept. 2011): 232–46.

10. Curtis P. Nettels, 'British Mercantilism and the Economic Development of the Thirteen Colonies', *Journal of Economic History* 12 (Spring 1952): 105–14; William Appleman Williams, 'The Age of Mercantilism: An Interpretation of the American Political Economy, 1763 to 1828', *William and Mary Quarterly* 15 (Oct. 1958): 419–37; Gautham Rao, *National Duties: Custom Houses and the Making of the American State* (Oxford: Oxford University Press, 2016).

11. Max M. Edling, *A Revolution in Favor of Government: Origins of the US Constitution and the Making of the American State* (Oxford: Oxford University Press, 2003).

12. Songho Ha, *The Rise and Fall of the American System: Nationalism and the Development of the American Economy, 1790–1837* (London: Routledge, 2016), 2; Maurice Glen Baxter, *Henry Clay and the American System* (Lexington: University of Kentucky Press, 1995), 27.

13. John R. Van Atta, 'Western Lands and the Political Economy of Henry Clay's American System, 1819–1832', *Journal of the Early Republic* 21 (Winter 2001): 633–65; Baxter, *Henry Clay*, 27, 23, 26.

14. Randolph B. Campbell, 'The Spanish American Aspect of Henry Clay's American System', *The Americas* 24 (July 1967): 3–17; George Dangerfield, *The Awakening of American Nationalism, 1815–1828* (New York: Harper & Row, 1965), 166; Baxter, *Henry Clay*, 56–59; Clay quoted in Ha, *Rise and Fall*, 3. The Latin American economic nationalist embrace of the American System at century's end would overlook this US imperial dimension. See Nicola Miller, *Republics of Knowledge: Nations of the Future in Latin America* (Princeton: Princeton University Press, 2020), ch. 8.

15. Arthur M. Lee, 'Henry C. Carey and the Republican Tariff', *Pennsylvania Magazine of History and Biography* 81 (July 1957): 280–302.

16. Roland Ringwalt, 'Friedrich List's American Years', *Protectionist* 31 (Oct. 1919), 372.

17. Onur Ulas Ince, 'Friedrich List and the Imperial Origins of the National Economy', *New Political Economy* 21 (2016): 380–400; Marc-William Palen, *The 'Conspiracy' of Free Trade: The Anglo-American Struggle over Empire and Economic Globalisation, 1846–1896* (Cambridge: Cambridge University Press, 2016), 4–7; Jens-Uwe Guettel, *German Expansionism, Imperial Liberalism, and the United States, 1776–1945* (Cambridge: Cambridge University Press, 2012), 63–64; Henryk Szlajfer, *Economic Nationalism and Globalization: Lessons from Latin America and Central Europe*, trans. by Maria Chmielewska-Szlajfer (Leiden: Brill, 2012), 56–57; Mauro Boianovsky, 'Friedrich List and the Economic Fate of Tropical Countries', *History of Political Economy* 45 (2013): 647–91.

18. Keith Tribe, 'Friedrich List and the Critique of "Cosmopolitical Economy"', *Manchester School of Economic and Social Studies* 56 (March 1988): 17–36; Ha-Joon Chang, *Kicking Away the Ladder: Development Strategy in Historical Perspective* (London: Anthem, 2002); Eric Helleiner, 'Economic Nationalism as a Challenge to Economic Liberalism? Lessons from the 19th Century', *International Studies Quarterly* 46 (Sept. 2002): 307–29; Ivo Lambi, *Free Trade and Protectionism in Germany, 1868–1879* (Wiesbaden: Steiner, 1963), 8–9; David Levi-Faur, 'Friedrich List and the Political Economy of the Nation-State', *Review of International Political Economy* 4 (Spring 1997): 154–78.

19. Richard Franklin Bensel, *Yankee Leviathan: The Origins of Central State Authority in America, 1859–1877* (Cambridge: Cambridge University Press, 1990); John Gerring, *Party Ideologies in America, 1828–1996* (Cambridge: Cambridge University Press, 1998), ch. 3.

20. Carl Mosk, *Nationalism and Economic Development in Modern Eurasia* (London: Routledge, 2013), 85–108; Max M. Edling, *A Hercules in the Cradle: War, Money, and the American State, 1783–1867* (Chicago: University of Chicago Press, 2014).

21. Palen, *'Conspiracy'*, ch. 6.

22. Palen, 'Empire by Imitation?'

23. David Todd, *Free Trade and its Enemies in France, 1814–1851* (Cambridge: Cambridge University Press, 2015), 125, 152–53, 27.

24. Alex Tyrrell, '"La Ligue Française": The Anti–Corn Law League and the Campaign for Economic Liberalism in France during the Last Days of the July Monarchy', in Anthony Howe

228 NOTES TO CHAPTER 1

and Simon Morgan, eds, *Rethinking Nineteenth-Century Liberalism: Richard Cobden Bicentenary Essays* (Aldershot: Ashgate, 2006), 99–116; Todd, *Free Trade and its Enemies*, ch. 3; David Todd, 'John Bowring and the Global Dissemination of Free Trade', *Historical Journal* 51 (June 2008): 373–97; W. O. Henderson, 'Friedrich List and the French Protectionists', *Zeitschrift fur die gesamte Staatswissenchaft* 138 (1982): 262–75.

25. Todd, *Free Trade and its Enemies*, 16.

26. Parker Moon, *Imperialism and World Politics* (New York: Macmillan, 1926), 44–47.

27. Todd, *Free Trade and its Enemies*, 233; Michael Smith, *Tariff Reform in France, 1860–1900* (Ithaca, NY: Cornell University Press, 1980), 181–88, 200–201; Eugene O. Golob, *The Méline Tariff: French Agriculture and Nationalist Economic Policy* (New York: Columbia University Press, 1944), 206–15; Thomas George Ganiats, 'The Rise of Protectionism in France from 1860 to 1892' (PhD diss., University of California, Berkeley, 1961); Andrew Gardner Brown, *Reluctant Partners: A History of Multilateral Trade Cooperation, 1850–2000* (Ann Arbor: University of Michigan Press, 2003), 63–64.

28. Eugen Wendler, *Friedrich List (1789–1846): A Visionary Economist with Social Responsibility* (Berlin: Springer, 2015), 183, quotation at 181.

29. Wendler, *Friedrich List*, 200–205.

30. Woodruff D. Smith, *The Ideological Origins of Nazi Imperialism* (Oxford: Oxford University Press, 1986), 30–40; Smith, *The German Colonial Empire* (Chapel Hill: University of North Carolina Press, 1978), 13–15.

31. Matthew P. Fitzpatrick, *Liberal Imperialism in Germany: Expansionism and Nationalism, 1848–1884* (New York: Berghahn, 2008), 56.

32. Wendler, *Friedrich List*, 214.

33. Fitzpatrick, *Liberal Imperialism in Germany*, 61–65.

34. Alfred Zimmermann, *Geschichte der deutschen Kolonialpolitik* (Berlin: Mittler, 1914), 5–6; Moon, *Imperialism and World Politics*, 48.

35. Moon, *Imperialism and World Politics*, 50; Smith, *German Colonial Empire*, 95.

36. Wendler, *Friedrich List*, 214.

37. Eric Helleiner, *The Neomercantilists: A Global Intellectual History* (Ithaca, NY: Cornell University Press, 2021), 170–72.

38. Helleiner, *Neomercantilists*, 172.

39. Wendler, *Friedrich List*, 213–14.

40. Torp, *Challenges of Globalization*, 89.

41. Fitzpatrick, *Liberal Imperialism in Germany*, 56; Torp, *Challenges of Globalization*, ch. 6; Smith, *German Colonial Empire*, 94–98.

42. Fitzpatrick, *Liberal Imperialism in Germany*, 59–61.

43. Evalyn A. Clark, 'Adolf Wagner: From National Economist to National Socialist', *Political Science Quarterly* 55 (Sept. 1940): 393–400.

44. James J. Sheehan, *German Liberalism in the Nineteenth Century* (Chicago: University of Chicago Press, 1983 [1978]), 159.

45. Szlajfer, *Economic Nationalism*, 56; Keith Tribe, *Strategies of Economic Order: German Economic Discourse, 1750–1950* (Cambridge: Cambridge University Press, 1995); Yuichi Shionoya, ed., *The German Historical School: The Historical and Ethical Approach to Economics* (London: Routledge, 2001); Shionoya, *The Soul of the German Historical School: Methodological Essays*

on *Schmoller, Weber and Schumpeter* (New York: Springer, 2005); Peter Koslowski, ed., *The Theory of Ethical Economy in the Historical School: Wilhelm Roscher, Lorenz von Stein, Gustav Schmoller, Wilhelm Dilthey and Contemporary Theory* (Berlin: Springer, 1997); Erik Grimmer-Solem, *The Rise of Historical Economics and Social Reform in Germany, 1864–1894* (New York: Oxford University Press, 2003); Lambi, *Free Trade and Protectionism.*

46. Luigi Cossa, *An Introduction to the Study of Political Economy* (New York: Macmillan, 1893), 477.

47. Daniel T. Rodgers, *Atlantic Crossings: Social Politics in a Progressive Age* (Cambridge, MA: Harvard University Press, 1998), ch. 3; Jurgen Herbst, *The German Historical School in American Scholarship: A Study in the Transfer of Culture* (Ithaca, NY: Cornell University Press, 1965), ch. 6; Brian Balogh, *A Government Out of Sight: The Mystery of National Authority in Nineteenth-Century America* (New York: Cambridge University Press, 2009), ch. 9; Axel R. Schafer, *American Progressives and German Social Reform, 1875–1920* (Stuttgart: Steiner, 2000), 37–40; Sidney Fine, 'Richard T. Ely, Forerunner of Progressivism, 1880–1901', *Mississippi Valley Historical Review* 37 (March 1951): 599–624; Jack C. Myles, 'German Historicism and American Economics: A Study of the Influence of the German Historical School on Economic Thought' (PhD diss., Princeton University, 1956); Carl Diehl, *Americans and German Scholarship, 1770–1870* (New Haven: Yale University Press, 1978); James T. Kloppenberg, *Uncertain Victory: Social Democracy and Progressivism in European and American Thought, 1870–1920* (New York: Oxford University Press, 1986).

48. Steven A. Sass and Barbara Copperman, 'Joseph Wharton's Argument for Protection', *Business and Economic History* 9 (1980): 51–60 at 51, 56.

49. Robert Ellis Thompson, *Social Science and National Economy* (Philadelphia: Porter and Coates, 1875), 28–29, 132; Palen, 'Conspiracy', 177, 180.

50. Craufurd D. W. Goodwin, *Economic Inquiry in Australia* (Durham, NC: Duke University Press, 1966), 45–51; Helleiner, *Neomercantilists*, 181–85.

51. Mel Watkins, 'The American System and Canada's National Policy', (reprinted) in Hugh Grant and David Wolfe, eds, *Staples and Beyond: Selected Writings of Mel Watkins* (Montreal: McGill-Queen's University Press, 2006 [1967]), 97–101.

52. Goodwin, *Economic Inquiry in Australia*, 47–59.

53. Palen, 'Conspiracy', ch. 8.

54. See especially Edmund Rogers, 'Free Trade versus Protectionism: New South Wales, Victoria, and the Tariff Debate in Britain, 1881–1900', *Australian Studies* 1 (2009): 1–16.

55. Goodwin, *Economic Inquiry in Australia*, 10, 13, 27–28; Helleiner, *Neomercantilists*, 185–89.

56. *The Protectionist's Handbook* (Melbourne, The Age Office, 1895), 28.

57. Benjamin H. Brown, *The Tariff Reform Movement in Great Britain, 1881–1895* (New York: Columbia University Press, 1943), 16–18.

58. Sampson Samuel Lloyd, translator's preface to List, *National System*, v–vii.

59. Gordon Bannerman, 'The Rise and Fall of Fair Trade in Britain, 1879–92', in Anthony Howe and Mark Duckenfield, eds, *Battles over Free Trade: Anglo-American Experiences with International Trade, 1776–2009*, vol. 3: *The Challenge of Economic Nationalism, 1879–1939* (London: Routledge, 2013 [2008]), 1–5.

60. Palen, 'Conspiracy', 212.

61. Marc-William Palen, 'Protection, Federation and Union: The Global Impact of the McKinley Tariff upon the British Empire, 1890–94', *Journal of Imperial and Commonwealth*

History 38 (2010): 395–418; Brown, *Tariff Reform Movement*, 16–18, 58; Sidney H. Zebel, 'Fair Trade: An English Reaction to the Breakdown of the Cobden Treaty System', *Journal of Modern History* 12 (June 1940): 161–85 at 182–84.

62. Palen, 'Imperialism of Economic Nationalism'.

63. On America's colonial empire, see especially Daniel Immerwahr, *How to Hide an Empire: A History of the Greater United States* (New York: Macmillan, 2019); and Hopkins, *American Empire*.

64. Sidney Sherwood, *Tendencies in American Economic Thought* (Baltimore: Johns Hopkins University Press, 1897), 12, 16.

65. 'The Best Open Door Policy', *American Economist*, 18 January 1901, 31; Benjamin B. Wallace, 'Preferential Tariffs and the Open Door', *Annals of the American Academy of Political and Social Science* 112 (March 1924), 211–13.

66. 'American Labor and the Puerto Rican Problem', *American Economist*, 6 April 1900, 165.

67. 'Was Wisely Settled', *American Economist*,16 March 1900, 128; 'Its Importance Overestimated', *American Economist*, 23 March 1900, 130; 'Make Them Colonies', *American Economist*, 19 January 1900, 31; George L. Bolen, 'Hawaii and Porto Rico as Colonies', *Gunton's Magazine* 18 (Jan. 1900): 26–32.

68. Palen, *'Conspiracy'*, chs 7–8; Palen, 'Imperialism of Economic Nationalism'.

69. Marc-William Palen, 'Pandemic Protectionism: Revisiting the 1918 "Spanish" Flu in the Era of COVID-19', *Diplomatic History* 45 (June 2021): 571–79.

70. *Protectionist Opposition to the League of Nations* (New York: Free Trade League, 1920), 'Free Trade League' Folder, Carton 4, Erving Winslow Papers, Massachusetts Historical Society, Boston, MA; 'Example of League of Nations Trickery', *American Economist*, 30 January 1920, 73; 'A Horse of Another Color', *American Economist*, 14 March 1919, 167.

71. Sarah Churchwell, *Behold, America: A History of America First and the American Dream* (London: Bloomsbury, 2018), 94, 145; Christopher McKnight Nichols, *Promise and Peril: America at the Dawn of a Global Age* (Cambridge, MA: Harvard University Press, 2011), 247–48; Charles A. Kupchan, *Isolationism: A History of America's Efforts to Shield Itself from the World* (New York: Oxford University Press, 2020), 257–58.

72. Rick Baldoz, *The Third Asiatic Invasion: Migration and Empire in Filipino America, 1898–1946* (New York: New York University Press, 2011), 161

73. Douglas A. Irwin, *Peddling Protectionism: Smoot-Hawley and the Great Depression* (Princeton: Princeton University Press, 2011); Joseph M. Jones Jr., *Tariff Retaliation: Repercussions of the Hawley-Smoot Bill* (Philadelphia: University of Pennsylvania Press, 1934).

74. Raymond Leslie Buell, *The Hull Trade Program and the American System* (New York: Foreign Policy Association, 1938), 32.

75. Brown, *Tariff Reform Movement*; Luke Trainor, 'The British Government and Imperial Economic Unity, 1890–1895', *Historical Journal* 13 (March 1970): 68–84; Trainor, 'The Imperial Federation League in Britain and Australia, c. 1884–1900', in Andrea Bosco and Alex May, eds, *The Round Table: The Empire/Commonwealth and British Foreign Policy* (London: Lothian Foundation Press, 1997), 161–76; Andrew S. Thompson, 'Tariff Reform: An Imperial Strategy, 1903–1913', *Historical Journal* 40 (Dec. 1997): 1033–54.

76. Marc-William Palen, 'Adam Smith as Advocate of Empire, c. 1870–1932', *Historical Journal* 57 (March 2014), 197.

77. Frederick Scott Oliver, *Alexander Hamilton: An Essay on American Union* (New York: G. P Putnam's Sons, 1906); John D. Fair, 'F. S. Oliver, Alexander Hamilton, and the "American

Plan" for Resolving Britain's Constitutional Crises, 1903–1921', *Twentieth Century British History* 10 (1999): 1–26; Patrick M. Kirkwood, 'Alexander Hamilton and the Early Republic in Edwardian Imperial Thought', *Britain and the World* 12 (March 2019): 28–50.

78. Erik Grimmer-Solem, *Learning Empire: Globalization and the German Quest for World Status, 1875–1919* (Cambridge: Cambridge University Press, 2019), 282–84.

79. L. S. Amery, *The Fundamental Fallacies of Free Trade* (London: National Review Office, 1906); Frank Trentmann, *Free Trade Nation: Commerce, Consumption, and Civil Society in Modern Britain* (Oxford: Oxford University Press, 2009), 231.

80. William Roger Louis, 'American Anti-Colonialism and the Dissolution of the British Empire', *International Affairs* 61 (Summer 1985), 398.

81. David Thackeray, 'Selling the Empire?: Marketing and the Demise of the British World, c. 1920–1960', *Journal of Imperial and Commonwealth History* 48 (April 2020): 679–705.

82. Leo Petritsch, 'The Fiscal Question and the Experience of the Austro-Hungarian Empire', *Economic Journal* 14 (March 1904), 26.

83. Samuel R. Williamson Jr., *Austria-Hungary and the Origins of the First World War* (New York: Macmillan, 1991), 104–8; Samuel Danziger, 'Protectionism Caused World War', *International Free Trader* 3 (Jan. 1920), 7.

84. Goodwin, *Economic Inquiry in Australia*, 31.

85. Benjamin Hoare, *Preference Trade* (London: Kegan Paul, Trench, Trubner, 1904), v–vi.

86. Todd, *Free Trade and its Enemies*, 233.

87. Owen White, *The Blood of the Colony: Wine and the Rise and Fall of French Algeria* (Cambridge, MA: Harvard University Press, 2021), 131, 139; Bùi Minh Dũng, 'Japan's Role in the Vietnamese Starvation of 1944–45', *Modern Asian Studies* 29 (July 1995): 573–618.

88. Haile M. Larebo, *The Building of an Empire: Italian Land Policy and Practice in Ethiopia 1935–1941* (Oxford: Oxford University Press, 1994); Michele Sollai, 'How to Feed an Empire? Agrarian Science, Indigenous Farming, and Wheat Autarky in Italian-Occupied Ethiopia, 1937–1941', *Agricultural History* 96 (2022): 379–416.

89. Alla Sheptun, 'The German Historical School and Russian Economic Thought', *Journal of Economic Studies* 32 (August 2005): 349–74 at 354–59.

90. Matthew P. Fitzpatrick, 'Introduction: Particular or Universal? Historicizing Liberal Approaches to Empire in Europe', in Fitzpatrick, ed., *Liberal Imperialism in Europe* (New York: Palgrave Macmillan, 2012), 1–24 at 13; T. H. von Laue, 'A Secret Memorandum of Sergei Witte on the Industrialization of Imperial Russia', *Journal of Modern History* 26 (March 1954): 60–74; Steven Marks, *Road to Power: The Trans-Siberian Railroad and the Colonization of Asian Russia, 1850–1917* (Ithaca, NY: Cornell University Press, 1991); Sidney Harcave, *Count Sergei Witte and the Twilight of Imperial Russia* (New York: Routledge, 2004), 49–57.

91. Harcave, *Count Sergei Witte*, 39.

92. Chia Yin Hsu, 'A Tale of Two Railroads: "Yellow Labor", Agrarian Colonization, and the Making of Russianness at the Far Eastern Frontier, 1890s–1910s', *Ab Imperio* 3 (2006): 217–53, esp. 221–25; Scott Reynolds Nelson, *Oceans of Grain: How American Wheat Remade the World* (New York: Basic Books, 2022), ch. 13.

93. Uğur Ümit Üngör and Eric Lohr, 'Economic Nationalism, Confiscation, and Genocide: A Comparison of the Ottoman and Russian Empires during World War I', *Journal of Modern European History* 12 (2014): 500–522.

94. Ruth AmEnde Roosa, *Russian Industrialists in an Era of Revolution: The Association of Industry and Trade, 1906–1917*, ed. by Thomas C. Owen (Armonk: M. E. Sharpe, 1997), 49–51; Roman Szporluk, *Communism and Nationalism: Karl Marx versus Friedrich List* (Oxford: Oxford University Press, 1988), 224, 219–20.

95. Grimmer-Solem, *Learning Empire*, 284.

96. Torp, *Challenges of Globalization*, 239–48.

97. Smith, *German Colonial Empire*, 117.

98. Henry Cord Meyer, *Mitteleuropa in German Thought and Action 1815–1945* (The Hague: Nijhoff, 1955), 96.

99. Bo Strath, 'Mitteleuropa: From List to Naumann', *European Journal of Social Theory* 11 (2008): 171–83.

100. Mark T. Kettler, 'Designing Empire for the Civilized East: Colonialism, Polish Nationhood, and German War Aims in the First World War', *Nationalities Papers* 47 (Nov. 2019): 936–52 at 937.

101. Mark Mazower, *Dark Continent: Europe's Twentieth Century* (New York: Allen Lane, 1998), 72; Meyer, *Mitteleuropa*, 317; Clark, 'Adolf Wagner'. On Nazism's roots, see also David Olusoga and Casper W. Erichsen, *The Kaiser's Holocaust: Germany's Forgotten Genocide and the Colonial Roots of Nazism* (London: Faber and Faber, 2010); Asaf Kedar, 'National Socialism before Nazism: Friedrich Naumann and Theodor Fritsch, 1890–1914' (PhD diss., University of California, Berkeley, 2010); Shelley Baranowski, *Nazi Empire: German Colonialism and Imperialism from Bismarck to Hitler* (Cambridge: Cambridge University Press, 2011).

102. C. W. Guillebaud, 'Hitler's New Economic Order for Europe', *Economic Journal* 50 (Dec. 1940): 449–60; Benjamin Madley, 'From Africa to Auschwitz: How German South West Africa Incubated Ideas and Methods Adopted and Developed by the Nazis in Eastern Europe', *European History Quarterly* 35 (2005): 429–64; Smith, *Ideological Origins*, 30–40, 106; Salvatore Prisco, 'Vampire Diplomacy: Nazi Economic Nationalism in Latin America, 1934–40', *Diplomacy and Statecraft* 2 (1991): 173–81; David Furber, 'Near as Far in the Colonies: The Nazi Occupation of Poland', *International History Review* 26 (2004): 541–79; Adam Tooze, *The Wages of Destruction: The Making and Breaking of the Nazi Economy* (New York: Penguin, 2006), 8–9, 28–29, 88, 113–14, 174–75.

103. Deniz T. Kılınçoğlu, *Economics and Capitalism in the Ottoman Empire* (New York: Routledge, 2015), 47–57, 65–67, 134; Sarp Balci, 'Two Versions of Enlightenment State in the Late Ottoman Era: Protectionist State versus Liberal State in the Works of Akyiğitzade Musa and Mehmed Cavid' (MSc diss., Middle East Technical University, 2004), 8; Kenan Demir, 'Akyiğitzade Musa and Conservation Thought', *Turkish Journal of Business Ethics* 11 (2018), 325; Hilmi Ozan Özavci, 'Liberalism in the Turkish Context and Its Historiography: Past and Present', *Anatolian Studies* 62 (2012): 141–51 at 144.

104. Cyrus Schayegh, 'Imperial and Transnational Developmentalisms: Middle Eastern Interplays, 1880s–1960s', in Stephen J. Macekura and Erez Manela, eds, *The Development Century: A Global History* (Cambridge: Cambridge University Press, 2018), 61–82 at 67.

105. Üngör and Lohr, 'Economic Nationalism', 501; Şevket Pamuk and Jeffrey G. Williamson, 'Ottoman De-industrialization, 1800–1913: Assessing the Magnitude, Impact and Response', *Economic History Review* 64 (2011): 159–84; Stefania Ecchia, 'The Economic Policy of the Ottoman Empire (1876–1922)', *MPRA Paper No. 42603* (2010), 5–6; Helleiner, *Neomercantilists*, 93–94.

106. Vedit İnal, 'Evolution of Economic Thought in the Ottoman Empire and Early Republican Turkey', *Middle Eastern Studies* 57 (2021): 14–36 at 26–27.

107. Cyrus Schayegh, *The Middle East and the Making of the Modern World* (Cambridge, MA: Harvard University Press, 2017), 204.

108. Mike Heffernan and Benjamin J. Thorpe, '"The Map That Would Save Europe": Clive Morrison-Bell, the Tariff Walls Map, and the Politics of Cartographic Display', *Journal of Historical Geography* 60 (2018): 24–40.

109. Chitoshi Yanaga, *Japan since Perry* (New York: McGraw-Hill, 1949), 72.

110. Mark Metzler, 'The Cosmopolitanism of National Economics: Friedrich List in a Japanese Mirror', in A. G. Hopkins, ed., *Global History: Interactions between the Universal and the Local* (New York: Palgrave MacMillan, 2006), 98–130; Helleiner, *Neomercantilists*, 85–89, 173–80; Yanaga, *Japan since Perry*, 73–75; Grimmer-Solem, *Learning Empire*, 29, 96–98.

111. Kazuo Hori, 'The Formation of Capitalism in East Asia', in Minoru Sawai, ed., *Economic Activities Under the Japanese Colonial Empire* (Tokyo: Springer Japan, 2016), 11–49 at 21.

112. Antony Best, 'Economic Appeasement or Economic Nationalism? A Political Perspective on the British Empire, Japan, and the Rise of Intra-Asian Trade, 1933–37', *Economic History Review* 30 (May 2002): 77–101.

113. Aaron Stephen Moore, 'The Technological Imaginary of Imperial Japan, 1931–1945' (PhD diss., Cornell University, 2006), 49–54, 56 n. 48.

114. Jeremy A. Yellen, *The Greater East Asia Co-Prosperity Sphere: When Total Empire Met Total War* (Ithaca, NY: Cornell University Press, 2019), 86–89.

115. Michael A. Barnhart, *Japan Prepares for Total War: The Search for Economic Security, 1919–1941* (Ithaca, NY: Cornell University Press, 1987), 177.

116. Ince, 'Friedrich List', 393.

117. Gary B. Magee and Andrew S. Thompson, *Empire and Globalisation: Networks of People, Goods and Capital in the British World, c. 1850–1914* (Cambridge: Cambridge University Press, 2010), 61; David Thackeray, *Forging a British World of Trade: Culture, Ethnicity, and Market in the Empire-Commonwealth, 1880–1975* (Oxford: Oxford University Press, 2019), 3–4. Stephen Howe, *Anticolonialism in British Politics: The Left and the End of Empire, 1918–1964* (Oxford: Oxford University Press, 1993), 30.

118. R. J. Moore, 'Imperialism and "Free Trade" Policy in India, 1853–4', *Economic History Review* 17 (1964): 135–45; Peter Harnetty, *Imperialism and Free Trade: Lancashire and India in the Mid-Nineteenth Century* (Manchester: Manchester University Press, 1972).

119. Romesh Dutt, *The Economic History of India* (London: Kegan Paul, Trench, Trubner, 1902), 302.

120. Antoinette Burton, *The Trouble with Empire: Challenges to Modern British Imperialism* (Oxford: Oxford University Press, 2015), 94–96.

121. Helleiner, *Neomercantilists*, 262–68.

122. Helleiner, *Neomercantilists*, 268–69; Mei Junjie, 'Friedrich List in China's Quest for Development', in Harald Hagemann, Stephan Selter, Eugen Wendler, eds, *The Economic Thought of Friedrich List* (New York: Routledge, 2019), 213–22.

123. Paul A. Pickering, '"Irish First": Daniel O'Connell, the Native Manufacture Campaign, and Economic Nationalism, 1840–44', *Albion* 32 (Winter 2000): 598–616 at 599–600.

124. Paul A. Pickering and Alex Tyrell, *The People's Bread: A History of the Anti–Corn Law League* (London: Leicester University Press, 2000), 73.

125. Carla King, 'Michael Davitt, Irish nationalism and the British Empire in the Late Nineteenth Century', in Peter Gray, ed., *Victoria's Ireland? Irishness and Britishness, 1837–1901* (Dublin:

234 NOTES TO CHAPTER 1

Four Courts Press, 2004), 116–30; Niamh Lynch, 'Defining Irish Nationalist Anti-imperialism: Thomas Davis and John Mitchel', *Éire-Ireland* 42 (Spring/Summer, 2007): 82–107.

126. Arthur Griffith, *The Sinn Fein Policy* (Dublin: James Duffy, 1906), 11; T. K. Whitaker, 'From Protection to Free Trade: The Irish Experience', *Social & Policy Administration* 8 (June 1974): 95–115 at 96; Thomas A. Boylan and Timothy P. Foley, *Political Economy and Colonial Ireland* (London: Routledge, 2005 [1992]), 156; Denis O'Hearn, *The Atlantic Economy: Britain, the US and Ireland* (Manchester: Manchester University Press, 2001), 108. Griffith, however, apparently overlooked the fact that List's advocacy for tariff protection was not suitable for small agrarian nations like Ireland. See Sean Cronin, *Irish Nationalism: A History of Its Roots and Ideology* (Dublin: Academy Press, 1980), 118.

127. Mary E. Daly, *Industrial Development and Irish National Identity, 1922–1939* (Dublin: Gill & Macmillan, 1992).

128. Whitaker, 'From Protection', 97–98

129. Mary Cumpston, 'Some Early Indian Nationalists and Their Allies in the British Empire', *English Historical Review* 76 (April 1961): 279–97; Howard Brasted, 'Indian Nationalist Development and the Influence of Irish Home Rule, 1870–1886', *Modern Asian Studies* 14 (1980): 37–63; Brasted, 'Irish Nationalism and the British Empire in the Late Nineteenth Century', in Oliver MacDonagh, W. F. Mandle, and Pauric Travers, eds, *Irish Culture and Nationalism, 1750–1950* (New York: St. Martin's Press, 1983), 83–103. Ireland and India's food insecurity provided a further point of anti-colonial convergence. See Peter Gray, 'Famine and Land in Ireland and India, 1845–1880: James Caird and the Political Economy of Hunger', *Historical Journal* 49 (March 2006): 193–215; Jill Bender, 'The Imperial Politics of Famine: The 1873–74 Bengal Famine and Irish Parliamentary Nationalism', *Éire-Ireland* 42 (Spring/Summer 2007): 132–56; Michael Silvestri, *Ireland and India: Nationalism, Empire and Memory* (London: Palgrave Macmillan, 2009).

130. Kris Manjapra, *Age of Entanglement: German and Indian Intellectuals Across Empire* (Cambridge, MA: Harvard University Press, 2014), 42.

131. Bipan Chandra, *The Rise and Growth of Economic Nationalism in India: Economic Policies of Indian National Leadership, 1880–1905* (New Delhi: People's Publishing House, 1960), 217–51, INC and Mehta respectively quoted on pp. 244, 245. More recently, see Shashi Tharoor, *Inglorious Empire: What the British Did to India* (London: Hurst, 2017).

132. Manjapra, *Age of Entanglement*, 49; Burton, *Trouble with Empire*, 99–100; Chandra, *Rise and Growth*, 87–89.

133. Aashish Velkar, 'Swadeshi Capitalism in Colonial Bombay', *Historical Journal* 64 (Sept. 2021): 1009–34.

134. M.G.K. Gokhale, 'The Swadeshi Movement in India', *Unity*, 1 March 1906, 13.

135. Matthew Stubbings, 'Free Trade Empire to Commonwealth of Nations: India, Britain and Imperial Preference, 1903–1932', *International History Review* 41 (2019): 323–44.

136. Seán Ó Lúing, 'Arthur Griffith, 1871–1922: Thoughts on a Centenary', *Studies: An Irish Quarterly Review* 60 (Summer 1971): 127–38 at 127–28.

137. On Gandhism and interwar debates over Indian development, see especially Benjamin Zachariah, *Developing India: An Intellectual and Social History, c. 1930–1950* (Oxford: Oxford University Press, 2005). For the broader interwar debates over India and tariffs, see Basudev Chatterji, *Trade, Tariffs and Empire: Lancashire and British Politics in India 1919–1939* (Oxford: Oxford University Press, 1992).

138. Anthony Howe, *Free Trade and Liberal England, 1846–1946* (Oxford: Clarendon Press, 1997), 294.

139. Manjapra, *Age of Entanglement*, 49; Burton, *Trouble with Empire*, 99–100; Chandra, *Rise and Growth*, 210–16.

140. Manu Goswami, *Producing India: From Colonial Economy to National Space* (Chicago: University of Chicago Press, 2004), 215–24, 336 n. 14; Bipan Chandra, ed., *Ranade's Economic Writings* (New Delhi: Gian Publishing House, 1990), xiv, xviii.

141. Quoted in Manjapra, *Age of Entanglement*, 148.

142. Velkar, 'Swadeshi Capitalism', 1019–20.

143. Jawaharlal Nehru, *Glimpses of World History* (New York: Asia Publishing House, 1934), 918–20, 431, 455–56, 715–16, 754.

144. Michele L. Louro, *Comrades against Imperialism* (Cambridge: Cambridge University Press, 2018), 214–15, 247.

145. Manjapra, *Age of Entanglement*, 150; Andrew Sartori, 'Beyond Culture-Contact and Colonial Discourse: "Germanism" in Colonial Bengal', in Shruti Kapila, ed., *An Intellectual History of India* (Cambridge: Cambridge University Press, 2010), 68–84 at 81–82.

146. Benjamin Zachariah, 'At the Fuzzy Edges of Fascism: Framing the Volk in India', *South Asia* 38 (Oct. 2015): 639–55.

147. Suruchi Thapar-Bjorkert, *Women in the Indian Nationalist Movement: Unseen Faces and Unheard Voices, 1930–42* (New Delhi: Sage, 2006), 47, 106–7.

148. James Campbell Ker, *Political Trouble in India 1907–1917* (Calcutta: Editions Indian, 1960 [1917]), 350–52.

149. Nancy Reynolds, *A City Consumed: Urban Commerce, the Cairo Fire, and the Politics of Decolonization in Egypt* (Palo Alto: Stanford University Press, 2012), 84–88; Margot Badran, *Feminists, Islam, and Nation* (Princeton: Princeton University Press, 1995), 74–88, 228; Huda Shaarawi, *Harem Years: The Memoirs of an Egyptian Feminist*, trans. by Margot Badran (New York: The Feminist Press, 1986), 130–31.

150. Mona L. Russell, *Creating the New Egyptian Woman: Consumerism, Education, and National Identity, 1863–1922* (New York: Palgrave Macmillan, 2004), 89–92; Noor-Aiman Khan, *Egyptian–Indian Nationalist Collaboration and the British Empire* (New York: Palgrave Macmillan, 2011), 93–94, 107–8, 113–14, 121–22; Beth Baron, *Egypt as a Woman* (Los Angeles: University of California Press, 2005), 176; Reynolds, *A City Consumed*, 84–86, 91–95, 103–8, 113.

151. Nico Slate, *Colored Cosmopolitanism: The Shared Struggle for Freedom in the United States and India* (Cambridge, MA: Harvard University Press, 2012), 36–39, 42, 72.

152. *Crusader* (March 1921), quoted in Gerald Horne, *The End of Empires: African Americans and India* (Philadelphia: Temple University Press, 2008), 81–82.

153. Johnson quoted in Slate, *Colored Cosmopolitanism*, 45.

154. Horne, *End of Empires*; Bill V. Mullen, 'Du Bois, Dark Princess, and the Afro-Asian International', *Positions* 11 (Spring 2003): 217–39; Vijay Prashad, 'Black Gandhi', *Social Scientist* 37 (Jan.–Feb. 2009): 3–20; Vinay Lal, 'Gandhi's West, the West's Gandhi', *New Literary History* 40 (Spring 2009): 281–313; Sean Chabot, *The Transnational Roots of the Civil Rights Movement: African American Explorations of the Gandhian Reportoire* (Lanham: Lexington Books, 2012).

155. W.E.B. Du Bois, *Dusk of Dawn: An Essay toward an Autobiography of a Race Concept* (New York: Oxford University Press, 2007 [1940]), 23–24. Indian reformers such as Swami

Vivekananda and Lajpat Rai were drawing similar connections during their turn-of-the-century travels through the Jim Crow South. See Slate, *Colored Cosmopolitanism*, 16–20, 39–42.

156. W.E.B. Du Bois, *Black Reconstruction in America, 1860–1880* (New York: The Free Press, 1998 [1935]), 237; Du Bois, 'Reconstruction, Seventy-Five Years After', *Phylon* 4 (third quarter, 1943), 211.

157. Patrick Anderson, 'Pan-Africanism and Economic Nationalism: W.E.B. Du Bois's *Black Reconstruction* and the Failings of the "Black Marxism" Thesis', *Journal of Black Studies* 48 (2017): 732–57.

158. Walter Rucker, '"A Negro Nation within the Nation": W.E.B. Du Bois and the Creation of a Revolutionary Pan-Africanist Tradition, 1903–1947', *Black Scholar* 32 (Fall/Winter 2002): 37–46 at 39.

159. Du Bois, *Dusk of Dawn*, 23, 20.

160. Lawrence J. Oliver, 'W.E.B. Du Bois and the Dismal Science: Economic Theory and Social Justice', *American Studies* 53 (2014): 49–70 at 54.

161. Du Bois, *Black Reconstruction*, 211.

162. Rucker, 'A Negro Nation', 38.

Chapter 2. The Anti-imperialism of Free Trade

1. Richard Cobden to Henry Ashworth, 12 April 1842, reprinted in Anthony Howe, ed., *The Letters of Richard Cobden*, vol. 1: *1815–1847*, Oxford online (by subscription), https://www.oxfordscholarlyeditions.com/view/10.1093/actrade/9780199211951.book.1/actrade-9780199211951-div2-172 (accessed 10 May 2023).

2. Henri Lambert, 'The Way of Salvation: An Economic Peace', *International Free Trader* 1 (June 1918), 2.

3. [Tom Taylor], 'The Exhibition of Industry—A Hint', *Punch* 18 (13 April 1850), 141.

4. 'As the Day for the Opening of the Great Exhibition Approaches, the Interest of the Public of This and Other Countries Increases in Intensity with Regard to It', *Illustrated London News*, 26 April 1851, 332.

5. 'The Great Exhibition', *Illustrated London News*, 3 May 1851, 343; 'London During the Great Exhibition', *Illustrated London News*, 17 May 1851, 423.

6. [Henry Mayhew], 'England's Peace-Offering', *Punch* 19 (28 Dec. 1850), 265.

7. *Morning Chronicle*, 14 January 1851, 3.

8. William Dyer Grampp, *The Manchester School of Economics* (Stanford: Stanford University Press, 1960).

9. Jeffrey A. Auerbach, *The Great Exhibition of 1851: A Nation on Display* (New Haven: Yale University Press, 1999), 163. See also Paul Young, 'Mission Impossible: Globalization and the Great Exhibition', in Jeffrey A. Auerbach and Peter H. Hoffenberg, eds, *Britain, The Empire, and the World at the Great Exhibition of 1851* (London: Routledge, 2008), 1–24 at 7; Young, *Globalization and the Great Exhibition: The Victorian New World Order* (London: Palgrave Macmillan, 2009).

10. Anthony Howe, *Free Trade and Liberal England, 1846–1946* (Oxford: Clarendon Press, 1997); Frank Trentmann, *Free Trade Nation: Commerce, Consumption, and Civil Society in Modern Britain* (Oxford: Oxford University Press, 2008).

11. Martin Ceadel, *The Origins of War Prevention: The British Peace Movement and International Relations, 1730–1854* (Oxford: Oxford University Press, 1996), 463–64; Geoffrey Cantor, *Religion and the Great Exhibition of 1851* (Oxford: Oxford University Press, 2011); Cobden quoted in Auerbach, *Great Exhibition*, 163.

12. Oliver MacDonagh, 'The Anti-Imperialism of Free Trade', *Economic History Review* 14 (April 1962): 489–501.

13. Anthony Howe, 'Free Trade and Global Order: The Rise and Fall of a Victorian Vision', in Duncan Bell, ed., *Victorian Visions of Global Order: Empire and International Relations in Nineteenth-Century Political Thought* (Cambridge: Cambridge University Press, 2009), 26–46 at 37.

14. Douglas Maynard, 'Reform and the Origin of the International Organization Movement', *Proceedings of the American Philosophical Society* 107 (19 June 1963): 220–31 at 220–21, 226, 223.

15. See, for instance, Duncan Bell, *Dreamworlds of Race: Empire and the Utopian Destiny of Anglo-America* (Princeton: Princeton University Press, 2020); Bell, *The Idea of Greater Britain: Empire and the Future of World Order, 1860–1900* (Princeton: Princeton University Press, 2007); Gregory Claeys, *Imperial Sceptics: British Critics of Empire, 1850–1920* (Cambridge: Cambridge University Press, 2010).

16. Anthony Howe, 'Liberals, Free Trade, and Europe: From Cobden to the Common Market', *Journal of Liberal History* 98 (Spring 2018): 4–11.

17. Roger Chickering, *Imperial Germany and a World without War: The Peace Movement and German Society, 1892–1914* (Princeton: Princeton University Press, 1975), 6–9; David S. Patterson, *Toward a Warless World: The Travail of the American Peace Movement, 1887–1914* (Bloomington: Indiana University Press, 1976), 11–14, 19, 32, 74–75, 78; Mark Mazower, *Governing the World: The History of an Idea, 1815 to the Present* (New York: Penguin, 2012), 42.

18. Chickering, *Imperial Germany*, 6–8; Marc-William Palen, 'The Transimperial Roots of American Anti-imperialism: The Transatlantic Radicalism of Free Trade, 1846–1920', in Jay Sexton and Kristin Hoganson, eds, *Crossing Empires: Taking US History into Transimperial Terrain* (Durham, NC: Duke University Press, 2020), 159–82.

19. Norman Etherington, 'The Capitalist Theory of Capitalist Imperialism', *History of Political Economy* 15 (1983): 38–62.

20. P. J. Cain, 'Capitalism, Aristocracy and Empire: Some "Classical" Theories of Imperialism Revisited', *Journal of Imperial and Commonwealth History* 35 (2007): 25–47.

21. Bell, *Victorian Visions*; Mazower, *Governing the World*.

22. Matt Karp, *This Vast Southern Empire* (Cambridge, MA: Harvard University Press, 2018); Simon Morgan, 'The Anti–Corn Law League and British Antislavery in Transatlantic Perspective, 1838–1846', *Historical Journal* 52 (March 2009): 87–107 at 104–5; Marc-William Palen, 'The Civil War's Forgotten Transatlantic Tariff Debate and the Confederacy's Free Trade Diplomacy', *Journal of the Civil War Era* 3 (March 2013): 35–61; Palen, *The 'Conspiracy' of Free Trade: The Anglo-American Struggle over Empire and Economic Globalisation, c. 1846–1896* (Cambridge: Cambridge University Press, 2016), chs 1–2; Glory M. Liu, *Adam Smith's America: How a Scottish Philosopher Became an Icon of American Capitalism* (Princeton: Princeton University Press, 2022), chs 1–3.

23. Marc-William Palen, 'Free-Trade Ideology and Transatlantic Abolitionism: A Historiography', *Journal of the History of Economic Thought* 37 (June 2015): 291–304 at 293, 298.

238 NOTES TO CHAPTER 2

24. Martin Ceadel, 'Cobden and Peace', in Anthony Howe and Simon Morgan, eds, *Rethinking Nineteenth Century Liberalism: Richard Cobden Bicentenary Essays* (Aldershot: Ashgate, 2006), 189–207 at 195–96.

25. Jonathan Parry, *The Politics of Patriotism: English Liberalism, National Identity and Europe, 1830–1886* (Cambridge: Cambridge University Press, 2006), ch. 4.

26. David Nicholls, 'Richard Cobden and the International Peace Congress Movement, 1848–1853', *Journal of British Studies* 30 (Oct. 1991): 351–76 at 352–54; Howe, 'Free Trade and Global Order', 30; Vanessa Lincoln Lambert, 'The Dynamics of Transnational Activism: The International Peace Congresses, 1843–51', *International History Review* 38 (2016): 126–47; C. Phelps Harris, *The Anglo-American Peace Movement in the Mid-Nineteenth Century* (New York: Columbia University Press, 1930); Mazower, *Governing the World*, xiv–xv, 21–22.

27. Cobden to Ashworth, 12 April 1842.

28. Richard Cobden, in John Bright and James E. Thorold Rogers, eds, *Speeches on Questions of Public Policy by Richard Cobden, M.P.*, 2 vols (London: Macmillan, 1870), 1: 362–63.

29. Peter J. Cain and Antony G. Hopkins, *British Imperialism, 1688–2000* (London: Longman, 2001).

30. Palen, 'Conspiracy', ch. 1; Morgan, 'Anti–Corn Law League'.

31. Cobden to Colonel Fitzmayer, 18 October 1857, reprinted in John Morley, *The Life of Richard Cobden* (Cambridge: Cambridge University Press, 2010 [1881]), 214; MacDonagh, 'Anti-Imperialism of Free Trade'; Simon Morgan, 'Richard Cobden and British Imperialism', *Journal of Liberal History* 45 (Winter 2004/5): 16–21; Peter Cain, 'Capitalism, War and Internationalism in the Thought of Richard Cobden', *British Journal of International Studies* 5 (Oct. 1979): 229–47; Anthony Howe, 'Radicalism, Free Trade, and Foreign Policy in Mid-Nineteenth-Century Britain', in William Mulligan and Brendan Simms, eds, *The Primacy of Foreign Policy in British History, 1660–2000* (Basingstoke: Palgrave Macmillan, 2010), 167–80; Howe, 'Free Trade and Global Order', 31–32; Stephen Frick, 'Joseph Sturge, Henry Richard, and the *Herald of Peace*: Pacifist Response to the Crimean War' (PhD diss., Cornell University, 1971).

32. Luke A. Heselwood, 'The Impact of Anglo–Chinese Relations on the Development of British Liberalism, 1842–1857' (PhD thesis, University of Manchester, 2016), 40–41, 52–57, 65–67, ch. 4; Stephen Conway, 'Bentham, the Benthamites, and the Nineteenth-Century British Peace Movement', *Utilitas* 2 (Nov. 1990): 221–43 at 224; Conway, 'John Bowring and the Nineteenth Century Peace Movement', *Historical Research* 64 (Oct. 1991): 344–58; David Todd, 'John Bowring and the Global Dissemination of Free Trade', *Historical Journal* 51 (June 2008): 373–97.

33. Palen, 'Conspiracy', ch. 1.

34. Todd, 'John Bowring'.

35. Maynard, 'Reform and the Origin', 226–29.

36. 'The Peace Congress at Paris, 1849', *Advocate of Peace* 8 (Nov./Dec. 1849), 138.

37. Howe, 'Free Trade and Global Order', 34–35.

38. Morgan, 'Anti–Corn Law League', 100–103; Maynard, 'Reform and Origin', 220–21, 226, 223.

39. Quoted in Morgan, 'Anti–Corn Law League', 91 (emphasis in original).

40. José María Serrano Sanz and Marcela Sabaté Sort, 'Between Ideas and Interests: The End of the Spanish Free Trade Movement, 1879–c. 1903', *Revista de Historia Industrial* 29 (Feb. 2020):

11–43 at 20, 23, 29; Christopher Schmidt-Nowara, 'National Economy and Atlantic Slavery: Protectionism and Resistance to Abolitionism in Spain and the Antilles, 1854–1874', *Hispanic American Historical Review* 78 (Nov. 1998): 603–29.

41. Chickering, *Imperial Germany*, 120.

42. John Breuilly, '"Ein Stück Englands"? A Contrast between the Free-Trade Movements in Hamburg and Manchester', in Andrew Marrison, ed., *Free Trade and Its Reception 1815–1960: Freedom and Trade, Volume One* (London: Routledge, 2003), 105–26 at 203; Serrano and Sort, 'Between Ideas and Interests', 16; Gustave Louis Maurice Strauss, *Reminiscences of an Old Bohemian* (London: Tinsley Brothers, 1883), 179; John Prince Smith quoted in Ralph Raico, 'John Prince Smith and the German Free-Trade Movement', in Walter Block and Llewellyn H. Rockwell Jr., eds, *Man, Economy, and Liberty: Essays in Honor of Murray N. Rothbard* (Auburn: Ludwig von Mises Institute, 1988), 345. See also Ivo Lambi, *Free Trade and Protection in Germany, 1868–1879* (Wiesbaden: Steiner, 1963).

43. Roberto Romani, 'The Cobdenian Moment in the Italian Risorgimento', in Howe and Morgan, *Rethinking Nineteenth Century Liberalism*, 129.

44. 'The Italian Commercial League', *The Economist*, 20 November 1847, 1338; Camille Palma Castorina, 'Richard Cobden and the Intellectual Development and Influence of the Manchester School of Economics' (PhD thesis, University of Manchester, 1976), 255–72, Montenelli quoted on p. 261, Minghetti on p. 270.

45. 'Grand Dinner Given to Mr Cobden in Paris', *The Economist*, 22 August 1846, 1084; 'Mr Cobden's Sojourn in and Departure From Paris', *The Economist*, 5 September 1846, 1156–57.

46. Vanessa Fabius Lincoln, 'Organizing International Society: The French Peace Movement and the Origins of Reformist Internationalism, 1821–1853' (PhD diss., University of California, Berkeley, 2013), 48–63.

47. David Todd, *A Velvet Empire: French Informal Imperialism in the Nineteenth Century* (Princeton: Princeton University Press, 2021), 25–71; Lincoln, 'Organizing International Society', 66; Pamela M. Pilbeam, *Saint-Simonians in Nineteenth-Century France: From Free Love to Algeria* (Basingstoke: Palgrave Macmillan, 2014), 173–86.

48. Lincoln, 'Organizing International Society', 63–68.

49. 'Letter From Jacques Courrier', *Advocate of Peace* 30 (April 1872), 170–71; Sandi Cooper, *Patriotic Pacifism: Waging War on War in Europe, 1815–1914* (Oxford: Oxford University Press, 1991), 31–32.

50. H. L. Malchow, *Gentlemen Capitalists: The Social and Political World of the Victorian Businessmen* (Stanford: Stanford University Press, 1992), 63; Cooper, *Patriotic Pacifism*, 53–54, 66.

51. *Address of the Free Trade Association of London, to the American Free Trade League, New York* (London: P. S. King, 1866), 4.

52. Palen, 'Conspiracy', 67–81.

53. Palen, 'Conspiracy', 157.

54. Charles Albro Barker, *Henry George* (New York: Oxford University Press, 1955), 72–78, 142; Henry George, *Protection or Free Trade: An Examination of the Tariff Question with Especial Regard to the Interests of Labor* (New York: Robert Schalkenbach Foundation, 1886), 352–53.

55. Palen, 'Conspiracy'; Marc-William Palen, 'Foreign Relations in the Gilded Age: A British Free-Trade Conspiracy?' *Diplomatic History* 37 (April 2013): 217–47; Henry Cabot Lodge, 'Our Blundering Foreign Policy', *Forum* 19 (March 1895), 15.

56. Letter of 10 October 1879, in Herbert Spencer, *An Autobiography*, 2 vols (New York: Appleton, 1904), 2: 329; Peter Cain, 'Radicalism, Gladstone, and the Liberal Critique of Disraelian "Imperialism"', in Bell, *Victorian Visions*, 215–38 at 217–18; Cain and Hopkins, *British Imperialism*.

57. Anthony Howe, 'Towards the "Hungry Forties": Free Trade in Britain, c. 1880–1906', in Eugenio F. Biagini, ed., *Citizenship and Community: Liberals, Radicals, and Collective Identities in the British Isles, 1865–1931* (Cambridge: Cambridge University Press, 2009), 193–218.

58. Schmidt-Nowara, 'National Economy'; Christopher Schmidt-Nowara, *Empire and Antislavery: Spain, Cuba, and Puerto Rico, 1833–1874* (Pittsburgh: University of Pittsburgh Press, 1999), 95–96, 139–76, Labra quotation at 139, Rodríguez quotation at 162.

59. Howe, 'Free Trade and Global Order', 34–35.

60. Frederick W. Haberman, ed., *Nobel Lectures: Peace 1901–1925* (Singapore: World Scientific, 1999), 9–10; Cooper, *Patriotic Pacifism*, 53.

61. Cooper, *Patriotic Pacifism*, 66.

62. René Maunier, *The Sociology of the Colonies: An Introduction to the Study of Race Contact; Part One*, ed. and trans. by E. O. Lorimer (London: Routledge, 2002 [1949]), 361; Yves Guyot, *The French Corn Laws* (London: Cassell, 1888); 'Yves Guyot on the Protection of National Labor', *Population and Development Review* 33 (June 2007): 401–4 at 403; Yves Guyot, *Boer Politics* (London: John Murray, 1900); Charles Gide, 'Yves Guyot (1843–1928)', *Economic Journal* 38 (June 1928): 332–34; Jean-Claude Wartelle, 'Yves Guyot ou le libéralisme de combat', *Revue française d'histoire des idées politiques* 7 (1998): 73–109.

63. Castorina, 'Richard Cobden', 238–55; Detlev Mares, '"Not Entirely a Manchester Man": Richard Cobden and the Construction of Manchesterism in Nineteenth-Century German Economic Thinking', in Howe and Morgan, *Rethinking Nineteenth Century Liberalism*, 141–60 at 155–57.

64. Pieter M. Judson, *Exclusive Revolutionaries: Liberal Politics, Social Experience, and National Identity in the Austrian Empire, 1848–1914* (Ann Arbor: University of Michigan Press, 1996), 101–2, 180–81.

65. Ralph Raico, 'Eugen Richter and Late German Manchester Liberalism: A Reevaluation', *Review of Austrian Economics* 4 (Dec. 1990): 3–25 at 17–19, Bismarck quoted at 12 n. 19.

66. Mariano Carreras y Gonzalez, *Philosophie de la science économique* (Madrid: Librairie de Fernando Fe, 1881), 260; Ferdinand Lassalle, *Herr Bastiat-Schulze von Delitzsch* (Berlin: Schlingmann, 1864). See also Julius Becker, *Das deutsche Manchestertum: Eine Studie zur Geschichte des wirtschaftspolitischen Individualismus* (Karlsruhe: Braun, 1907); Carl Brinkmann, *Richard Cobden und das Manchestertum* (Berlin: Hobbing, 1924).

67. James J. Sheehan, *German Liberalism in the Nineteenth Century* (Chicago: University of Chicago Press, 1983 [1978]), 153; 'A Signal Loss to the Cause', *Free Trade Broadside* 2 (July 1909), 5.

68. Chickering, *Imperial Germany*, 42–47; Sheehan, *German Liberalism*, 153; 'A Signal Loss', 5.

69. Theodor Barth, 'A Jubilee of Free Trade and Democracy', in Richard Gowing, ed., *Richard Cobden and the Jubilee of Free Trade* (London: T. Fisher Unwin, 1896), 129–65; Chickering, *Imperial Germany*, 50–53, 58, 62, 101–2, 120, Fried quoted at 101; Klaus Schlichtmann, 'Alfred Hermann Fried (1864–1921): Transitioning to World Order', *Peace Research* 48 (Jan. 2016): 33–65 at 50; Glenda Sluga, *Internationalism in the Age of Nationalism* (Philadelphia: University of Pennsylvania Press, 2013), 15–16.

70. Fiorenzo Mornati, *Vilfredo Pareto: An Intellectual Biography*, vol. 1: *From Science to Liberty (1848–1891)*, trans. by Paul Wilson (London: Palgrave Macmillan, 2018), 174–76; Mornati, *Vilfredo Pareto: An Intellectual Biography*, vol. 2: *The Illusions and Disillusions of Liberty (1891–1898)*, trans. by Paul Wilson (London: Palgrave Macmillan, 2018), 58–60; Terenzio Maccabelli, 'From Pacifism to Political Realism: The Economics and Sociology of War in Vilfredo Pareto', in Fabrizio Bientinesi and Rosario Patalano, eds, *Economists and War: A Heterodox Perspective* (New York: Routledge, 2017), 57–80 at 59–61.

71. Daniel Laqua, *The Age of Internationalism and Belgium, 1880–1930: Peace, Progress and Prestige* (Manchester: University of Manchester Press, 2013), 148–49.

72. Cooper, *Patriotic Pacifism*, 45; Howe, *Free Trade and Liberal England*, 120; Emile Arnaud and Elie Ducommun, 'The Proceedings of the Twelfth Universal Peace Congress', *Advocate of Peace* 65 (Nov. 1903), 205.

73. J. Novicow, 'Views of a Russian Cosmopolitan', *Free Trade Broadside* 16 (July 1905), 7; W. T. Stead, 'A Russian Cobden', in *The United States of Europe on the Eve of the Parliament of Peace* (London: *Review of Reviews* Office, 1899), 133–37.

74. Craufurd D. W. Goodwin, *Economic Enquiry in Australia* (Durham, NC: Duke University Press, 1966), 42; J. A. La Nauze, '"That fatal, that mischievous passage": Henry Parkes and Protection, 1859–1866', *Australian Quarterly* 19 (June 1947): 52–61 at 59–60; Howe, *Free Trade and Liberal England*, 120, 127, 140; Palen, 'Conspiracy', 220.

75. Dadabhai Naoroji, 'Congress Presidential Address, Lahore, 1893', in Naoroji, *Speeches and Writings of Dadabhai Naoroji* (Madras: Natesan, 1917), 42; 'Indian Famine Relief Fund Meeting, 1 July 1900', in ibid., 222.

76. Dadabhai Naoroji, *Poverty and Un-British Rule in India* (London: Swan Sonnenschein, 1901), 62.

77. Dadabhai Naoroji, 'Presidential Address to the Twenty-Second Congress, Calcutta, 1906', in Naoroji, *Speeches and Writings*, 95; Naoroji, 'Message to the Benares Congress', 26 November 1905, in ibid., 650–52.

78. Sluga, *Internationalism*, ch. 1.

79. Avner Offer, *Property and Politics, 1870–1914* (Cambridge: Cambridge University Press, 1981), 184.

80. Anthony Howe, 'The "Manchester School" and the Landlords: The Failure of Land Reform in Early Victorian Britain', in Matthew Cragoe and Paul Readman, eds, *The Land Question in Britain, 1750–1950* (Basingstoke: Palgrave Macmillan, 2010), 74–91; Antony Taylor, 'Richard Cobden, J. E. Thorold Rogers and Henry George', in Cragoe and Readman, *Land Question*, 146–66; F.M.L. Thompson, 'Cobden, Free Trade in Land, and the Road to the Abbey National', in Howe and Morgan, *Rethinking Nineteenth Century Liberalism*, 68–79.

81. 'Cobden on Land Value Tax', *The Public* 1 (16 April 1898), 13.

82. John M. Gates, 'Philippine Guerrillas, American Anti-Imperialists, and the Election of 1900', *Pacific Historical Review* 46 (Feb. 1977): 51–64 at 54; Harriet Hyman Alonso, *Growing Up Abolitionist: The Story of the Garrison Children* (Amherst: University of Massachusetts Press, 2002), 288–89.

83. John A. Farrell, *Clarence Darrow: Attorney for the Damned* (New York: Vintage Books, 2011), 97–98; Clarence Darrow, 'Free Trade or Protection?' *Current Topics* (April 1894), Box 13, Folder 1, Clarence Darrow Papers, Library of Congress, Washington, DC.

84. 'Land Value Taxation and Free Trade', *Land & Liberty*, July–August 1929, 146.

85. Howe, *Free Trade and Liberal England*, 277–78.

86. J. L. Hammond, ed., *Towards a Social Policy: or, Suggestions for Constructive Reform* (London: Speaker Publishing Company, 1905), 44. See also Peter Clarke, *Liberals and Social Democrats* (Cambridge: Cambridge University Press, 1978), 82.

87. Jane Cobden, *The Land Hunger: Life Under Monopoly* (London: T. Fisher Unwin, 1913).

88. Lucia Ames Mead, 'The Philippines and Naval Reductionism', *Advocate of Peace* 76 (May 1914), 110; John M. Craig, *Lucia Ames Mead and the American Peace Movement* (Lewiston, NY: Edwin Mellen Press, 1990), 57–61. For Mead's advocacy of free trade, interdependence, and peace, see Lucia Ames Mead, 'Economic Conditions of Permanent Peace', *Advocate of Peace* 80 (March 1918), 79–80; Mead, *Swords and Ploughshares* (New York: G. P. Putnam's Sons, 1912), ch. 3; John M. Craig, 'Lucia True Ames Mead: American Publicist for Peace and Internationalism', in Edward P. Crapol, ed., *Women and American Foreign Policy* (Westport, CT: The Greenwood Press, 1987), 67–91 at 72–73.

89. Hobson, in turn, had been influenced by imperial theorist Gaylord Wilshire. See P. J. Cain, 'Hobson, Wilshire, and the Capitalist Theory of Capitalism Imperialism', *History of Political Economy* (Fall 1985): 455–60. For Hobson and Cobdenism, see P. J. Cain, 'J. A. Hobson, Cobdenism and the Radical Theory of Economic Imperialism, 1898–1914', *Economic History Review* 31 (Nov. 1978): 565–84.

90. Patterson, *Toward a Warless World*, 69; Craig, 'Lucia True Ames Mead', 72–73.

91. *Report of the Fourth Annual Meeting of the New England Anti-Imperialist League* (Boston, MA: New England Anti-Imperialist League, 1902), 8; 'Imperialism: J. A. Hobson's New Book on Its Growth and Its Influence in British Politics', *New York Times*, 15 November 1902, BR5. The AIL's Philadelphia branch extended a similar invitation for a 1903 lecture tour to Cobden biographer John Morley. See George Mercer to Moorfield Storey, 18 June 1902, Box 2, '1902' Folder, Moorfield Storey Papers, Massachusetts Historical Society, Boston, MA [MHS].

92. Peter Cain, 'Free Trade, Social Reform and Imperialism: J. A. Hobson and the Dilemmas of Liberalism, 1890–1914', in Marrison, *Free Trade and Its Reception*, ch. 16 at 390, 392. See also P. J. Cain, *Hobson and Imperialism: Radicalism, New Liberalism, and Finance, 1887–1938* (Oxford: Oxford University Press, 2002).

93. April Merleaux, *Sugar and Civilization: Amerian Empire and the Cultural Politics of Sweetness* (Chapel Hill: University of North Carolina Press, 2015).

94. Erving Winslow to Herbert Welsh, December 7, 1901, Box 2, Herbert Welsh Papers, Special Collections Library, University of Michigan, Ann Arbor, MI.

95. 'Our Peace Number', *Free Trade Broadside* 1 (July 1905); William Lloyd Garrison, 'Chinese Exclusion', *Advocate of Peace* 64 (Feb. 1902), 35–39; 'The Closed American Door', ibid.: 22–23; Rick Baldoz, *The Third Asiatic Invasion: Migration and Empire in Filipino America, 1898–1946* (New York 2011), 161; Marc-William Palen, 'The Imperialism of Economic Nationalism', *Diplomatic History* 39 (Jan. 2015): 157–85 at 175–76. Numerous economic peace workers counted among the American Peace Society's officers, including Jane Addams, Edward Atkinson, Edwin Mead, Lucia Ames Mead, George Foster Peabody, and NAACP president Moorfield Storey.

96. US Congress, House, 'Reciprocity with Cuba', *Hearings before Committee on Ways and Means*, 57th Congress, 1st Session (Washington, DC: Government Printing Press, 1902), 144–45,

149, 91, 94–95. On the US insular empire, see especially A. G. Hopkins, *American Empire: A Global History* (Princeton: Princeton University Press, 2018).

97. Mary Speck, 'Closed-Door Imperialism: The Politics of Cuban–US Trade, 1902–1933' *Hispanic American Historical Review* 85 (Aug. 2005): 449–83 at 455–58.

98. Palen, 'Imperialism of Economic Nationalism', 176–77.

99. Excerpt reproduced in Charles Francis Adams Jr. to Moorfield Storey, 20 August 1904, Box 1, '1904 Aug.–Dec.' Folder, Moorfield Storey Papers, MHS.

100. Raul Rafael Ingles, *1908: The Way It Really Was* (Quezon City: University of the Philippines Press, 2008), 172; *El Renacimiento* [Manila], July 13, 1908, Box 178, Folder 15, Garrison Family Papers, Sophia Smith Collection, Smith College, Northampton, MA [hereafter SSC].

101. Sixto Lopez, *The 'Wild Tribes' and Other Filipinos* (Boston, MA: Anti-Imperialist League, 1911), Box 5, 'Misc. #3: Printed (Philippines)', Moorfield Storey Papers, MHS.

102. See Raymond L. Bridgman, *World Organization* (Boston, MA: Ginn & Company, 1905); Bridgman, *The Passing of the Tariff* (Boston, MA: Sherman, French & Company, 1909); Thomas Mott Osborne, *Democracy and Imperialism* (Cambridge, MA: Press of the *Cambridge Chronicle*, 1908).

103. Michale Silagi, *Henry George and Europe: The Far-Reaching Impact and Effect of the Ideas of the American Social Philosopher*, trans. by Susan N. Faulkner (New York: Robert Schalkenback Foundation, 2000), chs 7 and 8; Sein Lin, 'Sun Yat-Sen and Henry George: The Essential Role of Land Policy in their Doctrines', *American Journal of Economics and Sociology* 33 (April 1974): 201–20; 'Sun Yat-Sen's Economic Program for China', *The Public* 15 (12 April 1912), 349; Paul Myron Anthony Linebarger, *The Political Doctrines of Sun Yat-Sen* (Baltimore: Johns Hopkins University Press, 1957 [1937]), 134–36.

104. Eric Helleiner, *The Neomercantilists: A Global Intellectual History* (Ithaca, NY: Cornell University Press, 2021), ch. 9.

105. Sun Yat-Sen, *The International Development of China* (Singapore: Springer, 2021 [1921]), xv; Sun Yat-Sen, *San Min Chu I: The Three Principles of the People* (Taipei: China Pub. Co., 1924), 15, 161–62; Linebarger, *Political Doctrines*, 175–81.

106. Kenneth C. Wenzer, 'The Influence of Henry George's Philosophy on Lev Nikolaevich Tolstoy: The Period of Developing Economic Thought (1881–1897)', *Pennsylvania History* 63 (Spring 1996): 232–52 at 239, 243, Tolstoy quoted at 241, 244; Patrick Heyer, 'Revolution of Spirit: Henry George, Leo Tolstoy, and the Land Value Tax' (MA thesis, California State University, Fullerton, 2014).

107. *Proceedings of the International Free Trade Congress* (London: Unwin, 1908); *The Fourth Annual Report of the United Committee or the Taxation of Land Values. 1910–1911* (London: United Committee for the Taxation of Land Values, 1912), 31.

108. 'Syndicalism or Single Tax', *Everyman*, March 1913, 16; *1923 International Conference on the Taxation of Land Values Held in the Assembly Room of the Town Hall, Oxford, England, 13th to 19th August, 1923* (London: United Committee for the Taxation of Land Values, 1924), 23–27; Felix Vitale, 'The Struggle for Freedom in South America', *Land and Freedom* 40 (July–Aug. 1940): 103–5; C. Macintosh, 'The Movement in South America', *Single Tax Review* 15 (Sept.–Oct. 1915): 278–79; 'War is for Land Monopoly', *Everyman*, Aug.–Sept. 1914, 5–6, Box 14, Folder 2, Clarence Darrow Papers, Library of Congress, Washington, DC.

109. Paul Mulvey, *The Political Life of Josiah C. Wedgwood: Land, Liberty and Empire, 1872–1943* (Woodbridge: Boydell Press, 2010), 20, 5, 7, 10, 14, 17.

110. Mulvey, *Political Life of Wedgwood*, 43, 45, 46–47, 112.

111. Joseph Fels, 'Free Trade and the Single Tax vs. Imperialism: A Letter to Andrew Carnegie' (Dec. 1910), available at http://www.cooperative-individualism.org/fels-joseph_free-trade-and-the-single-tax-vs-imperialism-1910.htm (accessed 10 May 2023).

112. 'Public Opinion Force to End Great Wars, Mrs. Fels Declares', July 31, 1916 [unknown newspaper], Box 5, Folder 7, Joseph and Mary Fels Papers, Historical Society of Philadelphia [hereafter HSP].

113. Howe, *Free Trade and Liberal England*, 244–73.

114. Howe, *Free Trade and Liberal England*, 296.

115. Alexander Zevin, *Liberalism at Large: The World According to the Economist* (London: Verso Books, 2019), 143–65.

116. Paul Laity, *The British Peace Movement, 1870–1914* (Oxford: Oxford University Press, 2002), 190–91; Norman Angell, *The Great Illusion* (New York and London: G. P. Putnam's Sons, 1913 [1910]), 31–35.

117. Howard Weinroth, 'Norman Angell and *The Great Illusion*: An Episode in Pre-1914 Pacifism', *Historical Journal* 17 (Sept. 1974): 551–74 at 555–67.

118. Henri La Fontaine, *The Great Solution* (Boston, MA: World Peace Foundation, 1916), 25–26.

119. Morley, *Life of Richard Cobden*, 6–7.

120. H. Haneck, 'The Union of Democratic Control During the First World War', *Bulletin of the Institute of Historical Research* 36 (Nov. 1963): 168–80 See, for instance, J. A. Hobson, *Towards International Government* (New York: Macmillan, 1915); Hobson, *A League of Nations* (London: Union of Democratic Control, 1915).

121. J. A. Hobson, *Wealth and Life: A Study in Values* (London: Macmillan, 1929), 400.

122. J. A. Hobson, *Richard Cobden: The International Man* (London: T. Fisher Unwin, 1918), 408–9; Hobson, *Democracy and a Changing Civilization* (London, 1934), 146, 150–51, 141–24; David Weinstein, 'Consequentialist Cosmopolitanism', in Bell, *Victorian Visions*, 267–90 at 275–78; Trentmann, *Free Trade Nation*, 176; Duncan Bell, 'Democracy and Empire: J. A. Hobson, Leonard Hobhouse, and the Crisis of Liberalism', in Ian Hall and Lisa Hill, eds, *British International Thinkers from Hobbes to Namier* (New York: Palgrave Macmillan, 2009), 181–205 at 199; Jamie Martin, *The Meddlers: Sovereignty, Empire, and the Birth of Global Economic Governance* (Cambridge, MA: Harvard University Press, 2022), ch. 5.

123. Amalia Ribi Forclaz, *Humanitarian Imperialism: The Politics of Anti-Slavery Activism, 1880–1940* (Oxford: Oxford University Press, 2015).

124. See for instance Jean Bricmont, *Humanitarian Imperialism: Using Human Rights to Sell War*, trans. by Diana Johnstone (New York: Palgrave Macmillan, 2006); Ray Bush, Giuliano Martiniello, and Claire Mercer, 'Humanitarian Imperialism', *Review of African Political Economy* 38 (Sept. 2011): 357–65; Richard Drayton, 'Beyond Humanitarian Imperialism: The Dubious Origins of "Humanitarian Intervention" and Some Rules for Its Future', in Bronwen Everill and Josiah Kaplan, eds, *The History and Practice of Humanitarian Intervention and Aid in Africa* (London: Palgrave Macmillan, 2013), 217–31.

125. Stephen Howe, *Anticolonialism in British Politics: The Left and the End of Empire 1918–1964* (Oxford: Oxford University Press, 1993), 32.

126. Patterson, *Toward a Warless World*, 76–77.

127. 'Carnegie on Free Trade', *Free Trade Broadside* 2 (July 1909), 6; Erving Winslow, 'The Open vs. The Closed Door', *North American Review* 206 (Sept. 1917), 450.

128. Susan Pedersen, *The Guardians: The League of Nations and the Crisis of Empire* (Oxford: Oxford University Press, 2015), esp. ch. 8; Daniel Gorman, 'Liberal Internationalism, the League of Nations Union, and the Mandates System', *Canadian Journal of History* 40 (Dec. 2005): 449–77.

129. Winslow, 'Open vs. Closed Door'. See also Winslow, *Tariffs after the War* (Boston, MA: American Free Trade League, n.d. [1916?]); Winslow, 'War or Free Trade', *Advocate of Peace* 78 (May 1916), 145; Henri Lambert to Erving Winslow, 1918, n.d., '1918' Folder, Carton 2, Erving Winslow Papers, MHS.

130. Kenneth B. Elliman, Mary Ware Dennett, Walter L. Ehrich, Daniel Kiefer, Samuel Milliken, and Frank W. Garrison to Erving Winslow, undated (1917), '1917 n.d.' Folder, Carton 2, Winslow Papers, MHS.

131. Trentmann, *Free Trade Nation*, 255.

132. Joseph Fels to Louis Post, 5 Oct. 1910, Folder 5, Fels Papers, HSP.

133. Christopher William England, 'Land and Liberty: Henry George, the Single Tax Movement, and the Origins of 20th Century Liberalism' (PhD diss., Georgetown University, 2015), 347–49; Dominic Candeloro, 'The Single Tax Movement and Progressivism, 1880–1920', *American Journal of Economics and Sociology* 38 (April 1979): 113–27 at 120–22.

134. Matt Perry, ed., *The Global Challenge of Peace: 1919 as a Contested Threshold to a New World Order* (Liverpool: Liverpool University Press, 2021).

135. Herbert Quick, *From War to Peace* (Indianapolis: Bobbs-Merrill Co., 1919). For his critique of the 'civilizing mission' and imperialism, see also Quick, *On Board the Good Ship Earth: A Survey of World Problems* (Indianapolis: Bobbs-Merrill Co., 1913).

136. 'Free Trade Sentiment in Germany', *International Free Trader* 2 (June 1919), 4; Lida Gustava Heymann, 'Free Trade in Germany', *International Free Trader* 5 (May 1922), 3.

137. Joseph Schumpeter, 'The Sociology of Imperialisms [1919]', reprinted in *Imperialism and Social Classes* (New York: The World Publishing Co., 1966 [1955]); Cain, 'Capitalism, Aristocracy and Empire', 30–31.

138. Frederic C. Howe, *The Only Possible Peace* (New York: Charles Scribner's Sons, 1919), vii, x, 224–28.

139. Peter G. Forster, *The Esperanto Movement* (The Hague: Mouton Publishers, 1982), 170.

140. Sakai Toshihiki and Juroita Katsumi, *Chokugen*, 19 March 1905, quoted in Ian Rapley, 'Sekaigo: Esperanto, International Language, and the Transnational Dimension to Japan's Linguistic Modernity', *Japan Forum* 32 (Oct. 2020): 511–30 at 526.

141. Forster, *Esperanto Movement*, 179.

142. Dr. Foehr, 'Esperanto in the War', *The Public*, 20 August 1915, 815; George Winthrop Lee, 'Esperanto, An Instrument of Peace', *Advocate of Peace* 79 (Nov. 1917), 297; 'Esperanto as the Official Language of the League', 31 October 1920, File R1549/39/8935/579, League of Nations Archives, Geneva, Switzerland [hereafter LoN]; 'Paris Business Men Would Use Esperanto', *New York Times*, 16 February 1921, 12; Forster, *Esperanto Movement*, 181.

143. Forster, *Esperanto Movement*, 175–76.

144. Forster, *Esperanto Movement*, 183.

145. John Maynard Keynes, *The Economic Consequences of the Peace* (London: Labour Research Dept., 1920), 22, 225, 266–69; Donald Markwell, *John Maynard Keynes and International Relations: Economic Paths to War and Peace* (Oxford: Oxford University Press, 2006), 17–25.

146. Norman Angell, 'The Moral and Psychological Roots of Protectionism', *International Free Trader* 5 (May 1922), 5.

147. 'The League', *The Public*, 6 December 1919, 1131.

148. Candeloro, 'Single Tax Movement', 121.

149. Diary entries of 31 August 1922, 26 Oct. 1922, '1922–27', Box 10, Louis Freeland Post Papers, Library of Congress, Washington, DC.

150. 'Self-Determination for All Peoples', *The World Tomorrow* 2 (Dec. 1919), 349.

151. Arthur Upham Pope [temporary secretary of League of Oppressed Peoples] to W.E.B. Du Bois, 10 November 1919, W.E.B. Du Bois Papers, University of Massachusetts, Amherst, https://credo.library.umass.edu/view/pageturn/mums312-b014-i260/#page/1/mode/1up (accessed 10 May 2023).

152. Sheepshanks also noted that the Council was torn over the question of worldwide distribution of raw materials. Mary Sheepshanks to the Secretary, League of Nations, 16 November 1920, 10/7645/956, 'Economic and Financial', LoN.

153. *International Conference on the Taxation of Land Values Held in the Assembly Room of the Town Hall, Oxford, England, 13th to 19th August, 1923* (London: United Committee for the Taxation of Land Values, 1924), 17.

154. Charles O'Connor Hennessy, *The Interdependence of the Economic Causes of War and of Industrial Depression: Memorandum Addressed to the International Economic Conference of the League of Nations, Held at Geneva—May, 1927—by the International Union for Land-Value Taxation and Free Trade* (London: International Union for Land-Value Taxation and Free Trade, 1927), 3–8.

155. *The Fifty-Sixth Annual Co-operative Congress* (Manchester: Co-operative Union, 1924), 117.

156. *International Economic Conference, Geneva, May 1927*, 10/59345x/52566; 'Notes by Dr. Grendelenburg on the Work of the Special Session of the Economic Committee in July 1927', doc. no. 60506, doss. no. 51672, 'Economic and Financial', LoN.

157. Thomas R. Davies, 'Internationalism in a Divided World: The Experience of the International Federation of League of Nations Societies, 1919–1939', *Peace & Change* 37 (April 2012): 227–52 at 232.

158. Sir George Paish to Nicholas Murray Butler, 30 July 1925; Butler to Paish, 10 August 1925; H. S. Perris, *Dunford House as a Memorial of Richard Cobden* (s.p., 1926); 'Cobden's Home', *The Guardian*, 19 July 1928; Butler to Perris, 10 Dec. 1928, Box 18a, Carnegie Records, Columbia University Library, New York.

159. On the Kellogg-Briand Pact, see Oona A. Hathaway and Scott J. Shapiro, *The Internationalists: How a Radical Plan to Outlaw War Remade the World* (New York: Simon & Schuster, 2017).

160. H. S. Perris, 'To Dr. Nicholas Murray Butler, An Open Letter from a European Friend', (1929), Folder 18b, Carnegie Records.

161. Lionel Robbins, *The Economic Causes of War* (New York: Howard Fertig, 1968 [1939]), 98, 91, 101, 104–5.

162. Cordell Hull, *The Memoirs of Cordell Hull* (New York: Macmillan, 1948), 81, 84.

163. F. W. Hirst, 'Cobden and Cordell Hull', *Contemporary Review* 155 (1939): 10–17 at 10.

164. Alfred E. Eckes, *Opening America's Market: US Foreign Trade Policy since 1776* (Chapel Hill: University of North Carolina Press, 1995). See also Anthony Howe, 'Free Trade and the International Order', in Fred M. Leventhal and Roland Quinault, eds, *Anglo-American Attitudes: From Revolution to Partnership* (London: Routledge, 2000), 142–67; Howe, 'From Pax Britannica to Pax Americana: Free Trade, Empire and Globalisation, 1846–1946', *Bulletin of Asia-Pacific Studies* 13 (2003): 137–59; Howe, *Free Trade and Liberal England*, 274, 299, 304.

165. Robert David Johnson, 'Anti-Imperialism and the Good Neighbour Policy: Ernest Gruening and Puerto Rican Affairs, 1934–1939', *Journal of Latin American Studies* 29 (Feb. 1997): 89–110.

166. Arthur W. Schatz, 'The Anglo-American Trade Agreement and Cordell Hull's Search for Peace 1936–1938', *Journal of American History* 57 (June 1970): 85–103; Douglas A. Irwin, Petros C. Mavroidis, and Alan O. Sykes, *The Genesis of the GATT* (Cambridge: Cambridge University Press, 2008), 12–22; Richard Toye, 'The Attlee Government, the Imperial Preference System and the Creation of the GATT', *English Historical Review* 118 (Sept. 2003): 912–39.

167. Thomas W. Zeiler, *Capitalist Peace: A History of American Free-Trade Internationalism* (Oxford: Oxford University Press, 2022), 1, 22.

168. Douglas A. Irwin, *Clashing over Commerce: A History of US Trade Policy* (Chicago: University of Chicago Press, 2017), chs 9–10.

169. Amry Vandenbosch, 'Cordell Hull: Father of the United Nations', *World Affairs* 136 (Fall 1973): 99–120.

170. *Building a New World Economy* (Washington, DC, 1946).

171. Timothy Healey, 'Will Clayton, Negotiating the Marshall Plan, and European Economic Integration', *Diplomatic History* 35 (April 2011): 229–56.

172. Irwin, Mavroidis, and Sykes, *Genesis of the GATT*, 11–12; Thomas W. Zeiler, 'Closed Doors', in Akira Iriye, ed., *Global Interdependence: The World after 1945* (Cambridge, MA: Harvard University Press, 2014), 207–244 at 213. On the politico-ideological conflict surrounding the GATT regime, see especially Susan Ariel Aaronson, *Trade and the American Dream: A Social History of Postwar Trade Policy* (Lexington: University Press of Kentucky, 1996); Thomas W. Zeiler, *Free Trade, Free World: The Advent of GATT* (1999); Irwin, *Clashing over Commerce*, 483–508; and Francine McKenzie, *GATT and Global Order in the Postwar Era* (Cambridge: Cambridge University Press, 2020).

173. Oswald Garrison Villard, *Free Trade: Free World* (New York: Robert Schalkenbach Foundation, 1947), 78.

Chapter 3. Marx and Manchester

1. Karl Marx, 'Speech on the Question of Free Trade', Brussels, Belgium, 9 January 1848, reprinted in *Karl Marx/Frederick Engels Collected Works*, 50 vols (New York: International Publishers, 1975–2004 [hereafter *MECW*], vol. 6: *1845–1848*(1976), 465.

2. Reprinted in *The Liberator* 1 (Oct. 1918), 4.

3. *Protokoll über die Verhandlungen des Parteitages der Sozialdemokratischen Partei Deutschlands, Stuttgart* (Berlin: Dietz, 1898), 68, 200; Carlton J. H. Hayes, 'The History of German Socialism Reconsidered', *American Historical Review* 23 (Oct. 1917): 63–121 at 93–94; Cornelius Torp, *The Challenges of Globalization: Economy and Politics in Germany, 1860–1914* (New York:

Berghahn, 2014), 248; *Report of the Proceedings of the International Free Trade Congress, London, August, 1908* (London: Cobden Club, 1908), 28; Anthony Howe, *Free Trade and Liberal England, 1846–1946* (Oxford: Clarendon Press, 1997), 275.

4. See, for example, Friedrich Hayek, *Individualism and Economic Order* (Chicago: University of Chicago Press, 1948), 270–71; Michael A. Heilperin, *Studies in Economic Nationalism* (Paris: Librairie Minard, 1960), 43; Dorothy Ross, 'Socialism and American Liberalism: Academic Social Thought in the 1880's', *Perspectives in American History* 11 (1977–78): 5–79.

5. See, for instance, *Humanity's* Spring 2015 special issue, *Toward a History of the New International Economic Order*; Oscar Sanchez-Sibony, *Red Globalization: The Political Economy of the Soviet Cold War from Stalin to Khrushchev* (Cambridge: Cambridge University Press, 2014); Johanna Bockman, *Markets in the Name of Socialism: The Left-Wing Origins of Neoliberalism* (Stanford: Stanford University Press, 2011); James Mark, Bogdan Iacob, Tobias Rupprecht, and Ljubica Spaskovska, *1989: A Global History of Eastern Europe* (Cambridge: Cambridge University Press, 2019).

6. See, among others, Ha-Joon Chang, *Kicking Away the Ladder: Development Strategy in Historical Perspective* (London: Anthem, 2002); Henryk Szlajfer, *Economic Nationalism and Globalization*, trans. by Maria Chmielewska-Szlajfer (Leiden: Brill, 2012).

7. Bert F. Hoselitz, 'Socialism, Communism, and International Trade', *Journal of Political Economy* 57 (1949): 227–41; Michael Howard and John Edward King, *A History of Marxian Economics*, vol. 1: *1883–1929* (Princeton: Princeton University Press, 1989), 90–92; Pranab Bardhan, 'Marxist Ideas in Development Economics: A Brief Evaluation', *Economic and Political Weekly* 20 (30 March 1985): 550–55 at 550; Claudio Katz, 'The *Manifesto* and Globalization', trans. by Carlos Perez, *Latin American Perspectives* 28 (Nov. 2001): 5–16 at 7–8; Bill Dunn, *Neither Free Trade Nor Protection: A Critical Political Economy of Trade Theory and Practice* (Cheltenham: Edward Elgar, 2015), ch. 5.

8. This line of thought bore more than a few similarities to that of their interwar 'neoliberal' contemporaries. See, for instance, Ben Jackson, 'At the Origins of Neo-Liberalism: The Free Economy and the Strong State, 1930–1947', *Historical Journal* 53 (March 2010): 129–51; Quinn Slobodian, *Globalists: The End of Empire and the Birth of Neoliberalism* (Cambridge, MA: Harvard University Press, 2018).

9. C. P. Kindleberger, 'The Rise of Free Trade in Western Europe, 1820–1875', *Journal of Economic History* 35 (March 1975): 20–55; Scott C. James and David A. Lake, 'The Second Face of Hegemony: Britain's Repeal of the Corn Laws and the American Walker Tariff of 1846', *International Organization* 43 (Winter 1989): 1–29.

10. Richard Cobden, in John Bright and James E. Thorold Rogers, eds, *Speeches on Questions of Public Policy by Richard Cobden, M.P.*, 2 vols (London: Macmillan, 1870), 1: 362–63.

11. Debates surrounding 'material interests' in early-1840s Germany informed Marx's later free-trade position. Karl Marx, *A Contribution to the Critique of Political Economy* (Chicago: C. H. Kerr, 1904 [1859]), 10.

12. On the Irish exception, see Marx to Engels, 30 November 1867, reprinted in *Karl Marx and Frederick Engels: Selected Correspondence, 1846–1895* (New York: International Publishers, 1942), 229.

13. Reza Ghorashi, 'Marx on Free Trade', *Science & Society* 59 (Spring 1995): 38–51 at 43; Howard and King, *History of Marxian Economics*, 15; Samuel Hollander, *The Economics of Karl Marx: Analysis and Application*, 445–46; Hollander, *Friedrich Engels and Marxian Political*

Economy (Cambridge: Cambridge University Press, 2011), 132–34, 233, 275, 359–61; Friedrich Engels, preface to Karl Marx, 'On the Question of Free Trade' [1888], *MECW*, vol. 25: *Anti-Dühring; Dialectics of Nature* (1987), 521; Bert F. Hoselitz, 'Socialism, Communism, and International Trade', *Journal of Political Economy* 57 (June 1949): 227–41 at 233.

14. Karl Marx, 'The Industrialists of Hanover and Protective Tariffs', 22 November 1842, *MECW*, vol. 1: *1835–1843* (1975), 286.

15. Katz, 'The *Manifesto* and Globalization', 5.

16. Frederick Engels, 'The Free Trade Congress at Brussels', *MECW*, 6: 283; Engels, 'The Corn Laws', (22 Dec. 1842), *MECW*, vol. 2: *1838–1842* (1987), 380–82; W. O. Henderson, *The Life of Friedrich Engels*, 2 vols (London: Frank Cass, 1976), 1: 95.

17. Ghorashi, 'Marx on Free Trade', 46; Karl Marx, *The Eastern Question: A Reprint of Letters Written 1853–1856 Dealing with the Events of the Crimean War*, ed. by Eleanor Marx Aveling and Edward Aveling (London: Swan Sonnenschein & Co., 1897), 151; James Joll, 'The Second International and War', *Publications de l'École française de Rome* 54 (1981): 245–62 at 247.

18. Karl Marx, 'Speech of Dr. Marx on Protection, Free Trade, and the Working Classes', *Northern Star*, 9 October 1847, reprinted in *MECW*, 6: 290; Jorge Larrain, 'Classical Political Economists and Marx on Colonialism and "Backward" Nations', *World Development* 19 (Feb.–March 1991): 225–43 at 230–31; Alan Gilbert, 'Marx on Internationalism and War', *Philosophy & Public Affairs* 7 (Summer 1978): 346–69.

19. Marx, 'Speech on the Question of Free Trade', 465; Larrain, 'Classical Political Economists', 230–31; Alan Gilbert, 'Marx on Internationalism and War', *Philosophy & Public Affairs* 7 (Summer 1978): 346–69.

20. Per A. Hammarlund, *Liberal Internationalism and the Decline of the State: The Thought of Richard Cobden, David Mitrany and Kenichi Ohmae* (New York: Palgrave Macmillan, 2005); Mark Mazower, *Governing the World: The History of an Idea* (New York: Penguin, 2012), ch. 2.

21. Karl Marx, 'Draft of an Article on Friedrich List's Book: *Das Nationale System der Politischen Oekonomie*', *MECW*, vol. 4: *1844–1845* (1975), 275 (emphasis in original). See also Karl Marx, 'Speech of Dr. Marx on Protection, Free Trade, and the Working Classes', *Northern Star*,9 October 1847, reprinted in *MECW*, 6: 287–90; Roman Szporluk, *Communism and Nationalism: Karl Marx versus Friedrich List* (Oxford: Oxford University Press, 1988); Radhika Desai, 'Marx, List, and the Materiality of Nations', *Rethinking Marxism* 24 (2012): 47–67.

22. *MECW*, vol. 35: *'Capital', Volume 1* (1996), 744; Hollander, *Friedrich Engels*, 132–34.

23. Marx, 'Industrialists of Hanover', *MECW*, 1: 286 (emphasis in original); Edmund Silberner, *The Problem of War in Nineteenth Century Economic Thought* (Princeton: Princeton University Press, 1946), 261–62.

24. George Lichtheim, *Marxism: An Historical and Critical Study* (New York: Praeger, 1961), 216; Frederick Engels, preface to the 1888 American edition of Karl Marx's *On the Question of Free Trade*, available at https://www.marxists.org/archive/marx/works/1888/free-trade/ (accessed 10 May 2023).

25. Mori Kenzo argues, in 'Marx and "Underdevelopment": His Thesis on the "Historical Roles of British Free Trade" Revisited', *Annals of the Institute of Social Science* 19 (1978): 35–61, that Marx's views on free trade changed with respect to some developing countries.

26. Hoselitz, 'Socialism, Communism', 227; Howard and King, *History of Marxian Economics*, 15–16, 91.

27. Anthony Howe and Simon Morgan, eds, *Rethinking Nineteenth Century Liberalism: Richard Cobden Bicentenary Essays* (Aldershot: Ashgate, 2006).

28. Erik Grimmer-Solem, *The Rise of Historical Economics and Social Reform in Germany, 1864–1894* (New York, 2003); José Luís Cardos and Michalis Psalidopoulos, eds, *The German Historical School and European Economic Thought* (London: Routledge, 2016); Keith Tribe, *Strategies of Economic Order: German Economic Discourse, 1750–1950* (Cambridge: Cambridge University Press, 1995).

29. Howard and King, *History of Marxian Economics*, ch. 5.

30. Robert Thomas Tierney, *Monster of the Twentieth Century: Kōtoku Shūsui and Japan's First Anti-imperialist Movement* (Oakland: University of California Press, 2015), 2, 36, 38, 47–49, 52, 54–59; John Crump, *The Origins of Socialist Thought in Japan* (London: Routledge, 2011 [1983]), ch. 8.

31. Rudolf Hilferding, *Finance Capital: A Study of the Latest Phase of Capitalist Development* [1910], extracts reprinted in Peter J. Cain and Mark Harrison, eds, *Imperialism: Critical Concepts in Historical Studies*, 3 vols (London: Routledge, 2001), 1: 223–56 at 227.

32. Hilferding, *Finance Capital*; Lichtheim, *Marxism*, 310–12.

33. Howard and King, *History of Marxian Economics*, ch. 13.

34. V. I. Lenin, *The Economic Content of Narodism and the Criticism of It in Mr. Struve's Book* [1894/95], in *V. I. Lenin: Collected Works*, vol. 1: *1893–1894* (Moscow: Progress Publishers, 1971), 333–505 at 441.

35. V. I. Lenin, *Imperialism: The Highest Stage of Capitalism* (Sydney: Resistance Books, 1999 [1916]), 71.

36. Lenin, *Imperialism*, 111; A. M. Eckstein, 'Is There a "Hobson-Lenin Thesis" on Late Nineteenth-Century Colonial Expansion?' *Economic History Review* 44 (May 1991): 297–318. On Hobson's influence on Lenin, see also Anthony Brewer, *Marxist Theories of Imperialism: A Critical Survey* (London: Routledge & Kegan Paul, 1980); D. H. Kruger, 'Hobson, Lenin and Schumpeter on Imperialism', *Journal of the History of Ideas* 16 (1955): 252–59; John Willoughby, 'Evaluating the Leninist Theory of Imperialism', *Science & Society* 59 (Fall 1995): 320–38.

37. John H. Kautsky, *Karl Kautsky: Marxism, Revolution and Democracy* (London: Routledge, 1994), 143–44; L. Meldolesi, 'The Debate on Imperialism Just before Lenin', *Economic and Political Weekly* 19 (20–27 Oct. 1984): 1833–39.

38. Lichtheim, *Marxism*, 275; Kautsky, *Karl Kautsky*, 14.

39. Paul Probert, "Our Natural Ally': Anglo-German Relations and the Contradictory Agendas of Wilhelmine Socialism, 1897–1900', in Geoff Eley and James Retallack, eds, *Wilhelminism and Its Legacies* (New York: Berghahn, 2008), 123–37 at 126; L. Meldolesi, 'The Debate on Imperialism Just before Lenin', *Economic and Political Weekly* 19 (3 Nov. 1984), 1876; John H. Kautsky, 'J. A. Schumpeter and Karl Kautsky: Parallel Theories of Imperialism', *Midwest Journal of Political Science* 5 (May 1961): 101–28; P. J. Cain, 'Capitalism, Aristocracy and Empire: Some "Classical" Theories of Imperialism Revisited', *Journal of Imperial and Commonwealth History* 35 (March 2007): 25–47. Hobson and Schumpeter also owed an intellectual debt to Kautsky and other contemporary Marxist theorists of imperialism and monopoly capitalism. See, for instance, Ricardo Villanueva, 'Hobson's Theory of Imperialism and its Indebtedness to Socialism: A Challenge to Conventional Narratives of Early International Relations', *Australian Journal of*

Politics and History 63 (2017): 508–23; Nathan Rosenberg, 'Was Schumpeter a Marxist?' *Industrial and Corporate Change* 20 (Aug. 2011): 1215–22; Panayotis Michaelides and John Milios, 'Did Hilferding Influence Schumpeter?' *History of Economics Review* 41 (2005): 98–125; Kautsky, 'Schumpeter and Kautsky'.

40. Karl Kautsky, 'Ultra-Imperialism' [1914], partial translation reprinted in *New Left Review* I/59 (Jan.–Feb. 1970): 41–46 at 42, 44.

41. Dick Geary, *Karl Kautsky* (Manchester: Manchester University Press, 1987), 32, 46; Karl Kautsky, *Socialism and Colonial Policy*, trans. by Angela Clifford (Belfast: Athol Books, 1975 [1907]), 50–51, 91–92; John Milios and Dimitris P. Sotiropoulos, *Rethinking Imperialism: A Study of Capitalist Rule* (London: Palgrave Macmillan, 2009), 60–61; Mike Macnair, *Karl Kautsky on Colonialism* (London: November Publications, 2013), 15.

42. Brian Shaev, 'Liberalising Regional Trade: Socialists and European Economic Integration', *Contemporary European History* 27, special issue 2: *Continuity and Change in European Cooperation during the Twentieth Century* (May 2018): 258–79 at 261.

43. Macnair, *Kautsky on Colonialism*, 29.

44. On the broader influence of the Manchester School on German liberalism, see Detlev Mares, '"Not Entirely a Manchester Man": Richard Cobden and the Construction of Manchesterism in Nineteenth-Century German Economic Thinking', in Howe and Morgan, *Rethinking Nineteenth-Century Liberalism*, 141–60; Julius Becker, *Das deutsche Manchestertum: Eine Studie zur Geschichte des wirtschaftspolitischen Individualismus* (Karlsruhe: Braun, 1907).

45. Howard and King, *History of Marxian Economics*, 92; Becker, *Das deutsche Manchestertum*, 99.

46. Manfred Steger, *The Quest for Evolutionary Socialism: Eduard Bernstein and Social Democracy* (Cambridge: Cambridge University Press, 1997), 206.

47. R. A. Fletcher, 'Cobden as Educator: The Free-Trade Internationalism of Eduard Bernstein, 1899–1914', *American Historical Review* 88 (June 1983): 561–78 at 562; Fletcher, 'Bernstein in Britain: Revisionism and Foreign Affairs', *International History Review* 1 (July 1979): 349–75.

48. Eduard Bernstein, 'German Professors and Protectionism', *Contemporary Review* (1904): 18–31; R. A. Fletcher, 'In the Interest of Peace and Progress: Eduard Bernstein's Socialist Foreign Policy', *Review of International Studies* 9 (April 1983): 79–93 at 79–80, 82–84; Fletcher, 'Cobden as Educator', 564–68, 572.

49. These trade union leaders included, among others, Arthur Henderson, a founding member of the Labour Party, J. R. Clynes of the National Union of General Workers (and a member of the Labour Party Executive Committee from 1904 to 1939), G. H. Wardle of the Railwaymen's Union, and Tom Shaw of the Textile Trades Federation. Paul Bridgen, *The Labour Party and the Politics of War and Peace, 1900–1924* (London: Boydell & Brewer, 2009), 38–39; Jean Gaffin and David Thoms, *Caring and Sharing: The Centenary of the Co-operative Women's Guild* (Manchester: Co-operative Union, 1983), 54–55; Paul Laity, *The British Peace Movement 1870–1914* (Oxford: Oxford University Press, 2002), 10. On British socialism, see, among others, Mark Bevir, *The Making of British Socialism* (Princeton: Princeton University Press, 2011); Stanley Pierson, *Marxism and the Origins of British Socialism* (Ithaca, NY: Cornell University Press, 1973); Willard Wolfe, *From Radicalism to Socialism: Men and Ideas in the Formation of Fabian Socialist Doctrines, 1881–1889* (New Haven: Yale University Press, 1975); Keith Laybourn, *The Rise of Socialism in*

Britain, c. 1881–1951 (Stroud: Sutton, 1997); Raymond Challinor, *The Origins of British Bolshevism* (London: Croom Helm, 1977).

50. Bridgen, *Labour Party*, 24, 38–39; Robert E. Dowse, 'The Entry of the Liberals into the Labour Party, 1910–1920', *Bulletin of Economic Research* 13 (Nov. 1961): 78–87 at 85. See also Anthony Howe, 'Towards the "Hungry Forties": Free Trade in Britain, c. 1880–1906', in Eugenio F. Biagini, ed., *Citizenship and Community: Liberals, Radicals and Collective Identities in the British Isles, 1865–1931* (Cambridge: Cambridge University Press, 1996), 193–218 at 194, 208; Howe, *Free Trade and Liberal England*, 264; D. J. Newton, *British Labour, European Socialism and the Struggle for Peace, 1889–1914* (Oxford: Oxford University Press, 1985); Kenneth E. Miller, *Socialism and Foreign Policy: Theory and Practice in Britain to 1931* (The Hague: Nijhoff, 1967).

51. Peter d'Alroy Jones, *Christian Socialist Revival, 1877–1914* (Princeton: Princeton University Press, 1968), 53.

52. J. L. Hammond, ed., *Towards a Social Policy; or, Suggestions for Constructive Reform* (London: Speaker Publishing Company, 1905), 44. See also Peter Clarke, *Liberals and Social Democrats* (Cambridge: Cambridge University Press, 1978), 82.

53. Ezequiel Grisendi, 'Contra nuestro feudalismo: Intelectuales y política en la expansión del georgismo en Argentina (Córdoba, 1914–1924)', *Nuevo Mundo* (2015), https://doi.org/10.4000/nuevomundo.68743.

54. 'South America', *Land & Liberty*, February 1920, 344.

55. Edgar J. Dosman, *The Life and Times of Raúl Prebisch, 1901–1986* (McGill-Queen's University Press, 2008), 24–26; Carlos Rodríguez Braun, 'Early Liberal Socialism in Latin America: Juan B. Justo and the Argentine Socialist Party', *American Journal of Economics and Sociology* 67 (Oct. 2008): 567–604 at 571, 583, 575–76, 581, 592; 'South America'.

56. 'Productive Channels?' *American Economist* 62 (12 July 1918), 17.

57. Becker, *Das deutsche Manchestertum*; Fletcher, 'Cobden as Educator'; Torp, *Challenges of Globalization*; Volker Hentschel, *Die deutschen Freihändler und der Volkswirtschaftlich Kongress 1858 bis 1885* (Stuttgart: Klett, 1975), 17–22. Belgian socialists endorsed free trade a few years earlier. See Michael Huberman, "Ticket to Trade: Belgian Labour and Globalization Before 1914," *Economic History Review* 61 (May 2008): 326–359. Engels himself had long been encouraging the SPD to oppose these protectionist measures. Engels to Bebel, 24 November 1879, reprinted in *MECW*, vol. 45: *1874–1879* (1991), 423. Hoselitz, 'Socialism, Communism', 233. On Bebel's condemnation of colonialism and tariff wars, see his 'Socialism and Internationalism', *Social Democrat* 9 (15 Aug. 1905): 491–93.

58. Lichtheim, *Marxism*, 287n, 275n.

59. Roger Chickering, *Imperial Germany and a World without War: The Peace Movement and German Society, 1892–1914* (Princeton: Princeton University Press, 1975), 276.

60. William English Walling, *Socialists and the War* (New York: Henry Holt, 1915), 443, 444.

61. Philip D. Supina, 'The Norman Angell Peace Campaign in Germany', *Journal of Peace Research* 9 (1972): 161–64; Chickering, *Imperial Germany*, 180–81.

62. Gareth Dale, 'Karl Polanyi in Budapest: On his Political and Intellectual Formation', *European Journal of Sociology* 50 (April 2009): 97–130 at 120–21; Lee Congdon, 'Karl Polanyi in Hungary, 1900–19', *Journal of Contemporary History* 11 (Jan. 1976): 167–83 at 177; 'Radikális Párt és Polgári Párt', *Szabadgondolat* 8 (1918): 198–204, reprinted in Gareth Dale, ed., *Karl Polanyi: The Hungarian Writings* (Manchester: Manchester University Press, 2016): 191–196.

63. Daan Musters, 'Internationalism, Protectionism, Xenophobia: The Second International's Migration Debate (1889–1914)', *International Review of Social History* 68 (April 2023): 75–105 at 86–90.

64. 'Socialist Peace Conference', *Information Quarterly* 2 (Oct. 1916), 462. The delegates from Switzerland, Luxemburg, Norway, and Rumania were unable to attend.

65. *Report of the First American Conference for Democracy and Terms of Peace, May 30th and 31st, 1917* (New York City: s.p., 1917), 19–12, 33–34.

66. 'Brief Peace Notes', *Advocate for Peace* 79 (March 1917), 88.

67. Max Eastman, 'A World's Peace', *The Liberator* 1 (March 1918), 8.

68. 'Memorial: To the President and Congress of the United States from the NEC of the Socialist Party of America, February 1918', *Eye Opener* [Chicago] 9 (16 Feb. 1918), 4.

69. 'Socialist Party Congressional Program', reprinted in *The Liberator* 1 (Oct. 1918), 42.

70. David M. Kennedy, *Over Here: The First World War and American Society* (Oxford: Oxford University Press, 2004 [1980]), 70–86, 355–57; Arno Mayer, *Wilson versus Lenin: Political Origins of the New Diplomacy, 1917–1918* (New Haven: Yale University Press, 1959); Georg Schild, *Between Ideology and Realpolitik: Woodrow Wilson and the Russian Revolution, 1917–1921* (Westport, CT: Praeger, 1995). On the false Wilsonian promise to undermine the imperial order, see Erez Manela, *The Wilsonian Moment: Self-Determination and the International Origins of Anticolonial Nationalism* (Oxford: Oxford University Press, 2007); Susan Pedersen, *The Guardians: The League of Nations and the Crisis of Empire* (Oxford: Oxford University Press, 2015).

71. 'Program and Resolutions of the Labor, Socialist and Radical Movements of the United States', reprinted in *Bulletin of the People's Council of America* 1 (1 March 1918), 6; 'Pacifists Glorify Bolshevik 'Victory'', *New York Times*, 17 February 1918, 14; 'A Working-Class Peace', *The Liberator* 1 (April 1918), 7–8.

72. Frank Wright Garrison to William Lloyd Garrison III, 15 February 1918, Box 76, Folder 5, Garrison Family Papers, SSC.

73. 'Memorandum on War Aims. Adopted by the Inter-Allied Labour and Socialist Conference in London February 22, 1918', reprinted in *Labor's War Aims* (June 1918), 190, 192; *Proceedings of the Inter-Allied Labor Conference, London, September 17, 18, 19, 1918* (Washington, DC: American Federation of Labor, 1918), 10, 48. The conference's endorsement of the principle of the open door even earned it some reluctant praise from the *New York Times*. See 'Plans for Socialistic World', *New York Times*, 22 September 1918, 47.

74. Frank Garrison, 'In Praise of Socialists', *International Free Trader* 2 (Oct.–Nov. 1919), 3.

75. Onur Ulas Ince, 'Friedrich List and the Imperial Origins of the National Economy', *New Political Economy* 21 (2016): 380–400; Mauro Boianovsky, 'Friedrich List and the Economic Fate of Tropical Countries', *History of Political Economy* 45 (Winter 2013): 647–91; Keith Tribe, 'Friedrich List and the Critique of "Cosmopolitical Economy"', *Manchester School of Economic and Social Studies* 56 (March 1988): 17–36; Szlajfer, *Economic Nationalism*; David Levi-Faur, 'Friedrich List and the Political Economy of the Nation-State', *Review of International Political Economy* 4 (1997): 154–78.

76. David Todd, *Free Trade and Its Enemies in France, 1814–1851* (Cambridge: Cambridge University Press, 2015), 146–54, 187–89, 191, 216–20. Some French socialist internationalists came around to free trade by the turn of the century. See Suzanne Berger, *Notre première mondialisation: Leçons d'un échec oublié* (Paris: Le Seuil, 2003).

77. Gregory Claeys, *Imperial Sceptics: British Critics of Empire, 1850–1920* (Cambridge: Cambridge University Press, 2010), 185–98; Noel Thompson, 'Hobson and the Fabians: Two Roads to Socialism in the 1920s', *History of Political Economy* 26 (Summer 1994): 203–20 at 212–13; Frank Trentmann, 'Wealth versus Welfare: The British Left between Free Trade and National Political Economy before the First World War', *Historical Research* 70 (Feb. 1997): 70–98 at 88–96; Bernard Porter, *Critics of Empire: British Radicals and the Imperial Challenge* (London: I. B. Tauris, 2008), 111–23.

78. Mark Bevir, 'The Marxism of George Bernard Shaw 1883–1889', *History of Political Thought* 13 (Summer 1992): 299–318 at 305; George Bernard Shaw, *Fabianism and the Fiscal Question* (London: Fabian Society, 1904), 9; Clarke, *Liberals and Social Democrats* (Cambridge: Cambridge University Press, 1978), 89–90; Frank Trentmann, *Free Trade Nation: Commerce, Consumption, and Civil Society in Modern Britain* (Oxford: Oxford University Press, 2008), 182.

79. Trentmann, 'Wealth versus Welfare', 89–93.

80. H. M. Hyndman, 'Commercial Boycotts and Policies', *English Review* 21 (Oct. 1915): 283–94, available at https://www.marxists.org/archive/hyndman/1915/10/boycotts.htm (accessed 10 May 2023). On Hyndman's complex positions regarding British imperialism, see Bill Baker, 'The Social Democratic Federation and the Boer War', *Our History* 59 (Summer 1974): 3–16; Claeys, *Imperial Sceptics*, 140–59; Marcus Morris, 'From Anti-Colonialism to Anti-imperialism: The Evolution of H. M. Hyndman's Critique of Empire, c. 1875–1905', *Historical Research* 87 (May 2014): 293–314; Seamus Flaherty, 'H. M. Hyndman, E. B. Bax, and the Reception of Karl Marx's Thought in Late-Nineteenth Century Britain, c. 1881–1893' (PhD thesis, Queen Mary University of London, 2017).

81. Abraham Ascher, "'Radical' Imperialists within German Social Democracy, 1912–1918', *Political Science Quarterly* 76 (Dec. 1961): 555–75 at 561, 570–71; Lichtheim, *Marxism*, 96–99, 287. See, also, Alfred Meusel, *List und Marx* (Jena: Fischer, 1928); Erik van Ree, '"Socialism in One Country" before Stalin: German Origins', *Journal of Political Ideologies* 15 (2010): 143–59; Musters, 'Internationalism, Protectionism, Xenophobia'.

82. William English Walling, 'Free Trade League Used for Germany', *New York Times*, 16 August 1918, 5. For the free trade response, see Kenneth Elliman and Frank Garrison, 'The Free Trade League: Replies to the Charges of Aiding the German Cause Made by W. E. Walling', *New York Times*, 25 August 1918, 38.

83. Michael J. Saman, 'Du Bois and Marx, Du Bois and Marxism', *Du Bois Review* 17 (2020): 33–54; Patrick Anderson, 'Pan-Africanism and Economic Nationalism: W.E.B. Du Bois's Black Reconstruction and the Failings of the "Black Marxism" Thesis', *Journal of Black Studies* 48 (2017): 732–57; Yuichiro Onishi, 'The New Negro of the Pacific: How African Americans Forged Cross-Racial Solidarity with Japan, 1917–1922', *Journal of African American History* 92 (Spring 2007): 169–324; Seok-Won Lee, 'The Paradox of Racial Liberation: W.E.B. Du Bois and Pan-Asianism in Wartime Japan, 1931—1945', *Inter-Asia Cultural Studies* 16 (2015): 513–30.

84. Manu Goswami, *Producing India: From Colonial Economy to National Space* (Chicago: University of Chicago Press, 2004), ch. 7.

85. James Connolly, 'Sinn Fein, Socialism and the Nation', *Irish Nation*, 23 January 1909, available at https://www.marxists.org/archive/connolly/1909/01/sfsoclsm.htm (accessed 10 May 2023); Seán Ó Lúing, 'Arthur Griffith, 1871–1922: Thoughts on a Centenary', *Studies: An Irish Quarterly Review* 60 (Summer 1971): 127–38 at 131–32; Austen Morgan, *James Connolly: A*

Political Biography (Manchester: Manchester University Press, 1988), 79; Mary E. Daly, 'The Economic Ideals of Irish Nationalism: Frugal Comfort or Lavish Austerity?' *Éire-Ireland* 29 (Winter 1994): 77–100 at 83–85.

86. Mei Junjie, 'Friedrich List in China's Quest for Development', in Harald Hagemann, Stephan Selter, Eugen Wendler, eds, *The Economic Thought of Friedrich List* (New York: Routledge, 2019), 213–22.

87. Francis Neilson, *My Life in Two Worlds*, vol 2: *1915–1952* (Appleton, WI: C. C. Nelson, 1953), 144. See, also, Albert Einstein to Heinrich Zangger, 21 August 1917, Einstein Archives Online 89–523, https://einsteinpapers.press.princeton.edu/vol10-trans/101 (accessed 14 June 2023); David E. Rowe and Robert Schulmann, *Einstein on Politics* (Princeton: Princeton University Press, 2007), 77, 200; Albert Einstein, 'Statement on the Inauguration of the Institute for Intellectual Cooperation', before 16 January 1926, Einstein Archives Online 28–037, https://einsteinpapers.press.princeton.edu/vol15-trans/219 (accessed 14 June 2023). Einstein also found inspiration in Henry George's *Progress and Poverty*. See *United Committee for the Taxation of Land Values: Report 1936 on the Work Carried on by the United Committee for the Taxation of Land Values* (London, 1936), 2.

88. *International Socialism and World Peace: Resolutions of the Berne Conference, February, 1919* (London: Independent Labour Party, 1919), 4. Australian socialists were making similar motions. See 'The World's Peace', *Daily Standard* [Brisbane], 16 January 1919, 3.

89. 'Free Trade', *The Liberator* 2 (Jan. 1919), 2.

90. Katherine A. S. Siegel, *Loans and Legitimacy: The Evolution of Soviet-American Relations, 1919–1933* (Lexington: University Press of Kentucky, 1996); 'From Trade to Peace', *Soviet Russia*, 25 June 1920, 639. See also *Soviet Russia*, 7 June 1919, 11; 20 March 1920, 292. Crystal Eastman was similarly happy to note that the US Socialist Party platform included an anti-embargo call for free trade. Crystal Eastman, 'The Socialist Party Convention', *The Liberator* 3 (July 1920), 25.

91. Lucian M. Ashworth, 'Democratic Socialism and International Thought in Interwar Britain', in Ian Hall, ed., *Radicals and Reactionaries in Twentieth-Century International Thought* (New York: Palgrave Macmillan, 2015): 75–100; P. J. Cain, *Hobson and Imperialism: Radicalism, New Liberalism, and Finance 1887–1938* (Oxford: Oxford University Press, 2002), ch. 7; Thompson, 'Hobson and the Fabians, 212–13; Jules Townsend, 'Hobson and the Socialist Tradition', in J. Phelby, ed., *J. A. Hobson after Fifty Years: Freethinker of the Social Sciences* (Basingstoke: Palgrave Macmillan, 1994): 34–52; Paul Mulvey, *The Political Life of Josiah C. Wedgwood: Land, Liberty and Empire, 1872–1943* (Woodbridge: Boydell & Brewer, 2010), 125; Howard Weinroth, 'Norman Angell and *The Great Illusion*: An Episode in Pre-1914 Pacifism', *Historical Journal* 17 (Sept. 1974): 551–74 at 554 n. 9, 555–56, 562, 572–73; Trentmann, 'Wealth versus Welfare', 91; Frank Trentmann, 'The Strange Death of Free Trade: The Erosion of "Liberal Consensus" in Great Britain, c. 1903–1932', in Biagini, *Citizenship and Community*, 219–50 at 233–35, 242–45; J. E. King, 'Popular Philosophy and Popular Economics: Bertrand Russell, 1919–70', *Russell: Journal of Bertrand Russell Studies* 27 (Winter 2007/8): 193–219 at 203–5, 212–13. On Brailsford's socialist support for Cobdenism, see, for instance, Henry Noel Brailsford, *A League of Nations* (New York: Macmillan, 1917), ch. 9; Brailsford, *The War of Steel and Gold* (London: Bell, 1918), esp. 328–29.

92. *1923 Labour Party General Election Manifesto* (1923); Trentmann, *Free Trade Nation*, 311. On British socialism and anti-imperial and peace activism, see especially Claeys, *Imperial Sceptics*; Martin Ceadel, *Pacifism in Britain 1914–1945: The Defining of a Faith* (Oxford: Oxford

University Press, 1980); Stephen Howe, *Anticolonialism in British Politics: The Left and the End of Empire, 1918–64* (Oxford: Oxford University Press, 1993); Porter, *Critics of Empire*; Richard Price, *An Imperial War and the British Working Class* (London: Routledge, 1972); Partha Sarathi Gupta, *Imperialism and the British Labour Movement, 1914–1964* (London: Palgrave Macmillan, 1975); Billy Frank, Craig Horner, and David Stuart, eds, *The British Labour Movement and Imperialism* (Newcastle: Cambridge Scholars, 2010); Martin Shaw, 'War, Peace and British Marxism, 1895–1945', in Richard Taylor and Nigel Young, eds, *Campaigns for Peace: British Peace Movements in the Twentieth Century* (Manchester: Manchester University Press, 1987): 49–72; Lucian M. Ashworth, 'Democratic Socialism and International Thought in Interwar Britain', in Hall, *Radicals and Reactionaries*, 75–100; Peter Lamb, 'The British Left in the Problems of Peace Lectures, 1926–38: Diversity that E. H. Carr Ignored', *International History Review* 36 (2014): 530–49.

93. Labour Party, *For Socialism and Peace* (London, 1934), 8–9, 11; Labour Party—Advisory Committee on Imperial Questions, *The Demand for Colonial Territories and Equality of Economic Opportunity*, 48; R. M. Douglas, *The Labour Party, Nationalism and Internationalism, 1939–1951* (London: Routledge, 2004), 182–83; Richard Toye, *The Labour Party and the Planned Economy, 1931–1951* (Woodbridge: Boydell & Brewer, 2003), 158–62.

94. Daniel Laqua, 'Democratic Politics and the League of Nations: Labour and Socialist International as a Protagonist of Interwar Internationalism', *Contemporary European History* 24 (May 2015): 175–92 at 192.

95. *Resolutions of the International Labour Congress of Socialist Parties*, Hamburg 1923, 7, 14, 16–17; J. W. Brown, 'The International Trade Union Movement', *Journal of the Royal Institute of International Affairs* 7 (Jan. 1928): 29–41; Laqua, 'Democratic Politics'.

96. Peter Gurney, *Wanting and Having: Popular Politics and Liberal Consumerism in England, 1830–70* (Manchester, 2014), 263.

97. Katarina Friberg, 'A Co-operative Take on Free Trade: International Ambitions and Regional Initiatives in International Co-operative Trade', in Mary Hilson, Silke Neunsinger, and Greg Patmore, eds, *A Global History of Consumer Co-operation Since 1850* (Leiden: Brill, 2017), 201–25 at 211.

98. Rita Rhodes, *The International Co-operative Alliance During War and Peace 1910–1950* (Geneva: ICA, 1995), 28–31.

99. Friberg, 'Co-operative Take', 214–15, 218.

100. *Women's Free Trade Demonstration* (Manchester, 1903), in Folder DM 851, Miscellaneous 1901–1911, Jane Cobden Unwin Papers, Special Collections Library, University of Bristol, UK; Naomi Black, 'The Mothers' International: The Women's Co-operative Guild and Feminist Pacifism', *Women's Studies International Forum* 7 (1984): 467–76.

101. *Report of the Proceedings of the Ninth Congress of the International Co-operative Alliance held at Glasgow 1913*; Friberg, 'Co-operative Take', 211; Rhodes, *International Co-operative Alliance*, 28–31.

102. Friberg, 'Co-operative Take', 212.

103. See, for instance, Joy Emmanuel and Ian MacPherson, eds, *Co-operatives and the Pursuit of Peace* (Vancouver: New Rochdale Press, 2007).

104. Bruno Jossa, 'Marx, Marxism and the Cooperative Movement', *Cambridge Journal of Economics* 29 (2005): 3–18; Jossa, 'Marx, Lenin and the Cooperative Movement', *Review of Political Economy* 26 (May 2014): 282–302.

105. Friberg, 'Co-operative Take', 203–205, 219.

106. Rudolf Hilferding, quoted in Shaev, 'Liberalising Regional Trade', at 266.

107. Matthew Stubbings, 'Free Trade Empire to Commonwealth of Nations: India, Britain and Imperial Preference, 1903–1932', *International History Review* 41 (2019): 323–44; John Willoughby, 'The Changing Role of Protection in the World Economy', *Cambridge Journal of Economics* 6 (June 1982): 195–211 at 196; 'Extracts From the Theses of the Twelfth ECCI Plenum on the International Situation and the Tasks of the Comintern Sections', in Jane Degras, ed., *The Communist International, 1919–1943: Documents*, 3 vols (Oxford: Oxford University Press, 1956), 3: 223.

108. *Report and Manifesto of the World Anti-War Congress at Amsterdam August 27th–29th, 1932* (1932). British Marxist Sue Cockerill sounded this same free-trade internationalist note in 1980 in 'Reply to Left Reformism', *International Socialism* 2 (1980). Similarly, see 'Reply of the Young Communist International to the Questions Raised in the "Study Plan"', 8, Box 213.08.3, Student Christian Federation Papers, World Council of Churches, Geneva, Switzerland; 'The Programme of the Communist International Adopted at Its Sixth Congress', in Degras, ed., *Communist International*, 2: 478.

109. Friberg, 'Co-operative Take', 222–23.

110. Szporluk, *Communism and Nationalism,*

111. Massimo Salvadori, *Karl Kautsky and the Socialist Revolution, 1880–1938*, trans. by Jon Rothschild (London: Verso, 1990), 305, 350.

112. Shaev, 'Liberalising Regional Trade', 265.

113. Shaev, 'Liberalising Regional Trade', 269. By contrast, the Labour Party in Australia embraced the precepts of the British system of imperial preference and was wary of US-backed multilateral initiatives through the late 1930s and early 1940s. Roger Bell, 'Testing the Open Door Thesis in Australia, 1941–1946', *Pacific Historical Review* 51 (Aug. 1982): 283–311.

114. Franz Borkenau, *Socialism: National or International* (London: Routledge, 1942), 37–38, 91, 69, 89, 162. On mid-century transatlantic liberal and socialist debates over postwar 'federal union', see Tommaso Milani, 'From Laissez-Faire to Supranational Planning: The Economic Debate within Federal Union (1938–1945)', *European Review of History* 23 (March 2016): 664–85; Or Rosenboim, 'Barbara Wootton, Friedrich Hayek and the Debate on Democratic Federalism in the 1940s', *International History Review* 36 (2014): 894–918; Peter Lamb, 'Harold Laski's International Functionalism: A Socialist Challenge to Federalism', *International History Review* 41 (2019): 581–603.

115. Norman Thomas, *The Challenge of War: An Economic Interpretation* (New York: League for Industrial Democracy, 1923), 9–11, 32–33, 36–37.

116. Trentmann, 'Strange Death', 248; *Declaration of Principles of the Socialist Party in the 1930 Congressional Campaign* (Chicago, 1930), 1, in 'Socialism', Box 20, Folder 3, Alice Park Papers, Hoover Institution, Stanford University, Palo Alto, CA.

117. Scott Nearing, *Fascism* (Ridgewood, NJ, 1930), 47

118. Scott Nearing, *Europe: West and East* (Ridgewood, NJ, 1934), 42–45.

119. Shaev, 'Liberalising Regional Trade.'

120. Or Rosenboim, *The Emergence of Globalism: Visions of World Order in Britain and the United States, 1939–1950* (Princeton: Princeton University Press, 2016); Slobodian, *Globalists*; Richard Toye, 'Developing Multilateralism: The Havana Charter and the Fight for the International Trade Organization, 1947–1948', *International History Review* 25 (2003): 282–305;

Talbot C. Imlay, 'Exploring What Might Have Been: Parallel History, International History, and Post-War Socialist Internationalism', *International History Review* 31 (2009): 521–57; James Mark, Artemy M. Kalinovsky, and Steffi Marung, eds, *Alternative Globalizations: Eastern Europe and the Postcolonial World* (Bloomington: Indiana University Press, 2020); Mark, Iacob, Rupprecht, and Spaskovska, *1989*, ch. 1; Johanna Bockman, 'Socialist Globalization against Capitalist Neocolonialism: The Economic Ideas behind the New International Economic Order', *Humanity* 6 (Spring 2015): 109–28.

Chapter 4. Free Trade Feminism

1. *Report of the Third International Congress of Women, Vienna, July 10–17, 1921* (Geneva: WILPF, 1921), 149.

2. *Report of the Fourth Congress of the Women's International League for Peace and Freedom, Washington, May 1 to 7, 1924* (Washington, DC: WILPF, 1924), 93.

3. Julia Irwin, *Making the World Safe: The American Red Cross and a Nation's Humanitarian Awakening* (Oxford: Oxford University Press, 2013), ch. 5.

4. Bruna Bianchi, '"That massacre of the innocents has haunted us for years": Women Witnesses of Hunger in Central Europe', in Bruna Bianchi and Geraldine Ludbrook, eds, *Living War, Thinking Peace (1914–1924): Women's Experiences, Feminist Thought, and International Relations* (Newcastle: Cambridge Scholars, 2016), 64–92 at 82–85.

5. Jane Addams, *Peace and Bread in Time of War* (New York: Macmillan, 1922), 166–72.

6. Addams, *Peace and Bread*, 172, 88, 240–41.

7. On first-wave feminism's relationship to international peace activism, see, among others, Leila Rupp, *Worlds of Women: The Making of an International Women's Movement* (Princeton: Princeton University Press, 1997); Nitza Berkovitch, *From Motherhood to Citizenship: Women's Rights and International Organizations* (Baltimore: Johns Hopkins University Press, 1999); David S. Patterson, *The Search for Negotiated Peace: Women's Activism and Citizen Diplomacy in World War I* (New York: Routledge, 2008); Harriet Hyman Alonso, *Peace as a Women's Issue: A History of the US Movement for World Peace and Women's Rights* (Syracuse, NY: Syracuse University Press, 1993); Robert Johnson, *The Peace Progressives and American Foreign Relations* (Cambridge, MA: Harvard University Press, 1995); Frances H. Early, *A World without War: How US Feminists and Pacifists Resisted World War I* (Syracuse, NY: Syracuse University Press, 1997); Erika A. Kulman, *Reconstructing Patriarchy after the Great War: Women, Gender, and Postwar Reconciliation between Nations* (New York: Palgrave Macmillan, 2008).

8. Glenda Sluga, 'Women, Feminisms and Twentieth-Century Internationalisms', in Glenda Sluga and Patricia Clavin, eds, *Internationalisms: A Twentieth-Century History* (Cambridge: Cambridge University Press, 2017): 61–84.

9. Harriet Hyman Alonso, *The Women's Peace Union and the Outlawry of War, 1921–1942* (Syracuse, NY: Syracuse University Press, 1997), 9. For feminism and the antislavery movement, see, for instance, Jean Fagan Yellin, *Women and Sisters: The Antislavery Feminists in American Culture* (New Haven: Yale University Press, 1989); Blanche Glassman Hersch, *The Slavery of Sex: Feminist-Abolitionists in America* (Urbana: University of Illinois Press, 1978); Ellen DuBois, 'Women's Rights and Abolition: The Nature of the Connection', in Lewis Perry and Michael Fellman, eds, *Antislavery Reconsidered: New Perspectives on the Abolitionists* (Baton Rouge:

Louisiana State University Press, 1979), 238–51; Karen Sanchez-Eppler, 'Bodily Bonds: The Intersecting Rhetorics of Feminism and Abolition', *Representations* 24 (Fall 1988): 28–59; Louis Billington and Rosamund Billington, '"A burning zeal for righteousness": Women in the British Anti-Slavery Movement, 1820–1860', in Jane Rendall, ed., *Equal or Different: Women's Politics, 1800–1914* (Oxford: Blackwell, 1987), 82–111; Clare Midgley, *Women Against Slavery: The British Campaigns, 1780–1870* (London: Routledge, 1992); Midgley, 'Anti-Slavery and Feminism in Nineteenth-Century Britain', *Gender & History* 5 (Autumn 1993): 343–62; Clare Taylor, *Women of the Anti-Slavery Movement: The Weston Sisters* (London: Palgrave MacMillan, 1995).

10. Sluga, 'Women, Feminisms'.

11. For the former, see especially Patricia Owens and Katharina Rietzler, eds, *Women's International Thought: A New History* (Cambridge: Cambridge University Press, 2021).

12. Studies emphasizing the economic dimensions of feminist peace reform include Kristen E. Gwinn, *Emily Greene Balch: The Long Road to Internationalism* (Urbana: University of Illinois Press, 2010); Heloise Brown, *'The truest form of patriotism': Pacifist Feminism in Britain, 1870–1902* (Manchester: Manchester University Press, 2003); Rhodri Jeffreys-Jones, *Changing Differences: Women and the Shaping of American Foreign Policy, 1917–1995* (New Brunswick: Rutgers University Press, 1997), ch. 3; Corinna Oesch, 'Economics and Peace: Yella Hertzka (1873–1948)', in Bianchi and Ludbrook, *Living War, Thinking Peace*, 153–68. Jeffreys-Jones labels the feminists' free-trade advocacy as 'conservative' and antithetical to Marxism in *Changing Differences*, 30.

13. See, for instance, Gertrude Bussey and Margaret Tims, *Women's International League for Peace and Freedom* (London: WILPF British Section, 1980 [1965]); Carrie A. Foster, *The Women and the Warriors: The US Section of the Women's International League for Peace and Freedom, 1915–1946* (Syracuse, NY: Syracuse University Press, 1995); Joyce Blackwell, *No Peace Without Freedom: Race and the WILPF, 1915–1975* (Carbondale, IL: Southern Illinois University Press, 2004); Linda Schott, *Reconstructing Women's Thoughts: The Women's International League for Peace and Freedom before World War II* (Stanford: Stanford University Press, 1997).

14. See Deborah Stienstra, *Women's Movements and International Organizations* (New York: St. Martin's Press, 1994); David S. Patterson, *Toward a Warless World: The Travail of the American Peace Movement 1887–1914* (Bloomington: Indiana University Press, 1976), ch. 6; Karen Garner, *Shaping a Global Women's Agenda: Women's NGOs and Global Governance, 1925–85* (Manchester: Manchester University Press, 2010). On economic nationalism and the League of Nations, see Patricia Clavin, *Securing the World Economy: The Reinvention of the League of Nations, 1920–1946* (Oxford: Oxford University Press, 2013).

15. Marc-William Palen, 'Free-Trade Ideology and Transatlantic Abolitionism: A Historiography', *Journal of the History of Economic Thought* 37 (June 2015): 291–304.

16. Peter Cain, 'Capitalism, War, and Internationalism in the Thought of Richard Cobden', *British Journal of International Studies* 5 (1979): 229–47; Oliver MacDonagh, 'The Anti-Imperialism of Free Trade', *Economic History Review* 14 (April 1962): 489–501; David Nicholls, 'Richard Cobden and the International Peace Congress Movement, 1848–1853', *Journal of British Studies* 30 (1991): 351–76; Richard Francis Spall, 'Free Trade, Foreign Relations, and the Anti–Corn-Law League', *International History Review* 10 (1988): 405–32.

17. Sarah Richardson, '"You know your father's heart": The Cobden Sisterhood and the Legacy of Richard Cobden', in Anthony Howe and Simon Morgan, eds, *Rethinking Nineteenth-Century Liberalism: Richard Cobden Bicentenary Essays* (Aldershot: Ashgate, 2006), 229–46 at

233; Anna M. Stoddart, *Elizabeth Pease Nichol* (London: Dent, 1899), 132–34; Alonso, *Peace as a Women's Issue*; Kristin Hoganson, 'Garrisonian Abolitionists and the Rhetoric of Gender, 1850–1860', *American Quarterly* 45 (Dec. 1993): 558–95.

18. Simon Morgan, 'Domestic Economy and Political Agitation: Women and the Anti–Corn Law League, 1839–46', in Kathryn Gleadle and Sarah Richardson, eds, *Women in British Politics, 1760–1860* (New York: Palgrave, 2000), 115–33; W. Caleb McDaniel, *The Problem of Democracy in the Age of Slavery: Garrisonian Abolitionists and Transatlantic Reform* (Baton Rouge: Lousiana State University Press, 2013), 122, 165–66; Leslie Thorne-Murphy, 'Women, Free Trade, and Harriet Martineau's *Dawn Island* at the 1845 Anti–Corn Law League Bazaar', in Lana L. Dalley and Jill Rappoport, eds, *Economic Women: Essays on Desire and Dispossession in Nineteenth-Century British Culture* (Columbus: Ohio State University Press, 2013), 41–59.

19. Ayşe Çelikkol, *Romances of Free Trade: British Literature, Laissez-Faire, and the Global Nineteenth Century* (Oxford: Oxford University Press, 2011), 66, ch. 4; Deborah A. Logan, *Harriet Martineau, Victorian Imperialism, and the Civilizing Mission* (London: Routledge, 2016), 103.

20. Martineau, quoted in Deborah Logan, 'Fighting a War of Words: Harriet Martineau in the *National Anti-Slavery Standard*', *Victorian Periodicals Review* 37 (Spring 2004): 46–71 at 51–52. On the role of Northern protectionism upon Anglo–American Civil War diplomacy, see Marc-William Palen, 'The Civil War's Forgotten Transatlantic Tariff Debate and the Confederacy's Free Trade Diplomacy', *Journal of the Civil War Era* 3 (March 2013): 35–61. Anglo-American Cobdenites commonly associated protectionism with economic slavery throughout the latter half of the nineteenth century. Marc-William Palen, *The 'Conspiracy' of Free Trade: The Anglo-American Struggle over Empire and Economic Globalisation, 1846–1896* (Cambridge: Cambridge University Press, 2016).

21. Martineau to Chapman, 31 October 1861, reprinted in Maria Weston Chapman, *Memorials of Harriet Martineau*, ed. by Deborah A. Logan (Bethlehem, PA: Lehigh University Press, 2015), 359.

22. Simon Morgan, 'Richard Cobden and British Imperialism', *Journal of Liberal History* 45 (Winter 2004/5): 16–21.

23. Martineau, quoted in Logan, *Harriet Martineau, Victorian Imperialism*, 171. See also Catherine Hall, 'Writing History, Writing a Nation: Harriet Martineau's *History of the Peace*', in Ella Dzelzainis and Cora Kaplan, eds, *Harriet Martineau: Authorship, Society, and Empire* (Manchester: Manchester University Press, 2010), 231–53 at 248.

24. On J. S. Mill and colonialism, see Eric Stokes, *The English Utilitarians and India* (Oxford: Oxford University Press, 1959); Bernard Semmel, 'The Philosophic Radicals and Colonialism', *Journal of Economic History* 21 (Dec. 1961): 513–25; Eileen P. Sullivan, 'Liberalism and Imperialism: J. S. Mill's Defense of the British Empire', *Journal of the History of Ideas* 44 (Oct. 1983): 599–617; Lynn Zastoupil, 'J. S. Mill and India', *Victorian Studies* 32 (Autumn 1988): 31–54; Michael Levin, *J. S. Mill on Civilization and Barbarism* (London: Routledge, 2004); Beate Jahn, 'Barbarian Thoughts: Imperialism in the Philosophy of John Stuart Mill', *Review of International Studies* 31 (2005): 599–618; Jennifer Pitts, *A Turn to Empire; The Rise of Imperial Liberalism in Britain and France* (Princeton: Princeton University Press, 2006); Duncan Bell, 'John Stuart Mill on Colonies', *Political Theory* 38 (2010): 34–64.

25. Çelikkol, *Romances*, 65–70.

26. Harriet Martineau, 'Political Economy and Condition of Ireland', *London Daily News*, 4 May 1863, reprinted in Deborah A. Logan, ed., *Harriet Martineau and the Irish Question: Condition of Post-Famine Ireland* (Bethlehem, PA: Lehigh University Press, 2012), 82.

27. On the ambiguous feminist position toward imperialism, see Antoinette M. Burton, *Burdens of History: British Feminists, Indian Women, and Imperial Culture, 1865–1915* (Chapel Hill: University of North Carolina Press, 1994); Nupur Chaudhuri and Margaret Strobel, eds, *Western Women and Imperialism: Complicity and Resistance* (Bloomington: Indiana University Press, 1992); Leila Rupp, 'Challenging Imperialism in International Women's Organizations, 1888–1945', *NWSA Journal* 8 (April 1, 1996): 8–27; Clare Midgley, ed., *Gender and Imperialism* (Manchester, 1998); Midgley, *Feminism and Empire: Women Activists in Imperial Britain, 1790–1865* (London: Routledge, 2007); Ian C. Fletcher, Laura E. Nym Mayhall, and Philippa Levine, eds, *Women's Suffrage in the British Empire: Citizenship, Nation and Race* (London: Routledge, 2000); Angela Woollacott, *To Try Her Fortune in London: Australian Women, Colonialism and Modernity* (Oxford: Oxford University Press, 2001); Lora Wildenthal, *German Women for Empire, 1884–1945* (Durham, NC: Duke University Press, 2001); Kristin L. Hoganson, '"As badly off as the Filipinos": US Women's Suffragists and the Imperial Issue at the Turn of the Twentieth Century', *Journal of Women's History* 13 (Summer 2001): 9–33; Allison L. Sneider, *Suffragists in an Imperial Age: U. Expansion and the Woman Question, 1870–1929* (Oxford: Oxford University Press, 2008); Fiona Paisley, *Glamour in the Pacific: Cultural Internationalism and Race Politics in the Women's Pan-Pacific* (Honolulu: University of Hawai'i Press, 2009); Eliza Riedi, 'The Women Pro-Boers: Gender, Peace and the Critique of Empire in the South African War', *Historical Research* 86 (Feb. 2013): 92–115; Antoinette Burton, 'Race, Empire, and the Making of Western Feminism', in *Routledge Historical Resources: History of Feminism* (London: Routledge, 2016), available at https://www.routledgehistoricalresources.com/feminism/essays/race-empire-and-the-making-of-western-feminism (accessed 14 June 2023); Sumita Mukherjee, *Indian Suffragettes: Female Identities and Transnational Networks* (Oxford: Oxford University Press, 2018).

28. Judith Lissauer Cromwell, *Florence Nightingale, Feminist* (Jefferson, NC: McFarland, 2013), 1.

29. Florence Nightingale to Samuel Howe, June 20, 1852, reprinted in Lynn McDonald, ed., *Florence Nightingale on Society and Politics, Philosophy, Science* (Waterloo, Ontario: Wilfrid Laurier University Press, 2003), 335–36. Mary Poovey explores other aspects of Nightingale's economic thought in 'Florence Nightingale's Contributions to Economics', in Dalley and Rappoport, *Economic Women*, 77–96.

30. McDonald, *Nightingale on Society*, 289.

31. 'Annual Meeting', July 17, 1886, Cobden Club Manuscripts, Records Office, Chichester, West Sussex, England; Christopher J. L. Brock and Gilbert H. B. Jackson, eds, *A History of the Cobden Club, by Members of the Club* (London: Cobden Club, 1939), 38–39.

32. Nightingale to Sir Louis Mallet, May 30, 1878, reprinted in Gérard Vallée, ed., *Florence Nightingale on Social Change in India* (Waterloo, Ontario: Wilfrid Laurier University Press, 2007), 810. See also ibid., 464–66.

33. Florence Nightingale, 'The United Empire and the Indian Peasant', 7 May 1878, reprinted in Vallée, *Nightingale on Social Change*, 499.

34. Brown, 'Truest form of patriotism', 6.

35. Brown, 'Truest form of patriotism', 34, 40–41, 141.

36. 'Elizabeth Cady Stanton for Congress', 10 October 1866, in Ann D. Gordon, ed., *The Selected Papers of Elizabeth Cady Stanton and Susan B. Anthony*, vol. 1: *In the School of Anti-Slavery, 1840–1866* (New Brunswick: Rutgers University Press, 2001), 593.

37. Elizabeth Cady Stanton, 'Subjection of Women' (1875), reprinted in Ellen Carol DuBois and Richard Candida Smith, eds, *Elizabeth Cady Stanton, Feminist as Thinker: A Reader in Documents and Essays* (New York: NYU Press, 2007), 214–15.

38. Karl Marx, *Free Trade: A Speech Delivered before the Democratic Club, Brussels, Belgium, January 9, 1848*, trans. by Florence Kelley Wischnevetzky (Boston, MA: Lee and Shepard, 1888); Robert C. Tucker, ed., *The Marx-Engels Reader* (New York: W. W. Norton: 1972) 696n; Florence Kelley, quoted in Kathryn Kish Sklar, *Florence Kelley and the Nation's Work: The Rise of Women's Political Culture, 1830–1900* (New Haven: Yale University Press, 1995), 130. On the 'Great Debate' of 1888, see Palen, '*Conspiracy*'; Joanne Reitano, *The Tariff Question in the Gilded Age: The Great Debate of 1888* (University Park: Pennsylvania State University Press, 1994); Charles W. Calhoun, *Minority Victory: Gilded Age Politics and the Front Porch Campaign of 1888* (Lawrence: University Press of Kansas, 2008).

39. Ann Oakley, *Women, Peace and Welfare: A Suppressed History of Social Reform, 1880–1920* (Bristol: Bristol University Press, 2018), 250–51.

40. Kristin Hoganson, *Consumers' Imperium: The Global Production of American Domesticity, 1865–1920* (Chapel Hill: University of North Carolina Press, 2007), 11.

41. Jeffreys-Jones, *Changing Differences*, 40.

42. Hoganson, '"As badly off as the Filipinos"'; Burton, *Burdens of History*; Sneider, *Suffragists in an Imperial Age*; Ian R. Tyrrell, *Woman's World, Woman's Empire: The Woman's Christian Temperance Union in International Perspective, 1880–1930* (Chapel Hill: University of North Carolina Press, 1991); Rupp, *Worlds of Women*, 51–76; Blackwell, *No Peace Without Freedom*; Megan Threlkeld, *Pan American Women: US Internationalists and Revolutionary Mexico* (Philadelphia: University of Pennsylvania Press, 2014).

43. Hoganson, '"As badly off as the Filipinos"' 14–15.

44. Sozialdemokratische Partei Deutschlands, *Protokoll über die Verhandlungen des Parteitages der Sozialdemokratischen Partei Deutschlands, Stuttgart* (Berlin, 1898). Zietz afterwards became the first elected female executive committee member of the SPD in 1908, and helped spearhead the creation of the Independent Social Democratic Party and its women's movement in 1917.

45. Hella Pick, *Bertha von Suttner: Living for Peace* (Austrian Federal Ministry for Foreign Affairs, 2005), 10–11, https://www.bmeia.gv.at/fileadmin/user_upload/Zentrale/Publikationen /berthavonsuttner.pdf (accessed 12 May 2023); Bertha von Suttner, *Memoirs of Bertha von Suttner: The Records of an Eventful Life*, 2 vols (London: Ginn, 1910), 2: 49–50; Brigitte Hamann, *Bertha von Suttner: A Life for Peace* (Syracuse, NY: Syracuse University Press, 256), 256.

46. Naomi Black, 'The Mothers' International: The Women's Co-Operative Guild and Feminist Pacifism', *Women's Studies International Forum* 7 (1984): 467–76; Andrew Flinn, '"Mothers for Peace", Co-operation, Feminism and Peace: The Women's Co-operative Guild and the Antiwar Movement between the Wars', in Lawrence Black and Nicole Robertson, eds, *Consumerism and the Co-operative Movement in Modern British History* (Manchester: Manchester University Press, 2009), 138–54.

47. Richardson, '"You know your father's heart"', 231–32, 243–45.

48. Anne Hurley, 'Helena Mary Carroll Cobden Hirst, 1880–1965', pdf available at https:// www.hurleyskidmorehistory.com.au/cobden-women (accessed 12 May 2023); Riedi, 'Women pro-Boers', 97, 99.

49. Brown, 'Truest form of patriotism', 165.

50. 'Preferential Tariffs', *The Times*, 25 July 1903, 12.

51. Sue Millar, 'Middle Class Women and Public Politics in the Late Nineteenth and Early Twentieth Centuries: A Study of the Cobden Sisters' (MA dissertation, University of Sussex, 1985); Richardson, '"You know your father's heart"'.

52. Frank Trentmann, *Free Trade Nation: Commerce, Consumption, and Civil Society in Modern Britain* (Oxford: Oxford University Press, 2008), 52.

53. Frank Trentmann, 'Before "Fair Trade": Empire, Free Trade, and the Moral Economies of Food in the Modern World', *Environment and Planning D: Society and Space*, 25 (2007): 1079–102.

54. Sandra Stanley Holton, *Feminism and Democracy: Women's Suffrage and Reform Politics in Britain, 1900–1918* (Cambridge: Cambridge University Press, 1986), 138; *Report of the Fourth Congress of the Women's International League for Peace and Freedom, Washington, May 1 to 7, 1924* (Washington, DC: WILPF, 1924), 93.

55. David Thackeray, *Conservatism for the Democratic Age: Conservative Cultures and the Challenge of Mass Politics in Early Twentieth Century England* (Manchester: Manchester University Press, 2013).

56. John Sutherland, *Mrs. Humphry Ward: Eminent Victorian, Pre-eminent Edwardian* (Oxford: Oxford University Press, 1991), 197.

57. Donal Lowry, '"Making fresh Britains across the seas": Imperial Authority and Anti-feminism in Rhodesia', in Ian Christopher Fletcher, Philippa Levine, and Laura E. Nym Mayhall, eds, *Women's Suffrage in the British Empire: Citizenship, Nation and Race* (London: Routledge, 2012), 175–90 at 175–76, 179.

58. *Mary Maxse, 1870–1944: A Record Compiled by Her Family and Friends* (London: Rolls Publishing, 1946), 17, 43, 46, 48, 50, 70, 76, 95–105.

59. Trentmann, *Free Trade Nation*, 229–32. See also Erika Rappaport, 'Drink Empire Tea: Gender, Conservative Politics and Imperial Consumerism in Inter-war Britain', in Erika Rappaport, Sandra Trudgen Dawson, and Mark J. Crowley, eds, *Consuming Behaviours: Identity, Politics and Pleasure in Twentieth-Century Britain* (London: Bloomsbury, 2015), 139–58.

60. Marc-William Palen, 'The Transimperial Roots of American Anti-imperialism: The Transatlantic Radicalism of Free Trade, 1846–1920', in Jay Sexton and Kristin Hoganson, eds, *Crossing Empires: Taking US History into Transimperial Terrain* (Durham, NC: Duke University Press, 2020), 159–82.

61. C. Roland Marchand, *The American Peace Movement and Social Reform, 1889–1918* (Princeton: Princeton University Press, 1972), 196.

62. Harriet Hyman Alonso, *Growing Up Abolitionist: The Story of the Garrison Children* (Boston: University of Massachusetts Press, 2002), 321–22; Alonso, *Women's Peace Union*, 9.

63. Jane Addams, Emily G. Balch, and Alice Hamilton, *Women at The Hague. The International Congress of Women and its results* (New York: Macmillan, 1915), 136.

64. *Congressional Program of the Woman's Peace Party of New York State* (New York: s.p., 1918), 5.

65. WPS letterhead (italics added for emphasis), Peace Collection, Box 3, Folder 24, SSC.

66. Elinor Byrns, *The Women's Peace Society: Its Aim, Program and Arguments* (New York: WPS, [1921?]), 7–8, Box 1, Folder 3, Women's Peace Society Papers, Peace Collection, Swarthmore College, Swarthmore, PA [hereafter WPS Papers. In 1923, the WPS added the principle

of non-cooperation to its platform, inspired by Gandhi's Non-Cooperation movement in India and informed by Gandhi's friends and disciples in the United States. See Byrns, *The Women's Peace Society: Its Aim, Program and Arguments* (New York: WPS, 1923), 6; J. C. Chatterji to Elinor Byrns, August 5, 1921, and J. C. Chatterji to Elizabeth Black, August 5, 1921, WPS Papers, Box 1, Folder 4.

67. Jane Addams to Louis R. Ehrich, 29 June 1910, Judith Kaplan Private Collection, Jane Addams Papers Project, available at https://digital.janeaddams.ramapo.edu/items/show/2728 (accessed 12 May 2023).

68. See, also, the speech of Anita Augspurg, Germany's first woman judge, to the German Section of WILPF in April 1922 in Bremen, wherein the German Section dedicated itself to free trade.

69. *Report of the Third International Congress of Women, Vienna, July 10–17, 1921* (Geneva: WILPF, 1921), 79, 85, 149.

70. Draft copy, 'Report of the Business Committee of the WOMEN'S PEACE SOCIETY, Jan. 1–Jun. 1, 1921'; *From 'the Non-Resistant' of 1839* (WPS leaflet, c. 1920); Fanny Garrison Villard, *Objections to Non-resistance Answered* (leaflet, c. 1920); Box 1, Folder 1, WPS Papers. Field had been converted to Georgism by her sister Mary, a supporter of Cleveland, Ohio's Georgist mayor, Tom Johnson. She and fellow Georgist Clarence Darrow became close friends. See Tim Barnes, 'Sara Bard Field (1882–1974)', *Oregon Encyclopedia*, https://oregonencyclopedia.org /articles/field_sara_bard_1882_1974_/#.W2yfJ9hKiSM (accessed 12 May 2023).

71. *Disarmament Parade, November 12th, 1921, New York City* (leaflet) (New York: Women's Peace Society, 1921), 'Literature (1919–21)', Box 1, WPS Papers.

72. *News Letter Published by the Women's Peace Society* 2 (Feb. 1928), 4, 'Newsletters/Photographs', Box 1, WPS Papers. See also *News Letter Published by the Women's Peace Society* 3 (Aug. 1929), 1.

73. Kirsten Marie Delegard, *Battling Miss Bolsheviki: The Origins of Female Conservatism in the United States* (Philadelphia: University of Pennsylvania Press, 2012), ch. 3.

74. Martha Strayer, *The D.A.R.: An Informal History* (Washington, DC: Public Affairs Press, 1958), 98.

75. *Report of the Fourth Congress*, 93, 6, 64, 58, 84.

76. *Report of the Fifth Congress of the Women's International League for Peace and Freedom, Dublin, July 8 to 15, 1926* (Geneva: WILPF, 1926).

77. 'Women Delegates to the Economic Conference', *Pax International* 2 (June 1927), 3. Van Dorp had built up an impressive internationalist resumé by this point. She was the Netherland's first female lawyer; an officer of the Boston-based peace organization the International Free Trade League (IFTL); the only woman to have addressed the 1920 International Free Trade Congress in Westminster, London; an editorial board member of the Dutch journal *De Economist*; and a former representative of the Dutch Liberal Party (1922–1925).

78. Mary Sheepshanks, 'The Kellogg Peace Pact and After', *Pax International* 3 (Aug 1928), 2; 'German Section', *Pax International* 4 (Dec. 1928), 5.

79. Florence Hamilton, Annie E. Gray, and Mary Abbott, 'The Following Letter Speaks for Itself', *News Letter Published by the Women's Peace Society* (Aug. 1928).

80. 'International Alliance of Women for Suffrage and Equal Citizenship', Peace Collection, Box 3, Folder 28A, SSC.

81. *Resolutions Presented to the Peace Conference of the Powers in Paris* (Geneva: WILPF, 1919), League of Nations Archives, Box 1008, 1919–1927, Dossier no. 9176, doc. no. 9176 (*sic*), Geneva, Switzerland.

82. *Congressional Program of the Woman's Peace Party of New York State*, 8; Johan Hansson, 'The Colonial Question', *The Public*, 2 March 1918, 268–69; Emily Greene Balch, 'The White Man's Burden', *New World* 1 (Feb. 1918): 37–39; Melinda Plastas, 'A Different Burden: Race and the Social Thought of Emily Greene Balch', *Peace & Change* 33 (Oct. 2008), 479.

83. *Report of the Fourth Congress*, 30–33, 93, 169.

84. *Report of the Fourth Congress*, 58.

85. *Report of the Fourth Congress*, 74–77.

86. Catia C. Confortini, 'Race, Gender, Empire, and War in the International Thought of Emily Greene Balch', in Owens and Rietzler, *Women's International Thought*, 244–65.

87. 'How Many Members Has the W.I.L.?' *Pax International* 1 (April 1926), 6.

88. *Report of the Fifth Congress*, 85, 86.

89. *Report of the Fifth Congress*, 87.

90. *Report of the Fifth Congress*, 90.

91. *Report of the Fifth Congress*, 91–93.

92. Confortini, 'Race, Gender, Empire', 248.

93. Emily Greene Balch, 'Economic Aspects', *Report of the Fourth Congress*, 73.

94. *Report of the Fifth Congress*, 96–97.

95. Confortini, 'Race, Gender, Empire'

96. *Report of the Fifth Congress*, 97–99.

97. *Report of the Fifth Congress*, 106–7.

98. Rupp, *Worlds of Women*, 116; Threlkeld, *Pan American Women*, 195–96.

99. Emmy Freundlich, *Housewives Build a New World* (London, 1936), 9, 11.

100. *Report of the Fourth Congress*, 77–78.

101. Emmy Freundlich, 'Free Trade and Co-operation', *Report of the Sixth Congress of the Women's International League for Peace and Freedom, Prague August 24th to 28th, 1929* (Geneva: WILPF, 1929), 86–88.

102. International Cooperative Women's Guild, Peace Collection, Box 3, Folder 28A, SSC. See also Sarah Hellawell, '"A strong international spirit": The Influence of Internationalism on the Women's Co-operative Guild', *Twentieth Century British History* 32 (2021): 93–118.

103. 'Women Want Congress of Nations, Free Trade', *Cooperative Consumer* 10 (31 March 1943), 1, in Alice Park Papers, Hoover Institution Library and Archives, Stanford University, Palo Alto, CA.

104. 'Single Taxers in Boston; Massachusetts League Gives a Lunch to Members of the Woman's Suffrage Association', *New York Times*, 7 November 1897, 5; Arthur Nichols Young, *The Single Tax Movement in the United States* (Princeton: Princeton University Press, 1916), 248 n. 64.

105. 'Public Opinion Force to End Great Wars, Mrs. Fels Declares', July 31, 1916 (unknown newspaper), Box 5, Folder 7, Joseph and Mary Fels Papers, HSP.

106. Mary Pilon, *The Monopolists: Obsession, Fury, and the Scandal Behind the World's Favorite Board Game* (New York: Bloomsbury, 2015), 17–31, 49–50.

107. Louis F. Post diary entry, 31 August 1922, Louis F. Post Papers, Box 10, Folder 1922–27, Library of Congress, Washington, DC.

108. 'The Women's Henry George League Dinner', *Single Tax Review* 15 (March/April 1915), 116; Mary Ware Dennett, 'Free Trade—WHEN?' *International Free Trader* 1 (Dec. 1918), 1.

109. 'Women! March to Stop War! Disarmament Parade Organized by the Women's Peace Society and the Women's Peace Union of the Western Hemisphere, Nov. 12, 1921' (leaflet), Box 1, Folder 2, WPS Papers; 'News Notes and Personals', *Land and Freedom* 40 (July/Aug. 1940), 127.

110. Other IFTL members included Bavaria's trade union leader Lida Gustava Heymann; Aletta Jacobs of the Netherlands; Martha Larsen of Norway; Cecilia John and H. L. Bayly of Australia; Harriet Dunlop Prenter of Toronto, Canada; and Americans Crystal Eastman, Mary B. Ely, Zona Gale, Mary D. Hussey, Fay Lewis, and Anne Harriet Martin. AFTL members included single tax advocate Grace Isabel Colbron, lawyer and suffragist Catherine Waugh McCulloch, and Bertha Putnam, daughter of American Cobdenite publisher George Haven Putnam.

111. Anna Angela George de Mill, 'World Peace and Economic Freedom', *Land and Freedom* (1937), 24. Other Georgists included: Alice Stone Blackwell; Sara Barker Field; Jennie Bradley Roessing; AFTL member and secretary-treasurer of the IFTL Florence Garvin; AIL officer Josephine Shaw Lowell; novelist Fannie Hurst; Lydia Avery Coonley Ward; Ida B. Wells; Jane Dearborn Mills, who called for the creation of a Peace Branch of the single tax movement in 1903; AFTL member and secretary-treasurer of the IFTL Florence Garvin, a resident of the single tax colony of Arden, Delaware; Pittsburg's Jennie Bradley Roessing; and Haverford, Pennsylvania's IFTL officer and WILPF member Ellen Winsor.

112. Hedevig Sonne-Hald, 'Some Economic Causes of War', *Report of the Sixth Congress*, 88–89 (emphasis in original).

113. 'Letter From the Daughter of Count Leo Tolstoy', *Single Tax Review* 10 (Nov.–Dec. 1910), 60.

114. Eleanor M. Moore, *The Quest for Peace as I Have Known It in Australia* (Melbourne: Wilke & Co., 1949), 142.

115. On Angell's influence within the British and international peace movement, see Martin Ceadel, *Living the Great Illusion: Sir Norman Angell, 1872–1967* (Oxford: Oxford University Press, 2009); Ceadel, *Semi-Detached Idealists: The British Peace Movement and International Relations, 1854–1945* (Oxford: Oxford University Press, 2000); Ceadel, 'The Founding Text of International Relations? Norman Angell's Seminal yet Flawed *The Great Illusion* (1909–1938)', *Review of International Studies*, 37 (Oct. 2011): 1671–93; Paul Laity, *The British Peace Movement 1870–1914* (Oxford: Oxford University Press, 2001); Louis Bisceglia, *Norman Angell and Liberal Internationalism in Britain 1931–1935* (New York: Garland, 1982); Andrew Williams, 'Norman Angell and his French Contemporaries, 1905–1914', *Diplomacy & Statecraft* 21 (Dec. 2010): 574–92.

116. Julius Moritzen, *The Peace Movement of America* (New York: G. P. Putnam's Sons, 1912), 326.

117. Robert I. Rotberg, *A Leadership for Peace: How Edwin Ginn Tried to Change the World* (Stanford: Stanford University Press, 2007), 140.

118. On her single tax scepticism, see Fanny Garrison Villard to William Lloyd Garrison Jr., 20 January 1907, Box 57, Folder 10, Garrison Family Papers, SSC.

119. 'The Union for Democratic Control and Women', *Ius Suffragii* 10 (1 June 1916), reprinted in Sybil Oldfield, ed., *Ius Suffragii*, vol. 2: *November 1914–September 1916* (London, 2002), 99; Oldfield, ed., *Ius Suffragii*, vol. 1: *July 1913–October 1914* (London, 2002), 14; *Books and Pamphlets on International Problems Suggested for Reading Aloud* (Boston, MA: n.p., 1917), 3; For Hobson

as Cobdenite, see especially P. J. Cain, 'J. A. Hobson, Cobdenism, and the Radical Theory of Economic Imperialism, 1898–1914', *Economic History Review* 31 (1978): 565–84.

120. Recent studies include Julie Gottlieb and Judith Szapor, with Tiina Lintunen and Dagmar Wernitznig, 'Suffrage and Nationalism in Comparative Perspective: Britain, Hungary, Finland and the Transnational Experience of Rosika Schwimmer', in Ingrid Sharp and Matthew Stibbe, eds, *Women Activists between War and Peace: Europe, 1918–1923* (London: Bloomsbury, 2017), 29–75; Dagmar Wernitznig, 'Living Peace, Thinking Equality: Rosika Schwimmer's (1877–1948) War on War', in Bianchi and Ludbrook, *Living War, Thinking Peace*, 123–38.

121. Rosika Schwimmer to M. Talmadge, 6 July 1914, Rosika Schwimmer Papers, Box 1, Folder 1, Hoover Institution Library and Archives, Stanford University, Palo Alto, CA.

122. J. W. Bengough, 'Bursting the Bonds', *International Free Trader* 3 (April 1920), 5.

123. Moore, *Quest for Peace*, 145, 178, 189.

124. Jane Addams, 'Peace on Earth', *Ladies' Home Journal* 30 (Dec. 1913), 27, in Jane Addams Papers, Box 2, Folder 29, SSC.

125. Addams, *Peace and Bread*, 242.

126. Jane Addams interview transcript, NBC Radio Broadcast, p. 5, Jane Addams Papers, Box 1, Folder 21, SSC.

127. Beatrice Pitney Lamb, *Economic Causes of War and the Hope for the Future* (New York City: National League of Women Voters, 1932), 61–62, 71.

128. Carole Stanford Bucy, 'Exercising the Franchise, Building the Body Politic: The League of Women Voters and Public Policy, 1945–1964' (PhD diss., Vanderbilt University, 2002), 10–11, 34–36, 64, ch. 3.

129. 'If Goods Move Not across Boundaries, Soldiers Will', *Milwaukee Sentinel*, 21 June 1936, 4.

130. Mosa Anderson, 'Colonial Questions', in *Report of the Ninth Congress of the Women's International League for Peace and Freedom, Luhacovice, Czechoslovakia* (Geneva: WILPF, 1937), 65–67; *Women's International League for Peace and Freedom Program & Policies* (Washington, DC: WILPF, 1937).

131. Lola Maverick Lloyd and Rosika Schwimmer, *Chaos, War, or New World Order: What We Must Do to Establish the All-Inclusive, Non-Military, Democratic Federation of Nations* (Chicago: Campaign for World Government, 1942), 3–6. See also Megan Threlkeld, "Chaos, War, or a New World Order?' A Radical Plan for Peace and World Government in the 1930s', *Peace & Change* 43 (Oct. 2018): 473–97.

132. *The Peoples Want Peace, the Peoples Want Freedom, the Peoples Want to Live!* (Geneva: WILPF, 1939), File Number 1000/6/24, 'Women's Questions, Women's International League for Peace and Freedom, Emergency Session, Executive Committee', International Labour Organisation Archives, Geneva.

133. *Call to the Annual Meeting of the Women's International League for Peace and Freedom, May 4-5-6, 1939* (Washington, DC: WILPF, 1939), File Number 1000/6/24, 'Women's Questions, Women's International League for Peace and Freedom, Emergency Session, Executive Committee', International Labour Organisation Archives, Geneva.

134. B. W. Gearhart quoted in 'Stabbing in the Dark', *Washington News*, Box 52, Folder 2 Carnegie Endowment for International Peace Records, Columbia University, New York [hereafter CEIPR].

Chapter 5. Free Trade, Fraternity, and Federation

1. Quoted in Julie Salis Schwabe, ed., *Reminiscences of Richard Cobden* (London: T. Fisher Unwin, 1895), vii.

2. Liston Pope, *Religious Proposals for World Order: An Analysis of Thirty-Four Statements* (New York: Church Peace Council and World Alliance for International Friendship through the Churches, 1941), 16, in 'Program of Work, 1940–1941' Folder, World Alliance for International Friendship through the Churches Papers, Swarthmore Peace Collection, PA [hereafter WAP].

3. Patricia Appelbaum, *Kingdom to Commune: Protestant Pacifist Culture between World War I and the Vietnam Era* (Chapel Hill: University of North Carolina Press, 2009), 29.

4. *Platform for Campaign for World Economic Cooperation* (New York: Foreign Policy Association, 1937); 1937 Campaign for World Economic Cooperation leaflets: 'For Farm Prosperity'; 'Labor Hates War Wants Peace'; 'Business Prospers'; *Conference on World Economic Cooperation* (New York: Foreign Policy Association, 1938), all in YWCA of the USA records, Box 444, 'World Economic Conference 1937–1939' folder, SSC; Gale Kenny, '"The Christian Woman's Trusteeship": Protestant Churchwomen, Pacifism, and Economic Citizenship in the 1930s–1950s', paper presented at SHAFR conference, New Orleans, June 2022.

5. See, for instance, William R. Hutchison, *Errand to the World: American Protestant Thought and Foreign Missions* (Chicago: University of Chicago Press, 1993); William Inboden, *Religion and American Foreign Policy, 1945–1960* (Cambridge: Cambridge University Press, 2008); Andrew Preston, *Sword of the Spirit, Shield of Faith: Religion in American War and Diplomacy* (New York: Knopf, 2012); Gene Zubovich, 'US Protestants, Globalization, and the International Origins of the Sixties', *Diplomatic History* 45 (Jan. 2021): 28–49; Boyd Hilton, *The Age of Atonement: The Influence of Evangelicalism on Social and Economic Thought, 1795–1865* (New York: Clarendon Press, 1988).

6. See, among others, Amy Reynolds, *Free Trade and Faithful Globalization: Saving the Market* (Cambridge: Cambridge University Press, 2014); Benjamin M. Friedman, *Religion and the Rise of Capitalism* (New York: Penguin, 2022).

7. For the imperial side, see, for instance, Ian Tyrrell, *Woman's World/Woman's Empire: The Woman's Christian Temperance Union in International Perspective, 1880–1930* (Chapel Hill: University of North Carolina Press, 2010); Hilary Carey, *God's Empire: Religion and Colonialism in the British World, c. 1801–1908* (Cambridge: Cambridge University Press, 2011); Preston, *Sword of the Spirit*, chs 6–8; Emily Conroy-Krutz, *Christian Imperialism: Converting the World in the Early American Republic* (Cornell: Cornell University Press, 2015); Harald Fischer-Tiné, Stefan Huebner, and Ian Tyrrell, 'Introduction: The Rise and Growth of a Global "Moral Empire": The YMCA and YWCA during the Late Nineteenth and Early Twentieth Centuries', in Harald Fischer-Tiné, Stefan Huebner, and Ian Tyrrell, eds, *Spreading Protestant Modernity: Global Perspectives on the Social Work of the YMCA and YWCA, 1889–1970* (Honolulu: University of Hawai'i Press, 2021), 1–38.

8. Preston, *Sword of the Spirit*, 12–13, 248–49.

9. For recent studies of Christian left-wing peace activism, see, for instance, Michael Thompson, *For God and Globe: Christian Internationalism in the United States between the Great War and the Cold War* (Ithaca, NY: Cornell University Press, 2016); Gene Zubovich, *Before the Religious Right: Liberal Protestants, Human Rights, and the Polarization of the United States* (Philadelphia: University of Pennsylvania Press, 2022); Appelbaum, *Kingdom to Commune*.

10. Richard Francis Spall Jr., 'Reform Ideas of the Anti-Corn-Law Leaguers' (PhD diss., University of Illinois at Urbana-Champaign, 1985), 243.

11. F.S.L. Lyons, *Internationalism in Europe, 1815–1914* (Leiden: Sythoff, 1963), 311. The Christian free-trade tradition has been traced as far back as Thomas Aquinas, Martin Luther, and Adam Smith. See, respectively, Tihamér Tóth, 'Is There a Vatican School for Competition Policy?' *Chicago Law Journal* 46 (2015): 583–616; Kenneth G. Elzinga and Daniel A. Crane, 'Christianity and Antitrust: A Nexus', in Daniel A. Crane and Samuel Gregg, eds, *Christianity and Market Regulation* (Cambridge: Cambridge University Press, 2021), 74–100; Samuel Gregg, 'Commercial Order and the Scottish Enlightenment: The Christian Context', in Ian R. Harper and Samuel Gregg, eds, *Christian Theology and Market Economics* (Cheltenham: Edward Elgar, 2008), 43–59.

12. David Turley, *The Culture of English Antislavery, 1780–1860* (London: Routledge, 1994), 5–6, 111–12, 126–28.

13. Preston, *Sword of the Spirit*, 249–50.

14. Brian Stanley, '"Commerce and Christianity": Providence Theory, the Missionary Movement, and the Imperialism of Free Trade, 1842–1860', *Historical Journal* 26 (March 1983): 71–94 at 77–78, 81–84.

15. Quoted in R. K. Webb, 'John Bowring and Unitarianism', *Utilitas* 4 (May 1992): 43–79 at 44 n. 2.

16. Stanley, '"Commerce and Christianity"', 78–80.

17. Stanley, '"Commerce and Christianity"', 80; Julie L. Holcomb, *Moral Commerce: Quakers and the Transatlantic Boycott of the Slave Labor Economy* (Ithaca, NY: Cornell University Press, 2016), 147–55.

18. Stanley, '"Commerce and Christianity"', 82–84, 86–90.

19. Stanley, '"Commerce and Christianity"', 91.

20. Conroy-Krutz, *Christian Imperialism*, 3, 54. See also Emily Conroy-Krutz, 'Foreign Missions and Strategy, Foreign Missions as Strategy', in Elizabeth Borgwardt, Christopher McKnight Nichols, and Andrew Preston, eds, *Rethinking American Grand Strategy* (New York: Oxford University Press, 2021), 311–28; Michael C. Lazich, 'American Missionaries and the Opium Trade in Nineteenth-Century China', *Journal of World History* 17 (June 2006): 197–223; Dael A. Norwood, *Trading Freedom: How Trade with China Defined Early America* (Chicago: University of Chicago Press, 2001), 80, 88, 93.

21. Norwood, *Trading Freedom*, 82–86, 91; Nicholas Guyatt, 'The Righteous Cause: John Quincy Adams and the Limits of American Exceptionalism', in Christopher McKnight Nichols and David Milne, eds, *Ideology in US Foreign Relations: New Histories* (New York: Columbia University Press, 2022), 135–51.

22. Ian Tyrrell, *Transnational Nation: United States History in Global Perspective Since 1789* (London: Palgrave Macmillan, 2015), 158.

23. Alexander Tyrrell, 'Making the Millennium: The Mid-Nineteenth Century Peace Movement', *Historical Journal* 21 (March 1978): 75–95.

24. Spall, 'Reform Ideas', 245–46; Simon Morgan, 'Richard Cobden and British Imperialism', *Journal of Liberal History* 45 (Winter 2004/5): 16–21.

25. Quoted in Schwabe, ed., *Reminiscences*, vii.

26. Richard Cobden to Henry Ashworth, 12 April 1842, reprinted in Anthony Howe, ed., *The Letters of Richard Cobden*, vol. 1: *1815–1847*, Oxford online (by subscription), https://www

.oxfordscholarlyeditions.com/view/10.1093/actrade/9780199211951.book.1/actrade-9780199
211951-div2-172 (accessed 10 May 2023).

27. 'Song', *Anti-Bread-Tax Circular*, 7 March 1843, quoted in Spall, 'Reform Ideas', 236.

28. Simon Morgan, 'The Anti–Corn Law League and British Antislavery in Transatlantic Perspective, 1838–1846', *Historical Journal* 52 (March 2009): 87–107 at 90–92. Thompson's own conversion against the Corn Laws followed his rereading of the Biblical story of famine striking Jacob and his family when 'all countries came into Egypt to buy corn'. See Anna M. Stoddart, *Elizabeth Pease Nichol* (London: Dent & Co., 1899), 135.

29. Sarah Crabtree, *Holy Nation: The Transatlantic Quaker Ministry in an Age of Revolution* (Chicago: University of Chicago Press, 2015), 167. See also Thomas Schlereth, *The Cosmopolitan Ideal in Enlightenment Thought* (Notre Dame, IN: University of Notre Dame Press, 1977).

30. Whitehead, quoted in Tyrrell, 'Making the Millennium', 90.

31. *Report of the Proceedings of the Third General Peace Congress* (London: Charles Gilpin, 1851), 31.

32. Winter Jade Werner, 'The Gospel and the Globe: Missionary Enterprises and the Cosmopolitan Imagination, 1795–1860', (PhD. diss, Northwestern University, 2014), 47, 143, 148–57; Andrew Porter, '"Commerce and Christianity": The Rise and Fall of a Nineteenth-Century Missionary Slogan', *Historical Journal* 28 (1985): 597–621.

33. Geoffrey Cantor, *Religion and the Great Exhibition of 1851* (Oxford: Oxford University Press, 2011), 171, 174, 200–201.

34. Marshall, quoted in Cantor, *Religion*, 171, 175, 177. In a letter written on behalf of the London Peace Society, Sturge unsuccessfully urged Prince Albert to impose a ban on weapons at the Exhibition. See Cantor, *Religion*, 181–82.

35. Marx to Engels, 24 January 1852, quoted in Paul Young, *Globalization and the Great Exhibition: The Victorian New World Order* (London Palgrave Macmillan, 2009), 85; Werner, 'Gospel and the Globe', 48.

36. Radical Unitarians also spearheaded early feminism. See Kathryn Gleadle, *The Early Feminists: Radical Unitarians and the Emergence of the Women's Rights Movement, 1831–51* (New York: St. Martin's Press, 1995).

37. Cantor, *Religion*, 186–87.

38. Martin Ceadel, *The Origins of War Prevention: The British Peace Movement and International Relations, 1730–1854* (Oxford: Oxford University Press, 1996), 362.

39. Douglas Jerrold ['Juniper Hedgehog'] to Elihu Burritt, 2 April 1846, 'Extract of a Letter from Oxford, England', *Advocate of Peace and Universal Brotherhood* 1 (May 1846), 120–21.

40. Burritt, quoted in Tyrrell, 'Making the Millennium', 90.

41. Elihu Burritt, 'The Higher Law and Mission of Commerce', lecture to the Norwich Young Men's Christian Association, 27 October 1863, reprinted in *Lectures and Speeches by Elihu Burritt* (London: S. Low, Son, and Marston, 1869), 88–89 (emphasis in original).

42. Ceadel, *Origins of War Prevention*, 357.

43. Douglas H. Maynard, 'The World's Anti-Slavery Convention', *Mississippi Valley Historical Review* 47 (Dec. 1960): 452–71 at 455; *Proceedings of the General Anti-Slavery Convention* (London: John Snow, 1843), 154–58; Morgan, 'Anti–Corn Law League', 95–96; Marc-William Palen, *The 'Conspiracy' of Free Trade: The Anglo-American Struggle over Empire and Economic Globalisation, 1846–1896* (Cambridge: Cambridge University Press, 2016), 16–19.

44. Julie L. Holcomb, *Moral Commerce: Quakers and the Transatlantic Boycott of the Slave Labor Economy* (Ithaca, NY: Cornell University Press, 2016), 1, 6–7, 79–80, 114–15.

45. Bronwen Everill, *Not Made by Slaves: Ethical Capitalism in the Age of Abolition* (Cambridge, MA: Harvard University Press, 2020). See also Andrea Major, *Slavery, Abolitionism and Empire in India, 1772–1843* (Liverpool: Liverpool University Press, 2012), ch. 8; Richard Huzzey, *Freedom Burning* (Ithaca, NY: Cornell University Press, 2012), ch. 5; Zoë Laidlaw, *Protecting Empire's Humanity* (Cambridge: Cambridge University Press, 2021), ch. 5.

46. Carol Faulkner, 'The Root of the Evil: Free Produce and Radical Antislavery, 1820–1860', *Journal of the Early Republic* 27 (Fall 2007): 377–405; Morgan, 'Anti–Corn Law League', 92–94; Marc-William Palen, 'Free-Trade Ideology and Transatlantic Abolitionism: A Historiography', *Journal of the History of Economic Thought* 37 (June 2015): 291–304 at 294–96.

47. Henry Ward Beecher, *Henry Ward Beecher on Free Trade and Congressional Elections*, lecture, 22 November 1883, 'Free Trade and Tariff Reform', Box 80, Folder 4, Garrison Family Papers, SSC. See also Beecher, 'Protection Anti-Christian', *Free Trade Broadside* (July 1905), 5.

48. William Robertson, *The Life and Times of the Right Hon. John Bright* (Rochdale: s.p., 1877), 218.

49. John Bright, 'Introduction' to M. M. Trumbull, *The American Lesson of the Free Trade Struggle in England* (Chicago: Schumm and Simpson, 1884 [1882]), 7, 5; Palen, 'Conspiracy', 123–24.

50. Palen, 'Conspiracy', ch. 5.

51. Jennier Regan-Lefebvre, *Cosmopolitan Nationalism in the Victorian Empire: Ireland, India and the Politics of Alfred Webb* (Basingstoke: Palgrave Macmillan, 2009), 17–24, 3–4, 128–53.

52. James Jeremiah Green, 'The Impact of Henry George's Theories on American Catholics' (PhD diss., University of Notre Dame, 1956).

53. Walter Nugent, 'A Catholic Progressive? The Case of Judge E. O. Brown', *Journal of the Gilded Age and Progressive Era* 2 (Jan. 2003): 5–47 at 17–21, 26, 29–31. The Rev. Louis A. Lambert in upstate New York and Peoria's Bishop John Lancaster Spalding were two other prominent liberal Catholic followers of Henry George.

54. Henry George, *The Condition of Labor: An Open Letter to Pope Leo XIII* (New York: US Book Co., 1891), 3–4, pdf available at http://wealthandwant.com/pdf/George_The_Condition_of_Labor.pdf (accessed 12 May 2023)

55. Patrick Doyle, 'The Clergy, Economic Democracy, and the Co-operative Movement in Ireland, 1880–1932', *History of European Ideas* 46 (2020): 982–96; Joseph A. MacMahon, 'The Catholic Clergy and the Social Question in Ireland, 1891–1916', *Studies: An Irish Quarterly Review* 70 (Winter 1981): 263–88 at 277. See also Andrew Phemister, *Land and Liberalism: Henry George and the Irish Land War* (Cambridge: Cambridge University Press, 2023).

56. Patrick Mary Doyle, 'Reframing the "Irish Question": The Role of the Irish Co-operative Movement in the Formation of Irish Nationalism, 1900–22', *Irish Studies Review* 22 (2014): 267–84.

57. Stephen Meardon, 'From Religious Revivals to Tariff Rancor: Preaching Free Trade and Protection during the Second American Party System', *History of Political Economy* 40 (2008): 265–98 at 292–94.

58. Dorothy Ross, 'Socialism and American Liberalism: Academic Social Thought in the 1880s', *Perspectives in American History* 11 (1977–78): 7–79.

59. John A. Kasson, *Free Trade Not the International Law of the Almighty* (New York: Brooklyn Tariff Reform Club, 1884).

60. Palen, 'Conspiracy', 100–101, 134, 149, 173, 185, 195, 274.

61. 'Moral Value of Protection', *American Economist*, 17 March 1905, 123.

62. Carl Strikwerda, "'L'organisation, clé du succès!" European Christian Labor Movements in Comparative Perspective', in Lex Heerma van Voss, Patrick Pasture, and Jan De Maeyer, eds, *Between Cross and Class: Comparative Histories of Christian Labour in Europe 1840–2000* (Bern: Peter Lang, 2005), 333–78 at 367.

63. John S. Conway, 'Resisting Militarism: The Peace Movement in the German Evangelical Church during the Weimar Republic', *Kirchliche Zeitgeschichte* 4 (May 1991): 29–45 at 32, 34, 43–44; Stefan Grotefeld, 'Peace Enforcement through International Friendship of the Churches from 1919 to 1933. The Example of the German World Alliance', *Current Research on Peace and Violence* 13 (1990): 193–209.

64. Kenneth C. Wenzer, 'The Influence of Henry George's Philosophy on Lev Nikolaevich Tolstoy: The Period of Developing Economic Thought (1881–1897)', *Pennsylvania History* 63 (Spring 1996): 232–52, Tolstoy quoted at 241, 244; Patrick Heyer, 'Revolution of Spirit: Henry George, Leo Tolstoy, and the Land Value Tax' (MA thesis, California State University, Fullerton, 2014); Peter d'Alroy Jones, *Christian Socialist Revival, 1877–1914* (Princeton: Princeton University Press, 1968), 54.

65. Thomas E. Graham, 'Jones, Jenkin Lloyd', *American National Biography* (Oxford: Oxford University Press, 1999), https://doi-org.uoelibrary.idm.oclc.org/10.1093/anb/9780198606697.article.0800774.

66. C. Roland Marchand, *The American Peace Movement and Social Reform, 1889–1918* (Princeton: Princeton University Press, 1972), 302–3.

67. Benjamin F. Trueblood, *The Federation of the World* (Boston, MA: Houghton, Mifflin and Company, 1899), 65, 134–35.

68. Charles H. Brent, 'Tyranny or Democracy—Which?' *Outlook* 83 (May–Aug. 1906): 599–600; 'Wawbeek' Petition, New Hampshire Congregation of Christians, to F. D. Currier, September 6, 1906; Brent to Welsh, October 31, 1906; Brent to Welsh, November 15, 1906; 'Memorandum', July 25, 1907, Philippine Tariff Papers, Vol. 2, Herbert Welsh Papers, Special Collections Library, University of Michigan, Ann Arbor, MI; 'The Truth about Cotton Splits in the Philippines', *Textile World Record* 32 (Dec. 1906), 69–70.

69. Paul Laity, *The British Peace Movement 1870–1914* (Oxford: Oxford University Press, 2001), 193.

70. Martin Ceadel, 'Christian Pacifism in the Era of Two World Wars' *Studies in Church History* 20 (1983): 391–408, at 395.

71. Bert den Boggende, 'Richard Roberts' Vision and the Founding of the Fellowship of Reconciliation', *Albion* 36 (Winter 2004): 608–35 at 625; Boggende, 'The Fellowship of Reconciliation 1914–1945' (PhD diss., McMaster University, 1986), 19–20.

72. Charles F. Howlett, 'John Nevin Sayre and the American Fellowship of Reconciliation', *Pennsylvania Magazine of History and Biography* 114 (July 1990): 399–421 at 403.

73. Eleanor M. Moore, *The Quest for Peace as I Have Known It in Australia* (Melbourne: Wilke & Co., 1949), 145, 178, 189.

74. Cyril H. Powles, *Pacifism in Japan, 1918–1945* (Toronto: University of Toronto Press, 1999), 145–51, 162.

75. Preston, *Sword of the Spirit*, 241–42.

76. Yuzo Ota, 'Kagawa Toyohiko: A Pacifist?', in Nobuya Bamba and John F. Howes, eds, *Pacifism in Japan: The Christian and Socialist Tradition* (Vancouver: University of British Columbia, 1978), 172–79, Kagawa quoted at 177; David P. King, 'The West Looks East: The Influence of Toyohiko Kagawa on American Mainline Protestantism', *Church History* 80 (June 2011): 302–20 at 303–4, 315. See also Toyohiko Kagawa, 'The Economic Foundation of World Peace', *Friends of Jesus* 5 (Aug. 1932); Kagawa, *The Philosophy of the Co-operative Movement* (Chicago: Chicago Church Federation, 1936); Kagawa, 'Peace by World Cooperatives', *Christian Century* (29 April 1936); Brian G. Byrd and John Paul Loucky, 'Toyohiko Kagawa and Reinhold Niebuhr: The Church and Cooperatives', *Journal of Interdisciplinary Studies* 28 (2016): 63–88. On the FCC and the New Deal, see Zubovich, *Before the Religious Right*, ch. 1.

77. Thompson, *For God and Globe*, 27–46.

78. Preston, *Sword of the Spirit*, 258–68, 275–79; Cara Lea Burnidge, *A Peaceful Conquest: Woodrow Wilson, Religion, and the New World Order* (Chicago: University of Chicago Press, 2016), 78, 82, 91.

79. Sherwood Eddy and Kirby Page, *The Abolition of War* (New York: George H. Doran, 1924), 57, 66, 63.

80. Eddy and Page, *Abolition of War*, 1, 33–34, 85, 89–90, 92.

81. Kirby Page, *Christianity and Economic Problems* (New York: Association Press, 1926), 103–6, 110.

82. Norman Thomas, 'Afterthoughts on the Suffrage Victory', *The World Tomorrow* 4 (Jan. 1921), 20–21; 'The Shame of the Race Riots', *The World Tomorrow* 2 (Sept. 1919), 237; 'Mr. Garvey's Black Republic', *The World Tomorrow* 3 (Sept. 1920), 265.

83. Norman Thomas, 'What is Bolshevism?', *The World Tomorrow* 2 (Feb. 1919), 37–39; 'Is the British Empire Safe for Democracy?' *The World Tomorrow* 2 (June 1919), 151; Thomas, 'Reflections on Russia and Revolution', *The World Tomorrow* 3 (Sept. 1920), 259–62.

84. Oswald Garrison Villard, 'Germany in Collapse', *The World Tomorrow* 2 (June 1919), 154–59; Norman Angell, 'Shall We Fail Through Lack of Freedom?' *The World Tomorrow* 2 (Jan. 1919), 6–9.

85. For the latter, see *League of Nations: Outlines for Discussion* (New York: National Committee on the Churches and the Moral Aims of the War, n.d.), 9–10. On Protestant support for Wilson and the League, see Burnidge, *Peaceful Conquest*; James L. Lancaster, 'The Protestant Churches and the Fight for Ratification of the Versailles Treaty', *Public Opinion Quarterly* 31 (Winter 1967–1968): 597–619.

86. Henri Lambert, 'The Fundamentals of a League of Nations I & II—Free Trade and National Sovereignty', *The World Tomorrow* 1 (Dec. 1918), 313–15; Lambert, 'The Fundamentals of a League of Nations III & IV—Disarmament and Freedom of the Seas', *The World Tomorrow* 2 (Jan. 1919): 25–27; 'The Book of the Hour: Pax Economica', *The World Tomorrow* 2 (Feb. 1919). See, also, 'Sign of the Times', *The World Tomorrow* 1 (Aug. 1918), 183; 'By the Way', *The World Tomorrow* 1 (Sept. 1918), 217; 'The Fall Campaign', *The World Tomorrow* 1 (Oct. 1918), 261.

87. Lida Gustava Heymann, 'Towards Reconciliation', *The World Tomorrow* 7 (April 1924), 120.

88. Kurt Klaeber, 'The Uniting of France and German: A Communist View', *The World Tomorrow* 7 (April 1924), 115.

89. 'The Principles of a Righteous League', *The World Tomorrow* 2 (Jan. 1919), 24.

90. 'If Thine Enemy Hunger', *The World Tomorrow* 1 (Dec 1918), 294.

91. '"Another Scrap of Paper" Says Scott Nearing', *The World Tomorrow* 2 (March 1919), 66; 'Bishop Jones Sees the Way Open for World Brotherhood', *The World Tomorrow* 2 (March 1919), 67–68.

92. Charles F. Dole, 'What is Wrong in Profits?' *The World Tomorrow* 3 (Oct. 1920), 303.

93. 'The Barbed Wire Entanglements of "Peace"', *The World Tomorrow* 3 (Feb. 1920), 40.

94. 'No Peace Without Internationalism', *The World Tomorrow* 3 (May 1920), 135–36.

95. Arthur Wallace Calhoun, 'Spiritual Resources in the Cooperative Movement', *The World Tomorrow* 3 (Nov. 1920), 341–42.

96. 'Concerning Protective Tariffs', *The World Tomorrow* 4 (Aug. 1921), 230.

97. 'Mr. Harding's Cabinet', *The World Tomorrow* 4 (March 1921), 67.

98. Jessie Wallace Hughan, 'Why I Will Support Debs in 1920', *The World Tomorrow* 3 (Oct. 1920), 300.

99. J. A. Hobson, 'The New Intolerance', *The World Tomorrow* 5 (Oct. 1922), 291–93.

100. Albert D. Belden, 'The Two Internationals', *The World Tomorrow* 3 (May 1920), 151–52.

101. 'Death and Life in India', *The World Tomorrow* 3 (Jan. 1920), 20.

102. Norman Thomas, 'England, Ireland and America', *The World Tomorrow* 2 (April 1919), 105–9; Thomas, 'Ireland as an American Problem', *The World Tomorrow* 4 (Jan. 1921), 3.

103. Norman Thomas, 'Is the British Empire Safe for Democracy?' *The World Tomorrow* 2 (June 1919), 151.

104. 'A View from Within, "What of Japan?"' *The World Tomorrow* 3 (June 1920), 165–66; 'Japanese Imperialism—and American Bad Manners', *The World Tomorrow* 3 (Sept. 1920), 268.

105. David Starr Jordan, 'The Myth of the Yellow Peril', *The World Tomorrow* 1 (July 1918), 163.

106. 'Our Caribbean Empire', *The World Tomorrow* 3 (July 1920), 209; M. K. Gandhi, 'The Law of Suffering', *The World Tomorrow* 3 (Sept. 1920), 266–67.

107. See, for instance, Gilbert Reid, 'Japan, China and the League of Nations', *The World Tomorrow* 2 (Aug. 1919), 227–28; Norman Thomas, 'Soviet Russia and Its Critics', *The World Tomorrow* 2 (Aug. 1919), 229; Louis P. Lochner, 'Open Covenants of War, Openly Arrived At', *The World Tomorrow* 2 (Aug. 1919), 230–32.

108. Jeremy Sabella, 'The 1930s: Economic Crisis and the "End of an Era"', in Robin Lovin and Joshua Mauldin, eds, *The Oxford Handbook of Reinhold Niebuhr* (Oxford: Oxford University Press, 2021), https://doi.org/10.1093/oxfordhb/9780198813569.013.2; Daniel F. Rice, *Reinhold Niebuhr and His Circle of Influence* (Cambridge: Cambridge University Press, 2012): 80–112.

109. Niebuhr did make an exception for economic nationalism in anti-colonial contexts. For example, he heaped praise upon Gandhi's non-violent implementation of economic boycotts on behalf of Indian independence. In *Moral Man and Immoral Society* (1932), he even recommended Swadeshism (see chapter 1) as an effective method for Black Americans to obtain 'complete emancipation' from racist white capitalist exploitation. See Reinhold Niebuhr, *Moral Man and Immoral Society* (New York: Charles Scribner's Sons, 1932), 89–90, 240–54.

110. Paul Merkley, *Reinhold Niebuhr* (McGill-Queen's University Press, 1975), 120. See also, Niebuhr, 'Economic Perils to World Peace', *The World Tomorrow* 14 (May 1931), 154–56.

111. Preston, *Sword of the Spirit*, 304–9; C. Melissa Snarr, 'Economic Justice', in Lovin and Mauldin, *Oxford Handbook of Reinhold Niebuhr*, https://doi.org/10.1093/oxfordhb/9780198813569.013.29. See, for instance, Reinhold Niebuhr, *Christianity and Power Politics* (New York: Scribner's Sons, 1940), 138–39.

112. Charles E. Raven, *Christian Socialism, 1848–1854* (London: Macmillan, 1920), 31; Philip N. Backstron Jr., 'The Practical Side of Christian Socialism in Victorian England', *Victorian Studies* 6 (June 1963): 305–24.

113. J. Eerdekens, 'The National Federation of Christian Cooperatives', *Journal of Collective Economy* 29 (Nov. 1958): 659–64.

114. Noel Loos and Robyn Keast, 'The Radical Promise: The Aboriginal Christian Cooperative Movement', *Australian Historical Studies* 25 (1992): 286–301.

115. Sidney L. Gulick to the World Peace Foundation, 16 June 1917, 'World Alliance, 1928–1940'; Gulick and B. S. Winchester to Halland Hudson, 25 March 1929, 'Churches & World Peace, 1914–1930'; *The World Alliance of Churches for Promoting International Friendship* (Swarthmore, PA: Benjamin F. Battin, 1915), 6–8, 'World Alliance for International Friendship through the Churches, 1918–1922', Box 185, World Peace Foundation, Tisch Library, Tufts University, Boston, MA

116. *The New Task of the Church* (New York: World Alliance, n.d.), 'Program Work, 1914–19' Folder, WAP.

117. Sidney L. Gulick, *Helps for Leaders of Discussion Groups* (New York: World Alliance, n.d.), 21, 26, in 'Program Work, 1914–19' Folder, WAP.

118. Rev. Sidney Gulick, 'Christian Women and International Friendship', in 'Correspondence, 1917–1939' Folder, WAP.

119. *The World Alliance for International Friendship Through the Churches, American Council: History, Work, Plans and Program* (New York, s.p., n.d. [c. 1920]), 14, in 'Correspondence, 1917–1939' Folder, WAP.

120. See, for instance, Sidney L Gulick, *The Christian Crusade for a Warless World* (New York: The Macmillan Company, 1922).

121. *International Goodwill Congress*, 4, in 'Program Work, 1932' Folder, WAP.

122. *Report of the Committee on Message and Recommendations of the Annual Meeting of the World Alliance, November 1933*, 'Program Work, 1933' Folder, WAP, 4.

123. *Report of the Committee on Message and Recommendations of the Annual Meeting of the World Alliance for International Friendship, November, 1934*, 'Program Work, 1934' Folder, WAP.

124. 'Shantung—Japan's Unholy Grab', *Christian Century* 36 (7 Aug. 1919), 16.

125. Harold A. Hatch, 'What the Layman Expects of the Church', *Christian Century* 38 (31 March 1921), 10.

126. Kirby Page, 'What Shall We Do about War?' *Christian Century* 40 (12 July 1923), 879–80.

127. John Herman Randall, 'The Ideal of World Unity I', *World Unity* 1 (Oct. 1927), 10–11.

128. John Herman Randall, 'The Ideal of World Unity II', *World Unity* 1 (Nov. 1927), 76–77.

129. Parker T. Moon, *Causes of War: Security, Old and New* (Washington, DC: Catholic Association for International Peace, 1930), 12–13. Moon's radical critique of imperialism gets an oft-overlooked treatment, alongside those of Hobson and Lenin, in John Gallagher and Ronald Robinson, 'The Imperialism of Free Trade', *Economic History Review* 6 (1953): 1–15 at 2.

130. Europe Committee, *Europe and the United States: Elements in Their Relationship* (Washington, DC: Catholic Association for International Peace, 1931), 38.

131. Thomas F. Divine, *Tariffs and World Peace* (Washington, DC: CAIP, 1933), 12, 2, 6, 16, 19–21, 40.

132. *America's Peace Aims* (Washington, DC: CAIP, 1941), 34. See also Rev. John A. Ryan, Dr. Parker T. Moon, and Rev. R. A. McGowan, *International Economic Life* (Washington, DC: CAIP, 1934); Rev. Dr. Edgar Schmiedeler, *Agriculture and International Life* (Washington, DC: CAIP, 1937); Charles Fenwick, *A Primer of Peace* (Washington, DC: CAIP, 1937); Ethics Committee, *The Obligation of Catholics to Promote Peace* (Washington, DC: CAIP, 1940); Post-War World Committee, *A Peace Agenda for the United Nations* (Washington, DC: CAIP, 1943). Divine himself would create the Catholic Economic Association in 1941 to address questions surrounding global economic development and poverty. See Thomas F. Divine, 'The Origin of the Challenge of the Future', *Review of Social Economy* 49 (1991): 542–45.

133. Zubovich, *Before the Religious Right*, ch. 2.

134. *The Message and Decisions of Oxford on Church, Community and State* (Chicago: Universal Christian Council, 1937), 32, 36–50; Heather A. Warren, *Theologians of a New World Order: Reinhold Niebuhr and the Christian Realists 1920–1948* (Oxford: Oxford University Press, 1997), 59–60; Thompson, *For God and Globe*, 147, chs 5–6.

135. Thompson, *For God and Globe*, 7–8.

136. Preston, *Sword of the Spirit*, 298–99.

137. Walter W. Van Kirk, *Religion Renounces War* (Chicago: Willet, Clark, 1934), 49, 56–57.

138. *Report of the Committee on Message and Recommendations of the Annual Meeting of the World Alliance for International Friendship through the Churches, 1936*, 'Program Work, 1936' Folder, WAP.

139. Preston, *Sword of the Spirit*, 301; *Report of the Committee on Message and Recommendations of the Annual Meeting of the World Alliance for International Friendship, Nov. 1937*, 'Program of Work, 1937' Folder, WAP; John A. Hutchison, *We Are Not Divided: A Critical and Historical Study of the Federal Council of the Churches of Christ in America* (New York: Round Table Press, 1941), 212.

140. Pope, *Religious Proposals*, 16–17, in 'Program of Work, 1940–1941' Folder, WAP.

141. In 1947, Dulles admitted privately to being a strong believer 'in the free enterprise system [. . .]. I have that economic belief just as I have my own personal religious belief.' See Zubovich, *Before the Religious Right*, 264.

142. Zubovich, *Before the Religious Right*, 81, 84.

143. *Social Justice and Economic Reconstruction* (New York: Federal Council of the Churches of Christ in America, 1942), 10–11, 14–22, 25, in 'Program Work 1942' Folder, WAP.

144. Ian Tyrrell, 'Vectors of Practicality: Social Gospel, the North American YMCA in Asia, and the Global Context', in Fischer-Tiné, Huebner, and Tyrrell, eds, *Spreading Protestant Modernity*, 39–40.

145. Zubovich, 'US Protestants', 35.

146. *Toward a New Economic Society: A Program for Students* (New York: Council of Christian Associations, 1931), 84–85.

147. John Swomley, 'Program of the Youth Committee Against War', in *National Youth Anti-War Congress* (New York: Youth Committee Against War, 1940), 29.

148. Richard M. Fagley, *To Build a Better World: International Problems for Religious Young People* (New York: World Alliance and Church Peace Union, 1941), 7–11, in 'Program of Work, 1940–1941' Folder, WAP.

149. Sherwood Eddy, *A Century with Youth* (New York: Association Press, 1944), 10.

150. See especially Thompson, *For God and Globe*.

151. Paul David Hines, 'Norman Angell: Peace Movement 1911–1915' (PhD diss., Ball State Teachers College, Muncie, 1965), 47

152. Oswald F. Schuette, 'Text Book Used by Y.M.C.A. Misrepresents Protection', *American Economist* 64 (5 Dec. 1919), 244.

153. *Henry George News* (New York: Henry George School of Social Science, 1953), 7.

154. The NCCCW, created by Carrie Chapman Catt in 1924, was composed of eleven women's organizations: the YWCA USA, the NLWV, the American Association of University Women, the Council of Women for Home Missions, the National Conference of American Ethical Union, the Committee on Women's Work—the Foreign Missions Conference of North America, the General Federation of Women's Club's, the National Council of Jewish Women, the National Federation of Business and Professional Women's Clubs, the National Women's Trade Union League, and the National Woman's Christian Temperance Union. By 1935 the umbrella organization claimed a combined membership of more than five million women across the nation. Harriet Hyman Alonso, *Peace as a Woman's Issue* (Syracuse, NY: Syracuse University Press, 1993), 106–8.

155. 'Plan for bringing economic forces into cooperation with the women's peace movement', 1935; Edgar Smith to Clara Guthrie d'Arcis [copy], 13 September 1935, YWCA of the USA records, Box 444, 'Role of industrialists' folder, SSC.

156. Emerson to Doughton, 22 January 1927; 'World Economic Conference 1937–1939', YWCA of the USA records, Box 444, 'Role of industrialists' folder, SSC.

157. *A Primer on the Trade Agreements* (New York: National Peace Conference, 1940), 19, Box 462.

158. Zubovich, *Before the Religious Right*, ch. 3; Inboden, *Religion and American Foreign Policy*, 5–6.

159. Joseph S. Rossi, *American Catholics and the United Nations* (Lanham: University Press of America, 1993), 17.

160. Zubovich, *Before the Religious Right*, 114–17.

161. Walter W. Van Kirk, *Technical Assistance Programs, 1st Sess. 84th Cong.* (Washington, DC: US Government Printing Office, 1955), 100.

162. David Starr Jordan to Hamilton Holt, 18 October 1910, Folder 25, 'Hamilton Holt, 1910–1922', Box 23, David Starr Jordan Papers, Hoover Institution Library and Archives, Stanford University, Palo Alto, CA.

163. *The World Alliance of Churches for Promoting International Friendship*, 17; Crystal Eastman to David Starr Jordan, 11 June 1916, Box 19, Folder 12, 'Crystal Eastman, 1916–1917', Jordan Papers; Hamilton Holt, 'A Declaration of Interdependence', *Independent* (5 June 1916), 357.

164. 'School for League of Nations', *American Economist* 71 (27 April 1923), 148.

165. Hamilton Holt to Charles Oscar Andrews, 11 July 1945, reprinted in *The Charter of the United Nations* (Washington, DC: US Government Printing Office, 1945), 457; Joseph Preston Baratta, *The Politics of World Federation* (Westport, CT: Praeger, 2004), 156–57.

166. Hamilton Holt and George C. Holt, 'An Appeal to the Peoples of the World', *World Affairs* 109 (June 1946): 83–86; Anna Virena Rice, *A History of the World's Young Women's Christian Association* (New York, 1948), 267.

Chapter 6. Pax Economica vs. Pax Americana

1. 'United States: Statement by H. E. Mr. William J. Clinton, President', *World Trade Organization*, 'Geneva WTO Ministerial 1998: Statement' (18 May), https://www.wto.org /english/thewto_e/minist_e/min98_e/anniv_e/clinton_e.htm (accessed 12 May 2023).

2. Simon Schama, 'When Britain Chose Europe', *Financial Times*, 28 February 2019.

3. O'Regan interview, *99% Invisible*, Episode 477, 'Call of Duty: Free' podcast [25-min. mark], https://99percentinvisible.org/episode/call-of-duty-free/ (accessed 12 May 2023).

4. Karen Duffin and Robert Smith, NPR *Planet Money*, Episode 841, 'The Land of Duty Free', 11 May 2018, https://www.npr.org/sections/money/2018/05/11/610516972/episode -841-the-land-of-duty-free (accessed 12 May 2023); Brian O'Connell and Cian O'Carroll, *Brendan O'Regan: Irish Innovator, Visionary and Peacemaker* (Kildare: Irish Academic Press, 2018).

5. Or Rosenboim, *The Emergence of Globalism: Visions of World Order in Britain and the United States, 1939–1950* (Princeton: Princeton University Press, 2017); Akira Iriye, *Global Community: The Role of International Organizations in the Making of the Contemporary World* (Berkeley: University of California Press, 2002).

6. Eric Helleiner, *Forgotten Foundations of Bretton Woods: International Development and the Making of the Postwar Order* (Ithaca, NY: Cornell University Press, 2014).

7. Martin Daunton, 'The Inconsistent Quartet: Free Trade Versus Competing Goals', in Martin Daunton, Amrita Narlikar, and Robert M. Stern, eds, *Oxford Handbook on the World Trade Organization* (Oxford: Oxford University Press, 2012), https://doi.org/10.1093/oxfordhb /9780199586103.013.0003.

8. Stephen Wertheim, *Tomorrow, the World: The Birth of US Global Supremacy* (Cambridge, MA: Harvard University Press, 2020).

9. Marc-William Palen, 'The Open Door Empire', in Christopher Dietrich, ed., *A Companion to US Foreign Relations: Colonial Era to the Present*, 2 vols (Hoboken: Wiley-Blackwell, 2020), 1: 271–87; Jo Grady and Chris Grocott, eds, *The Continuing Imperialism of Free Trade* (London: Routledge, 2018).

10. Paul Adler, *No Globalization without Representation: US Activists and World Inequality* (Philadelphia: University of Pennsylvania Press, 2021). The terms 'Global South' and 'developing states' are used interchangeably with 'Third World' here. Alessandro Inadolo makes a compelling case for the continued historical utility of 'Third World' in *Arrested Development: The Soviet Union in Ghana, Guinea, and Mali, 1955–1968* (Ithaca, NY: Cornell University Press, 2022), 4–6.

11. Christy Thornton, *Revolution in Development: Mexico and the Governance of the Global Economy* (Oakland: University of California Press, 2021); Amy C. Offner, *Sorting Out the Mixed Economy: The Rise and Fall of Welfare and Developmental States in the Americas* (Princeton: Princeton University Press, 2019); Helleiner, *Forgotten Foundations*.

12. 'Absolute Free Trade Opposed by Mexico', *New York Times*, 20 November 1947, 3. See also Thornton, *Revolution in Development*, ch. 6.

13. Martin Thomas and Andrew Thompson, 'Empire and Globalisation: From "High Imperialism" to Decolonisation', *International History Review* 36 (Sept. 2014): 142–70 at 157; Dierk Walter, *Colonial Violence: European Empires and the Use of Force* (Oxford: Oxford University

Press, 2017); Martin Thomas, 'Violence, Insurgency, and the End of Empires', in Martin Thomas and Andrew S. Thompson, eds, *Oxford Handbook of the Ends of Empire* (Oxford: Oxford University Press, 2017), https://doi.org/10.1093/oxfordhb/9780198713197.001.0001.

14. Caroline Elkins, *Legacy of Violence: A History of the British Empire* (New York: Penguin, 2022); Martin Thomas, *Fight or Flight: Britain, France, and the Roads from Empire* (Oxford: Oxford University Press, 2014); Stuart Ward, 'A Matter of Preference: The EEC and the Erosion of the Old Commonwealth Relationship', in Alex May, ed., *Britain, The Commonwealth and Europe* (London: Palgrave Macmillan, 2001), 156–80; Richard Toye, 'The Attlee Government, the Imperial Preference System and the Creation of the GATT', *English Historical Review* 478 (Sept. 2003): 912–39; Catherine R. Schenk, 'Decolonization and European Economic Integration: The Free Trade Area negotiations, 1956–58', *Journal of Imperial and Commonwealth History* 24 (1996): 443–63.

15. Oscar Sanchez-Sibony, *Red Globalization: The Political Economy of the Soviet Cold War from Stalin to Krushchev* (Cambridge: Cambridge University Press, 2014), 94–96, 119–21; Tobias Rupprecht, *Soviet Internationalism after Stalin: Interaction and Exchange between the USSR and Latin America during the Cold War* (Cambridge: Cambridge University Press, 2015); James Mark and Paul Betts, eds, *Socialism Goes Global: The Soviet Union and Eastern Europe in the Age of Decolonization* (Oxford: Oxford University Press, 2022); James Mark, Artemy M. Kalinovsky, and Steffi Marung, eds, *Alternative Globalizations: Eastern Europe and the Postcolonial World* (Bloomington: Indiana University Press, 2020); Anna Calori, Anne-Kristin Hartmetz, Bence Kocsev, James Mark, and Jan Zofka, eds, *Between East and South: Spaces of Interaction in the Globalizing Economy of the Cold War* (Berlin: Degruyter, 2019).

16. Michael Cox and Caroline Kennedy-Pipe, 'The Tragedy of American Diplomacy? Rethinking the Marshall Plan', *Journal of Cold War Studies* 7 (Winter 2005): 97–134.

17. Richard Toye, 'Developing Multilateralism: The Havana Charter and the Fight for the International Trade Organization, 1947–1948', *International History Review* 25 (June 2003): 282–305; Francine McKenzie, 'Free Trade and Freedom to Trade: The Development Challenge to GATT, 1947–1968', in Marc Frey, Sönke Kunkel, and Corinna R. Unger, *International Organizations and Development, 1945–1990* (London: Palgrave Macmillan, 2014), 150–70. For the GATT and WTO as neoliberal projects, see, among others, Kendall Stiles, 'Negotiating Institutional Reform: The Uruguay Round, the GATT, and the WTO', *Global Governance* 2 (Jan. 1996): 119–48; Elaine Hartwick and Richard Peet, 'Neoliberalism and Nature: The Case of the WTO', *Annals of the American Academy of Political and Social Science* 590 (Nov. 2003): 188–211; Nitsan Chorev and Sarah Babb, 'The Crisis of Neoliberalism and the Future of International Institutions: A Comparison of the IMF and the WTO', *Theory and Society* 38 (Sept. 2009): 459–84; Quinn Slobodian, *Globalists: The End of Empire and the Birth of Neoliberalism* (Cambridge, MA: Harvard University Press, 2018).

18. Thomas W. Zeiler, 'Closed Doors', in Akira Iriye, ed., *Global Interdependence: The World After 1945* (Cambridge, MA: Harvard University Press, 2014), 207–44 at 214–15.

19. Daniel J. Sargent, *A Superpower Transformed: The Remaking of American Foreign Relations in the 1970s* (Oxford: Oxford University Press, 2014), ch. 1.

20. Mark Atwood Lawrence, *The End of Ambition: The United States and the Third World in the Vietnam Era* (Princeton: Princeton University Press, 2021).

21. Zeiler, 'Closed Doors', 234, 238–39.

22. Zeiler, 'Closed Doors', 223–24, 227, 228; Thomas W. Zeiler, *Free Trade, Free World: The Advent of GATT* (Chapel Hill: University of North Carolina Press, 1999), 4.

23. R. Joseph Parrott and Mark Atwood Lawrence, eds, *The Tricontinental Revolution: Third World Radicalism and the Cold War* (Cambridge: Cambridge University Press, 2022).

24. Gavin Kitching, *Development and Underdevelopment in Historical Perspective: Populism, Nationalism and Industrialisation* (London: Routledge, 2011), 145.

25. Gunnar Myrdal, *Beyond the Welfare State: Economic Planning in the Welfare States and its International Implications* (London: Duckworth, 1960), 109.

26. Mauro Boianovsky, 'Friedrich List and the Economic Fate of Tropical Countries', *History of Political Economy* 45 (2013): 647–91.

27. Theodore H. von Laue, *The Global City: Freedom, Power and Necessity in the Age of World Revolutions* (Philadelphia: J. B. Lippincott, 1969), 147–48n.

28. W. O. Henderson, *Friedrich List: Economist and Visionary, 1789–1846* (London: Frank Cass, 1983), 163.

29. Leonard Gomes, *The Economics and Ideology of Free Trade: A Historical Review* (Cheltenham: Edward Elgar, 2003), 66, 83–89.

30. Ha-Joon Chang, *Kicking Away the Ladder: Development Strategy in Historical Perspective* (London: Anthem, 2002).

31. Aashish Velkar, '*Swadeshi* Capitalism in Colonial Bombay', *Historical Journal* 64 (Sept. 2021): 1009–34.

32. Kwame Nimako, 'Nkrumah, African Awakening and Neocolonialism: How Black America Awakened Nkrumah and Nkrumah Awakened Black America', *Black Scholar* 40 (Summer 2010): 54–70 at 67–68.

33. Richard Toye, *The Labour Party and the Planned Economy, 1931–1951* (Woodbridge: Boydell & Brewer, 2003); Everett W. Ferrill, 'Sir Norman Angell: Critic of Appeasement, 1935–1940' (D.Ed thesis, Ball State University, 1977); J.D.B. Miller, *Norman Angell and the Futility of War* (London: Palgrave Macmillan, 1986).

34. Gerald Swope (chair of the Citizens' Committee for Reciprocal World Trade) to the Senate Committee on Finance, 1 June 1948; Testimony of Alger Hiss before the Senate Finance Committee, 2 June 1948, Box 52, Folder 2, CEIPR.

35. Melvin J. Fox to Milton Gelman, 30 December 1946, Box 297a, CEIPR; 'World Trade Foundation Purpose and Plans', Box 297b, CEIPR.

36. YWCA National Board, 'Filling the World's Market Basket', *Public Affairs News Service* 10 (Jan. 1946); Edward Yardley (executive secretary of the Committee for Reciprocity Information) to Mrs. Arthur Forrest Anderson (president of the National Board of the YWCA), 21 January 1947, YWCA of the USA records, Box 462, Folder 2, SSC, and Marjorie Taggart White (executive secretary Of the Citizens' Committee for Reciprocal World Trade), open letter, 26 March 1948, YWCA of the USA records, Box 462, Folder 3, SSC.

37. 'Statement by the Women's Action Committee for Lasting Peace in Support of Extension of the Trade Agreements Act', 'Statement of Mrs. Margaret F. Stone, Representing the National Women's Trade Union League of America, in support of Extension of the Reciprocal Trade Agreements Program', 'Statement of Mrs. William Johnstone, Member of the National Board of Directors, League of Women Voters, at the People's Hearings on Reciprocal Trade, May 14, 1948', Box 294, Folder 294.5, CEIPR; Gale Kenny, '"The Christian Woman's Trusteeship":

Protestant Churchwomen, Pacifism, and Economic Citizenship in the 1930s–1950s', paper presented at SHAFR conference, New Orleans, June 2022. Other RTAA supporters in 1948 included the General Federation of Women's Clubs, the League of Women Shoppers, the League of Women Voters, and the Pan Pacific Women's Association. See *The Citizens Speak* (New York: CCRWT, 1948), Box 294, Folder 294.4, CEIPR.

38. Carole Stanford Bucy, 'Exercising the Franchise, Building the Body Politic: The League of Women Voters and Public Policy, 1945–1964' (PhD diss., Vanderbilt University, 2002), 10–11, 34–36, 64, ch. 3.

39. Doreen L. Brown, chair, 'Statement on Behalf of the Consumer Education Council on World Trade', March 1974, YWCA of the USA records, Folder 7, Box 462, SSC.

40. Jessica M. Frazier, *Women's Antiwar Diplomacy During the Vietnam War Era* (Chapel Hill: University of North Carolina Press, 2017), 136–37.

41. Robin Lovin, 'Reinhold Niebuhr in Contemporary Scholarship: A Review Essay', *Journal of Religious Ethics* 31 (Oct. 2003): 489–505 at 493–94.

42. 'The People's Hearings on RTA', 14 May 1948, Washington, DC, CCRWT, Box 294d, CEIPR.

43. Gene Zubovich, *Before the Religious Right: Liberal Protestants, Human Rights, and the Polarization of the United States* (Philadelphia: University of Pennsylvania Press, 2022).

44. *The Commission of the Churches on International Affairs: Report 1964–1965* (New York: World Council of Churches, 1965), 20–23, 47, 52–53.

45. Amy Reynolds, *Free Trade and Faithful Globalization: Saving the Market* (Cambridge: Cambridge University Press, 2014), ch. 2.

46. *The Uppsala Report 1968* (Geneva: World Council of Churches, 1968), 40.

47. *Uppsala Report*, 40–42, 47–49, 68–69.

48. See, for instance, *We Take Our Stand! 1940 Socialist Platform*, pamphlet in Box 20, 'Socialism' folder 3, Alice Park Papers, Hoover Institution Library and Archives, Stanford University, Palo Alto, CA.

49. 'Socialist Party Platform, 1948', reprinted in *The Wisconsin Blue Book 1950* (Madison: State of Wisconsin, 1950), 553.

50. *Platform, Socialist Party, 1952* (New York, 1952), 8–9.

51. *Tribune* [Sydney], 27 May 1953, 9; 28 October 1959, 5.

52. Terence Renaud, *New Lefts: The Making of a Radical Tradition* (Princeton: Princeton University Press, 2021), 197–98, suggests that 'the Marxist holdouts in the party likely cringed' at the call for free trade and peace.

53. Stephanie L. Mudge, *Leftism Reinvented: Western Parties from Socialism to Neoliberalism* (Cambridge, MA: Harvard University Press, 2018).

54. Hubert H. Humphrey, 'A Time for Compassion, a Time for Excellence' (address to the National Conference on International Economic and Social Development, Washington, DC, 16 June 1961), pdf available at http://www2.mnhs.org/library/findaids/00442/pdfa/00442 -01062.pdf (accessed 12 May 2023); Nicole Sackley, 'Selling Cooperative Capitalism Abroad: The US Cooperative Movement and International Development During the Cold War', in Christopher R. W. Dietrich, ed., *Diplomacy and Capitalism: The Political Economy of US Foreign Relations* (Philadelphia: University of Pennsylvania Press, 2022), 133–53 at 133–34, 148–53; Daniel Immerwahr, *Thinking Small: The United States and the Lure of Community Development* (Cambridge, MA: Harvard University Press, 2015), 139.

55. 'Schuman Declaration May 1950', European Union, text available at https://european -union.europa.eu/principles-countries-history/history-eu/1945-59/schuman-declaration-may -1950_en (accessed 12 May 2023).

56. Brian Shaev, 'Liberalising Regional Trade: Socialists and European Economic Integration', *Contemporary European History* 27, special issue 2: *Continuity and Change in European Cooperation during the Twentieth Century* (May 2018): 258–79 at 258–59, 271–73; Talbot C. Imlay, '"The Policy of Social Democracy Is Self-Consciously Internationalist": The German Social Democratic Party's Internationalism after 1945', *Journal of Modern History* 86 (March 2014): 81–123 at 92, 97, 113–15, 119; Imlay, 'Socialist Internationalism after 1914', in Glenda Sluga and Patricia Clavin, eds, *Internationalisms: A Twentieth-Century History* (Cambridge: Cambridge University Press, 2016), 213–42 at 215, 222, 226; Imlay, *The Practice of Socialist Internationalism: European Socialists and International Politics, 1914–1960* (Oxford: Oxford University Press, 2018), ch. 7; Aurélie Dianara Andry, *Social Europe, The Road Not Taken: The Left and European Integration in the Long 1970s* (Oxford: Oxford University Press, 2022); Kirin Klaus Patel, *Project Europe: A History* (Cambridge: Cambridge University Press, 2020), 72.

57. Giuliano Garavani, 'The Colonies Strike Back: The Impact of the Third World on Western Europe, 1968–1975', *Contemporary European History* 16 (Aug. 2007): 299–319 at 317.

58. Sarah B. Snyder, *Human Rights Activism and the End of the Cold War: A Transnational History of the Helsinki Network* (Cambridge: Cambridge University Press, 2011); Stella Ghervas, *Conquering Peace: From the Enlightenment to the European Union* (Cambridge, MA: Harvard University Press, 2021), 290–91.

59. Anthony Howe, 'Liberals, Free Trade, and Europe from Cobden to the Common Market', *Journal of Liberal History* 98 (Spring 2018): 5–11 at 10.

60. Slobodian, *Globalists*, 184–93; Philip Mirowski and Dieter Plehwe, eds, *The Road from Mount Pèlerin: The Making of the Neoliberal Thought Collective* (Cambridge, MA: Harvard University Press, 2009).

61. F. A. Hayek, *Individualism and Economic Order* (Chicago: University of Chicago Press, 1948), 270, 255, 269. For 'neoliberal' associations of free trade, supranational governance, and peace, see, for instance, Lionel Robbins, *Economic Planning and International Order* (London, 1937); Ludwig von Mises, *Liberalism in the Classical Tradition*, trans. by Ralph Raico (San Francisco: Cobden Press, 1985); Rosenboim, *Emergence of Globalism*; Slobodian, *Globalists*, chs 3, 6, and 7. Hayek's support for European integration has since contributed to the common association of the EU with 'neoliberal globalism'.

62. Sean Ehrlich, *The Politics of Fair Trade: Moving beyond Free Trade and Protection* (Oxford: Oxford University Press, 2018), chs 2–4; Adler, *No Globalization*, ch. 2.

63. See also Lawrence B. Glickman, *Buying Power: A History of Consumer Activism in America* (Chicago: University of Chicago Press, 2009); Mimi Sheller, 'Bleeding Humanity and Gendered Embodiments: From Antislavery Sugar Boycotts to Ethical Consumers', *Humanity* 2 (Summer 2011): 171–92.

64. Laurence Whitehead, *The United States and Bolivia: A Case Study of Neocolonialism* (Oxford: Haslemere Group, 1969); Andrea Franc, 'What "Fair Trade" Was Originally About: The Haslemere Declaration of 1968', Centre for Imperial and Global History, University of Exeter, *Imperial & Global Forum*, 3 May 2018, https://imperialglobalexeter.com/2018/05/03/what-fair -trade-was-originally-about-the-haslemere-declaration-of-1968/ (accessed 12 May 2023).

65. Rabasa quoted in Christopher R. W. Dietrich, *Oil Revolution: Anticolonial Elites, Sovereign Rights, and the Economic Culture of Decolonization* (Cambridge: Cambridge University Press, 2017), 276; Jenny Andersson, 'The Future of the Western World: The OECD and the Interfutures Project', *Journal of Global History* 14 (2019): 126–44; Giuliano Garavini, 'Completing Decolonization: The 1973 "Oil Shock" and the Struggle for Economic Rights', *International History Review* 33 (Sept. 2011): 473–87.

66. Milton S. Katz, *Ban the Bomb: A History of SANE, the Committee for a Sane Nuclear Policy* (New York: Prager, 1986); Robert Kleidman, *Organizing for Peace: Neutrality, the Test Ban, and the Freeze* (Syracuse, NY: Syracuse University Press, 1993); Samuel Moyn, *The Last Utopia: Human Rights in History* (Cambridge, MA: Harvard University Press, 2010); Zubovich, *Before the Religious Right*

67. Slobodian, *Globalists*; Daniel Stedman Jones, *Masters of the Universe: Hayek, Friedman, and the Birth of Neoliberal Politics* (Princeton: Princeton University Press, 2012); Simon Reid-Henry, *Empire of Democracy: The Remaking of the West since the Cold War, 1971–2017* (New York: Simon & Schuster, 2019); Michael A. Wilkinson, 'Authoritarian Liberalism in Europe: A Common Critique of Neoliberalism and Ordoliberalism', *Critical Sociology* 45 (2019): 1023–34.

68. Samuel Moyn, *Not Enough: Human Rights in an Unequal World* (Cambridge, MA: Harvard University Press, 2018), 178–79; Benjamin Selwyn, Andrew Farrant, Edward McPhail, and Sebastian Berger, 'Preventing the "Abuses" of Democracy: Hayek, the "Military Usurper" and Transitional Dictatorship in Chile?' *American Journal of Economics and Sociology* 71 (July 2012): 513–38; Benjamin Selwyn, 'Friedrich Hayek: In Defence of Dictatorship', *Open Democracy*, 9 June 2015, https://www.opendemocracy.net/en/friedrich-hayek-dictatorship/ (accessed 12 May 2023); Juan Gabriel Valdés, *Pinochet's Economists: The Chicago School in Chile* (New York: Cambridge University Press, 1995); Karin Fischer, 'The Influence of Neoliberals in Chile before, during, and after Pinochet', in Mirowski and Plewhe, *Road from Mount Pèlerin*, 305–46; Timothy David Clark, 'Rethinking Chile's "Chicago Boys": Neoliberal Technocrats or Revolutionary Vanguard?' *Third World Quarterly* 38 (2017): 1350–65; Tobias Rupprecht, 'Global Varieties of Neoliberalism: Ideas on Free markets and Strong States in Late Twentieth-Century Chile and Russia', *Global Perspectives* 1 (2020): 1–13; Quinn Slobodian, 'The World Economy and the Color Line: Wilhelm Röpke, Apartheid, and the White Atlantic', *German Historical Institute Bulletin Supplement* (2014): 61–87.

69. Lars Cornelissen, "How Can the People Be Restricted?': The Mont Pèlerin Society and the Problem of Democracy, 1947–1998', *History of European Ideas* 43 (2017): 507–24; Wendy Brown, *Undoing the Demos: Neoliberalism's Stealth Revolution* (New York: Zone, 2015); Thomas Biebricher, 'Neoliberalism and Democracy', *Constellations* 22 (2015): 255–66; Slobodian, *Globalists*.

70. Slobodian, *Globalists*, ch. 7, 16.

71. Moyn, *Not Enough*, 178; Slobodian, *Globalists*, 113–17.

72. Zubovich, *Before the Religious Right*, ch. 9, 270, 2; Darren Dochuk, *From Bible Belt to Sunbelt* (New York: W. W. Norton, 2011), 64–65, 187; William Inboden, *Religion and American Foreign Policy, 1945–1960: The Soul of Containment* (Cambridge: Cambridge University Press, 2008), 81, ch. 2.

73. Falwell quoted in Gary Gerstle, *The Rise and Fall of the Neoliberal Order* (Oxford: Oxford University Press, 2022), 120; Lauren Turek, *To Bring the Good News to All Nations: Evangelical*

Influence on Human Rights and US Foreign Relations (Ithaca, NY: Cornell University Press, 2020), 152, 174–75; Melani McAlister, *The Kingdom of God Has No Borders: A Global History of American Evangelicals* (Oxford: Oxford University Press, 2018), 136–37; Bethany Moreton, *To Serve God and Wal-Mart: The Making of Christian Free Enterprise* (Cambridge, MA: Harvard University Press, 2009), 8.

74. Gerstle, *Rise and Fall*, 121, 129–30.

75. Jeremy Shearmur, 'Hayek, *The Road to Serfdom*, and the British Conservatives', *Journal of the History of Economic Thought* 28 (Sept. 2006): 309–14 at 309 n. 1.

76. Andrew Farrant and Edward McPhail, 'Hayek, Thatcher, and the Muddle of the Middle', in Robert Leeson, ed., *Hayek: A Collaborative Biography* (London: Palgrave Macmillan, 2017), 263–84.

77. Moyn, *Not Enough*, 113–18, ch. 5; Adom Getachew, *Worldmaking after Empire: The Rise and Fall of Self-Determination* (Princeton: Princeton University Press, 2019), ch. 5.

78. Edgar J. Dosman, *The Life and Times of Raúl Prebisch, 1901–1986* (McGill-Queen's University Press, 2008), ch. 2; Diego Gastón Araya, 'El sistema nacional de economía política (1840) para una nueva Argentina (1940): Friedrich List en Alejandro E. Bunge', *Cuestiones de Sociología* 15 (Dec. 2016), available at https://www.cuestionessociologia.fahce.unlp.edu.ar/article/view /CSe019 (accessed 12 May 2023); María Cristina Lucchini, Teodoro V. Blanco, and Ángel Cerra, 'El pensamiento industrialista arentino en el período de entreguerras—El estudio de un caso: La influencia de List en Bunge', *Estudios Interdisciplinarios de America Latina y el Caribe* 11 (June 2000), available at https://eial.tau.ac.il/index.php/eial/article/view/1005 (accessed 12 May 2023); Eric Helleiner, *The Neomercantilists: A Global Intellectual History* (Ithaca, NY: Cornell University Press, 2021), 98–99.

79. Raúl Prebisch, 'El problema de la tierra', address given at the Henry George Club, Melbourne, April 1924, reprinted in *Raúl Prebisch: Obras 1919–1949*, 5 vols (Buenos Aires: Fundación Raúl Prebisch, 1991), 1: 376–80. See also Marcelo Rougier and Juan Odisio, *Industry and Development in Argentina: An Intellectual History, 1914–1980* (New York: Routledge, 2023).

80. Dosman, *Life and Times*, ch. 4.

81. Dosman, *Life and Times*, 92–97.

82. Dosman, *Life and Times*, 282–83.

83. Victor McFarland, 'The New International Economic Order, Interdependence, and Globalization', *Humanity* 6 (Spring 2015): 217–33 at 221–22' Samir Amin, 'NIEO: How to Put Third World Surpluses to Effective Use', *Third World Quarterly* 1 (Jan. 1979): 65–72.

84. Dosman, *Life and Times*, 398–400, 403.

85. 'Statement Made by H.E. Mr Ernesto Guevara Serna, Minister for Industry of Cuba, Head of the Delegation', 25 March 1964, in *Proceedings of the United Nations Conference on Trade and Development, Geneva, 23 March–16 June 1964*, vol. 2: *Policy Statements* (New York: United Nations, 1964), 161–70 at 167, 169.

86. 'Statement by H.E. Mr Kiço Ngjela, Minister of Trade, Albania', 1 April 1964, in *Proceedings of the United Nations Conference*, 89–94 at 91; Raúl Prebisch, 'Report by the Secretary-General of the Conference, Part 1: The Problem of International Trade and Development", in *Proceedings of the United Nations Conference*, 5–23 at 10–13; Johanna Bockman, 'Socialist Globalization against Capitalist Neocolonialism: The Economic Ideas behind the New International Economic Order', *Humanity* 6 (March 2015): 109–28 at 110; Mark and Betts, *Socialism Goes Global*.

87. 'Declaration on the Establishment of a New International Economic Order', *UN General Assembly, 6th Special Session*, A/RES/S-6/3201, 1 May 1974, available at http://www.un -documents.net/s6r3201.htm (accessed 12 May 2023).

88. 'Programme of Action on the Establishment of a New International Economic Order', *UN General Assembly, 6th^h Special Session*, A/RES/S-6/3202, 1 May 1974, 5–12 at 6, 9, available at https://digitallibrary.un.org/record/218451?ln=en (accessed 12 May 2023).

89. 'Charter of Economic Rights and Duties of States', *UN General Assembly, 29th Session*, A/RES/3281, 12 Dec. 1974, 50–55 at 51–54, available at https://digitallibrary.un.org/record /190150?ln=en (accessed 12 May 2023); Thornton, *Revolution in Development*, ch. 8.

90. For the debates surrounding British free-trade imperialism in Argentina, see, for instance, John Gallagher and Ronald Robinson, 'The Imperialism of Free Trade', *Economic History Review* 6 (1953): 1–15; Andrew Thompson, 'Informal Empire? An Exploration of Anglo–Argentine Relations, 1810–1914', *Journal of Latin American Studies* 24 (May 1992): 419–36; A. G. Hopkins, 'Informal Empire in Argentina: An Alternative View', *Journal of Latin American Studies* 26 (May 1994): 469–84; Matthew Brown, ed., *Informal Empire in Latin America* (Oxford: Blackwell, 2008).

91. Michael Franczak, *Global Inequality and American Foreign Policy in the 1970s* (Ithaca, NY: Cornell University Press, 2022), ch. 7; Gerstle, *Rise and Fall*, 116; John Toye and Richard Toye, 'From New Era to Neo-liberalism: US Strategy on Trade, Finance and Development in the United Nations, 1964–82', *Forum of Development Studies* 32 (2005): 151–80; McFarland, 'New International Economic Order', 229–30.

92. James Mark, Bogdan C. Iacob, Tobias Rupprecht, and Ljubica Spaskovska, eds, *1989: A Global History of Eastern Europe* (Cambridge: Cambridge University Press, 2019).

93. Thomas W. Pogge, 'Cosmopolitanism and Sovereignty', *Ethics* 103 (Oct. 1992): 48–75 at 48.

94. Among many others, see Jean-Marie Guéhenno, *The End of the Nation-State* (Minneapolis: University of Minnesota Press, 1995); Kenichi Ohmae, *The End of the Nation State: The Rise of Regional Economies* (New York: Free Press, 1995); Anthony D. Smith, 'Towards a Global Culture?', in Michael Featherstone, ed., *Global Culture: Nationalism, Globalization and Modernity* (London: SAGE, 1995), 171–92; Gerard Delanty, *Citizenship in a Global Age: Society, Culture, Politics* (Buckingham: Open University Press, 2000); Joseph S. Nye Jr. and John D. Donahue, eds, *Governance in a Globalizing World* (Washington, DC: Brookings Institution Press, 2000); Derek Heater, *World Citizenship: Cosmopolitan Thinking and Its Opponents* (London: Continuum, 2002); John Hoffman, *Citizenship beyond the State* (London: SAGE Publications, 2004).

95. Slobodian, *Globalists*, 1.

96. Moyn, *Not Enough*, ch. 7.

97. See, among others, Peter Rutland, 'Neoliberalism and the Russian Transition', *Review of International Political Economy* 20 (2013): 332–62; Rosalind Bresnahan, 'Chile since 1990: The Contradictions of Neoliberal Democratization', *Latin American Perspectives* 39 (2003): 3–15; Aldo Madariaga, *Neoliberal Resilience: Lessons in Democracy and Development from Latin America and Eastern Europe* (Princeton: Princeton University Press, 2020); Tobias Rupprecht, 'Pinochet in Prague: Authoritarian Visions of Economic Reforms and the State in Eastern Europe, 1980–2000', *Journal of Modern European History* 18 (2020): 312–23; Johanna Bockman, *Markets in the Name of Socialism: The Left-Wing Origins of Neoliberalism* (Palo Alto, CA: Stanford University Press, 2011), ch. 7; Hui Wang and Rebecca E. Karl, 'The Year 1989 and the Historical Roots of Neoliberalism

in China', *Positions* 12 (Spring 2004): 7–70; Ian Bruff, 'Neoliberalism and Authoritarianism', in Simon Springer, Kean Birch, and Julie MacLeavy, eds, *The Handbook of Neoliberalism* (London: Routledge, 2016), 107–17; Jason Hickel, 'The End of Democracy', in ibid., 142–52.

98. George H. W. Bush, 'The State of the Union', *Congressional Record*, 29 January 1991, available at http://webarchive.loc.gov/congressional-record/20160429182832/http://thomas.loc.gov/cgi-bin/query/F?r102:2:./temp/~r102Y1hYMD:e0: (accessed 12 May 2023); George H. W. Bush, 'Remarks on Presenting the Presidential Medal of Freedom Awards', 18 November 1991, available at George H. W. Bush Presidential Library and Museum, *Public Papers*, https://bush41library.tamu.edu/archives/public-papers/3642 (accessed 12 May 2023); Slobodian, *Globalists*, 263.

99. Gerstle, *Rise and Fall*, ch. 5.

100. Alfred E. Eckes, 'Cobden's Pyrrhic Victory', *Chronicles*, 1 October 1995, https://chroniclesmagazine.org/web/cobdens-pyrrhic-victory/ (accessed 12 May 2023).

101. 'President Bush Speaks in Support of CAFTA at the OAS', *OAS Press Release*, 22 July 2005, https://www.oas.org/en/media_center/press_release.asp?sCodigo=E-149/05 (accessed 12 May 2023).

102. 'Aristide Condemns Clinton's Haiti Policy as Racist', *New York Times*, 22 April 1994, 1; 'Haiti: Different Coup, Same Paramilitary Leaders', *Democracy Now!*, 26 February 2004, https://www.democracynow.org/2004/2/26/haiti_different_coup_same_paramilitary_leaders (accessed 12 May 2023); Jeffrey D. Sachs, 'From His First Day in Office, Bush Was Ousting Aristide', *Los Angeles Times*, 4 March 2004, https://www.latimes.com/archives/la-xpm-2004-mar-04-oe-sachs4-story.html (accessed 12 May 2023); 'Demanding Reparations, and Ending Up in Exile', *New York Times*, 20 May 2022, https://www.nytimes.com/2022/05/20/world/americas/haiti-aristide-reparations-france.html (accessed 12 May 2023).

103. Samuel Moyn, *Humane: How the United States Abandoned Peace and Reinvented War* (London: Verso, 2022).

104. Melvyn P. Leffler, '9/11 in Retrospect: George W. Bush's Grand Strategy, Reconsidered', *Foreign Affairs* 90 (Sept./Oct. 2011): 33–44 at 33; Gerstle, *Rise and Fall*, ch. 6.

105. Bertrand Russell, *Marriage and Morals* (New York: Liveright Publishing, 1970 [1929]), 81.

106. Gerstle, *Rise and Fall*, ch. 7.

107. For a recent example of the former, see Jason Brennan, *Against Democracy* (Princeton: Princeton University Press, 2016).

108. Valentine M. Moghadam, 'Economic Empowerment, Peace, and Security: Connections, Opportunities, onstraints', *Peace and Freedom* 77 (Spring/Summer 2017), 8–9, 22; Gloria Malinalli, 'Fair Trade Better than Free Trade: WILPF Gathers in Costa Rica', *Peace and Freedom* 64 (Spring 2004), 24; Lisa Valanti, 'Cuba Action', *Peace and Freedom* 59 (May 1999), 29; 'Campaign Proposal: Cuba', *Peace and Freedom* 65 (Fall 2004), 10; Leni Villagomez Reeves, 'Women Lead Cuba Solidarity Activism', *Peace and Freedom* 80 (Spring/Summer 2020), 10–11, 23. See also Gwen Braxton and Mary Zepernick, 'Racism and Global Corporatization', *Peace and Freedom* 61 (Fall 2001), 20; Nancy Price, 'Movement Growing in America to Build Real Democracy of, for, and by the People', *Peace and Freedom* 71 (Spring 2011), 13, 28–29; Nancy Price, 'A Global Corporate Coup in the Making', *Peace and Freedom* 73 (Spring 2013), 9–10; 'CODEPINK and the U.N. Call on US to End the Cuba Embargo', *CODEPINK Press Release*, 3 November 2022 https://www.codepink.org/u_n_strongly_condemns_the_u_s_blockade_of_cuba (accessed 12 May 2023).

109. 'End the Blockade! Solidarity with Cuba! Free and Sovereign Latin America!' *World Peace Council*, 23 July 2022, https://www.wpc-in.org/statements/end-blockade-solidarity-cuba-free-and-sovereign-latin-america (accessed 12 May 2023); 'Our Cuban Friends Need Our Help . . .' *IFCO Pastors for Peace* (2022), 'News and Events', https://ifconews.org/news-events/ (accessed 12 May 2023).

110. Reynolds, *Free Trade*, ch. 3.

111. Rosa Balfour, 'Transatlantic Woes: Neither Side Can Have It All', *Carnegie Europe*, 1 December 2022, https://carnegieeurope.eu/strategiceurope/88524 (accessed 12 May 2023). See, also, Fareed Zakaria, 'American Protectionism Could Imperil a Golden Age of Western Unity', *Washington Post*, 8 December 2022; Anna Cooben, '"Not how you treat friends." Biden's Climate Plan Strains Trade Ties with Europe', *CNN*, 6 December 2022, https://edition.cnn.com /2022/12/06/business/eu-us-trade-tensions-ira/index.html (accessed 12 May 2023).

112. Bryn Jones and Mike O'Donnell, eds, *Alternatives to Neoliberalism: Toward Equality and Democracy* (Bristol: Policy Press, 2017); James Vernon, 'Heathrow and the Making of Neoliberal Britain', *Past & Present* 252 (Aug. 2021): 213–47.

113. Adler, *No Globalization*; Laura Sawyer, *American Fair Trade: Proprietary Capitalism, Corporatism, and the 'New Competition', 1890–1940* (Cambridge: Cambridge University Press, 2018); Matt Stoller, *Goliath: The 100-Year War between Monopoly Power and Democracy* (New York: Simon & Schuster, 2019).

114. Vicki L. Birchfield, John Krige, and Alasdair R. Young, 'European Integration as a Peace Project', *British Journal of Politics and International Relations* 19 (2017): 3–12; Ghervas, *Conquering Peace*; Jussi M. Hanhimäki, *Pax Transatlantica: America and Europe in the Post–Cold War Era* (Oxford: Oxford University Press, 2021).

115. 'Free Trade Deal Boosts Africa's Economic Development', *World Bank*, 30 June 2022, https://www.worldbank.org/en/topic/trade/publication/free-trade-deal-boosts-africa-economic-development (accessed 12 May 2023); Alan W. Wolff, 'AfCFTA and WTO Can Help "Knit Together" Africa in Peace and Prosperity', *World Trade Organization*, 4 March 2021, https://www.wto.org/english/news_e/news21_e/ddgaw_04mar21_e.htm (accessed 12 May 2023); Nadira Bayat and David Luke, 'Linking the Women, Peace and Security Agenda and the African Continental Free Trade Area', *Accord*, 18 December 2020, https://www.accord.org .za/analysis/linking-the-women-peace-and-security-agenda-and-the-african-continental-free-trade-area-afcfta/ (accessed 12 May 2023).

116. Samuel Moyn, 'Beyond Liberal Internationalism', *Dissent*, Winter 2017, https://www .dissentmagazine.org/article/left-foreign-policy-beyond-liberal-internationalism (accessed 12 May 2023); Aziz Rana, 'The Return of Left Internationalism', *Jacobin*, 2 June 2019, https://jacobin .com/2019/02/left-foreign-policy-internationalism-security-solidarity (accessed 12 May 2023). See also Michael Walzer, *A Foreign Policy for the Left* (New Haven: Yale University Press, 2018), 107; Aaron Ettinger, 'Is There an Emerging Left-Wing Foreign Policy in the United States?' *International Journal* 75 (2020): 24–48; Aziz Rana, 'Left Internationalism in the Heart of Empire', *Dissent*, 23 May 2022, https://www.dissentmagazine.org/online_articles/left-internationalism-in-the -heart-of-empire (accessed 12 May 2023); 'Responses to Aziz Rana', *Dissent*, Summer 2022, https://www.dissentmagazine.org/article/responses-to-aziz-rana (accessed 12 May 2023); Daniel Bessner, 'Empire Burlesque: What Comes After the American Century?', *Harper's*, July 2022, https://harpers.org/archive/2022/07/what-comes-after-the-american-century/ (accessed 12

May 2023); Adler, *No Globalization*, chs 13–20; Chris Murphy, 'The Wreckage of Neoliberalism', *The Atlantic*, 25 October 2022, https://www.theatlantic.com/ideas/archive/2022/10/democrats -should-reject-neoliberalism/671850/ (accessed 12 May 2023).

117. See, among others, Wolfgang Streeck, 'Exploding Europe: Germany, the Refugees and the British Vote to Leave', University of Sheffield, SPERI Paper No. 31 (Sept. 2016), pdf available at https://pure.mpg.de/rest/items/item_2342475/component/file_2342473/content (accessed 12 May 2023); Streeck, 'Ins and Outs', *New Left Review*, 19 Jan. 2021, https://newleftreview.org /sidecar/posts/ins-and-outs (accessed 12 May 2023); Streeck, 'The EU Is a Doomed Empire', *Le Monde diplomatique* (May 2019), https://mondediplo.com/2019/05/06eu (accessed 12 May 2023).

118. On the last of these, see also Patrick O. Cohrs, *The New Atlantic Order: The Transformation of International Politics, 1860–1933* (Cambridge: Cambridge University Press, 2022).

119. Nicholas Mulder, *The Economic Weapon: The Rise of Sanctions as a Tool of Modern War* (New Haven: Yale University Press, 2022); Benjamin A. Coates, 'The Secret Life of Statutes: A Century of the Trading with the Enemy Act', *Modern American History* 1 (July 2018): 151–72.

120. Marc-William Palen, 'Pandemic Protectionism: Revisiting the 1918 "Spanish" Flu in the Era of COVID-19', *Diplomatic History* 45 (June 2021): 571–79.

121. Edmund Fawcett, *Liberalism: The Life of an Idea* (Princeton: Princeton University Press), ch. 14.

INDEX

commercial peace movement; in Argentina, 79–80, 103–106; in Australia, 63, 70–71, 74, 82, 146, 148, 166–167, 174, 183, 202; in Austria, 68, 85–86, 100, 111, 127–128, 135, 142; in Belgium, 51, 58–59, 70–71, 82, 84–85, 135, 171, 252n57; in Brazil, 79–80; in Britain, 5, 7, 13–14, 51–76, 80–89, 91–92, 94–97, 102–104, 107, 111–113, 116, 118, 120–124, 128–131, 133, 135, 137–143, 145–147, 152, 155–159, 162, 164–166, 174, 179, 184, 186, 198, 205–206; in Canada, 64, 74, 135, 144, 166, 183; in China, 78; in Cuba, 76–77; in Czechoslovakia, 135; in Denmark, 69, 79–80, 87, 106, 134, 146; in Finland, 86, 111; in France, 7, 59, 61–63, 66–68, 82, 85–86, 133, 137, 204; in Germany, 60–61, 68–70, 82, 85–86, 93–94, 98–99, 101–103, 105–107, 111, 113–115, 127, 135–136, 171, 186, 202, 204; in Hungary, 106, 111, 132, 135, 147–148; in India, 45, 71; in Ireland, 41, 161–163, 189–190; in Italy, 11, 54, 61, 70, 79; in Japan, 78, 82, 86, 88, 99–100, 135, 140, 155, 165, 167–169, 186; in the Netherlands, 85, 135, 266n110; in New Zealand, 74, 85, 183; in the Philippines, 77–78, 166; in Puerto Rico, 66, 79; in Russia, 70–71, 78–79, 100, 146, 164; in Spain, 59–60, 65–66, 68, 76, 79, 86, 106; in Sweden, 79, 106, 137; in Switzerland, 79, 105, 111, 184; in the United States, 53, 56, 59, 63–65, 72–74, 76, 78–79, 82–92, 105–106, 108, 111, 114, 127, 132–133, 143–151, 153–167, 169–187, 198–204, 206, 218–221
Commercial Union League, 64
Commission of the Churches for International Friendship and Social Responsibility, 179–180, 182
Committee on Free Trade, 78
communism, 4, 11, 96–98, 100, 107, 170–171, 193–194, 200, 202–203, 207–208. See also Engels, Friedrich; Marx, Karl; socialism
Communist Youth Movement, 171
Confederacy, 56
Confucianism, 78

Congo, 65
Congrès des économistes, 58–59
congress of nations, 55–56, 96, 142. See also governance, supranational; world federalism
Connolly, James, 110
Conroy-Krutz, Emily, 156
Conservative Party: British, 1, 3, 25–26, 31, 37, 130–131, 204, 209; Canadian, 24; French, 20; German, 22–23
conservativism, 22, 60, 66, 81, 83, 104, 132, 134, 148, 164, 185, 192, 194, 206, 208–209, 216 259n12
Constant, Emmanuel, 217
Consumer Education Council on World Trade, 200
consumerism, 5, 19, 40, 68, 77, 104, 110, 118, 121–122, 124–126, 131, 134, 141, 151, 160, 163, 182, 189, 194, 198, 200, 205, 219–220
Conway, John, 164
Co-operation North, 189
Co-Operative League of America, 171
co-operativism, 45, 63, 68, 87–88, 104, 113–114, 116, 120, 128, 130, 141–143, 146, 163, 165, 167, 169, 171–172, 174, 179, 182, 187, 192, 198, 203, 206, 219. See also International Co-Operative Alliance; International Co-Operative Women's Guild; Women's Co-Operative Guild
Corn Laws, 13–14, 17, 54, 57–58, 67, 121, 123, 129, 155, 157, 159, 163, 198. See also Anti-Corn Law League
Corporaciones Económicas, 77
Cortney, Philip, 194
Cosmopolitan Clubs, 175
Cossa, Luigi, 23
Costa Rica, 21, 173
Council for Social Action of the Congregational and Christian Churches, 185, 200
COVID-19, 2–3, 222
Crabtree, Sarah, 157
Crimea, 220
Crimean War, 58

Preston, Andrew, 155, 167
pro-Boer, 68, 129
pro-slavery, 55–56, 59
Progress and Poverty, 73, 143
Progressive Party: British, 129; German, 68, 70
proletarian revolution, 4, 97–98, 100
protectionism. *See* American System; economic nationalism; German Historical School; infant industries; import substitution industrialization
Puerto Rico, 26, 30, 60, 66, 79
Pugh, Sarah, 160

Qichao, Liang, 10, 40
Qing Empire. *See* China
Quakerism, 56–57, 82, 118, 155, 157, 160–162, 165–166, 169, 205. *See also* Christianity
Quesnay, François, 61
Quick, Herbert, 85
Quintana, Ramón Beteta, 192

Rabasa, Emilio, 206–207
Radical Bourgeois Party, 106
Rai, Lala Lajpat, 87
railway, 15, 20, 24, 33–36, 43, 52, 123, 133, 158, 177, 211; transcontinental, 19, 24, 54
Ralston, Jackson H., 73
Rambaud, Alfred, 20
Rana, Aziz, 220
Ranade, Mahadev Govind, 43–44
Randall, John Herman, 167, 176–177
Rani, Swarup, 46
raw materials, 16, 18, 22, 38, 40, 73, 76, 83, 88, 101, 108, 110–113, 116, 135–136, 138–139, 149–151, 169–170, 176–178, 181, 184, 207, 211, 214, 246n152
Reagan, Ronald, 209–210, 215
Reciprocal Trade Agreements Act, 90, 151, 154, 180–181, 186–187, 191, 199–200, 206
reciprocity: conditional, 26, 90; Cuban, 76–77; unconditional, 26, 91. *See also* Cobden-Chevalier Treaty; General Agreement on Tariffs and Trade; Reciprocal Trade Agreements Act

Reconstruction, 48
Red Scare, 134, 194
Reformist Party, 104
Renoir, Jean, 82
Republican Party; US, 1, 3, 14, 18–19, 23–27, 29–31, 35, 44, 56, 63–65, 73, 76–78, 88, 90, 92, 99, 115–116, 122, 125, 150–151, 163–166, 172, 184, 193–194, 199, 206, 209, 211, 216–217, 221
Reynolds, Nancy, 47
Rhodesia, 130
Ricardo, David, 121
Richard, Henry, 57–59
Richter, Adolf, 69–70
Richter, Eugen, 68–69
Rinder, W. Gladys, 130, 137
Robbins, Lionel, 89
Robert, Richard, 166
Rodríguez, Gabriel, 60, 66
Roelofs, Henrietta, 184
Romani, Roberto, 61
Romania, 19
Roosevelt, Franklin, 31, 89–90, 149, 169, 179, 181, 184, 190
Röpke, Wilhelm, 208
Roscher, Wilhelm, 21–22
Ross, Dorothy, 163
Royal Colonial Institute, 130
Rucker, Walter, 49
Russell, Bertrand, 81–82, 112, 218
Russell, Charles Edward, 106
Russia, 2–4, 11, 16, 19, 22, 33–35, 38, 50, 70–72, 78–80, 99, 100–101, 107, 109, 111, 115, 137, 146, 148, 150, 164, 167, 169–170, 173,177, 182, 216, 219–220, 222. *See also* Soviet Union
Russo-Japanese War, 72, 80, 100, 167, 177

Sadamusu, Oshima, 37
Saint-Simonians, 62
salt tax, 46
Samoa, 26, 65
sanctions, economic, 4, 38, 137, 181, 209, 217, 221–222. *See also* embargo
San Francisco Conference, 90, 185–186

A NOTE ON THE TYPE

This book has been composed in Arno, an Old-style serif typeface in the
classic Venetian tradition, designed by Robert Slimbach at Adobe.